THE *PREMIERE* GUIDE TO MOVIES ON VIDEO

THE
PREMIERE
GUIDE TO
MOVIES
ON VIDEO

BY PREMIERE MAGAZINE

EDITED BY HOWARD KARREN

HarperPerennial
A Division of HarperCollins *Publishers*

FIRST EDITION

Designed by Charles Kreloff

Library of Congress Cataloging-in-
Publication Data
The Premiere guide to movies on
   video/edited by Howard Karren.—
   1st HarperPerennial ed.
       p.   cm.
   Includes index.
   ISBN 0-06-273019-3 (paper)
   1. Video   recordings—Catalogs.
2. Motion pictures—Plots, themes,
etc. I. Karren, Howard, 1956–   .
PN1992.95.P74   1991   89-46485
016.7914375—dc20

91 92 93 94 95 DT/RRD
10 9 8 7 6 5 4 3 2 1

CONTENTS

———•———

CONTENTS

THE GREATEST MOVIES OF THE '80s

HARDWARE

APPENDIX

PREFACE

———•———

The curse of the home video revolution is also its biggest advance: choice. No longer are we bound by theater showtimes or TV schedules. Video stores, whether they're located in the most isolated of rural main streets or the most sophisticated enclaves of urban bohemia, offer *thousands* of movies on cassette at once. How do you narrow it down? For most people, the problem isn't avoiding the duds, it's deciding *which* of many titles is going to be the perfect one (or two) to entertain you properly that night (or day). And it is this quandary that inspired *The* PREMIERE *Guide to Movies on Video*. Reference books will tell you about *all* movies, but we set out to tell you about *specific* movies: movies to match a particular mood, a special interest, an individual taste. What follows are 32 video guides, each containing an exacting selection of titles that belong to one genre, such as science fiction or screwball comedy, or that follow a more unusual theme, such as virginity or small towns. We've also thrown in an end-of-the-decade roundup on the Greatest Movies of the '80s, some helpful hints about video hardware, a useful guide to mail-order video companies, and an encyclopedic index of every movie title in the book. We hope that consulting *The* PREMIERE *Guide to Movies on Video* will make your trips to the video store a little less taxing. But mostly, we hope that your home viewing will be a first-class cinematic adventure and, of course, as much fun as possible.

THE

VIDEO

GUIDES

DIRECTORS' CHOICE I

By HOWARD KARREN AND
SCOTT IMMERGUT

DAVID LYNCH

Thwarted emotions, unbridled perversions lying just beneath an ordered surface—these are the obsessions of David Lynch, a director *(Eraserhead, The Elephant Man, Dune, Blue Velvet, Wild at Heart)* with a vision of America that's hardly apple pie. His choices for home viewing are classic examinations of the tormented psyche.

SUNSET BOULEVARD (1950). Billy Wilder's black valentine to the obsolescent veterans of Hollywood's silent era was a casting triumph. Gloria Swanson, an actress whose real-life history is a chilling parallel to her character's, plays Norma Desmond, the silent-movie superstar whose career was ruined with the advent of sound in 1929; the legendary Erich von Stroheim, Swanson's director for 1928's *Queen Kelly* (until she had him fired), plays her butler and ex-director. The images in this merciless, decadent depiction of an aspiring screenwriter (William Holden) who becomes the aging star's kept boy are camp at its most poetic: Swanson

screaming at a projector, movie images lighting her grotesque face; the funeral of her pet chimpanzee; Swanson, deranged, descending a stairway into the flashing of photographer's bulbs, meekly announcing, "All right, Mr. De Mille, I'm ready for my close-up." Check for Buster Keaton in a cameo.

LOLITA (1962). Vladimir Nabokov's novel, told in the delectable gentlemanly voice of Humbert Humbert, describes how Humbert's life is gradually undone through his all-encompassing erotic obsession with the prepubescent Lolita. Nabokov's glittering prose had such a passionate following that it was inevitable any filmed adaptation would be unfavorably compared. But Stanley Kubrick's movie, scripted by Nabokov, has managed to make a place for itself in the hearts of Humberts everywhere. It's filled with marvelous performances: James Mason as the tormented Humbert; Peter Sellers as the degenerate writer Clare Quilty, who, in various disguises, chases Humbert and his Lolita as they journey across the American wasteland; Shelley Winters as Lolita's mother, the repellent, hopelessly middle-brow Charlotte

Haze, whom Humbert expediently marries. The film only hints at sex—a response, presumably, to the realities of releasing movies in the early '60s.

8½ (1963). Federico Fellini's autobiographical film-within-a-film epic is a transitional marker between his early neorealist tragedies and the fantasy-filled extravaganzas of his later years. Marcello Mastroianni is Guido, a filmmaker creatively blocked and romantically confused (between Anouk Aimée as his wife, Sandra Milo as his mistress, and Claudia Cardinale as his ideal woman and leading lady). But the real story of *8½* is Guido's fantasies—claustrophobic, erotic, nostalgic, suicidal. The movie has often been imitated (Woody Allen's *Stardust Memories* is an example) and was adapted into the Broadway musical *Nine*.

PERSONA (1966). Probing deeper into the psyches of his two female stars (Liv Ullmann and Bibi Andersson) than the wary may wish to venture, Ingmar Bergman comes up with a visual climax that will satisfy and shock the most jaded psychoanalyst. Ullmann plays a major actress who has suddenly become mute and withdrawn. Andersson is her nurse. Frustrated by Ullmann's silence, Andersson keeps talking, talking, talking, essentially to herself, revealing more and more of her own problems, until the boundaries of nurse and patient begin to break down. *Persona* is Bergman at the height of his career. Cinematography by Sven Nykvist.

MARTIN SCORSESE

———————•———————

The characters that populate Martin Scorsese's movies *(Mean Streets, Taxi Driver, Raging Bull, GoodFellas)* are bombs waiting to go off, and they frequently do, erupting with a torrent of emotion. Each of the movies Scorsese recommends for home viewing focus on characters who are driven by their passions.

CITIZEN KANE (1941). Orson Welles co-wrote, directed, and starred in this, his first feature, called both the greatest American film and a "kitsch" classic. It is guaranteed not to disappoint you no matter how many times you've seen it. The virtuosity of Welles's cinematic style is evident from the opening sequence, in which the word "Rosebud" is first uttered, to the final shot of a sled being burned inside the great castle Xanadu. A portrait of multimillionaire Charles Foster Kane, the story is told elliptically, through a newsreel, a memoir, and testimonials. Kane's story bore obvious similarities to that of William Randolph Hearst (and his love for Marion Davies); the movie was panned by Louella Parsons and the Hearst press.

THE SEARCHERS (1956). Emotionally devastating, John Ford's western saga reaches as far as film can go toward expressing the longings and disillusionments of the human condition. The shadow of a Comanche chief envelops the image of young Debbie Edwards (Lana Wood, and later, as a teenager, Natalie Wood): She's been kidnapped and her family has been murdered. Her uncle Ethan (John Wayne) and her informally adopted brother, Martin Pawley (Jeffrey

Hunter), set out to find her. Ethan Edwards, the brave and bitter ex-Confederate soldier, is perhaps the greatest role of Wayne's career; he seems to effortlessly embody the character's deepest contradictions. In brilliant color, Ford's charged visual compositions have a stark poetic simplicity. From its ominous beginning to its climactic end, *The Searchers* is the western at its zenith, an American classic.

THE RED SHOES (1948). When fairy tales come true it's enchanting, but not always for happily-ever-after. Expanding the Hans Christian Andersen story that tells of a magical pair of shoes that once put on will not stop dancing, filmmakers Michael Powell and Emeric Pressburger (the team that made *Black Narcissus* and *The Tales of Hoffmann*) concocted a dazzling backstage movie about ballet dancers and the sacrifices they make for their art. Beautiful Moira Shearer stars as an aspiring young ballerina who, torn between her composer-husband (Marius Goring) and her ballet master (Anton Walbrook), dances herself to death. The movie contains lavishly produced ballet performances that are arguably the best ever put on film—for generations of aspiring dancers, the first viewing of *The Red Shoes* is often compared to a religious experience.

PHILIP KAUFMAN

———————●———————

Here is an international sampler of mind-and-soul feasts from the director of *The Right Stuff*, the acclaimed 1978 remake of *Invasion of the Body Snatchers, The Unbearable Lightness of Being,* and *Henry and June.*

THE BICYCLE THIEF (1948). The horrors of social injustice and the suffering of innocents has never been conveyed more acutely than in this story of an Italian laborer whose bicycle, his only means of getting to work and feeding his family, has been stolen. Vittorio De Sica's simple yet compassionate story of the focused search by the man and his son for the stolen bicycle grips any audience's heart. The documentarylike cinematography reveals the nightmarish poverty of postwar Rome.

THE THIRD MAN (1949). A blacker film noir there never was, and Vienna, wounded and bitter from World War II, never looked more sinister. Joseph Cotten, playing a pulp fiction writer, arrives to meet with his friend Harry Lime (Orson Welles), only to find he's just in time for Harry's funeral. After discovering the ugly truth about his friend, Cotten, along with British intelligence, ends up chasing a not-so-mysterious "third man" through Vienna's sewers. Directed by Carol Reed and written by Graham Greene, *The Third Man* was the follow-up to *The Fallen Idol.* The Oscar-winning cinematography by Robert Krasker features shots tilted at disorienting angles; the zither music by Anton Karas became an international sensation.

YOJIMBO (1961). Japanese movie maestro Akira Kurosawa has borrowed many stories from Western culture, adapting Shakespeare for his *Throne of Blood* and, more recently, for *Ran.* But the debt weighs heavily in his favor: Kurosawa's *The Seven Samurai* became *The Magnificent Seven,* his 1958 *The Hidden Fortress* inspired George Lucas's *Star Wars,* and this film, a satirical orgy of violence between feuding merchants, was the source for Sergio Leone's spaghetti western *A Fistful of Dollars*. In place of *Fistful's* laconic Eastwood, *Yojimbo* features the legendary Toshiro Mifune as a samurai who cleverly hires himself out to both merchants, then allows them to kill each other off as he walks away, a job well done. A spirited alternative to the regal formality of Kurosawa's later works.

JOE DANTE

———•———

In his segment of *Twilight Zone—The Movie*, Joe Dante imagined a world in which Warner Bros. animation became real. Along with two cartoon compilations, the director of *Innerspace, Gremlins,* and *Gremlins 2* has some eclectic recommendations, from camp horror to the classiest of westerns.

THE BUGS BUNNY/ROAD RUNNER MOVIE (1979); **THE LOONEY LOONEY LOONEY BUGS BUNNY MOVIE** (1981). Thoroughly adult and thoroughly childlike, the animated shorts of the Warner Bros. studio are a national treasure. These two compilations focus on the works of Chuck Jones *(Bugs Bunny/Road Runner)* and Friz Freleng *(Looney Looney Looney),* two of the most creative artists of the studio's remarkable staff. Each movie features Bugs, Daffy Duck, Elmer Fudd, Porky Pig, and many more indelible characters, each with a precise, achingly funny voice by Mel Blanc. Home video is the perfect vehicle for these animated compilations: You can watch as many cartoons as you wish, concentrate on the vintage greats (and scan past the new and mediocre linking material), and even watch one or two shorts the way they were meant to be watched—as a prelude to a live-action feature.

THE BRIDE OF FRANKENSTEIN (1935). Perhaps the best of James Whale's quasi-expressionist gothic tales, this sequel to his 1931 *Frankenstein* is once again introduced by Mary Shelley (Elsa Lanchester) and features the momentous debut of the creature's bizarre bride (Lanchester again) and her signature hairdo. Underrated because of their exaggerated drama, prurient violence, and mass-market packaging, the original *Frankenstein* films are far more imaginative and visually refined than later imitators. Starring Boris Karloff, who imbued the creature with a profound sadness, Colin Clive as Frankenstein, and Ernest Thesiger as the evil Dr. Pretorius.

THE MAN WHO SHOT LIBERTY VALANCE (1962). This is the movie for the skeptic who doubts the brilliance of John Ford or questions the validity of James Stewart's or John Wayne's stardom. Ford's moral and narrative complexity, typically submerged, is quite apparent here. The myths of the West are the subjects at hand, from the identity of the man in the title to the resolution of each character's fate. Stewart is the story's narrator, retelling at Wayne's funeral how gunman Liberty Valance (Lee Marvin) had the town of Shinbone quivering with fear and explaining loner Wayne's role in the establishment of law and order. Valance's death is re-enacted with resonant ambiguity—flashbacks within a flashback. Marvin plays the beast Valance with riveting power; Wayne and Stewart fill out their archetypal characters with rich emotional detail.

PATHS OF GLORY (1957). Stanley Kubrick achieves gut-twisting intensity in this examination of a futile massacre inflicted on French soldiers on the front lines of World War I by their upper-class superiors. The endless tracking shots of boot-camp Marines at attention in *Full Metal Jacket* are the direct descendants of the dollies through the trenches in this earlier, less self-consciously bizarre war movie. Throughout *Paths of Glory,* Kubrick's direction displays a relentless, creative intelligence. Kirk Douglas, as the colonel who hopelessly defends three soldiers scapegoated and executed for their company's "cowardice," is superb. With Adolphe Menjou and George Macready.

SUSAN SEIDELMAN

The guiding intelligence behind *Smithereens, Desperately Seeking Susan,* and *She-Devil,* director Susan Seidelman has chosen videos that reflect a film buff's sophistication and a filmgoer's desire to sit back and be entertained.

TOUCH OF EVIL (1958). The opening shot of *Touch of Evil*—an incredibly long take that begins with a close-up of a bomb being put in a car, continues with liquid crane movements up and down the streets of a U.S.–Mexico border town, introduces stars Charlton Heston and Janet Leigh while credits roll and the bomb ticks, ticks, and then goes off—is by itself enough to make the movie a classic. But that's not all: Add Mercedes McCambridge in leather and a motorcycle gang molesting Leigh in a deserted motel (yes, a deserted motel); Orson Welles as a bigoted, homicidal American cop; and Marlene Deitrich, enigmatic as ever. This is not your standard '50s film noir but an unforgettable thriller written and directed by Welles, based on Whit Masterson's novel *Badge of Evil.*

PLAN 9 FROM OUTER SPACE (1959). "It's not actually the worst film ever made, but it's the most entertaining bad one you'll find." So says Michael Weldon, "psychotronic" film specialist, of Edward Wood, Jr.'s low-budget sci-fi drama about the invasion of aliens. Wood used footage of Bela Lugosi shot for a different project only days before he died, hired a group of actors with names like Vampira and Dudley Manlove, and orchestrated some of the most laughably unpersuasive stunts and special effects ever put before an audience. Veterans insist that repeated viewings are a must, preferably late at night.

CABARET (1972). Bob Fosse's film version of the Fred Ebb–John Kander Broadway musical is show-biz artistry at its finest. Based on Christopher Isherwood's stories of Berlin in the early 1930s, *Cabaret* follows the exploits of a bunch of young expatriates and hedonists uninhibitedly living it up as the Nazis insinuate themselves into German life. The cinematography by Geoffrey Unsworth is breathtaking; the show-stopping numbers, featuring Joel Grey, Liza Minelli, and Fosse's choreography, have almost too much talent. In virtually every scene, Fosse sustains the mood of decadence and imminent evil. With Michael York, Marisa Berenson, and Helmut Griem.

ALL OF ME (1984). The best of Carl Reiner's comedies starring Steve Martin. Martin plays a lawyer who becomes the host, through an accident, of the soul of a dying millionairess (Lily Tomlin). The central joke—a man and a woman cohabiting a man's body—is executed by Martin with some extraordinary physical gags, such as Martin/Tomlin's difficulties at a urinal and having foreplay in bed with Victoria Tennant. Richard Libertini is hilarious as Tomlin's personal guru, a well-meaning foreigner with a peculiar grasp of English and American customs. Charming, good-natured fun.

STUART GORDON

———————●———————

The connection between horror movies and comedies has been noted by critics for years. Stuart Gordon, maverick director of *Re-Animator* and *From Beyond,* has chosen films that mix both horror and comedy.

THE PRODUCERS (1968). Mel Brooks's first feature is also his most outrageously funny: the story of how the ultimate flop, a musical called *Springtime for Hitler,* got to Broadway and, despite the best intentions of its producers, became a hit. Zero Mostel is Max Bialystock, sleazeball impresario extraordinaire, who descends into "little-old-lady-land" to finance the doomed project. Gene Wilder is Leo Bloom, Max's nebbish accountant who, between hysterical fits, contrives a way to make a fortune out of a flop. With Dick Shawn as a hippie who wins the part of the Führer and Kenneth Mars as the insane playwright.

DR. STRANGELOVE, OR HOW I LEARNED TO STOP WORRYING AND LOVE THE BOMB (1964). Stanley Kubrick's absurdist masterpiece about nuclear holocaust has as its centerpiece a three-role tour de force by Peter Sellers: He's prissy British officer Lionel Mandrake; the bald wimp of a U.S. President; and Dr. Strangelove, the Wernher von Braun–like weapons designer. As the inevitable moment approaches when the Soviet "Doomsday Machine" will go off, insane General Jack D. Ripper (Sterling Hayden) talks about "precious bodily fluids" and General "Buck" Turgidson (George C. Scott) casts aspersions on the Soviet ambassador. The serious bomb-scare novel *Red Alert,* by Peter George, is credited as the source material, but at some point during the adaptation it became obvious to the filmmakers that the story was too preposterous to be treated with a straight face.

PSYCHO (1960). Alfred Hitchcock to François Truffaut: "It wasn't a message that stirred the audiences, nor was it a great performance or their enjoyment of the novel. They were aroused by pure film . . . *Psycho,* more than any of my other pictures, is a film that belongs to filmmakers." It was Hitchcock's biggest success, a low-budget black-and-white horror movie shot with a TV crew, in which the heroine gets killed off less than halfway through. Though not as scary after repeated viewings, the movie becomes even more mesmerizing, and with the benefit of slow motion, you can see why the infamous shower scene took a week to shoot. Bernard Herrmann's goose-pimpling score uses only string instruments. With Anthony Perkins as the troubled Norman Bates, Janet Leigh as the unfortunate Marion Crane, and is-there-any-doubt-as-to-whom as the murderous Mrs. Bates.

ROSEMARY'S BABY (1968). Poor Mia Farrow. After moving into a creepy old apartment in Manhattan with her husband (John Cassavetes), odd, unpleasant things begin to happen. Cassavetes becomes enchanted with some nosy elderly neighbors (Ruth Gordon and Sidney Blackmer), and soon the older couple's ward commits suicide. Then Farrow gets pregnant after a bad dream in which a horrible creature makes love to her. Gordon (who won an Oscar for her sweet-and-sinister performance) keeps giving her some weird concoction for the pregnancy and Farrow doesn't feel at all well. People they know keep getting murdered. The only solution is, as the movie ads once said, to "pray for Rosemary's baby." Directed by Roman Polanski, who based his script on Ira Levin's best-selling novel.

ROBERT TOWNSEND

The actor-writer-director of *Hollywood Shuffle,* the man who only wanted not to be cast as a pimp or a thug, has chosen two standards from his beloved Hollywood and two made by outsiders.

HERE COMES MR. JORDAN (1941). Warren Beatty's 1978 hit *Heaven Can Wait* was based not on its 1943 Lubitsch namesake but on this delightful comedy starring Robert Montgomery as an up-and-coming boxer who dies before his time and is reincarnated in the body of a murdered millionaire. Despite pressure from his financial backers, Columbia mogul Harry Cohn decided to produce a movie based on this crazy premise; its success spawned numerous imitators. Also starring Claude Rains as Mr. Jordan, the man with a heavenly checklist, and James Gleason as Montgomery's coach. Directed by Alexander Hall.

THE WIZARD OF OZ (1939). Why wait for its next network broadcast? The characters and scenes from this movie are an essential part of American con-

sciousness. Though most of the principals have died, they will live forever onscreen: Judy Garland as Dorothy; Ray Bolger as the Scarecrow; Jack Haley as the Tin Woodsman; Bert Lahr as the Cowardly Lion; Margaret Hamilton as the Wicked Witch who threatens, "I'll get you, my pretty! And your little dog, too!" And yes, Munchkins, Flying Monkeys, and much, much more. Directed by Victor Fleming, whose *Gone With the Wind* was released in the same year.

THE MACK (1973). One of the more successful "blaxploitation" films of the '70s, this violent drama of an Oakland pimp's rise to power could have been the inspiration for the film Robert Townsend auditions for in *Hollywood Shuffle.* A presuperstardom Richard Pryor is on hand as the pimp's friend. Written by Robert J. Poole and directed by Michael Campus.

ONCE UPON A TIME IN AMERICA (1984). When this fascinating Sergio Leone epic of Jewish criminals in turn-of-the-century New York was first released in the U.S., the distributor, the Ladd Company, removed 88 minutes and had it completely re-edited to the point of incomprehensibility. The public and critical reaction was understandably lukewarm. Only later, and too late, was Leone's original version released; make sure the version you pick up is the full 227 minutes. Despite its length, Leone's film is never boring; as the dense plot builds, the effect of his jumping in time from past to present to future can be devastating. With Robert De Niro, James Woods, and Elizabeth McGovern.

JAMES L. BROOKS

———————————•———————————

A selection of polished commercial entertainments from the writer-director of *Terms of Endearment* and *Broadcast News*.

MANHATTAN (1979). Woody Allen fans can usually be divided into two camps: those who prefer *Annie Hall* to *Manhattan,* and vice versa. Devotees of Woody's earlier, more anarchic romps *(Bananas, Sleeper)* belong to the *Annie Hall* group; those who see his later works *(Crimes and Misdemeanors, Hannah and Her Sisters)* as more mature and accomplished belong to the other. No matter which side you're on, this romantic comedy about a successful, guilt-ridden television writer (Allen) and his teenage lover (Mariel Hemingway) is a witty and touching romantic comedy. Featuring Diane Keaton as one of Woody's neurotic-intellectual friends, Meryl Streep as his lesbian ex-wife, and a rousing George Gershwin score that's a perfect aural complement to cinematographer Gordon Willis's glistening black-and-white New York vistas.

ALL ABOUT EVE (1950). If there were such a thing as the ultimate Hollywood screenplay, it might well be this witty drama of ruthlessness in the theater world by Joseph L. Mankiewicz (from a story by Mary Orr). The classic characters—Margo Channing (Bette Davis), the vain, aging star; Eve Harrington (Anne Baxter), her icily manipulative, ambitious secretary; and Addison De Witt (George Sanders), the amoral critic—are etched with crystalline precision by the script's acid dialogue. Mankiewicz, who also directed, coached some fine performances, notably Davis's. This kind of refined bitchiness has become rarer and rarer in a movie industry dominated by adolescent fantasy.

THE MALTESE FALCON (1941). With just two seminal roles—Raymond Chandler's Philip Marlowe in *The Big Sleep* and Dashiell Hammett's Sam Spade in this, John Huston's directorial debut—Humphrey Bogart created a mythic standard for the hard-boiled private eye against which every other will forever be judged. A purist's genre film, rooted in its era, *The Maltese Falcon* refuses to grow old. Huston's script for the movie has an unsentimental world view that's in perfect harmony with Hammett's novel. The plot, rich with intricate detail, defies simple summary. In the superb cast: Mary Astor, Sydney Greenstreet, Peter Lorre, and Elisha Cook, Jr.

THE CANDIDATE (1972). Michael Ritchie's stunningly crafted political drama *The Candidate,* which seemed uncomfortably "real" at the time of its release, feels even less like fiction today. Robert Redford, an idealistic young lawyer and son of an ex-governor (Melvyn Douglas), plunges into a tough senatorial race when media whiz Peter Boyle promises him a campaign without compromise. The movie's pivotal irony—that Redford's candor and altruism are pleasing to the electorate but have nothing to do with government—is compounded by the fact that since the Reagan era Redford need only be himself, a Hollywood star, to be a legitimate candidate. Jeremy Larner wrote the prophetic screenplay.

TEN FROM YOUR SHOW OF SHOWS (1973). The NBC series *Your Show of Shows* (1950–54) was a magical live-television phenomenon, an earlier generation's *Saturday Night Live.* Week after week, the show's extraordinarily talented performers (Sid Caesar, Imogene Coca, Carl Reiner, and Howard Morris) and writers (Mel Brooks, Neil Simon, Woody Allen, Larry Gelbart, and many others) put together achingly funny sketches and routines. This compilation by producer Max Liebman includes several classic bits, including send-ups of *From Here to Eternity* and *This Is Your Life.* Born on the small screen, *Ten From Your Show of Shows* is ideal home-video fare.

CRITICS' CHOICE

BY DAVID DENBY, SHEILA BENSON, AND J. HOBERMAN

DAVID DENBY

NEW YORK

Here are ten recent American pictures, all provocative, funny, intense—in a word, terrific—that didn't make it, for one reason or another, into box-office heaven. Some were abandoned by distributors who just didn't think it worth their time to promote them properly; some had offbeat subjects and offended a few of the more conventional-minded reviewers; and some were simply ornery, stubbornly individualistic movies that would never have been successful no matter what was done on their behalf. Their video revival gives them a chance to overcome their unfounded reputations as losers.

SALVADOR (1986). Before *Platoon,* there was *Salvador,* Oliver Stone's impassioned, enraging, corrupt, but all in all thrilling piece of filmmaking on the mess in El Salvador at the beginning of the '80s. Stone's hero is the real-life photojournalist Richard Boyle, an infuriating crumbum idealist who drives down to San Salvador to make money and to look up an old girlfriend. He gets involved, willy-nilly, in trying to argue the CIA out of supporting a sinister death-squad commander. As this rasping, insanely bitter egotist, James Woods is maniacally alive; he gives an acid but deeply humane performance. And Stone works in a looser, more spontaneous way than he did in *Platoon*—though the paranoid mood, the sense of danger breaking out on all sides, is the same. With James Belushi as the cowardly, dope-smoking sidekick.

THE BOUNTY (1984). A fascinating, somberly powerful revisionist version of *Mutiny on the Bounty,* written by Robert Bolt and directed by Roger Donaldson, *The Bounty* is a big, spectacular piece of filmmaking with the usual complement of storms, floggings, and naked Tahitian girls flinging themselves at bony Englishmen, yet there's hardly a cliché in sight. This time, Captain Bligh (Anthony Hopkins) is no sadist. Instead, he's a stiff and angry man who loses control of his crew in Tahiti—after a few months of sensual pleasure, the men are simply unwilling to accept military discipline anymore. And Fletcher Christian (Mel Gibson) is no heroic antiauthoritarian but a callow young man who seems to have little idea of what he's doing.

PENNIES FROM HEAVEN (1981). Director Herbert Ross and writer Dennis Potter turn the American disillusion of the '30s—lonely hard times in bars and diners and cheap hotels—into a bad dream of ambiguous glamour. The saddened, frustrated characters open their mouths to speak, and out pops the lulling, honeyed popular music of the '30s—Connie Boswell and Fred Astaire. *Pennies From Heaven* reverses the usual procedure of musicals: The numbers (including some highly inventive dance sequences choreographed by Danny Daniels) tell us what the characters think but will never say to one another. The gap between fantasy and reality is painful (probably the reason the movie was a commercial failure). Starring an overly antagonistic Steve Martin, with Bernadette Peters and Jessica Harper.

CUTTER'S WAY (1981). A rich and entertaining thriller fueled by the peculiar, volatile tensions of intimate friendships. Jeff Bridges, tanned and sleek, with full, swept-back blond hair, plays Richard Bone, a thirtyish Santa Barbara yacht salesman and gigolo. The gifted John Heard, in a great hambone performance, is Bone's friend, a peg-legged Vietnam vet named Alex Cutter—a man who is crazy, sometimes merely obnoxious, but still an authentic American hero. When Bone is falsely accused of murdering a teenaged girl, Cutter concocts a plan to clear him and trap

the real killer, an oil magnate living in the hills. Director Ivan Passer captures both the dreamy, sun-blessed Santa Barbara high life and the desperation and squalor of the post '60s types who didn't make it.

DRAGONSLAYER (1981). By far the best of the sword-and-sorcery pictures of the early '80s, this production has a frightening, fairy-tale grandeur that takes one's breath away. In particular, the gigantic, vile, fire-breathing dragon is a triumph of imagination. Peter MacNicol plays the young man who takes on the beast, and the late Ralph Richardson, in a sublime performance, is his mentor, the half-mad sorcerer Ulrich. Directed by Matthew Robbins and produced by Hal Barwood; they both worked on the screenplay. Too scary for young children, but young teens should love it.

8 MILLION WAYS TO DIE (1986). Hal Ashby brings a shaggy narrative looseness and a tone of crazed aggression to this Los Angeles crime-thriller. In a strong, idiosyncratic cast, Jeff Bridges is the dour, alcoholic ex-cop Matthew Scudder, a seedy man of honor; Alexandra Paul plays the fluttery-eyed, masochistic prostitute whose murder Bridges avenges; Andy Garcia, coiffed with a ponytail, is the vicious Colombian drug dealer; and television actor Randy Brooks is a swank pimp outraged by other people's low estimation of his character. The movie has a druggy atmosphere that some critics deplored (without acknowledging that Ashby used the staggering, stoned-out tempo as a wonderful comic style).

CITIZENS BAND (1977). Jonathan Demme's lovely ensemble comedy, about CB radio as the great web of fantasy and connection, was dumped on the market by Paramount. To no one's surprise, it quickly failed. Later revived by critics and the New York Film Festival, it has still not reached the audience that it deserves. *Citizens Band* is a series of overlapping vignettes about smalltown Texans who are confused or screwed up in their lives and who feel powerful only when they're on the CB radio. Among the dreamers and lovers are Paul Le Mat, Candy Clark, and Charles Napier. And in one memorable scene, Marcia Rodd and Ann Wedgeworth play two ladies who meet on a bus and discover that they are married to the same man. Written by Paul Brickman, who later directed *Risky Business.*

MELVIN AND HOWARD (1980). Jonathan Demme's perfect, heartbreaking comedy about the real-life Melvin Dummar (Paul Le Mat), a failure at many occupations, who picks up a bearded, skinny old bum (Jason Robards) along the side of a desert road and tries to cheer him up by making him sing a song. The bum, who finally sings "Bye, Bye Blackbird" in a cracked, gravelly voice, is Howard Hughes, and after Hughes's death a handwritten document (the "Mormon Will"), leaving a fortune to Dummar, is found. Did the meeting happen, or did Dummar imagine it, long for it, make it up? The movie, which treats the meeting as factual, is mostly about Dummar's cheerful, debt-ridden marriages. Dummar fantasizes an instant fortune, and what links the two men is the legendary American life of which they are both a part. With Mary Steenburgen and Pamela Reed. Screenplay by Bo Goldman.

SHOOT THE MOON (1982). Diane Keaton, as Faith Dunlap, a housewife who married young and relied too much on her husband, and Albert Finney, as George, the choleric writer who has grown bored with Faith, are quite extraordinarily moving in this fierce, even violent, portrait of a couple coming apart. Screenwriter Bo Goldman has a genius for transforming commonplace affections and miseries into something vibrant and funny, and director Alan Parker, whose career has had more valleys than peaks, works sensitively without relinquishing the show-business vitality that gives his many bad movies some heat. The movie was excoriated by some feminists, who were horrified that Faith would suffer the overbearing George even for a minute. *Shoot the Moon* shows us not how people should behave but how they do behave. Set in Marin County, California. With Karen Allen and Peter Weller.

STRAIGHT TIME (1978). What is Dustin Hoffman's best movie performance? As Benjamin in *The Graduate?* Ratso Rizzo in *Midnight Cowboy?* Carl Bernstein? Tootsie? No, no, no, and no. Dustin Hoffman's best performance is as Max Dembo in *Straight Time,* a remarkably tough-minded movie about a lifelong petty criminal, a man who cannot bear normal life. Working with a scraggly mustache, greasy hair, and a strange, furtive way of moving his eyes, Hoffman uses candor as a come-on, but when people begin to trust his Max, he turns vicious. Hoffman preserves the mystery of Max's personality in all its wounding perversity. Ulu Grosbard's direction shows little regard for the camera but great virtuosity with the actors. With Theresa Russell and Harry Dean Stanton. Written by Alvin Sargent, Jeffrey Boam, and Edward Bunker.

SHEILA BENSON

LOS ANGELES TIMES

———————●———————

A mixed bag, these: A couple are lightweight but redeeming for special reasons; one is a deeply loved favorite; and one is a work that I truly suspect will become a classic. All are meant as useful catch-up, and are offered with the heartfelt suggestion that although video (as we know it today) is better than nothing, the *best* way to see movies is in a movie theater.

BLUE VELVET (1986). This brilliantly original American gothic dream of innocence, experience, and a peculiarly home-grown evil is also laced with a true deadpan humor. The small screen and the television version of sound are certainly not the ideal way to experience *Blue Velvet* for the first time, since its lush cinematography and music create so much of its power; but nothing dissipates the performances of Dennis Hopper and Isabella Rossellini (those lovers in horrifying experience) or those of Kyle MacLachlan and Laura Dern (lovers in as much innocence as Lynch allows) or Dean Stockwell, as Hopper's draggy drug connection.

MALCOLM (1986). Australia's spunkily endearing *Malcolm,* directed by Nadia Tass, works very nicely on the home screen. Its hero, Malcolm (Colin Friels), is a mechanical genius whom the world thinks of as "slow." When a dim but worldly-wise ex-con and his buxom moll move in with Malcolm, he comes out of his shell, inventing gadgets that have the sass and joy of animated cartoons for the "crims' " illegal schemes. Set to the grand sounds of the Penguin Café Orchestra, this fresh and unpretentious character comedy won eight Australian Film Institute Awards, including best picture and best director.

THE MORNING AFTER (1986). Occasionally, buried in the rubble of a bum movie is a superlative performance, such as Jane Fonda's marvelous work here as an alcoholic actress who has poured too much of her life into indifferent men and second-rate movies. Jeff Bridges gives a funny and equally inventive performance as the cheerfully bigoted, almost washed-up cop she picks up. Given brisk dialogue and a great first half-hour, the question is how James Hicks's screenplay became so derailed thereafter, degenerating into such a highly improbable little mystery. Still, if you savor good performances, try these two, directed by Sidney Lumet.

CHOOSE ME (1984). Today's romantics, the ones who are afraid of love, might take this hip, beautiful, and lyric rondelet as their own. Alan Rudolph's film concerns the funny and very complex love lives of a bunch of characters played by Lesley Ann Warren, Keith Carradine, Rae Dawn Chong, and Patrick Bauchau, all of whom inhabit a neon-lit bar called Eve's Place. They are linked together by the radio sex-academician, Geneviève Bujold, who throatily dispenses advice to *tout* L.A. The film's music (featuring the throbbing voice of Teddy Pendergrass), art direction, costumes, even flower arrangements, all make sly comments on this scene —today's version of *La Ronde,* perfectly played.

MY BEAUTIFUL LAUNDRETTE (1985). Amazing, the levels that writer Hanif Kureishi was able to address in this sleeper, directed by Stephen Frears for Britain's Channel 4. It may someday be remembered as one of the two movies that launched the remarkable Daniel Day-Lewis, here a bristle-haired and incidentally gay London punk. This fast and intelligent movie is a love story that's also about race, class, age, mortality, and sexuality, in Britain's Pakistani population, by now in its second prosperous generation.

SMOOTH TALK (1985). Surely one of the most harrowing coming-of-age movies ever made. Joyce Carol Oates's spare short story "Where Are You Going, Where Have You Been?" has been beautifully adapted by screenwriter Tom Cole and given precisely the right voice and weight by director Joyce Chopra. One of the real injustices at the 1985 Academy Awards was that Laura Dern was not nominated for her translucently fine performance as a small-town teenager, caught between dreams of romance and the dangerous sensuality of a glib and frightening stranger played by Treat Williams. Video only intensifies the experience.

VAGABOND (1985). This haunting look at the life and death of a young French nomad becomes something exceptional in the hands of actress Sandrine Bonnaire—rising out of the sea like some full-breasted goddess or lying sprawled and frozen in a ditch. In addition to this unsparing pivotal performance, there also are splendid subsidiary roles, played by actors who bear witness to Bonnaire's last, lost, meandering months. In a series of seemingly unrelated vignettes, director Agnès Varda shows the interrelation of each life and each action and the price of everything, including, and especially, mindless "freedom." Scary and lingering, this.

F/X (1986). There is a gee-whiz air to these proceedings that lets you know that the filmmakers are real movie fans themselves, which is part of the secret of its unabashed fun. You'll spot the villain early, but it hardly matters as special-effects wiz Bryan Brown unloads one sensational trick after another to foil his pursuers. Directed by Robert Mandel, *F/X* is crammed with great inventiveness and nifty performances, like Brian Dennehy's.

GEORGE STEVENS: A FILMMAKER'S JOURNEY (1984). Stevens *père* liked to have people believe he was part American Indian, his handy explanation for his unusual uncommunicativeness. But his son George Stevens, Jr., has caught the man whole, even caught him in a deadpan joke as he directed Tracy and Hepburn in a perilous piece of physical farce for *Woman of the Year.* Crisp, wide-ranging interviews and lavish use of clips *(Swing Time, Alice Adams, Gunga Din, A Place in the Sun, Giant,* and more) illuminate Stevens, Sr.'s craft as well as the volatile political climate in which he stood stubbornly for what he believed was right. This is a touching, spellbinding biography for the layman; mandatory for lovers of movies, movie lore, movie history.

COUP DE TORCHON (1981). Jim Thompson's bleak novels of seedy crime finally have been rediscovered in his own country, but the ubiquitous Bertrand Tavernier, who knows parts of our culture rather better than we do *('Round Midnight),* got to Thompson's *Pop. 1280* first. He changed the setting to French Equatorial Africa in the '30s and turned it into a strong and shamelessly enjoyable black comedy. Here, Philippe Noiret plays an amiable policeman in a flyspeck colonial town in the Congo. When he finds himself caught between a philandering wife (Stéphane Audran) and a scheming, manipulative mistress (Isabelle Huppert), he discovers the deep-seated pleasure of the upper hand.

J. HOBERMAN

THE VILLAGE VOICE

———•———

Most of these movies are genre flicks, but that doesn't make them any less offbeat. Domestic or foreign, they're films that are drunk on a love of filmmaking. (In every case, the director is the star.) There are wide-screen movies I admire just as much—Akira Kurosawa's *Yojimbo,* Sergio Leone's *The Good, the Bad and the Ugly,* Frank Tashlin's *The Girl Can't Help It*—but face it, the CinemaScope format is murdered by the small screen. The following ten films are tough enough to stand up to repeated viewings as well as the video format.

DETOUR (1946). This two-bit Greek tragedy, the story of a doomed hitchhiker implicated in a murder, is film noir at its most fatalistic, paranoid, and stringently minimal. A onetime set designer for Max Reinhardt, director Edgar G. Ulmer transforms all of the production's low-budget liabilities (three sets, talentless actors, a sixty-five-minute running time) into formal elements. So visually compelling as to be virtually indestructible, *Detour* is effective in a third-generation 16mm dupe, works on television even when interrupted by commercials for Kitchen Magician or *The Monkees' Greatest Hits,* and could doubtless survive even the loss of its moody, pulp-ridden soundtrack.

THE LADY EVE (1941). As blithe as *Detour* is hard-boiled, writer-director Preston Sturges's screwball farce is the epitome of inspired professionalism. Everyone involved is in top form, and although neither star is exactly known for comedy, both appear here as if they were born to it: Barbara Stanwyck plays one of the most entertaining fortune-hunters in the history of movies, while Henry Fonda, as the unworldly son of a millionaire brewer, is resilient putty in Stanwyck's assertive hands. Sturges's snappy pacing and off-speed slapstick humor, his rogue's gallery of vivid secondaries, and his gift for pungent, slangy dialogue should be required viewing for anyone who would like either to write or to direct comedy.

LOS OLVIDADOS (1950). Not for the faint-hearted, Luis Buñuel's ferocious slum-drama is no less shocking (or timely) than it was when it jolted the jury of the 1951 Cannes Film Festival. The most haunting part of this mordant account of starving juvenile delinquents and the dog-eat-dog conditions of their Mexico City barrio is an unexpected dream sequence. By including it, Buñuel contaminates his typical naturalistic style with a quality of fevered hallucination. *The Young and the Damned,* the film's lurid American title, gets the neosurrealist flavor —at once outraged and outrageous.

JOHNNY GUITAR (1954). As romantic as it is subversive, Nicholas Ray's wonderfully eccentric oat opera is the hippest Hollywood gibe of the '50s: *Shanghai Express* transposed to a back-lot western town, given an anti-HUAC subtext, set against a voluptuously melancholy backbeat of Mexicana brass, and acted by a quintessential B-movie cast (Joan Crawford, Sterling Hayden, Ernest Borgnine, Mercedes McCambridge, Ward Bond, John Carradine). The film opens with a forty-minute series of barroom confrontations and proceeds through a maze of crisscrossing loyalties and vendettas to end with a shootout between two female gunslingers. In France, this campy western is considered a masterpiece.

BLACK NARCISSUS (1947). Another gorgeous color film, this perverse *Lost Horizon* cum *The King and I,* by Michael Powell and Emeric Pressburger, posits a group of nuns setting up shop in a Himalayan kingdom—and each, in her own entertaining way, being driven out of her mind. Deborah Kerr is properly repressed as the youthful mother superior, while, tightly wrapped in a sari with a ring in her nose, Jean Simmons gives a memorably seductive performance as a wayward teenager. Still, the star of the film is India, or rather "India"—the fantastic studio dreamscape where jungles sprout at the foot of mountains, primal drums trigger savage dances, and a bearded sadhu perches atop the cliff like a cosmic garden-gnome.

TOUCH OF EVIL (1958). Orson Welles was at the height of his powers when he transformed this routine cop story into a marvel of pure filmmaking. From the magnificently convoluted tracking shot that opens the film to the looming, echoey grandeur of the last sequence, *Touch of Evil* is a masterpiece of orchestration—every crazy element contributes to the mad mambo expressionism. An uptight Mexican narcotics cop (Charlton Heston) takes his avid and beautiful American bride (Janet Leigh) to a Tijuana-esque hellhole for their honeymoon, only to have all of her worst fears of Mexico come true. ("This isn't the real Mexico. You know that," Heston vainly tries to reassure the miserable Leigh, who by this time has had it with bordertown sleaze.) Welles's own pop-eyed portrayal of a lawman gone to seed tops a raft of exuberant, hammy performances.

ASHES AND DIAMONDS (1958). A charged thunderstorm of a film, Andrzej Wajda's atmospheric evocation of post–World War II chaos may be the definitive on-screen expression of Polish romanticism. Still, in many respects, it's a very American movie— the action and locations suggest film noir, while Wajda's muscular compositions strain against the confines of the small screen. Among other things, *Ashes and Diamonds* is a treasure trove of now-fashionable '50s styles, not the least in Zbigniew Cybulski's charismatic turn as the doomed assassin of a Communist functionary.

FASTER, PUSSYCAT! KILL! KILL! (1965). This early Russ Meyer flick is nearly without redeeming social value —the title alone tells you that. If Meyer has made far more explicit films, none has ever been more deliriously iconic. Set entirely in the California desert, this goofy saga of three drag-racing, larcenous, top-heavy go-go girls is distinguished by its monumental compositions, lurid cartoon characterizations, and blaring Ventures-like rock score. *Faster, Pussycat!* is blatantly degenerate entertainment, but Meyer's sense of grim purpose imbues the mayhem with the convoluted quality of a gothic novel.

THE ATOMIC CAFE (1982). Detailing America's response to the first decade of the nuclear era, this unnarrated assemblage of Cold War newsreels, radio broadcasts, and TV shows proceeds through a series of thematic montages to a climax fashioned from the pseudo-nuclear-attack film clips of a dozen mid-'50s educational films. It's a comic horror film—entertaining, harrowing, and filled with surprising bits of business. When Hugh Beaumont (who played Ward Cleaver on TV's *Leave It to Beaver*) has a cameo as a friendly Pentagon honcho, you realize that this triumph of archival perseverance has as much to do with official representations of the nuclear family as it does with official reassurances regarding nuclear holocaust.

HAMMETT (1983). The dubious premise has Frederic Forrest playing Dashiell Hammett involved in a kind of "real-life" dry run for *The Maltese Falcon* as well as some of Hammett's earlier short stories. But interwoven as it is with dreams, fantasies, overhead angles, an insistent, world-weary theme, and baroque close-ups of Forrest's typewriter, Wim Wenders's American debut is more suggestive of smoking opium than of smoking Chesterfields. A fastidious studio reconstruction of 1920s San Francisco, every wall dappled by sun coming through the venetian blinds, *Hammett* is one film that actually gains by transfer to video.

ENHANCING YOUR BAD MOODS

BY ED SIKOV

One of the most persistent myths about Hollywood movies is that they are escapist in nature. This bizarre theory, promoted by certain producers, clergymen, and film reviewers, says that we want to see movies that distract us from the everyday cruelties in which we are presumed to live. Not so. In the annals of film history, there are literally thousands of movies that have been aimed not at people who want to escape from their problems but at those who wish to *wallow* in them.

These films serve a vast cultural need—to enable billions of individuals to see that their gloom is not unique. What follows is a guide to movies for the disenchanted. Ever sensitive to the demands of the marketplace, Hollywood distributors have made all of these films available on videocassette, so the bitterness they celebrate can be relished in the privacy of one's home.

ROMANTIC DESPAIR

WHAT THE WORLD NEEDS NOW

Few things are more satisfying to the miserable than a messed-up love affair between two stars. Not only do you get to feel their pain wash over you like a drenching summer shower, but you can also delight in the romantic torture of people you're supposed to admire. In this section are films of blighted love, linked together by the impossibility of their protagonists' relationships. In only one *(Autumn Leaves)* is there a happy ending, and even then its hero has to be committed to an asylum before he can enjoy it.

LAURA (1944). There is little room for optimism when the man is virile but the woman is dead. Something about the situation suggests that it's not going to work out, and in Otto Preminger's *Laura,* it doesn't. Dana Andrews is a police detective trying to figure out who murdered socialite Laura Hunt (Gene Tierney). Obsessed and depressed, the morbid Andrews can't help falling in love with the dead woman's portrait. Preminger treats this dark attraction with a surprising even-handedness, as if losing one's heart to a ghost might, in certain circumstances, be the only rational thing to do. Clifton Webb is hilarious as columnist Waldo Lydecker, who doesn't have a nice word to say about anyone—anyone, that is, but Laura.

DAYS OF WINE AND ROSES (1962). In this classic "problem drama," Blake Edwards uses alcoholism as a central metaphor for the decline and fall of the American family. Joe (Jack Lemmon), a public relations lackey, falls in love with Kirsten (Lee Remick), a pretty secretary. Neither has been blessed with a high self-image; when they take a walk by the ocean, they see their future in the form of garbage floating in the moonlight. Sure enough, the romance degenerates into an alcoholic nightmare: Kirsten sets fire to their apartment; Joe has to be straitjacketed and institutionalized; Kirsten starts sleeping around. . . .

AUTUMN LEAVES (1956). Lonely typist Millicent Wetherby (Joan Crawford) can't seem to find a date until she meets pleasant, good-looking Burt Hanson (Cliff Robertson). Trouble is, Burt's psychotic—the victim of a castrating ex-wife (Vera Miles) and an evil, manipulative father (Lorne Greene), who, to top it all off, are having an affair. It's worth noting that Millicent plunges into this demented situation with remarkable speed, which suggests that her fingers aren't exactly on the home keys either. Directed by Robert Aldrich, *Autumn Leaves* is a mid-'50s "women's weepie" twisted into a horror show. Crawford is her usual overwrought self, but the real surprise is Robertson, who turns out to be a superb crackpot.

VERTIGO (1958). The most romantic vision of despair ever filmed. Alfred Hitchcock makes his hero, Scottie (James Stewart), fall desperately in love with a woman who thinks she's fated to die (Kim Novak). Then Hitchcock kills her off, driving Scottie insane. Poor Scottie is forced to repeat the whole fiasco in its entirety, giving the already unstable man the unique opportunity to lose the love of his life twice. *Vertigo* is a symphony of lurid morbidity, with Bernard Herrmann's resonant score complementing Hitchcock's overripe visuals. And for the hard-core neurotic, there's even a nightmare sequence in which Scottie sees the worst events of his life played out as a cartoon.

DREAMCHILD (1985). In this enchanting, disturbing film, director Gavin Millar and screenwriter Dennis Potter use a real-life event—the 1932 appearance, at Columbia University, of Alice Hargreaves, the inspiration for *Alice's Adventures in Wonderland*—as a starting point for a meditation on time, memory, and childhood cruelty. Alice (Coral Browne), now a flustered and confused old woman, is incessantly drawn to distant memories of the ridiculous Reverend Dodgson (Ian Holm), who had expressed his love for her through fantastic tales published under the pen name Lewis Carroll. *Dreamchild* is about failed love—that of a stuttering middle-aged man for a little girl who laughs at him, and of an old woman for a suitor who's been dead for years.

MRS. SOFFEL (1984). The critics really blew it with *Mrs. Soffel,* carping that Gillian Armstrong's exquisite romance was visually too dark. What did they expect a film set in a turn-of-the-century Pittsburgh prison to look like? *Mrs. Soffel* is about a warden's wife (Diane Keaton), a neurasthenic woman who is trapped and maddened by Victorian social constrictions. Relief comes in the form of Ed Biddle (Mel Gibson), a dashing killer slated for execution. Since both parties are essentially hopeless, they fall passionately in love and engineer their mutual escape. It doesn't end well, though they do enjoy a few moments of cold sunlight in a rural Pennsylvania farmhouse.

A PLACE IN THE SUN (1951). George Stevens turns Theodore Dreiser's *An American Tragedy* into a '50s melodrama in which Montgomery Clift has a fling with Shelley Winters and ends up on death row. Clift plays George Eastman, an enterprising young man who gets a job at a relative's factory. There he meets Winters, a drab working girl who latches onto him like a clamp. Clift gets Winters pregnant before falling in love with Elizabeth Taylor, the belle of everyone's ball, and nobody ends up very happy: Winters drowns, Clift is found guilty of her murder, and Taylor is sent away to protect her reputation. The only respite from this extended calamity comes when Taylor gets the chance to say a few kind words to Clift before he's led away to the electric chair.

RAW PARANOIA

REASONS TO BE FEARFUL

———●———

Whether it takes the form of bad dreams, oppressive realism, or off-the-wall horror absurdities, there is a strain of Hollywood moviemaking that relishes how an evil world closes in for the kill. In each of the following movies, pleasure lies in the confirmation that the world is, in fact, out to get you—and, what's more, you deserve it.

INVASION OF THE BODY SNATCHERS (1956). In Don Siegel's definitive paranoid fantasy, the good folks of Santa Mira, California, are turned one by one into smiling, glad-handing optimists. These new citizens aren't born—they pop out of weird pods under the cover of darkness. This proliferation of human agriculture is not going to end until everyone on Earth is a happy vegetable, a fact that terrorizes and finally maddens hero Kevin McCarthy. One can see from Siegel's tense, nervous style that he genuinely believes in the idea of a massive pod takeover. ("Many of my associates are pods," the veteran director once declared.) It's not hard to read *Invasion of the Body Snatchers* as an allegory of the '50s, but the film is as timely today as it was when it was made. If you don't believe it, take a long, hard look at your neighbors.

THE WRONG MAN (1957). Except for supervising a documentary about Nazi concentration camps, this is as close as Alfred Hitchcock came to basing his work on fact. Perhaps for that reason, it's the bleakest-looking film of his career. *The Wrong Man* is the true story of Manny Balestrero (Henry Fonda), a musician unjustly convicted of armed robbery. In classic Hitchcock form, Balestrero vehemently protests his innocence but acts thoroughly guilty, leading a host of policemen and witnesses to finger him as the thief. His wife (Vera Miles) falls apart under the strain of his imprisonment, and even after the real crook is discovered and Balestrero is released from jail, Hitchcock keeps his camera so far from the reunited family that their happiness seems as remote as it is unlikely.

I WANT TO LIVE! (1958). Incredible as it may seem, Susan Hayward, the most brittle actress of the '50s, garnered an Oscar for her performance in this Robert Wise drama. The movie also won the endorsement of Albert Camus, who applauded its stand against capital punishment. Respectability aside, it's the prolonged gas-chamber sequence that makes *I Want to Live!* a paranoiac's dream. In the course of the film, California's criminal justice system becomes completely preoccupied with the task of killing Hayward, who may or may not be guilty of murder, but who is definitely guilty of irritating everybody from the judge and jury down to the matron on death row. Hayward is forced to spend what feels like an eternity in a holding pen next to the gas chamber, where the silence is broken only by her grating voice and the mechanical sounds of the death machine being readied for her.

PLAY MISTY FOR ME (1971). Clint Eastwood made his directorial debut with this exceedingly paranoid film about a disc jockey, Dave Garland (played by Eastwood), who attracts the amorous attentions of a demented fan named Evelyn (Jessica Walter). Dave and Evelyn pick each other up at a bar; later, at her apartment, Evelyn admits that she is the cooing caller who repeatedly asks Dave to play the Erroll Garner chestnut "Misty." From then on, *Play Misty for Me* is a lesson in how one bad date can turn your whole life around: Evelyn stalks Dave everywhere, ruins his business lunch, assaults his maid, mutilates his house and all of his belongings, and finally threatens to butcher his girlfriend (Donna Mills). You'll never be able to hear that song again without looking over your shoulder.

AFTER HOURS (1985). In Martin Scorsese's antisocial comedy, Griffin Dunne plays a New York City computer technician whose casual trip to SoHo turns into a deranged odyssey of guilt, farce, and humiliation. More than any other director listed here,

DAVE CALVER

Scorsese takes palpable, visceral joy in his hero's paranoia. His fictional SoHo is a modern hell, where everyone lives suspended in a state of fashion-oriented misery. The movie's lighting effects mix the dark spirit of film noir with the raucous amusement of camp and cartoons, with characters to match. Standouts are Rosanna Arquette as Dunne's scarred and suicidal date and Teri Garr as a mad '60s throwback (note the shelf full of hairspray in her mod apartment) who first offers Dunne refuge, then turns on him.

A NIGHTMARE ON ELM STREET, PART 2: FREDDY'S REVENGE (1985). This sequel to Wes Craven's original isn't as visually stylish as its predecessor, but it's a more intriguing film nonetheless. *Part 2* marks the return of Freddy Krueger, the decomposing phantasm with steel fingernails. Though the movie is subtitled "Freddy's Revenge," its villain is less an incarnation of vengeance than an expression of the young hero's repressed sexuality. The poor kid does little more than fall asleep, and Freddy takes over; the next thing he knows, he's talking to his phys-ed coach in an S&M bar, accompanying the older man to the gym, and tying him up and slaughtering him. Director Jack Sholder cuts right to the heart of a teenage boy's most secret and paranoid fears of homosexuality. How else can you read the scene where the boy starts making love to his girlfriend only to have a hideous appendage burst out of his mouth? (Keep in mind that this event causes him to flee the girl and lock himself in the bedroom of his hunky best friend, whom he can't help stabbing.)

UTTER CYNICISM

THE BITTER END

———●———

Beyond depressed romanticism and paranoid fantasy lies the numbed realm of empty bitterness. But a sour view of the world isn't enough. To make it into this category, a film has to suggest that things aren't going to get better, ever—that what you're seeing is the rotten outer limits of a way of life that wasn't much good to begin with.

WHAT EVER HAPPENED TO BABY JANE? (1962). In this dazzlingly unbalanced film, Hollywood takes a long look at Hollywood, which necessarily makes everything jaundiced. Joan Crawford plays a has-been actress named Blanche who lives with her wacko sister, the former child star Baby Jane (Bette Davis). Blanche is in a wheelchair, Jane is out of her mind, and together they spend their forced retirement playing out jealousies ranging from petty to murderous. (The best scene, of course, is when Jane serves Blanche a dead parakeet for lunch.) *Baby Jane* asks to be laughed at, but it's what Milan Kundera calls the Devil's laughter—sardonic and mean. The film concludes abjectly, with Blanche dying on a beach as the demented Baby Jane performs an old dance routine in front of a crowd of unimpressed onlookers. Endings don't come much more bitter.

NOTHING SACRED (1937). It was 1937's most corrosive box-office smash, and it remains just as potent today. A sparkling screwball comedy about radium poisoning and the corruption of the free press, *Nothing Sacred* features a central romantic couple

(Carole Lombard and Fredric March) who seem to detest each other and who, in fact, engage in a violent, knock-down brawl midway through the movie. The film soars with wit, comic invention, and Lombard's extraordinary radiance, yet underneath the gloss is Ben Hecht's bilious script, a foundation of pure misanthropy. Hecht's New York City is a world of calculating deceit and relentless stupidity. His nihilism never apologizes for itself, and even the obligatory happy ending can't undo it.

ZABRISKIE POINT (1970). Some think the flip side of *Woodstock* is *Gimme Shelter*. No, it's *Zabriskie Point*. Harshly panned by just about everyone, Michelangelo Antonioni's enervated vision of the late '60s presents American youth as genuinely disaffected— bored, spoiled, and dull. Antonioni cast two nonprofessionals, Mark Frechette and Daria Halprin, in the leading roles, and although they're terrible actors, they certainly succeed in conveying a sense of flat anomie better than any pros, who would have found a way to make themselves seem engaging. The story is ridiculously simple: Frechette shoots a cop, steals a plane, meets Halprin in Death Valley, leaves Halprin in Death Valley, and gets killed. But the point of *Zabriskie Point* is its dreary mood, not its plot. And the ending—Halprin mentally blows up somebody's house—is one of the great pop-culture spectacles in history.

BUDDY, BUDDY (1981). This is Billy Wilder's last film—a callous comedy for inveterate cynics only. Walter Matthau plays a hit man trying to assassinate a star witness, but he can't get the job done because Jack Lemmon is in the next room trying to kill himself. *Buddy, Buddy* marks the third collaborative effort of Wilder, Matthau, and Lemmon *(The Fortune Cookie* and *The Front Page* are the other two), and never have the two stars looked worse. The growling Matthau really does seem to despise Lemmon, and Lemmon, his face blotchy and haggard, keeps his already nervous voice pitched at a shrill whine. Klaus Kinski makes a very unpleasant appearance as the sex therapist who has stolen Lemmon's wife, and the whole film is in the worst possible taste. Still, one cannot come away from *Buddy, Buddy* without the redeeming sense that Wilder meant every word of it from the bottom of his acidic heart.

VIDEODROME (1983). The grotesquery of *Videodrome,* a science fiction/horror film about television as a medium, has a special kind of impact when viewed on your TV at home. Director David Cronenberg leads his rather sleazy protagonist, a cable-porn distributor (James Woods), to the un-

DAVE CALVER

known frontiers of Western civilization, then pushes him into another dimension. In the past, art and literature have dealt with the conflict between man and machine; in *Videodrome,* the conflict becomes unified within Woods's body as he is transformed biokinetically into a kind of human VCR, at one point actually inserting a videocassette into his belly. It's not a pretty sight, but Cronenberg films it with an unnervingly open mind, a kind of engrossed acceptance that transcends optimism and pessimism and makes way for a whole new era of hypermodern alienation.

VENGEANCE IS MINE

MAKE YOUR DAY

———●———

There are times when discontent gets out of hand and spills over into cruel vindictiveness. For those occasions, Hollywood has come up with a number of films that rejoice in returning evil for evil. To enjoy these dramas of violent retaliation fully, one must be flexible in choosing a character with whom to identify. This is especially true when watching a horror movie—an alliance with the forces of good is probably not a wise move.

THE KING OF COMEDY (1983). As Rupert Pupkin, the deluded hero of this Martin Scorsese black comedy, Robert De Niro embodies the link between paranoia and vengeance. An aspiring and nauseatingly unfunny comedian, Pupkin is so frustrated by his lack of success that he kidnaps his idol, talk-show host Jerry Langford (played with eerie gravity by Jerry Lewis), and threatens to kill him unless he gets a chance to appear on the show. Pupkin works in collusion with an obsessive autograph hound named Masha (Sandra Bernhard). Sick of being passive spectators to their beloved Langford's stardom, both Pupkin and Masha fight back the only way they know how. It's a Pyrrhic victory for Pupkin (unless one interprets the ending as anything more than a demented fantasy), but there are lots of little triumphs along the way. Even Lewis's most loyal fans will thrill at seeing the babbling, fidgeting comic bound and gagged at gunpoint.

THE BIG HEAT (1953). Corruption reigns in this Fritz Lang police drama, and Glenn Ford has to leave the force in order to clean it all up. This is the film in which the extravagantly sadistic Lee Marvin throws a pot of scalding coffee in Gloria Grahame's face, leaving her distraught, disfigured, and mighty furious at herself for ever having put up with him and his mobster friends. For Ford, life gets rough when the gangsters blow up his wife with a car bomb meant for him. Both Ford and Grahame want revenge, and they get it, too. Ford solves the crime, and Grahame gets to hurl some steaming java in Marvin's face and cry, "The lid's off the garbage can, and I did it!" Her revenge is sweet but regrettably short; she's shot and killed soon afterward.

CARRIE (1976). In grand operatic style, Brian De Palma brings to life the secret dream of millions of outcast American teenagers in Stephen King's tale of a gawky girl who ruins everybody's good time at the prom. Carrie (Sissy Spacek), the graceless daughter of a Bible-thumping madwoman (Piper Laurie), puts up with countless indignities at home and at school. But when the kids dump a bucket of pig's blood on her head, that's the final straw. De Palma's flashy technique looks more and more shopworn as the years go by, but he does know how to orchestrate a vision of hellish vengeance and uncompromising bleakness. In *Carrie,* he's helped immeasurably by the young Spacek's painfully evocative performance.

DAWN OF THE DEAD (1979). Sick of consumerism? Want to get even? In the second part of George Romero's zombie trilogy (begun in 1968 with *Night of the Living Dead* and ending in 1985 with *Day of the Dead,* both of which are also recommended), a large suburban shopping mall is overrun with thousands of staggering, rotting corpses, creating an appropriately cadaverous tableau of American culture. Retaliation runs rampant on both sides: the zombies seem to have an axe to grind against the living, and the living rapidly lose respect for the dead. Romero's popular reputation rests on his liberal and terribly effective use of stage blood and fake human entrails, but take a second look at his cutting skills (celluloid, not flesh). The horror in *Dawn of the Dead* has the kind of kinetic formal energy Hitchcock called "pure film."

IT'S ALIVE (1974) and **IT LIVES AGAIN** (1978). "There's only one thing wrong with the Davis baby," said the ads for the original. "It's *alive.*" In these two horror cheapies by writer–director Larry Cohen, the suppressed tensions of typical American families explode into the open when mutant babies appear on the scene demanding love, care, and civil rights. Cohen delights in the idea of a new strain of human beings equipped with claws and fangs, the better to deal with the pressures of the modern world. The parents sure have their hands full with these aggressive little tykes. Born with a chip on their shoulder, the snaggle-toothed kids won't take no for an answer. Pity the poor milkman who stands in their way.

TALES OF THREE CITIES

—•—

BY LUC SANTE

New York, Paris, and Los Angeles have been generating movie dreams on-screen and off- since the birth of the medium. Take your VCR on a cinematic journey into the heart of urban civilization.

NEW YORK

THE ETERNAL STREETSCAPE

——•——

New York is one of the great icons of the cinema, having appeared as a character in productions ranging from the shorts D. W. Griffith filmed before 1910 on the roof of the Fourteenth Street Biograph studios to whatever will emerge from the cluster of Winnebagos and rental trucks parked around the corner this morning. With its motley mix of old and new, upscale and down-, New York is always New York, even in movies shot on the "New York street" in the Paramount back lot. Its stoops, bodegas, subway stations, alleys, and docks have a greater consistency of presence through the decades than most actors could hope for.

IT SHOULD HAPPEN TO YOU (1954). Judy Holliday, perhaps the quintessential New York actress, stars as Gladys Glover, a lingerie model who's just been fired. She has only enough cash to make it back home to Binghamton, New York, but then she spots an empty billboard facing Columbus Circle: THIS SPACE FOR RENT. Soon the city is plastered with the name and likeness of the irrepressible Gladys, on rooftops, in the subway, even live on television. Simultaneously a hymn to New York ambition and a satire of it, this movie rockets around like a tourist on a shopping spree. Directed by George Cukor and co-starring a somewhat stiff Jack Lemmon, in his first screen appearance.

SHAFT (1971). They say this cat Shaft is in a bad (shut your mouth) movie, a typically degrading example of '70s blaxploitation, but then it's seldom given credit for its humor, or for the visceral satisfaction of its premise: trashing the Mafia without benefit of the law. Gordon Parks's direction is perhaps a bit too television-slick, and star Richard Roundtree perhaps too macho for his own good. But the movie glides along at a steady pace, fueled by Isaac Hayes's def score, and it just about eats up Manhattan, from Times Square up to Harlem and down to the deadbeat pseudo-bohemian cafés of Bleecker Street.

BROADWAY DANNY ROSE (1984). No Woody Allen comedy can really be said to have been neglected, but this one comes the closest. With its black-and-white pallor and its pursuit of nearly surrealistic cheesiness, the movie is an ode to a particular demimonde: the fringe of New York show biz. Danny Rose is an agent specializing in losers who spends more time at the Carnegie Deli (how can he afford it?) than in his office, and his task is to represent a lowlife crooner (Nick Apollo Forte) in spite of such hazards as New Jersey, the mob, and the stupefying gargoyle played by Mia Farrow. The result is a very funny horror movie, a boon for anthropologists of the future.

TAXI DRIVER (1976). Martin Scorsese's saga of psychotic ex-Marine Travis Bickle and his confused sense of mission has stood the test of time quite well. The irony is that, after Hinckley, Chapman, and Goetz, it now seems far less contrived and more credible than when it came out. It has an inevitability that is mesmerizing, even if marred by a ponderous ending, and it is marked by definitive performances: Robert De Niro, Jodie Foster, and Harvey Keitel create characters that have entered the popular unconscious. Scorsese is a great director of New York and its street life. In this one, connoisseurs will note such vanished landmarks as the Belmore Cafeteria, the Snow White Coffee Shop, and the little drummer with the bad hair-dye job.

KING KONG (1933). Much of it may take place on that island with the skull-shaped mountain in the South Seas, but *King Kong* is really a New York story. Kong, like Travis Bickle, is just a hayseed who comes to the big town and runs amok, upset by noise and commotion and frustrated by blondes. Ernest B. Schoedsack and Merian C. Cooper's use of miniatures and back projections is so seamless that it is hard to tell just where reality leaves off. The city certainly looks real enough as Kong, like any tourist of his day, takes in the Great White Way and the Third Avenue El before moving on to the (then) Tallest Building in the World, which he easily upstages. Not bad for a greenhorn.

ALICE IN THE CITIES (1974). Wim Wenders's loveliest movie has a story that sounds cute, even cloying: disaffected German journalist (Rüdiger Vogler) passing through New York is entrusted with the care of willful nine-year-old moppet (the amazing Yella Rottländer). Both initially suspicious and resentful, they wind up adopting each other. The result is a lyrical semi-comedy, languid but not dull, with sitcom cuteness held at bay. It displays an entertainingly garbled tourist's New York, a perspiration-and-vertigo-inducing maze where geography makes no sense and plot developments can be glimpsed through the binoculars atop the Empire State Building. For contrast, it goes on to show us Amsterdam and Wuppertal (Wuppertal?).

PARIS

LIFE AS ART

———————●———————

Not for nothing do they call it the City of Light. Paris has seen its share of film crews on location, since the French seem never to have thought it necessary to build in a studio what was already available on the street. But there are nearly as many versions of Paris as there have been movies shot there: the romantic city, the fleabag city, the tourist city, the surrealist city, the high-tech city. Which of these representations is the truest, the most essential, the closest to the core? Answer: All of them.

BOUDU SAVED FROM DROWNING (1932). Everybody suddenly remembered this film when it was "remade" as *Down and Out in Beverly Hills,* but no one should think the two movies have anything in common beyond a skeleton of plot. Under Jean Renoir's delicately rapturous direction, the great Michel Simon gives an incomparable performance as the noble savage who arrives in a bourgeois bookseller's household and proceeds to wreak every kind of havoc. The movie is all about drifting—it begins and ends in the Seine—and it makes Paris look as pastoral as any great city could be.

ALPHAVILLE (1965). This Jean-Luc Godard oddity is set in a futuristic city of logic and order, where poetry and emotions are banned and where all the details of life are dictated by a monster computer, but the joke is that the whole thing was shot on real locations in the horrific high-rise complexes that surround Paris and keep spreading toward the city's center. The glacial impersonality of these places is caught on black-and-white stock so grainy it looks like a surveillance video; and with cartoon-noir performances by Eddie Constantine and the woefully beautiful Anna Karina, it is all so alienated as to be romantic, and so futuristic it could have been made only in the era of pop art.

PLAYTIME (1967). Jacques Tati sets his Monsieur Hulot down on locations that match those of *Alphaville* and manages to make a movie that is even more alienated simply by virtue of being jolly. The plot is simplicity itself: Hulot appears in a high-rise office building for an appointment, but through one misunderstanding after another spends twenty-four hours failing to keep it. Although rich in ambient sound and overheard talk, the film is essentially silent, and Tati's hapless Hulot is a latter-day silent clown. But the proceedings have a weirdly chill edge. Here, too, Paris is part of the joke: Its landmarks are seen only as reflections on glass doors. English dialogue by Art Buchwald.

BOB LE FLAMBEUR (1955). Once known only to film buffs, and not released in the U.S. until 1982, this Jean-Pierre Melville gangster drama is finally being considered a true classic. It's the story of an aging crook, gracefully played by Roger Duchesne, who plans to make one last, impossible score, a strike against the casino at Deauville. The tone is unexpectedly tender, as the film focuses on group loyalty, on Bob's paternal feelings toward his son, and on his chivalry toward the lost girl played by the gorgeous Isabelle Corey. The Paris here is one that has just about vanished: the raffishly exciting Pigalle of nightclubs and private gambling houses at dawn.

AN AMERICAN IN PARIS (1951). Vincente Minnelli's Oscar-winning musical presents a Paris that never was but always is, dig? All those artists in garrets, lovable concierges, children playing in the little winding streets, understanding café proprietors, and golden-hearted soubrettes haven't been in evidence since the days of the Bateau Lavoir, if not before the Franco-

Prussian War, but who would argue with this kandy-kolored phantasmagoria? Hollywood has been building imaginary Parises just about forever; some were more literally faithful, but none has more poetic integrity. *An American in Paris* is the apotheosis of corn. Bonuses include Gershwin's score, Gene Kelly, that monument to dyspepsia Oscar Levant, and the splendid Leslie Caron.

THE 400 BLOWS (1959). Antoine Doinel (Jean-Pierre Léaud) is a youthful miscreant in the first installment of François Truffaut's series (which also includes *Stolen Kisses, Bed and Board,* and *Love on the Run*). He skips school, sneaks into movies, runs away from home, steals things, and tries (disastrously) to return them. Like most kids, he gets into more trouble for things he thinks are right than for his actual trespasses. Unlike most kids, he gets whacked with the big stick. He inhabits a Paris of dingy flats, seedy arcades, abandoned factories, and workaday streets, a city that seems big and full of possibilities only to a kid's eye. To the viewer it is just a slum embellished with grandiose masonry.

LOS ANGELES

THE WASTE LAND

———●———

Even though movies have been shot in Los Angeles since the studios moved there in the early teens, most of the tales being told were supposed to be taking place somewhere else. Thus, Griffith Park might become the Scottish heath, Topanga Canyon the forest primeval, and numerous former farm plots on the outskirts everything from ancient Rome to Mars. It's only in relatively recent years that filmmakers seem to have become interested in L.A. as a real place with real inhabitants unconnected to the movie industry. Is it just a coincidence that what they have found is seldom a romantic, carefree kind of town where the natives laugh and sing?

BLADE RUNNER (1982). This Ridley Scott sci-fi epic has its share of problems: an ill-considered voice-over narration, a wooden Harrison Ford, and a plot, extrapolated from a few paragraphs in the Philip K. Dick novel *Do Androids Dream of Electric Sheep?* that can most kindly be described as evasive. Nevertheless, the movie features an absorbing and fully realized vision of the city of the future, which is inevitably Los Angeles. There are giant hovering video billboards, a slang with elements of Japanese, Spanish, and German, a black market in byproducts of genetic engineering. A good deal of the action takes place in a preposterous apartment house, the Bradbury, which looks like it was constructed for the film, except that it is actually an office building and figured in *D.O.A.* thirty-three years earlier.

D.O.A. (1949). The Bradbury was relatively youthful when this was made, and Los Angeles still had streetcars. In fact, downtown looked more like Chicago or Cleveland than the litter of glass fronts it has since become. This riveting, if none too plausible, yarn is directed by Rudolph Maté and stars Edmond O'Brien as a man who has been poisoned and has just one day to find his killer. As for the 1988 remake with Dennis Quaid—could anyone have improved on the hectoring O'Brien or the splendidly creepy Neville Brand (a true specialist in playing sadistic killers)? And get a load of those ridiculous wolf whistles on the soundtrack.

REPO MAN (1984). Emilio Estevez, who seems to be playing an ineffectual punk no matter what role he's cast in, here plays a punk of the slam-dancing variety who semiaccidentally takes up the trade of auto repossession, with Harry Dean Stanton as his deadpan mentor. There's a confusing science-fiction by-plot that does little for the film, and the movie as a whole suffers from the usual Alex Cox rush job, especially in the editing. But it's entertaining and often very funny nevertheless, with a bevy of vivid secondary characters and a great soundtrack. L.A. here is, appropriately, all fringe and no center, a desperate string of junkyards, taco stands, convenience stores, and the eminently cinematic monstrosity known as the Los Angeles River.

CHINATOWN (1974). The L.A. River looms large here, too; in fact it is nearly the leading character. The movie is all about water supply, a prominent skeleton in the L.A. closet and one that has continually rattled its bones for the better part of a century.

In this sun-drenched film noir, water pipes become a conduit for the most intricate and perverse kinds of evil. Along the way, of course, there is the fine, clipped direction of Roman Polanski (and his fine work with a stiletto), great acting by Jack Nicholson, Faye Dunaway, and John Huston, and a script by Robert Towne that might have been dictated by the ghost of Raymond Chandler.

SUBURBIA (1984). This extremely low-budget film by Penelope Spheeris is exactly the kind of thing film cultists are always looking for: a poverty-row production that makes the most of its limitations and transcends them by collective will. The story of a group of kids—L.A. white-trash punks—who live in an abandoned tract house and stick together against overwhelming odds, it has numerous trash-film hallmarks: gratuitous violence, amateur acting, weak color processing. *Suburbia* is also moving, heartfelt, and resonant, and it says a mouthful about cities and where they're going, specifically L.A., which is here taken to its logical extreme: the instant slums of suburbia.

TROMPE L'OEIL

●

BY MASON WILEY

When Thomas Edison and the Lumière brothers pioneered motion pictures in the late nineteenth century, they demonstrated the new medium's ability to record reality, but when magician Georges Méliès got his hands on a camera in 1896, the cinema expanded its realm to include the world of make-believe and illusion. Ever since, the magic of special effects and the occasional mindlessness of Hollywood have combined to create movies that trick audiences into believing that the impossible is possible and that some actors are wearing their natural hair. Here's a selection of movies in which actors are allowed, through cinematic tomfoolery, to go blond, change sex, and play as many characters as they wish.

DOUBLES

ONE'S A CROWD

———●———

Actors would play every part in a movie if they could, but only a few have been given the opportunity to ham it up in multiple roles. No one benefited more from this trick than Lee Marvin, who grabbed a Best Actor Oscar for playing both the comic drunk and the bad guy in *Cat Ballou,* the 1965 western spoof that in-

spires few laughs today. Below are some more films that feature actors co-starring with themselves, but these have better stood the test of time.

KIND HEARTS AND CORONETS (1949). A young Briton (Dennis Price) seeks revenge against his mother's family after it cruelly disinherits her and allows her to die impoverished. Alec Guinness plays the entire family in this delicious black comedy, and what a family the D'Ascoynes are: most of them old, mean bores (a duke, a general, an admiral, a banker, a clergyman, and, all too briefly, a suffragette), and two of them young descendants (a cad and a nice guy with an attractive wife). Abetted by Ernest Taylor and Harry Frampton's makeup, Guinness makes each family member a vivid victim of the hero's murderous scheme, which we witness, as Hitchcock might, with pleasure in a job well done. Price is appropriately urbane as the hero, and Joan Greenwood practically purrs every one of her lines as his vixenish childhood friend. The exemplary screenplay is by John Dighton and Robert Hamer; Hamer directed.

THE PARENT TRAP (1961). A pair of teenage identical twins who have never met are accidentally sent to the same summer camp by their divorced parents. When they figure out what's up, the twins plot to reunite their parents before a gold digger takes Dad to the altar. It should have been another *Awful Truth,* but in Walt Disney's hands, it's just another arch, smutty romantic comedy. Brian Keith and Maureen O'Hara, as the parents, are stuck with such obvious routines as his finding her bra in his shower, har-de-har-har. The one thing Disney did right was to cast fifteen-year-old Hayley Mills as the twins; her charm and skill humanize the split-screen gimmick so that the girls are funny and individual. Just like the cousins in the later television sitcom *The Patty Duke Show,* one is repressed and the other a swinger. The best part of *The Parent Trap* is the beginning, when they meet at the camp run by Nancy Kulp, legendary star of *The Beverly Hillbillies* —the fur flies in an orgy of youthful slapstick as the girls battle it out until deciding to join forces.

FAHRENHEIT 451 (1967). Who could ask for more than two Julie Christies? Oskar Werner has both of them in this adaptation of Ray Bradbury's story set in a fascist near-future. Werner plays a "fireman" who burns books for a totalitarian government. When Christie's hair is down in the *Darling*

JOHN PIRMAN

style, she's Werner's wife, a vapid beauty who longs to be the Vanna White of the government's television show. When her hair is up in *Doctor Zhivago* fashion, she's a member of the rebel underground, tempting Werner to abandon his job and wife and run away with her to a colony where people go around memorizing books. This was François Truffaut's only film in English, and his unemotional handling of the drama mirrors the film's bleak vision of tomorrow as a world of apathy and mediocrity. Christie plays both of her roles sympathetically, so Werner's ambivalence seems entirely understandable.

THE PURPLE ROSE OF CAIRO (1985). Mia Farrow has one of her best roles in this Woody Allen fantasy about a Depression-era movie fanatic whose dream comes true when her favorite character in a film walks off the screen and into her arms. Jeff Daniels plays both the movie character and the Hollywood actor who rushes to New Jersey to persuade his screen incarnation to go back into the picture he deserted. As the actor, Daniels is a vain smoothy who woos Farrow with ostensible conviction. His innocent screen character, meanwhile, starts babbling like Woody Allen, wondering what life would be like without religion. "It'd be like a movie with no point and no happy ending," Farrow tells him. The movie has a point, but its own ending is definitely bittersweet. Not to worry—Woody does have fun with the movie within a movie, a parody of a '30s RKO musical he'd probably love to make but wouldn't dare to in real life.

DEAD OF WINTER (1987). Mary Steenburgen has three roles in Arthur Penn's entertaining throwback to thrillers in the mode of *Wait Until Dark,* which he directed on Broadway twenty years earlier. This time the damsel in distress is a young actress desperate for work who ventures off to a snowbound house in New England for a screen test. As things grow increasingly ominous, she learns she's been used to impersonate the murdered twin sister of a wealthy bitch, who's out for blood. Steenburgen has the look and spunk of a Victorian heroine as she plays the quick-thinking actress trying to save herself by outwitting everyone else. In contrast, her evil look-alike seems to have ice in her veins. To find out what her third role is, you'll have to watch the movie, preferably in the dark on a stormy night.

DRAG

A WALK ON THE WILD SIDE

———————●———————

When an actor puts on a costume, he begins to create the illusion that he's another person; but somehow when he dons the garb of the opposite sex, illusion becomes secondary and satire is the name of the game. The guy/girl can't help commenting on the follies of the gender that he/she is impersonating. Linda Hunt won an Oscar for her serious

> ### REAL NAMES
> ———————●———————
>
> **ALLEN STEWART KONIGSBERG**
> Woody Allen
>
> **ERNEST FREDERICK MCINTYRE BICKEL**
> Fredric March
>
> **PEGGY YVONNE MIDDLETON**
> Yvonne de Carlo
>
> **ZELMA KATHRYN HEDRICK**
> Kathryn Grayson
>
> **DORIS VON KAPPELHOFF**
> Doris Day
>
> **HAROLD CLIFFORD LEEK**
> Howard Keel
>
> **LEONARD ROSENBERG**
> Tony Randall
>
> **CHARLES BUNCHINSKY**
> Charles Bronson
>
> **JANE ALICE PETERS**
> Carole Lombard
>
> **ARTHUR GELIEN**
> Tab Hunter
>
> **IVO LIVI**
> Yves Montand

portrayal of a man in *The Year of Living Dangerously,* but most movies that feature a cross-dressing star are satirical romps. And why not? The word "satire" is, after all, derived from the Latin *satura,* meaning "fruit salad." *Bon appétit!*

OUTRAGEOUS! (1977). The star of this backstage saga is Craig Russell, a female impersonator on the nightclub circuit who is a one-man *That's Entertainment!* Bette Davis, Barbra Streisand (in her *Star Is Born* phase), Tallulah Bankhead, and Pearl Bailey are just a few of the personalities living inside Russell. He plays a lonely

Canadian hairdresser whose show-biz dreams are ridiculed by his boss—"A drag queen in my shop? Never!" His personal life is a mess, too; even a one-night stand asks him for money afterward, citing his personal policy: "I usually don't make drag queens at all." Through the encouragement of his schizophrenic, pregnant roommate (Hollis McLaren), Russell finds the courage to try his luck in New York City. Upon arriving, he's taken in by an ambitious cab driver who finds him gigs through his network of myriad sexual partners. "And all these years," sighs a disappointed Russell, "I thought it was the star who got to whore her way to the top." *Outrageous!* is not a slick Hollywood package—it was produced by the Film Consortium of Canada, Inc. (imagine the meeting when they decided to finance this script)—and technically it's on the crude side; but Russell's buoyant wit makes the film a hilarious and liberating experience.

VICTOR/VICTORIA (1982). Julie Andrews doesn't strive for Lon Chaney realism when she poses as a man in this musical comedy; instead she pulls off an amusing David Bowie androgyny. Robert Preston is her accomplice in gender deception, and he gets in the act himself at the end. Blake Edwards's farce focuses on the battle of the sexual preferences: When both Lesley Ann Warren and Alex Karras compete for Preston, Edwards lets Karras win. When gangster James Garner falls for Andrews in drag, he is allowed to have his heterosexuality confirmed, but only in private; in this film's crazy world, in order to go out with her he has to go along with her ruse and appear gay in public. While the sexual politics are modern, the film feels like Hollywood movies of the '30s: stylish sets and costumes and a story of a person down on her luck who makes a fortune by playing the world for a bunch of suckers. Some viewers complain that Julie sings one too many songs, the fools.

TOOTSIE (1982). Dustin Hoffman explains that drag is "one of the great acting challenges an actor can have," and he rises to the challenge with his funniest, most likable screen character since Benjamin in *The Graduate*. His Dorothy Michaels is prissy, sensible, outspoken, and thoroughly convincing; when Hoffman switches back to his male self, it's hard to believe he's the same person. Unfortunately, *Tootsie* can't resist spelling out a moral to the story; to wit, Hoffman becomes a better person by drawing upon the feminine part of himself. The film thus becomes a consciousness-raising lesson, but only Hoffman benefits from his newfound sensitivity. He's rewarded with cuddly Jessica Lange in the contrived epilogue, while poor Teri Garr, as a lovable klutz who charms the audience from the first scene on, is left alone and betrayed, as if her feelings don't count. So much for the sensitivity of *Tootsie*'s filmmakers.

YENTL (1983). Like Hoffman in *Tootsie,* Barbra Streisand uses drag to explore gender differences, taking on the traditional social divisions between men and women in Jewish culture. Set in turn-of-the-century Eastern Europe, the film has the lush look of Streisand's road-show musicals of the late '60s, but this time Barbra is directing, and the point of view is distinctly feminist. She makes it clear in one simple cut that she considers the women sequestered behind railings in a synagogue just as imprisoned as a peddler's chickens in their wooden box. But no one's gonna rain on *her* parade. Streisand dresses up as a boy and calls herself Yentl; when she's accepted in a yeshiva and states, "I'm a student," she recalls *Funny Girl's* Fanny Brice gloating, "I'm a Ziegfeld girl." The second half of the movie is devoted to the sexual tension that erupts when Streisand swoons over male chauvinist pig Mandy Patinkin and grows jealous of sex object Amy Irving, only it's Streisand who winds up marrying Irving. The score serves as interior soliloquies for Streisand as she ponders every step of her odyssey, and climaxes with her belting out the final song from the deck of a ship. So she's got a thing about singing on boats—if you've got a good gimmick, shtick with it.

FEMALE TROUBLE (1974). No discussion of drag in film is complete without a mention of Divine, whose work with director John Waters rivals Dietrich's with Sternberg. As marvelous as Divine is in the delightful *Polyester,* there's no doubt his tour de force is this epic melodrama. He plays Dawn Davenport from her fat-girl-dom in a Baltimore high school in the '60s to her *I Want to Live!*–style death years later, and a lot happens in between, none of it pleasant. The action begins when Dawn fails to receive a coveted pair of cha-cha heels at Christmas, and soon our heroine is mixed up with Mink Stole, as her wayward daughter, and Edith Massey, as her nemesis-neighbor, who learns why the caged bird sings. The versatile Divine sings the title song and also portrays the man who sires Dawn's daughter, thus earning him the distinction of being the only actor in film history to play a sex scene with himself; to his credit, the effect is not narcissistic, because he permits himself to be upstaged by a Waters sight gag (a stain on his underwear).

Though the director's trademark bad taste is always evident, Divine wears a stunning wardrobe and wigs by Van Smith.

BLONDES

IF YOU'VE GOT ONE LIFE TO LIVE

———————●———————

Is it true that blondes have more fun? They usually *are* fun lovers in movies, particularly the dumb blonde, who's always good for a laugh. Hollywood has often asked performers with hair of a darker hue to become blond onscreen in order to project that je ne sais quoi that audiences love. Below are films featuring stars who made the tonsorial switch to blond, either for their characters or for their careers.

DINNER AT EIGHT (1933). After playing the title role in *Platinum Blonde* at Columbia, twenty-one-year-old Jean Harlow signed a star contract at MGM the year the studio enjoyed a monster hit, *Grand Hotel,* which ushered in a vogue for "all-star casts." The very next year, she was shuffled into Metro's star-heavy adaptation of this Edna Ferber and George S. Kaufman Broadway hit about the Depression-era travails of the upper crust. Harlow plays a nouveau riche wife who lies around in bed all day eating chocolates and concocting illnesses for her good-looking doctor to cure. Even her maid, Tina (a hilarious Hilda Vaughn), is slatternly and lazy. Alas, there are a lot of other, far less interesting characters, and Harlow isn't on screen much. This movie is one a VCR actually improves; if Harlow or Billie Burke (as a flighty society wife) or the great Marie Dressler (as a former actress she's Harlow's match in the Laugh Department) aren't on screen, press fast forward until one of them shows up, and you won't have to endure the other subplots. In addition to her white coiffure, Harlow popularized the no-bra look, and designer Adrian provides plenty of negligees and gowns so she can strut her stuff. Director George Cukor keeps the poetry in motion by keeping Harlow on the move until the last scene, in which she wears a satin number so tight she can't even sit down.

REAL NAMES

●

RICHARD WALTER JENKINS, JR.
Richard Burton

RODOLFO ALFONZO RAFFAELE PIERRE PHILIBERT GUGLIELMI
Rudolph Valentino

HEDWIG EVA MARIA KIESLER
Hedy Lamarr

ISAIAH EDWIN LEOPOLD
Ed Wynn

TULA ELLICE FINKLEA
Cyd Charisse

ISSUR DANIELOVITCH
Kirk Douglas

EDNA RAE GILLOOLY
Ellen Burstyn

HARRIETTE LAKE
Ann Sothern

NATASHA GURDIN
Natalie Wood

SHIRLEY SCHRIFT
Shelley Winters

PHYLLIS ISLEY
Jennifer Jones

DIANE HALL
Diane Keaton

GENTLEMEN PREFER BLONDES (1953). "This type of movie lets you sleep at night without a care in the world," director Howard Hawks confessed to Andrew Sarris. "The two girls, Jane Russell and Marilyn Monroe, were so good together that any time I had trouble figuring out any business, I simply had them walking back and forth, and the audiences adored it." The twenty-seven-year-old Monroe was rising fast at Fox—she also made *Niagara* and *How to Marry a Millionaire* for the studio that year—and the role of Anita Loos's Lorelei Lee fit her like a kid glove. Certainly Monroe speaks Lorelei's lines with conviction. "I can be smart when it's important," she says, "but men don't like it." Or: "I won't let myself fall in love with a man who won't trust me no matter what I do." Even Russell, who plays Monroe's brunette chaperone, sheds her Wonder Woman look toward the end to do her own imitation of a dumb blonde. The leading men are dorks, but they don't get in the way of the women in their Travillas, in Technicolor that can only be described as yummy. And, as Madonna proved in her "Material Girl" video, Marilyn's "Diamonds Are a Girl's Best Friend" number is inimitable.

VERTIGO (1958). Leave it to Alfred Hitchcock to make a bleach job a hair-raising moment; the audience knows that Kim Novak is heading for trouble when she consents to obsessed James Stewart's wish that she switch from trampy brown to pristine platinum. At the same time, the audience can enjoy Novak's transformation from the not-so-bright Judy to the brilliantly serene Madeleine, since it means that she'll win Stewart's love. Or will she? Competing for Stewart is Barbara Bel Geddes, as an authentic blonde who pales next to Novak's manufactured glamour. As an actress, Novak never exuded self-assurance, making her the perfect pawn for this Hitchcock exercise in sexual melodrama, and Bernard Herrmann's score is as haunting as Novak's performance.

BONNIE AND CLYDE (1967). Before she was Evelyn Mulwray, Diana Christensen, Joan Crawford, or Wanda the Barfly, Faye Dunaway was a twenty-seven-year-old actress waiting for her big break, and she must have felt this movie was it. She reportedly prepared for stardom by returning a part of her salary in exchange for above-the-title billing and by bleaching her hair in a style resembling that of the actress who had turned down the part—Jane Fonda, then near the end of her sex-kitten period. Arthur Penn's film recreates the Depression-era Southwest with an overall period accuracy, but Dunaway's Bonnie has a swinging '60s look, starting in the opening scene, when she nakedly prowls her bedroom, banging the metal headboard like a cat in a cage. Her hair gets a workout in the rest of the movie, especially during her car scenes: making out with Warren Beatty on their first getaway, screaming at Estelle Parsons after the first police raid, and, of course, dying in the final ambush. Dunaway's then-contemporary look is appropriate, since the film is very antiestablishment; robbing a bank is equated with running a bank. But it isn't politics that motivates Faye's character—she spends the whole picture trying to seduce Beatty. "Honey, don't you ever just want to be alone with me?" she pleads, sprawled across yet another bed.

HAMLET (1948). "This is the tragedy of a man who could not make up his mind," begins the movie, but that didn't stop him from changing his hair color. Actor-director-producer Laurence Olivier toiled in Hollywood long enough to know how to spruce up a classic for the masses, and this British production is particularly reminiscent of his 1940 hit *Rebecca*. The castle at Elsinore is just as mysterious as Manderley, William Walton's music is as thunderous as Franz Waxman's, and Olivier shares David O. Selznick's disregard for the sanctity of any screenwriter's work. Shakespeare's scenes are deleted or rearranged in any order that pleases Olivier; Rosencrantz and Guildenstern, for instance, aren't dead, they're on the cutting-room floor. Olivier the actor never forgets about Olivier the movie star; he plays the hero as the only blond in Denmark, save for Jean Simmons, who portrays Ophelia in a Goldilocks wig. Although the exteriors were filmed on location in Elsinore, most of the movie takes place in a studio castle filled with long halls and staircases so that Olivier's camera can have a lot of places to roam when it's not focused on his blond crew cut.

FOOD

●

BY MICHAEL ZIMBALIST

Home viewing expands movie munching options far beyond the oversized sweets and prepopped corn offered at most theater concessions. Thanks to VCRs, any conceivable edible—from take-out Chinese to a six-course meal—can now accompany the film of your choice. But what about the characters in the movie that you're watching? *They* have to eat, too. Home viewing lets you match the food on-screen and off-, the way you might pick the right wine to go with meat or fish. What follows is a veritable cornucopia of films in which eating and food are central elements.

BALANCED DIET

MINIMUM DAILY REQUIREMENTS

────────●────────

The guiding principle here is three meals a day, your basic breakfast, lunch, and dinner, but each with a nourishing movie to help digest the roughage. If you still insist on cheating, a nostalgic Baltimore diner that's perfect for late-night snacks is included at the end.

BREAKFAST AT TIFFANY'S (1961). When we first see Holly Golightly, it's daybreak in New York City, and she's slipping out of a taxi. Sipping coffee and nibbling on a Danish, she peeks at jewels in the window of Tif-

fany's. Clearly, she's not up early— she's out late. In Blake Edwards's adaptation of Truman Capote's novella, Audrey Hepburn is irresistible as the free-spirited Golightly, a spunky, mischievous playgirl of the Warhol '60s. When Paul (George Peppard), a struggling writer, takes the apartment upstairs from hers and quickly falls for his neighbor, it seems we might be in for fare as light as Holly's breakfast. Then Doc Golightly (Buddy Ebsen) shows up. He's the backwoods veterinarian who married Miss Holly when she was just a Texas bumpkin by the name of Lulumae Barnes, and he brings out rich layers of sensitivity in Hepburn's high-gloss performance. By the time she and Peppard are wrapped in their happy-ending embrace, this love story has become something you can really sink your teeth into.

THE PLOUGHMAN'S LUNCH (1983). James Penfield (Jonathan Pryce) works for BBC Radio and is writing a book about the Suez Crisis of 1956. He either is or isn't a socialist, depending on who asks him. Inhabiting a London that's the flip side of Hanif Kureishi's immigrant slums, Penfield and his friends are privileged, opportunistic cynics. The script by Ian McEwan relentlessly advances the idea that history is a deception serving the purposes of its creators. Even the title hammers home this theme. Lunching with a television adman,

Penfield has a Spartan meal of bread and cheddar cheese, known in England as the "ploughman's lunch." Because it was the hearty fare of farmers, a time-honored tradition? Guess again. The name comes from a '60s advertising campaign designed to get people to eat in pubs.

MY DINNER WITH ANDRE (1981). Playwright Wallace Shawn meets ex–theater director Andre Gregory for a dinner of potato soup, fish paté, and roast quail. Wally peppers Andre with questions about his recent experiences. The answers are extraordinary, if longwinded; questing for life's essence. Andre has been through just about every self-actualization movement imaginable. He's been to India. He's been to Tibet. He's done improvisational theater in the forest, and he's even been buried alive in a rebirth ritual. Wally listens, sipping and chewing. He's a man who loves his electric blanket and is content simply to wake up and find that no roach has died in the coffee he left out overnight. In sum, he tells Andre, "I don't really know what you're talking about." What these two *do* share is a craving for honest personal interaction in a world cluttered with distractions. And Louis Malle's surprisingly successful film suggests that dinner might provide the occasion for just that.

DINER (1982). Eating at the diner has sacramental significance for Eddie (Steve Guttenberg), Shrevie (Daniel Stern), Boogie (Mickey Rourke), Billy (Timothy Daly), and Fenwick (Kevin Bacon). Reunited in Baltimore for Eddie's wedding the week between Christmas, 1959, and New Year's, the boys talk through the night in their favorite booth. If only daytime difficulties didn't complicate their lives. Eddie suffers from pre-marital ambivalence. Shrevie can't communicate with his wife (Ellen Barkin), Fenwick has a drinking problem, and Boogie has gambling debts. The diner is a sanctuary where the illusion of their innocence remains intact. Writer-director Barry Levinson proves that shared roast beef sandwiches and french fries contribute as much to male bonding as football or hazing do.

GLUTTONY

ENOUGH IS NEVER ENOUGH

————•————

Excess and overindulgence take center stage in these four obese films—eating becomes an end in itself, perversely divorced from any satisfaction. (The great extravaganza *La Grande Bouffe* is regrettably not available on cassette.)

THE DISCREET CHARM OF THE BOURGEOISIE (1972). Dinner guests arrive on the wrong night. They retreat to a nearby inn, where the manager has just died. They make another date, only to find their hosts indisposed at the appointed hour by a fit of passionate lovemaking. Despite persistent mealtime obstacles, this hungry group will not be deterred in its desire to dine. No synopsis can convey the magic of this movie—it's a visual poem, structured as a dream within dreams. And whenever director Luis Buñuel's knife cuts too deeply under the skin of bourgeois good manners, the dreamers awaken and seek out their next meal.

THE TIN DRUM (1979). Through Volker Schlöndorff's savage lens, Günter Grass's epic fable about

Oskar, the boy who refuses to grow, becomes a story of life feeding on death. As the Nazis prey on Poland, Hitler's power expands, causing Oskar's mother, Agnes, to be torn between her Nazi husband and her Polish lover. Sickened by the sight of eels teeming in every crevice of a severed horse's head, she embarks on a self-destructive orgy of bulimia. And all the while, the Reich advances, celebrating each conquest by devouring its enemies' food, be it Hungarian salami or Dutch chocolates. Winner of the Academy Award for Best Foreign Language Film and co-winner (with Francis Coppola's *Apocalypse Now*) of the coveted Palme d'or at Cannes.

MONTY PYTHON'S THE MEANING OF LIFE (1983). Beginning with "The Miracle of Birth" (set in the "fetus frightening room"), the Pythons elaborate Life's stages in a rambling series of vignettes that dissipate into comic chaos. Food is a persistent theme, stuffing one's soul with meaning like bread crumbs in a turkey. And featured in "The Autumn Years" is absolutely the fattest man ever, dining in an elegant club. When he's finished eating everything on the menu, the waiter insists on force-feeding him one "wafer thin" mint to top it all off. Be warned—that's the bite that bursts the glutton's buttons. Thank heaven, Life's final stage, "Death," arrives shortly thereafter. In it, the Grim Reaper interrupts a dinner party. How could all the guests have died at the same time? The salmon mousse, of course.

FRENZY (1972). While an innocent man is hunted down by police, a serial killer stalks London, sexually assaulting his victims before strangling them with a necktie. Alfred Hitchcock returned to England after thirty years in Hollywood to film this "wrong man" scenario with a cast unfamiliar to most Americans, but the real star of *Frenzy* is food, used as a metaphor for violence. The killer, Robert Rusk, a vegetable monger, informs one of his victims of a saying in his trade: "Don't squeeze the goods until they're yours." He stashes a corpse in a sack of potatoes, then has to dig the poor woman out to retrieve the monogrammed silver lapel pin he uses as a toothpick, which is clutched in her fist. Meanwhile, the wife of the police inspector on the case is taking a gourmet cooking class. Discussing various leads with her husband, she serves him truly horrifying meals of *soupe de poisson,* roast quail with grapes, and pigs' feet in tripe sauce. His reaction to her unsavory gustatory innovations is "Lovely, lovely," the same haunting chorus that the murderer intones while ravishing his human prey.

SEXUAL APPETITES

SUGAR AND SPICE

———————●———————

A sumptuous culinary creation can inspire passionate desires to smell and to touch as well as to taste. In the following films, characters hunger for more than just food.

TOM JONES (1963). This commercial and critical blockbuster not only garnered Oscars for Best Picture, Director, Adapted Screenplay, and Score, it also vaulted Henry Fielding back onto the best-seller list for the first time in two hundred years. Director Tony Richardson's narrative zips forward with Keystone Kop craziness—using such self-conscious flourishes as titles, wipes, freeze frames, and asides to the camera—and Albert Finney, as the foundling Tom Jones, romps with relish through the English countryside. On his way to London, Tom encounters Mrs. Waters (Joyce Redman), and the two share a leering, lusty-eyed feast that is arguably the most erotic food scene in movie history. They devour lobsters, fowl, and mutton, slurp oysters, and conclude their repast with crisp apples and juicy pears. Still unsated, they race from dinner table to bedroom. How they manage to couple with such bloated bellies is a question the film successfully eludes.

THE DECLINE OF THE AMERICAN EMPIRE (1986). At a health club in contemporary Quebec, four women frankly discuss their multifarious sex lives. In a country kitchen, four men, preparing dinner, do the same. Dominique, a historian, claims that the frantic pursuit of personal happiness typifies a civilization in decline; at the same time, Remy, a professor who once visited a brothel on the way to see his mistress, argues that decline is always marked by women's rise to power. Midway through the movie, the women arrive for the dinner: *coulibiac* of trout in mousseline sauce. This is sophisticated fare indeed, but pillow talk is never far from the lips of these effete academics. (After all, even Wittgenstein believed the only certainty is our ability to act with the body.) Following dinner, Dominique reveals that she's slept with Remy, devastating his wife. Yet by morning the insatiable eightsome is back in the kitchen, frying up bacon and eggs and talking about what they know best.

SLEEPER (1973). Frozen in tinfoil like a leftover, writer-director-star Woody Allen, as Miles Monroe, is thawed and awakens in the distant future, where vegetables grow to gargantuan size and sex has been abandoned in favor of a machine called the orgasmatron. Two hundred years earlier, Miles was part owner of the Happy Carrot Health Food Store, so, naturally, his first request upon reviving is for wheat germ, organic honey, and tiger's milk. His doctor is nonplussed. Why "no deep fat, no steak or cream pies or hot fudge?" she asks. A colleague explains that back in 1973, such goodies "were thought to be unhealthy. Precisely the opposite of what we now know to be true." Disguised as a domestic robot, Woody woos dilettante poet Luna Schlosser, played by Diane Keaton, and confesses to her that all he believes in is sex and death, "but at least after death you're not nauseous." Woody must have added BHT to this one—nothing else could explain why his nonstop barrage of sight gags and cultural barbs retains such freshness.

ACQUIRED TASTES

NOT FOR EVERYBODY

———————•———————

Certain brands of cinematic cuisine may prove difficult for some to swallow. The following smorgasbord of cult movies is not recommended for those with weak stomachs or a low tolerance for utter silliness; but for those who can take it, each is a gourmet's delight.

SOYLENT GREEN (1973). The year is 2022. The residents of squalid, overpopulated New York City queue up for their ration of soylent green, "the miracle food of high-energy plankton, gathered from the oceans of the world." Or is it? Charlton Heston stars as Detective Thorn, sharing his seedy digs with Edward G. Robinson, as Sol Roth, an old police librarian who likes to reminisce, "When I was a kid, food was food." He actually cries at the sight of real beef. Thorn and Roth feast on a pathetic meal of mottled meat, wilted lettuce, and gnarled apples, savoring every precious bite. In the end, Thorn discovers something about soylent green that's sure to leave a bad taste in your mouth. (Note: The exterior shots are *supposed* to appear green. Don't adjust your set.)

EATING RAOUL (1982). This deadpan farce teams Paul Bartel and Mary Woronov as Paul and Mary Bland, a frigid California couple who dream of opening a restaurant where the specialty would be "the Bland enchilada." Paul and Mary detest the oversexed swingers who seem to be everywhere, and they need money to finance their dream, so they devise a scheme: Lure the happy swingers into their apartment with the promise of kinky sex, then kill them and snatch their cash. After all, as Mary observes, "these swinger types always seem to have money." Bartel, who directed, makes this outrageous premise almost disappear into humdrum banality. Such lines as "Why don't you go to bed, honey; I'll bag the Nazi and straighten up around here" go down as easy as warm milk.

THE STUFF (1985). A night watchman notices something peculiar frothing up in the snow, so what does he do? What you or I or anyone would do: He dips in his finger and has a taste! "Sure is smooth," he says. "Tasty. Sweet." And before you can say "Twinkie," the whole country can't get enough of the Stuff, a nutritious, low-calorie dessert that, oddly enough, looks a lot like shaving cream. Whipped up by writer-director Larry Cohen, this free-wheeling tale of our sweet-toothed culture lampoons advertising, government, industry, suburbia, and even paramilitary survivalist groups. The near-bankrupt ice cream industry hires ex-FBI agent Mo Rutherford (Michael Moriarty) to find out what this Stuff is. Hooking up with Chocolate Chip Charlie (Garrett Morris), Mo learns that it's actually alive, destroying the insides of Stuff junkies until it erupts, lavalike, from their distended mouths. Yum!

LOVE AND MARRIAGE

• ———

BY MARJORIE ROSEN

When it's time for Dad to strain his bankbook as strains of *Lohengrin* and Mendelssohn accompany his little darling down the aisle, it's time for America to get married—and, in fact, marriage seems to be more fashionable today than ever. And so, forthwith, a bouquet of choice movies on videocassette that celebrate brides, grooms, and honeymoons, both happy and sad.

LOVE IN BLOOM

FLOWERS AND PLEDGES OF "FOREVER"

———— • ————

It's been said that the music of a wedding procession resembles the music of soldiers going into battle, and one might even argue that in Hollywood, at least, the war often begins

DANIEL TORRES

not with the nuptial event but with the courtship.

THE PHILADELPHIA STORY (1940). Katharine Hepburn, voted box-office poison by movie exhibitors in the late '30s, cleverly gained control of the film rights to this Philip Barry love song to the rich after starring in it on Broadway. When the property went Hollywood, Ms. B. O. Poison negotiated herself back onto the screen. Good thing: The picture, and her comeback, were a smash. In the most sophisticated and scrumptious of all screwball comedies, a Kate of breathtaking grace plays headstrong heiress Tracy Lord, who, on the eve of her wedding to a sleazy politico, finds that she's also a little bit in love with hayseed reporter James Stewart and with her debonair upper-crust ex, Cary Grant, as well. The burning question: Will she or won't she walk down the aisle—and with whom? If you never regarded Hepburn—or Stewart—as sexy, take a gander as the two of them drink themselves silly on the eve of the Big Event. Who steals Kate's heart? I won't tell, but Stewart steals the picture and got an Oscar to boot.

MARTY (1955). It wasn't George Bush, it was the late screenwriter Paddy Chayefsky who invented the Wimp Factor, in this story of the courtship between a pair of "dogs"— Marty (Ernest Borgnine), the fat Bronx butcher too awkward to find himself a girl, and Clara (Betsy Blair), the plain schoolteacher he meets at a local dance hall. "You get kicked around enough, you get to be a real professor of pain," Marty indiscreetly tells the timid wallflower, who has just been ditched by her date and seems to be chairing the Pain Department. Natch, in no time at all they're a twosome, much to the chagrin of Marty's Italian mama and his best friend, Angie, who prefer him available and around. Originally written for television, the movie is as self-conscious in its attempt at naturalism as Marty is. Yet Borgnine, in the performance of his life, does his best to keep Chayefsky honest.

THE GRADUATE (1967). This smash hit surprised some industry veterans, who didn't anticipate how strongly youthful audiences would identify with the middle-class angst of the movie's naive hero, Benjamin Braddock (Dustin Hoffman). Back then, he seemed quite the rebel, carrying on with his dad's partner's wife, Mrs. Robinson (Anne Bancroft), and then carrying off her daughter (Katharine Ross) in a wedding scene that crosses *It Happened One Night* with *Tarzan and His Mate*. *The Graduate*'s "small triumph," wrote Pauline Kael, was that it "domesticated alienation." Perhaps; yet what truly plugged it into the '60s sensibility was its contempt for everyone over thirty, especially Mrs. R., who probably ate nails for breakfast and would have frightened Casanova. Paradoxically, it's still courtship and marriage that act as balms for our hero's alienation—or maybe Ben, emulating Mommy, Daddy, and all those wretchedly bourgeois grown-ups, is, after all, a dull boy. No matter, Mike Nichols, stunning audiences with high-tech images and wry comedy, won the Best Director Oscar for this, his second picture.

THE HEARTBREAK KID (1972). As the young Jewish newlyweds drive down to Miami, telltale signs of dissatisfaction become etched like a road map on the face of the groom (Charles Grodin). First, the bride (Jeannie Berlin) sings off-key, and he's annoyed.

They make love, and he's unmoved. She gets a bad sunburn, and he's repelled. No wonder he flips when Wasp goddess Cybill Shepherd appears. "I made the big mistake about five days ago," Grodin moans about his marriage, "and when I say *big*, I mean Radio City Music Hall big." Neil Simon wrote it, Elaine May directed it, the cast is perfect, and the picture is as hilarious today as when it came out. It's also such an exercise in Jewish self-loathing that any self-respecting JAP like *moi* will squirm. The most memorable—and heart-breaking—moment: the bride (Berlin is May's real-life daughter) eating a double egg-salad sandwich, unaware of the egg dribbling down her chin or of her brand-new husband watching it with unremitting revulsion.

A WEDDING (1978). Director Robert Altman's mischievous sensibility shapes every frame of this frenetic, all-star black comedy about that venerable institution the wedding reception. The entire film takes place on the festive day, and whatever can go wrong does. Granny (Lillian Gish) dies in her upstairs bedroom as the reception begins; later on, gale winds blow the party apart. Every alternative permutation of coupling is thrown into the mix: the wedding co-ordinator (Geraldine Chaplin) puts the make on the bride (Amy Stryker); the groom's uncle (Pat McCormack) puts the make on the bride's mother (Carol Burnett); and the bride's sister (Mia Farrow) announces she's pregnant by the groom (Desi Arnaz, Jr.). Meanwhile, the groom's mother (Nina van Pallandt) mainlines drugs in the bathroom. And that's just during the hors d'oeuvres. Only one thing's missing from this one: a plot. But why be picky? *A Wedding* surprises with its spirit. Burnett and McCormack get

STAR MARRIAGES
IF AT FIRST YOU DON'T SUCCEED

—————⬤—————

CARY GRANT
Virginia Cherrill
Barbara Hutton
Betsy Drake
Dyan Cannon
Barbara Harris

ZSA ZSA GABOR
Burhan Belge
Conrad Hilton
George Sanders
Hebert Hutner
Joshua Cosden
Jack Ryan
Michael O'Hara
Felipe de Alba
Prince Frederic von Anhalt

MICKEY ROONEY
Ava Gardner
Betty Jane Rase
Martha Vickers
Elaine Mahnken
Barbara Thomason
Margie Lang
Carolyn Hockett
Jan Chamberlain

HENRY FONDA
Margaret Sullavan
Frances Seymour Brokaw
Susan Blanchard
Afdera Franchetti
Shirlee Adams

GLORIA SWANSON
Wallace Beery
Herbert K. Somborn
Marquis Henri de la Falaise de la Coudraye
Michael Farmer
William N. Davey
William Dufty

my vote for best couple: they make middle-aged passion seem funny and poignant.

DOMESTIC BLISS

HONEYMOON TO HOUSE OF HORROR

———————●———————

In its heyday, Hollywood sold fairy tales about love and marriage. Anything less than perfect harmony between spouses was treated as high drama *(Gaslight)* or flippant comedy *(Adam's Rib),* and not until the influx of postwar pictures from abroad and the rise of post-'60s independent film-makers here at home did movies begin to explore the marriage circle more realistically.

GASLIGHT (1944). "If the story is anything, it is that of a woman desperately, hopelessly in love with a monster," mogul David O. Selznick once wrote to producer Louis B. Mayer about *Gaslight.* Fear has many faces, and the astonishing Ingrid Bergman captures them all in her subtle and voluptuous Oscar-winning performance as a devoted wife being driven insane by a diabolical and greedy husband (Charles Boyer). "Bergman wasn't normally a timid woman; she was healthy," director George Cukor aptly pointed out. "To reduce someone like that to a scared, jittering creature is interesting and dramatic." The picture, adapted from Patrick Hamilton's play *Angel Street,* boasts lavish and evocative Victorian interiors (which won an Oscar, too). Also noteworthy: Boyer's cold-as-death eyes and the self-assured movie debut of eighteen-year-old Angela Lansbury, as the tarty housemaid.

ADAM'S RIB (1949). When husband and wife Adam and Amanda Bonner (Spencer Tracy and Katharine Hepburn), both attorneys, wind up on opposite sides of a court case, their domestic bliss is sorely tried as well. The case? A crime of passion committed by a jealous wife (Judy Holliday) against her philandering husband. Ruth Gordon and Garson Kanin's razor-sharp screenplay and the palpable dynamic between cool Tracy and ardent Hepburn (an off-screen item) make this skirmish in the War Between the Sexes truly grand and so modern it could have

DANIEL TORRES

been written yesterday. When Amanda continually one-ups poor Adam in court, he complains, "All of a sudden I don't like being married to what is known as a *new woman*." In another priceless scene, a hefty female demonstrates that "woman can be quite the equal of man" by picking up the stalwart Adam and raising him aloft like a trophy.

SMASH PALACE (1981). A strong shot of marriage on the rocks, New Zealand style. Al, a loner with a short fuse, owns an auto-wrecking company called, yes, Smash Palace, which just happens to describe his mismatched marriage as well. Jacqui, his wife, a civilized sort, hates living in the "graveyard" of his smashed cars, violent lovemaking, and vicious temper. When she gets fed up and leaves, taking with her their young daughter, Al snaps and kidnaps the child. The fury of his response is fascinating, horrifying, and, in the end, touching. As portrayed by Bruno Lawrence and cowritten and directed by Roger Donaldson, Al emerges as not just a brute out of control but a pathetic figure eaten up by his own irrational behavior.

BETRAYAL (1983). Harold Pinter, who adapted this film from his play, is arguably the finest scenarist in the business. (He also brilliantly adapted John Fowles's *The French Lieutenant's Woman* and wrote an extraordinary unproduced screenplay based on Proust's *Remembrance of Things Past*.) Here he explores the anatomy of an affair—and the dissolution of a marriage—by going backward in time with a triangle of friends and lovers who've been inextricably involved for seven years. Jeremy Irons plays a literary agent, the best friend of publisher Ben Kingsley; Patricia Hodge is

---

STAR MARRIAGES
SO HAPPY TOGETHER, TILL DEATH DO US PART

———◉———

HUMPHREY BOGART AND LAUREN BACALL
Married in 1945;
Bogart died in 1957

PAUL NEWMAN AND JOANNE WOODWARD
Married in 1958

GEORGE BURNS AND GRACIE ALLEN
Married in 1926;
Allen died in 1964

HUME CRONYN AND JESSICA TANDY
Married in 1942

LAURENCE OLIVIER AND JOAN PLOWRIGHT
Married in 1961;
Olivier died in 1989

ROBERT WAGNER AND NATALIE WOOD
Married in 1957;
divorced in 1962;
remarried in 1972;
Wood died in 1981

BLAKE EDWARDS AND JULIE ANDREWS
Married in 1969

CHARLES LAUGHTON AND ELSA LANCHESTER
Married in 1929;
Laughton died in 1962
Lanchester died in 1986

ELI WALLACH AND ANNE JACKSON
Married in 1948

Kingsley's wife and Irons's mistress. His eyes gleaming with the knowledge and humiliation of his betrayal, Kingsley stands out in an outstanding ensemble. David Jones's directorial understatements faithfully serve Pinter's sharp dramatic truths.

DIVORCE

THANKS FOR THE MEMORIES

●

Hollywood's view of divorce is typically comical or clichéd. If you're seeking more resonant truths about heartbreak, you'll have to look across the Atlantic.

THE AWFUL TRUTH (1937). The blueprint is simple enough: A hotheaded (but witty) couple begin divorce pro-

---

STAR MARRIAGES
FREE SPIRITS: THE SINGLE FILE

●

GRETA GARBO

LILLIAN GISH

DIANE KEATON

MONTGOMERY CLIFT

LIZABETH SCOTT

VINCENT GARDENIA

RODDY MCDOWALL

TAB HUNTER

ANJELICA HUSTON

AL PACINO

JULIE CHRISTIE

JOHN TRAVOLTA

RICHARD GERE

---

ceedings, but as soon as one—or both—are about to take the Big Step with someone else, they realize that they're still in love. In screwball comedies as good as this one, however, the road to reconciliation is paved with inspired lunacy: When former marrieds Irene Dunne and Cary Grant begin battling for custody of their dog, the judge asks the animal to take the stand. Producer-director Leo McCarey's classic confection contains many daffy bits, including a hilarious payoff scene with the dog and a hat. It also sports a stuffy Ralph Bellamy as the rich country boy whom Dunne is trying to loosen from his domineering mother's grip; he has the distinction of singing one of the most tuneless versions of "Home on the Range" ever heard, and practically steals the picture from seasoned charmers Grant and Dunne.

THE WOMEN (1939). Wild bitchery and high camp as Norma Shearer, Rosalind Russell, Paulette Goddard, Mary Boland, and Joan Crawford paint their nails Jungle Red, dab Summer Rain behind their ears, steal each other's husbands, lovers, and fashion secrets, and await their Reno divorces (along with a meek Joan Fontaine). George Cukor directed this all-female cast in a script based on Clare Boothe's play. The plot revolves around Shearer's determination to win back her hubby from gold digger Crawford. "A woman in love has no pride," Shearer gloats, victorious, at the film's finale. Not exactly a feminist anthem, this Paleolithic relic of male-female relations nevertheless has a certain je ne sais quoi. Best scene: the ladies'-room wrestling match between Crawford and a hilariously nearsighted Roz Russell.

SCENES FROM A MARRIAGE (1974).

Aching with recognitions, this may be the best film ever made about a marriage and the pain of its subsequent dissolution. In a mere half-dozen episodes (lasting 168 minutes), Bergman probes the relationship between Marianne (Liv Ullmann) and Johan (Erland Josephson), who at first seem to be the perfect couple. Married ten years, they have two daughters (whom we never meet) and solid careers, and they talk constantly about how happy they are. Then Johan startles Marianne by leaving her. The movie, originally made for Swedish television, charts their passions, boredom, deceptions, dependencies, and loneliness. "I'm not getting at the truth of our relationship," Johan tells Marianne, the two now lovers again years after their divorce. "I don't think there exists *one* truth." Bergman dissects human ambivalence better than anyone else, and you don't have to be an aficionado of his work to be devastated by *Scenes*.

THE WAY WE WERE (1973). What a great woman's fantasy: a loud-mouthed Jewish girl hooks a gorgeous guy by dint of her brains, because, as spunky Katie Morosky keeps telling Wasp Hubbell Gardiner, "I love the way you write." This is Hollywood schmaltz at its most romantic and ambitious—the story of an unlikely courtship and a marriage that fails not for lack of love but for lack of, or at least difference in, principles. Opening in the '30s and continuing through the McCarthy era, the story focuses on how Katie (Barbra Streisand) eats, sleeps, and breathes commitment—picketing Franco, marching against McCarthy, handing out Ban the Bomb flyers. Though she looks plain, her intelligence and spirit transform her into a beauty. On the other hand, Hubbell (Robert Redford), the writer for whom "everything came too easy," may look like a dreamboat, but inside he's empty, a sellout. *He* knows it, *we* know it, but poor Katie never does. In its day, the Streisand-Redford chemistry dazzled so—especially in the tearjerker finale—that even today, Ray Stark is seriously considering a sequel.

SHOOT THE MOON (1982). George Dunlap (Albert Finney) sits alone in his tux, crying. Faith Dunlap (Diane Keaton) reclines in her bath, singing a Beatles tune as tears roll down her face. George loses control and beats his fourteen-year-old daughter with a hanger. Shades of *Mommie Dearest?* Wrong. British director Alan Parker and screenwriter Bo Goldman avoid cheap melodrama in their searing portrait not just of a marriage gone sour but of an entire family torn apart by divorce. The four young Dunlap girls are the real thing—kids who fight, whine, and take worm medicine. They're also furious that their father has deserted them. "I don't think he left you," Faith explains. "He left *me*." There are remarkable insights and performances here (the cast includes Dana Hill, Karen Allen, and Peter Weller); Keaton's especially is a wonder of delicacy. As for the title, it refers to hearts, the card game, in which the player can risk all by "shooting the moon." The movie does, too, and the risk pays off.

TV ACTORS IN THE MOVIES

BY CHRISTOPHER CONNELLY

When season reruns drone on ad infinitum, you can catch the stars of your favorite TV series in some surprising big-screen roles.

SITCOMS

THAT'S A LAUGH

Time was when actors in situation comedies were doomed to an eternal retirement in the TV ghetto. If you can see them free every week, why pay to see them in a movie theater? But thanks to the successful crossovers of such performers as Michael J. Fox and Shelley Long, sitcom stars are now judged to be ripe prospects for big-screen work. And some of those mentioned below have slipped the bonds of their sitcom stereotypes to create fresh, enduring characterizations in the movies.

JUST BETWEEN FRIENDS (1986). For an actor so indelibly identified with a television role, *Cheers'* Ted Danson has had a surprisingly variegated film career. In this little-seen movie, Danson uses Sam Malone's rakish charm to invigorate what is otherwise a rather tepid tearjerker. Directed by Allan Burns, who co-created *The Mary Tyler Moore Show* with James L. Brooks, *Just Between Friends* stars Danson as a Southern California seismologist who's married to Mary Tyler Moore but is also having an affair with local newscaster Christine Lahti. Lahti and Moore meet at an aerobics class and become pals, little suspecting that they're sleeping with the same man. Unfortunately, the comic payoffs are slim, and the movie soon swerves into *Terms of Endearment*–style pathos that Burns isn't as deft at handling as his old cohort Brooks was. Moore seems uncharacteristically stiff and awkward throughout, but Danson's performance is filled with small touches that make it enjoyable. Watch for his light, easy flirting with Lahti as she adjusts his tie before interviewing him on live TV—and his mischievous reaction when he catches his son watching an R-rated movie on cable.

LIGHT OF DAY (1987). Paul Schrader's tale of a Cleveland bar band has grit to spare, but even an appropriately glum performance by Michael J. Fox—moonlighting from *Family Ties*—couldn't make this movie a hit. *Light of Day* presents Fox and real-life rocker Joan Jett as a brother-and-sister team grappling with family upheaval while they're looking for that million-dollar sound. Schrader expertly captures the joyless anomie of a struggling band (no drugs or wild times for these guys—they don't have the money), but his honesty sandbags the movie. As a unit, the band has to be mediocre, or we'd wonder why they haven't made it big. It's no surprise that Fox is preternaturally charming, especially when he and his toddler nephew improvise a song called "You Got No Place to Go." But Jett, a sturdy survivor of those teeny-bait terrors the Runaways, is miscast—not because she can't act (she can) but because she can't sing well enough. And when Bruce Springsteen gives a band a made-for-radio hit on the order of "Light of Day" for its finale, it's advisable to have some top chops on hand.

PLENTY (1985). It's postwar England, and there's nothing worth living for, and poor Meryl Streep is losing her marbles, and, uh . . . well, thank God there's also Tracey Ullman (of Fox Broadcasting's the late, great *The Tracey Ullman Show*). As Streep's boho buddy, Ullman makes for one hot-dog soubrette. Ullman's Alice—a cheeky, libidinous fun-lover lost in an avalanche of anhedonics—saucily sends up everyone in sight, particularly Streep's hopeless foreign-service spouse (Charles Dance). Streep's performance is sublime, but toward the ninety-minute mark, things get awfully slow. Use of the fast-forward

button is encouraged, so long as you don't miss the film's best scene: an exquisitely funny dinner-party-from-hell sequence on the eve of the Suez Crisis, featuring John Gielgud.

BILL COSBY—"HIMSELF" (1982). Before *The Cosby Show*'s creator became America's sitcom icon, he was the greatest stand-up comedian this side of Richard Pryor. Marvel at how he quotes a Carol Burnett remark about labor pains ("It's like someone

---

VIDEO TRANSFER

MOVIE DIRECTORS WHO FIRST BUILT A REPUTATION IN TELEVISION

⎯⎯⎯⎯⎯●⎯⎯⎯⎯⎯

MEL BROOKS

CARL REINER

JOHN FRANKENHEIMER

JAMES L. BROOKS

GARRY MARSHALL

PENNY MARSHALL

ROB REINER

ALAN ALDA

LEONARD NIMOY

RON HOWARD

ROBERT ALTMAN

STEVEN SPIELBERG

KEN RUSSELL

ARTHUR PENN

SIDNEY LUMET

STUART ROSENBERG

NORMAN JEWISON

taking your lower lip and pulling it over your head"), drops it, and then pays it off with a killer punch line ten minutes later. Yes, before the sweaters, before the best-sellers, even before that so-cute-you-could-just-eat-her-with-a-spoon Keshia Knight Pulliam, Cosby was the master of this form, and *Bill Cosby—"Himself"* shows him at his best: live and in concert.

SOAPS

THE NEVER-ENDING STORY

————●————

Okay, so *L.A. Law* and *St. Elsewhere* aren't really soaps—perhaps "continuing dramas" would be closer to the mark—but any way you slice it, the intelligence and acting challenges these shows provide have enabled them to attract the services of some truly top-of-the-line performers, many of them having already offered considerable achievements on film.

BETWEEN THE LINES (1977). Before becoming *L.A. Law*'s estimable shiksa goddess, Jill Eikenberry made her film debut in this enjoyable Joan Micklin Silver effort about the staff of an alternative Boston newspaper that's being sold to a more money-minded owner. *Between the Lines* may be virtually plotless, but its young ensemble cast (assembled by Juliet Taylor) is teeming with the best and brightest of the late '70s, John Heard, Jeff Goldblum, Stephen Collins, Bruno Kirby, and Lindsay Crouse among them. Goldblum revs up for his spree-to-come in *The Big Chill* with a dazzling turn as the paper's music critic, explaining to a class of wide-eyed Radcliffe students that if rock 'n' roll really is here to stay, then it won't be at his house—he doesn't have the room. The lovely Eikenberry handles her wholesome role as the paper's receptionist with consummate grace: supplying joints to Goldblum, calmly fending off the advances of Lewis J. Stadlen's ad director (at least until she socks him in the crotch with a telephone), and breezily sashaying through some girl-group lip-synching. She plays her decision to quit the paper with just enough embarrassment—she's not used to being the center of attention—so the moment doesn't have too self-satisfied a taste to it. This wistful, slightly sentimental movie also features *Taxi* mainstay Marilu Henner as a stripper and Southside Johnny and the Asbury Jukes pumping out the party-time classic "I Don't Want to Go Home."

MOVIE MOVIE (1978). *L.A. Law*'s Harry Hamlin has seen his film career judged by the unintentionally laughable *Making Love*. But Hamlin's underexplored flair for comedy turns up in "Dynamite Hands," the first half of this hilarious parody of a 1930s double feature, directed by Stanley *(Singin' in the Rain)* Donen. Hamlin stars as Joey Popchik, a would-be lawyer who becomes a professional boxer to finance an eye operation for his sister (Kathleen Beller). Under the tutelage of George C. Scott's prototypical manager, Popchik ascends to boxing greatness—but finds his head turned by the ultra-vampy "Troubles" Moran (Ann Reinking). The laughs flow like liniment, with malaprops and mix-and-match metaphors abounding in Larry Gelbart and Sheldon Keller's script. "How hard it is to say what there are no words for," intones Hamlin as the end nears. "But when a man speaks what's true and what's right, then his mouth is ten feet tall."

Don't forget to stick around for part two ("Baxter's Beauties of 1933"), so you can hear Scott, as a dying Broadway producer, give one of filmdom's best exit lines: "Funny, isn't it? One minute, you're standing in the wings. Next minute, you're wearing them."

ECHO PARK (1986). *L.A. Law*'s Susan Dey as a struggling-actress-turned-Strip-O-Grammer? Tom Hulce as a pizza delivery man? Hey, why not? Everything else seems pleasantly off-kilter in this easygoing Austrian-funded comedy about a handful of Los Angeles outcasts. And while some of you may be flinging shoes at the screen when Hulce uncorks his now-infamous laugh, Dey is truly a delight. The way she taps her young son on the arm with the back of her hand as she leaves for work, and the way she reacts when he catches her stripping at a party—each is a perfectly observed moment. There's some fine work in smaller roles here, too, especially by Timothy Carey as a pizza shop owner, John Paragon (Jambi on *Pee-wee's Playhouse*) as Dey's stripping instructor, and Cassandra Peterson, who takes off her Elvira makeup for a nifty comic turn as a health club receptionist.

SABOTEUR (1942). Norman Lloyd, *St. Elsewhere*'s Dr. Auschlander, plays the title role—and the MacGuffin—in this Alfred Hitchcock suspenser. It is he who concocts the destruction of a fighter-plane factory and the death of a plant worker, implicating the worker's best friend (Robert Cummings), who then sets out to track Lloyd down. The film has been faulted for its lurching plot development and its unsatisfying ending, but if you're like me, you'll be too caught up to notice. The young Lloyd is creepy as you

please, a wonderfully banal villain—and a far cry from his good-hearted, if cranky, medical persona.

VIDEO TRANSFER
MOVIE STARS WHO GOT THEIR FIRST BIG BREAK ON TELEVISION

STEVE MCQUEEN
Wanted: Dead or Alive

CLINT EASTWOOD
Rawhide

ANNETTE FUNICELLO
The Mickey Mouse Club

GOLDIE HAWN
Good Morning World
Rowan & Martin's Laugh-In

BURT REYNOLDS
Riverboat
Gunsmoke
Hawk
Dan August

JOHN TRAVOLTA
Welcome Back, Kotter

MIA FARROW AND RYAN O'NEAL
Peyton Place

MICHAEL DOUGLAS
The Streets of San Francisco

TOM HANKS
Bosom Buddies

WARREN BEATTY
The Many Loves of Dobie Gillis

SALLY FIELD
Gidget
The Flying Nun
Alias Smith and Jones
The Girl With Something Extra

ROBIN WILLIAMS
Mork & Mindy

DRAMAS

TUBULAR HELLS

———————●———————

It seems surprising that, out of all small-screen performers, actors in TV dramas have had the most difficult time breaking into movies. Is it the dead-earnest looks on their faces as they get their jobs done? The often mind-numbing plots? Even Tom Selleck had to make it through *High Road to China, Lassiter,* and *Runaway* before hitting it big with *Three Men and a Baby*. And while TV drama has attracted such notable names as the ones below (and others, such as Angela Lansbury and Howard E. Rollins, Jr.), it seems to be a hard line of work to leave.

THE HARRAD EXPERIMENT (1973). Maybe they should have called this *The Importance of Being Easy*. Harrad College, declares a professor (James Whitmore), is trying "a controlled group experiment in premarital relations." And later: "You're going to be expected—no, I mean encouraged—to have sexual intimacy." Heeeeeeeewack! A drawling Don Johnson—still sporting some pre-*Miami Vice* baby fat around the face—and Victoria Thompson are the "fast" teens; Bruno Kirby (here billed as "B. Kirby, Jr.") and Laurie Walters are the slow (ahem) pokes. Though there's nudity aplenty—even Johnson goes full-frontal about ten minutes in—there aren't any love scenes to speak of. Actually, the acting from the fellas isn't all that bad; Whitmore spins out line readings with as much wicked inventiveness as, say, Laurence Olivier in *The Betsy,* and Johnson and Kirby give it the old college try. God knows, they don't make 'em like this anymore. And if they did, it would be about New Age instead of sex, and instead of a guest appearance from the Ace Trucking Company, you'd get Ramtha.

BREAKER MORANT (1980). With his portrayal of Lieutenant Harry "Breaker" Morant, Edward Woodward (the suave avenger of CBS's *The Equalizer*) helped kick off the burst of American interest in this trial drama from down under about the leader of an Australian unit (Morant is an Englishman) accused of killing prisoners during the Boer War. Morant and his men—whose tactics are among the only effective countermeasures to the Boer resistance—have become the scapegoats for their British superiors, who are seeking a way to disguise the officially sanctioned brutality of their South African rule. The courtroom sequences are as taut and dramatic as you'd like, and Woodward showcases the same steely pride that's made him one of America's most unlikely sex symbols. Directed by Bruce Beresford *(Driving Miss Daisy)*.

DRAMADIES

MIXED COMPANY

———————●———————

The distinctly uneuphonious genre tag bestowed on such comedy-drama hybrids as *The Days and Nights of Molly Dodd* and the lab experiment in audience torture known as *thirtysomething* ("But what about *my* needs?") does at least pay tribute to the considerable skills of its performers. On TV and in their movie work as well, Blair Brown and Dennis Franz have played both sides of the comedy-drama dichotomy.

ALTERED STATES (1980). A hallucinogen-laden movie starring William Hurt (in his film debut), directed by Ken Russell, and written by Paddy Chayefsky? Let's just say that there must have been easier times for Blair Brown, of *The Days and Nights of Molly Dodd*. The svelte, alluring Brown races pell-mell through Chayefsky's dialogue, just as Hurt does, gasping for breath like a lummox on a Lifecycle. Most of you will howl when Hurt takes some mysterious psychedelic drug, descends the evolutionary ladder, and pops out of a sensory deprivation tank as an ape—at which point Russell cuts to a barely bestirred night watchman giving it all a lazy gee-what-*was*-that? glance. Poor Chayefsky insisted that his name be removed from the credits. As for Brown, she spunkily holds her own throughout Russell's psychosexual fantasies—even the final one, in which her naked body suddenly turns into what looks like an electric blanket gone haywire.

BLOW OUT (1981). Fans of the last year of *Hill Street Blues* know what an excellent actor Dennis Franz is. Blessed with a physiognomy that fairly screams "sleazeball," Franz nevertheless imbues his characters with an unlikely grace. The relationship that his *Hill Street* character, Norman Buntz, crafted with Sid the Snitch (Peter Jurasik) probably deserved feature-length exploration, instead of the garish, misfiring spin-off series *Beverly Hills Buntz*. Those eager to sample Franz's finer skills can check out this Brian De Palma masterwork, as brilliant and heartless as a gemstone. Franz plays an Oil Can Harry who helps cause the tire blowout—and subsequent fatal car crash—that the hero, played by John Travolta, inadvertently captures on audio tape. The victim is a political candidate, and

the event sets in motion a series of horrifyingly eerie events that recall the John F. Kennedy assassination, Chappaquiddick, and Watergate (and Michelangelo Antonioni's *Blow-Up*). When the stakes get raised, you can feel Franz's distress—he wasn't figuring on anything quite this heavy.

VIDEO TRANSFER

FILM FLOPS STARRING HOT TELEVISION ACTORS

———————●———————

Somebody Killed Her Husband
FARRAH FAWCETT-MAJORS

High Road to China
TOM SELLECK

Leonard Part 6
BILL COSBY

Head
THE MONKEES

Hero at Large
JOHN RITTER

On the Right Track
GARY COLEMAN

Satisfaction
JUSTINE BATEMAN

Heroes
HENRY WINKLER

Going Ape!
TONY DANZA

A Fine Mess
TED DANSON AND HOWIE MANDEL

Zapped!
SCOTT BAIO

Hard to Hold
RICK SPRINGFIELD

Goin' Coconuts
DONNY AND MARIE OSMOND

School Days

By Terri Minsky

Personally, I hated my tenth high school reunion. After all this time, I had thought, there would be no more cliques and no more tough kids, and I could finally talk to the boys whom I admired from afar and gossip with the cheerleaders, who were never my friends. But once I was in the room with those people, I found myself feeling neither popular nor outcast, just as I had a decade before—stuck in the vast nowhere-land that distinguished my undistinguished four years. I swore I would never go to another reunion; any desire I might have to recall school (fondly or otherwise) will now be satisfied by the movies.

FUTURE PROMISE

Most Likely to Succeed

————————————●————————————

You've gotten your diploma, tossed your mortarboard in the air—now what? Only time will tell if you've just ended the best years of your life or the worst. For the students in this group of movies, the lessons they learn in school—from teachers, friends, lovers—are the best preparation there is for the struggles beyond. For some of them, however, it's not enough.

THE GROUP (1966). Lots of movies—*The Big Chill, Diner,* and *St. Elmo's Fire* among them—follow school friends as they cope with the difficul-

ties of life after graduation, but none better than this Sidney Lumet film about eight Vassar girls from the class of 1933. It's based on Mary McCarthy's catty novel and cast brilliantly—here is one of the very rare times when characters in a well-loved book come to the screen just as readers envisioned them. Larry Hagman, known at the time as the harried astronaut in television's *I Dream of Jeannie*, plays one girl's husband, a callous, cheating lush; a twenty-year-old Candice Bergen is the icy beauty idolized by her friends; Jessica Walter is the two-faced busybody prone to gossip viciously. It would be impos-

sible to credit all the players here—Lumet fully creates no fewer than twelve characters (the proper Bostonian, the good-hearted girl with bad luck, the old-maid-to-be), making the two-and-a-half-hour running time seem all too brief.

TO SIR, WITH LOVE (1967). The kids in Sidney Poitier's class may not be the toughest hoods ever to terrorize a teacher, but they are certainly the most sentimental. Poitier plays an unorthodox teacher (the good ones always are, in movies) in an East London slum; when his lessons in history and geography fall on deaf ears, he re-

places them with lessons in life. "No man likes a slut for long," he says to the girls. To the boys: "I've seen garbage collectors who are cleaner." His victories are small but sweet—taking them to museums, teaching them how to make a salad, getting them to address him as "sir." When pop singer Lulu (who plays a student) belts out the title song at the school dance, make sure the Kleenex is close by.

BREAKING AWAY (1979). I hope no one ever makes a sequel to this perfect little movie, though its star, Dennis Christopher, who gives a noble and touching performance, could certainly use the work. Dave (Christopher) and his three best friends—Mike (Dennis Quaid, who had great abs even then), Cyril (Daniel Stern), and Moocher (Jackie Earle Haley)—don't know what to do with themselves now that high school has ended. But it's becoming painfully clear that they can't spend the rest of their lives swimming in the abandoned quarries of their hometown (Bloomington, Indiana) and staring wistfully at the self-assured coeds attending the local university. Dave does have one ambition—to become a champion bicycle racer, like the Italians of the Cinzano team—and so he affects an Italian accent and plays operas at top volume. Steve Tesich's Oscar-winning screenplay is never emotionally false and is filled with unpredictable details. We may not know exactly what happens to these four guys after that summer, but it's enough to know that they probably turn out just like you and me.

CARNAL KNOWLEDGE (1971). You'll have to suspend your disbelief to buy the sight of Jack Nicholson and Art Garfunkel as virginal Amherst College seniors checking out the girls at a mixer; Nicholson was thirty-four years old at the time, and Garfunkel was thirty. But Jules Feiffer's scathing script lends the lacking credibility and confirms women's worst fears about the way men talk. "The first time I do it," says Jonathan (Nicholson), "I want her beautiful. I don't want to waste it on some beast." As Sandy, his roommate, Garfunkel is awkward but determined; when he takes his girlfriend, Susan (Candice Bergen), to bed—not knowing that she's already been seduced by Jonathan—he wears his BVD's, a shirt, *and* a tie. *Carnal Knowledge* traces the two men's sexual relationships from the repressive '50s through the free-love '60s, ending with Nicholson as a nearly impotent chauvinist and Garfunkel as a middle-aged hippie. They're more pathetic than hateful, perfectly capturing the sort of men made passé by the women's movement and Alan Alda.

CLIQUES

YOU'VE GOT TO HAVE FRIENDS

———————●———————

Sometimes they're friends for life; sometimes they're friends just as long as you let them copy your homework. What matters is *who* they are—at school, belonging to the right crowd can change the way you feel about everything.

THE BREAKFAST CLUB (1985). No guide to movies about school would be complete without a John Hughes film, and this one is emblematic of his teenage oeuvre. According to Hughes, any high school population can be broken down into five distinct types: the princess, the jock, the delinquent, the brain, and the basket case. In *The Breakfast Club,* he's locked a representative of each in a weekend detention hall and written an extended group therapy session in which they bond by realizing that they all have the same problem—their parents don't understand them. (Even the titles of songs on the soundtrack reflect their pathos: "Don't You Forget About Me," "We Are Not Alone," "Heart Too Hot to Hold.") While Hughes's characters may seem familiar, their ultimate rapport is pure fantasy. But it's a compelling fantasy for those of us who longed to better our social standing at the age of sixteen. Look for Hughes in a cameo appearance as the parent who comes to pick up Anthony Michael Hall.

HEAVEN HELP US (1985). Catholic school is hell for Michael Dunn and his friends, not one of whom intends to be a priest. Andrew McCarthy plays Dunn, and for once the expressionless stares on McCarthy's baby face that so often pass for acting seem to work. His crew certainly qualifies as motley—a smarmy intellectual, an abusive punk, an overstimulated urchin who masturbates an average of 5.6 times a day, and a sweet local girl (Mary Stuart Masterson, looking unusually plain). The plot is just a mishmash of vignettes, the most memorable being the torturous punishments inflicted for minor infractions. In one scene, Dunn and his classmate Rooney (Kevin Dillon) have to kneel with their arms outstretched, balancing a weighty tome in each palm. It looks horrid. And Wallace Shawn has a show-stealing cameo as the priest who opens a school mixer with a speech on lust: "It's the beast that wants to *spit* you into the eternal fires of hell, where for all eternity your flesh will be *ripped* from your body by serpents with razor-sharp teeth!"

MY BODYGUARD (1980). This is the

NYU FILM SCHOOL'S ILLUSTRIOUS ALUMNI

●

OLIVER STONE

MARTIN SCORSESE

SPIKE LEE

SUSAN SEIDELMAN

AMY HECKERLING

MARTHA COOLIDGE

JIM JARMUSCH

JOEL COEN

CHRISTOPHER COLUMBUS

JONATHAN KAPLAN

MARTIN BREST

---

movie to watch the day before starting high school. Clifford (Chris Makepeace) is the new boy, and the tough crowd, led by Moody (Matt Dillon), is the unwelcome wagon. Moody demands a dollar a day in protection money to ensure that Cliff won't get beat up. Instead, Cliff enlists as his bodyguard the one kid in school even Moody is scared of: a big, silent lug named Linderman (Adam Baldwin), who is rumored to be a serial killer. The denouement is hardly surprising —Linderman isn't as mean as he looks, Moody isn't as tough as *he* looks, and Cliff isn't as helpless as he thinks he is. Still, it's a pleasantly unassuming—and uplifting—reminder of the appearances-can-be-deceiving lesson. Martin Mull is affable as Cliff's father, Ruth Gordon chews her usual portion of the scenery as Cliff's grandmother, and Jennifer Beals lurks in the background as one of his classmates.

USC FILM SCHOOL'S ILLUSTRIOUS ALUMNI

———————●———————

GEORGE LUCAS

MARCIA LUCAS

RANDAL KLEISER

JOHN MILIUS

IRVIN KERSHNER

DAVID WOLPER

GARY KURTZ

RON HOWARD

ROBERT ZEMECKIS

JOHN CARPENTER

JAMES IVORY

LES BLANK

FRENCH POSTCARDS (1979). One never knows what to expect from Willard Huyck and Gloria Katz. They wrote one classic (*American Graffiti*, with George Lucas) and one classic dud *(Howard the Duck);* this collaboration, which Huyck also directed and Katz produced, falls into that forgettable chasm in between. A group of college students spend their junior year abroad; there's no sex to speak of (or rather, there's some sex, but it's not worth speaking of), and the kids are reduced to stereotypes. You got your mama's boy who learns of love and adventure; you got your lonely girl who has more friends than she realizes; you got your free spirit who has his wings clipped. Nevertheless, movie buffs can pass a diverting ninety-two minutes spotting actors (Debra Winger, Mandy Patinkin) who later went on to more notable roles.

ROCK 'N' ROLL HIGH SCHOOL (1979). Though it's no longer the cult favorite it once was, this decade-old example of teeny-bopper camp has aged extremely well (perhaps because veteran campmeister Roger Corman was executive producer). P. J. Soles, as the totally cool Riff Randell, is still every boy's dream girl in her spandex tights and hightop sneakers. (Footnote to cinema history: Soles, who also has small roles in both *Carrie* and *Breaking Away,* is Dennis Quaid's ex-wife.) The nominal plot: Vince Lombardi High has a new, militant principal, Evelyn Togar (Mary Woronov, sporting a Big Nurse hairdo), who wants to put a stop to all the fun of being a teenager. Riff rallies the students to save the day by blowing up the school. Along the way, there's a rock concert by Riff's favorite group, the Ramones, and some foxy dancing by Riff and her gym class to the title song. But it's a sure sign you're getting older when you find yourself looking at Riff's dream guy—the dour, stoop-shouldered Joey Ramone—and agreeing with a policeman's assessment of him as "ugly, ugly, ugly."

FAST TIMES AT RIDGEMONT HIGH (1982). Most movies about high school aren't believable; this one is. The tiniest details are well observed: history students inhaling a freshly mimeographed handout; the pride a guy takes in working at the cool fast-food joint; the advice one friend gives another before a big date ("When it comes down to making out, this is most important: Put on side one of *Led Zeppelin IV*"). Some of the students at this Southern California school are sexually precocious—Stacy (Jennifer Jason Leigh) willingly sacrifices her virginity to the cute stereo salesman she meets at the mall, even though he can barely sustain a decent conversation about the weather and takes her to a graffiti-riddled baseball dugout for the tryst. The scene may not be romantic, but it is realistic. Sean Penn's turn as the stoned surfer Spicoli is already near-legend, and rightly so, but the rest of the cast—Judge Reinhold, Phoebe Cates, Robert Romanus, and Forest Whitaker, to name a few—are just as impressive in their less flashy roles.

TROUBLEMAKERS

HELL IS FOR CHILDREN

————•————

Every school has them—the kids who smoke in the bathroom when they're supposed to be in history and who wear green Army jackets no matter what the weather. Even the teachers are scared of them. But those are just your generic juvenile delinquents. The kids in this last group of movies aren't just bad, they're possessed.

CARRIE (1976). A telekinetic teenager kills her classmates, her teachers, her principal, and her mother and then brings her home down around her own head, leaving a pile of rubble—and I thought *I* had a bad time at the prom. It's ob-

vious that Carrie White is having a little trouble at school. She's clumsy and withdrawn, so the kids ridicule her. Home provides no respite; her mother is a Bible-toting loony who pours fire and brimstone on the typical travails of youth. "Pimples," Mrs. White intones, "are the Lord's way of chastising you." Of all the Stephen King horror novels that have been translated to the screen, *Carrie* is the best (*Christine,* another parable about a nerdy high schooler who wreaks havoc, runs a close second). Sissy Spacek is perfect in the title role; her pale eyes and fragile frame capture all the elements of Carrie's complex personality—the awkward wallflower, the beauty she might have been, and the powerful avenger of the penultimate scene. Director Brian De Palma makes his requisite homage to Alfred Hitchcock by naming Carrie's school Bates High.

SUSAN FAIOLA

THESE THREE (1936). In the '30s, Hollywood apparently couldn't tolerate a faithful adaptation of *The Children's Hour,* Lillian Hellman's play about a rumored lesbian affair between teachers at a private girls' school. So the affair in question was changed into a heterosexual one, a bowdlerization that might have irreparably dated the movie were it not for thirteen-year-old Bonita Granville's Oscar-nominated performance as the tale-telling student. Miriam Hopkins and Merle Oberon play two college graduates whose only apparent career choice is teaching; with the help of a friendly neighbor (Joel McCrea), they renovate a crumbling mansion and open a boarding school. Hopkins falls for McCrea, but he's in love with Oberon; it's all perfectly ordinary stuff until Granville starts fabricating lies designed to let her play hookey. "They've got secrets, funny secrets," she says to her grandmother. "I can't say them out loud. I've got to whisper them." Director William Wyler filmed a remake with the original plot twenty-five years later, but this is nevertheless a superior version. Cameos by Walter Brennan and Margaret Hamilton (not yet the Wicked Witch of the West) also help.

THE BAD SEED (1956). Rhoda Penmark never forgets to curtsy or say "please" and "thank you"; her clothes are never dirty, her shoes never scuffed. She seems the perfect child, until she throws a tantrum for not winning her third-grade class's penmanship medal. And when the little boy who did win mysteriously drowns at a school picnic, we know (even if Rhoda's parents don't) who killed him. As it happens, it's neither her first murder nor her last; she's an efficient, unremorseful killer. *The Bad Seed* is not a gory horror movie; it's mostly about Mrs. Penmark's slow and painful discovery of the evil nature lurking beneath her daughter's starched pinafore. As Rhoda, Patty McCormack is chilling; though we never see her actually commit a crime, her saccharine smile is more frightening than any explicit violence ever could be. The movie's single disappointment is its cop-out ending; director Mervyn LeRoy abandons the memorably creepy climax of the stage play, in which Mrs. Penmark, reluctantly facing the truth, poisons Rhoda and then shoots herself (the mother dies; Rhoda survives). But don't rewind until it's over: LeRoy offers a bit of inspired sickness in the closing credits.

THE BEGUILED (1971). The premise sounds vaguely pornographic: During the Civil War, a wounded Union soldier finds refuge in a Confederate girls' school. There are nine lonely females, and he is a handsome man—in fact, the only man they've seen in quite some time. But the *Dirty Harry*

UCLA FILM SCHOOL'S
ILLUSTRIOUS ALUMNI

●

FRANCIS COPPOLA

COLIN HIGGINS

GLORIA KATZ

HARVE BENNETT

ALEX COX

CARROLL BALLARD

SHANE BLACK

MIKE MINER

ED NEUMEIER

team of Clint Eastwood and director Don Siegel have given the story a gritty, nightmarish twist. As Corporal John McBurney, Eastwood will do anything—lie, flirt, seduce—to keep these women from turning him in. "Do you ever think of yourself as the sleeping beauty of a castle," he asks the spinsterish teacher played by Elizabeth Hartman, "waiting for a prince to awaken you with a kiss?" Suffice it to say that classes in napkin-folding are not as diverting as this enticing stranger. In short order, the teacher, two students, and the headmistress (a creepy turn by the estimable Geraldine Page) are in love with him. The trouble is, McBurney has drastically underestimated the wrath of a woman scorned—these southern belles turn out to be much more dangerous than the Confederate Army.

———————●———————

WINTER ANTIDOTES

By Ed Sikov

The cold, blue days of winter are the best time to watch a long, involving epic or a movie that warms you with its tropical setting. Go get blankets and the microwave popcorn and pop in one of these cassettes.

THE LONG RUN

When Time Is on Your Side

Moviegoers frequently complain that movies are too long, but as has been said, for everything there is a season, and the season for length is now. The titles below are filled with many hours of serious thoughts and intense drama—each demands a large investment of time and rewards it handsomely.

BERLIN ALEXANDERPLATZ (1980). When Rainer Werner Fassbinder's fifteen-and-a-half-hour epic was shown in American theaters, several critics announced that although it had been made for German television, *Berlin Alexanderplatz* was nonetheless a *film*. Actually, it makes more sense to see it the way it was originally meant to be seen—in installments on TV, rather than in one or two sense-numbing marathons in a theater. Episodic, in-

tensely detailed, and thoroughly entertaining, *Berlin Alexanderplatz* traces the life (or more accurately the low-life) of hulking Franz Biberkopf (Günter Lamprecht), who tries to lead what he thinks is an honest existence. Poor Franz doesn't succeed, surrounded as he is by a pack of petty thieves, whores, pimps, killers, and Nazis. The final episode is a letdown, but the first thirteen are superb, what with Peer Raben's elegant score, Xaver Schwarzenberger's rich cinematography, and star turns by Elisabeth Trissenaar, Hanna Schygulla, and Barbara Sukowa as Franz's three girlfriends.

THE GODFATHER, 1902—1959: THE COMPLETE EPIC (1981). Now that the expression "made him an offer he couldn't refuse" is as stale as the automobile horns that honk out the theme from *The Godfather,* it's time to look at the original material once again in a fresh, less pop-culture-choked light. Both *The Godfather* and *The Godfather, Part II* are available on videotape, but for dull winter weekends, try *The Complete Epic*—the massively resequenced and chronologized compilation that was edited under the supervision of Francis Coppola himself. Beginning in turn-of-the-century Sicily with the young Vito Corleone, age nine, witnessing the cold-blooded slaughter of several family members at the hands of the Cosa Nostra and ending with Vito's son Michael having iced his own brother, *The Complete Epic* wraps the two eras of *Part II* around the more linear original *Godfather* to produce the most expansive gangster film ever made.

SHOAH (1985). Dismissed by *The New Yorker's* Pauline Kael as "a long moan," *Shoah* is, rather, a steady-minded but relentless damnation of everyone who helped murder the Jews of Europe during World War II. The film's director, Claude Lanzmann, is scarcely an objective documentarian. He obtrudes into the film whenever possible, methodically repeating shots of trains pulling into the station at Treblinka, pressing and even badgering his subjects to reveal what they know, deliberately etching a sense of daily horror into the minds of his audience. In one harrowing sequence, an Israeli barber and former concentration camp inmate, a man who has been relating his experiences with peculiar dispassion, suddenly snaps; Lanzmann keeps the camera rolling to record the man's wretched pleas to stop the interview. It is a supremely uncomfortable moment, but it reveals more about the death of six million men, women, and children than any number of tidier, more typical efforts at explaining an event that resists comprehension.

GIANT (1956). No doubt about it: in George Stevens's WarnerColor adaptation of Edna Ferber's novel, bigness is the look, bigness is the theme, and passion is the primary plot motivator. The film traces the rising and falling fortunes of two generations of Texans, thus enabling makeup artists to force Rock Hudson, Elizabeth Taylor,

and James Dean to grow old before our eyes. (In keeping with the film's obsession with plenitude, there isn't just one tour de force, there are *three*.) Miscegenation, moral dissipation, racism, the oppression of women, the

---

SLOW MOTION

HERE ARE SOME SCENES THAT LOOK ESPECIALLY INTERESTING WHEN SLOWED DOWN ON YOUR VCR.

———⬤———

MAD FOR MONTAGE
Janet Leigh taking her last shower in *Psycho*

BALLET MÉCANIQUE
The gang fight in a subway men's room in *The Warriors*

GUILTY PLEASURES
Mel Gibson and friends frolicking naked in the sea in *Gallipoli*

Julie Christie and Donald Sutherland rustling the sheets in *Don't Look Now*

Susan Sarandon getting *very* close to Catherine Deneuve in *The Hunger*

An anatomically correct Tom Cruise making *All the Right Moves* with Lea Thompson

PROTRACTED MISERY
David Naughton metamorphosing in *An American Werewolf in London*

A screaming Pia Zadora's nervous breakdown in *The Lonely Lady*

Nicholas Clay removing a sword from his side in *Excalibur*

---

hollowness of *lumpenproletariat* dreams . . . lots of topics are brought forth during the film's 201 minutes, and though Stevens doesn't handle them in the most decisive way, he still bowls us over with the Texas-style scale of his ambition.

HEAT WAVE

STEAMY FILMS FOR SUBZERO DAYS

———————●———————

Warmth, like erotica, is often in the eye of the beholder. Here is a selection of high-temperature movies to help that eye of yours behold something unlike the bitter cold outside.

ONCE UPON A TIME IN THE WEST (1969). Sergio Leone's convoluted western opens with the sweatiest credit sequence in history, an attenuated prelude to a speedy gunfight. The film is an oblique allegory of American history in which Henry Fonda, cast radically against type, plays a gunslinging desperado hired by an evil but pathetic railroad baron to help ensure the future of corporate capitalism on the frontier. Nothing in the western genre quite equals the horrifying scene in which Fonda calmly blows away an innocent child. Claudia Cardinale is a young widow-turned-entrepreneur who aims to build the town of Sweetwater, but she can't do it without the help of Jason Robards, Charles Bronson, and Bronson's unremittingly eerie harmonica.

I WALKED WITH A ZOMBIE (1943). A surly country gentleman hires a sympathetic young woman to be his demented wife's nurse. Sound familiar? It's *Jane Eyre,* only this time around,

producer Val Lewton and director Jacques Tourneur give the story a voodoo spin. Set on a hot, morbid West Indies island, *Zombie* leaves many of its plot developments unresolved—such as whether or not this woman really is a zombie, not to mention how she got that way. Exquisite high-contrast black-and-white photography, together with the filmmakers' uncommon intelligence, brings alive each twist and turn of this fantastic tale, while the nebulous quality of the goings-on makes the whole spectacle unnerving.

TARZAN, THE APE MAN (1932). No, *not* the Bo Derek bomb, but the original, with Johnny Weismuller (which was, by the way, already a remake of a silent *Tarzan,* also available on videotape). What better cure for winter doldrums than the sight of a former Olympic swimmer in a loincloth hurtling through the treetops on a vine, yodeling as he flies? Don't laugh—Weismuller is great, though he's not exactly the erudite Lord Greystoke of Burroughs's novel. Less of a surprise is Maureen O'Sullivan, who is unusually poised in a role that could easily have been ridiculous. O'Sullivan's Jane Parker (presumably *not* of the A&P line of baked goods) is amusingly dazed by the apeman's body, which is really what the Tarzan series is all about. Just listen to the faint irony in her delivery of the deathless line "Tarzan? What am I doing here . . . alone . . . with *you?*"

THE EMERALD FOREST (1985). Echoing John Ford's *The Searchers,* director John Boorman tells the tale (based on a true story) of an American civil engineer (Powers Boothe) whose little boy is kidnapped by aborigines in the Amazon. He spends years pursuing his son's abductors through the brilliant green jungles of Brazil, only to find the child grown up, immersed in his adopted culture, and pluckily unwilling to come home. *The Emerald Forest* gets a bit bogged down in a schematic subplot involving rival tribes, and its right-minded concern for the rain forest probably played better on the page than it does on the screen. But Charley Boorman, the director's son, gives a quietly nuanced performance as the grown boy; through subtle gestures and mannerisms, he conveys a sense of genuine cultural *difference,* without which the story would be meaningless.

DONOVAN'S REEF (1963). According to one critic, this John Ford film is "close to a cinematic experience of pure form." Another declares that it's "Ford's most escapist film ever." Leaving grand declarations to others, let's just say that *Donovan's Reef* is colorful, warm-blooded, and ramblingly good-natured. Under the palms and thatched huts of a Tahitian village, "Uncle Guns" Donovan (John Wayne) and his brawling pal Gilhooley (Lee Marvin) engage in classic American buddyism against a backdrop of interracial family melodrama, yet Ford plays the whole business for comedy. Is this Polynesian extravaganza lyrical or merely protracted? And is the scene in which Wayne spanks Elizabeth Allen meant to be obnoxious, or does it just turn out that way? See for yourself.

BLUE HAWAII (1961). In his book *Elvis Presley,* British fan W. A. Harbinson pooh-poohs the King's eighth movie as "the first of the real trash," describing the hero as an "all-singing, girl-chasing, virginal Elvis in his swimming trunks and thongs, with his surfboards and sports cars." As if that's what's *wrong* with the film!

FAST FORWARD
HERE ARE SOME SCENES WE RECOMMEND FOR HIGH-SPEED SCANNING.

———●———

DANCING FEATS
Fred Astaire's "Let's Say It With Firecrackers" number in *Holiday Inn*

John Travolta's solo at *Saturday Night Fever*'s 2001 Odyssey disco

WHO WAS THAT GIRL?
All of *Shanghai Surprise*

CAR WARS
Chasing the bad guys in *The French Connection* and chasing the good guys in *To Live and Die in L.A.*

Steve McQueen taking the ups and downs of San Francisco in *Bullitt*

BORN TO CHOP
Bruce Lee versus everyone at the end of *Enter the Dragon*

SEE & SKI
Olympic skier Robert Redford competing in *Downhill Racer*

Okay, Elvis's character, Chad, might have been a little tougher and more rebellious (he demonstrates his contempt for the family pineapple empire by opening a travel agency). But hey—it was '61, the surf was up, bikinis were in, and millions of folks back on the mainland were dying to go with Elvis, singing "Rock-a-Hula Baby," on a Technicolor tour of the fiftieth state. You'd have to be John Simon to fail to appreciate the dramatic process shots of Elvis "surfing" on rear-projected neon-blue waves.

MACAO (1952). The spectacle of Jane Russell attacking Robert Mitchum with an electric fan may not be to everyone's taste, but director Josef von Sternberg clearly adored it. In Macao, a picturesque thermometer tells us, the temperature is "Healthy for plants, unhealthy for humans," a state of mind duplicated by the hothouse quality of the film. Forget the plot, a labored affair involving stolen jewelry, a wanted man, and knife-hurling coolies. Savor the mood and scenery instead—the netting that spreads over the docks, the shadow of a ceiling fan playing on a wall, the little shimmy Gloria Grahame employs to throw dice. Russell and Mitchum couldn't be better; a more languorous duo would be hard to find.

THE YEAR OF LIVING DANGER-OUSLY (1983). Peter Weir's tale of political turmoil in Indonesia was greeted with skepticism by many reviewers, who complained that neither its politics nor its philosophy was clear enough. It's true that the world would be more comforting to Westerners if we could impose our own rational order on the East, but we don't seem to be able to. That's exactly what journalist Guy Hamilton (Mel Gibson) discovers as he follows Sukarno's downfall with his half-Australian, half-Chinese photographer, Billy Kwan (Linda Hunt, as a man). Art and politics aside, Gibson and co-star Sigourney Weaver look spectacular in thin, tropical cotton clothes, the kind that get damp and cling to the skin when things heat up on Java.

JASON AND THE ARGONAUTS (1963). Tacky Greek-mythology movies set on sizzling Mediterranean islands are the guilty pleasures of more than a few film buffs, but magnificent special effects by Ray Harryhausen put this film in another league. For *Jason,* in which the future henpecked husband of Medea goes looking for the Golden Fleece, Harryhausen created a surreal world of animated plastic marvels. The creatures look patently and wonderfully artificial, but a system of prisms and stop-action photography places them alongside real actors with frightening precision. The best scene is the battle between Jason's men and a group of feisty skeletons who materialize out of sand—it's the masterpiece of Harryhausen's career.

IN REVERSE

GET A NEW PERSPECTIVE ON THESE FAMILIAR SCENES BY WATCHING THEM BACKWARD.

●

EAT TO THE BEAT
Albert Finney and Joyce Redman having a feast in *Tom Jones*

DANCING WATERS
Esther Williams in the finale of *Million Dollar Mermaid*

The diving sequence in *Olympia*

HOW DO YOU SPELL RELIEF?
The hideous creature bursting out of John Hurt's stomach in *Alien*

Linda Blair losing her lunch in *The Exorcist*

A man's head exploding in David Cronenberg's *Scanners*

BOAT PEOPLE
The topsy-turvy New Year's Eve in *The Poseidon Adventure*

COUNTERREVOLUTION
Sylvester Stallone shooting commies in *Rambo: First Blood Part II*

BODY HEAT (1981). *Body Heat* is such a quintessentially steamy film noir that it teeters on the edge of self-parody, though it never quite tips over. Director Lawrence Kasdan plays around with noir's sinister shades of gray, only he uses the most vivid hues Eastmancolor can muster. With William Hurt as Ned Racine, the film's morally collapsing protagonist, and Kathleen Turner as Matty Walker, his femme fatale, Kasdan pumps up the genre's conventional gynephobia to nearly obscene proportions: lust, hate, and deceit reign as a trinity. In *Body Heat,* perspiration becomes a self-conscious aesthetic device, especially when Racine's sweat turns cold. If you find yourself asking why nobody in the film has air-conditioning, you've probably missed the point.

ONE CRAZY SUMMER (1986). Director Savage Steve Holland doesn't transcend the teen-nerd-comedy genre with this broad farce about how America's youth spends its summer vacations, but his vision is hardly mainstream, either. Nantucket seems sunny and warm on the surface, but underneath lies New England's answer to jungle rot. The film's hero, Hoops (John Cusack), imagines his failed love life in the form of animated cartoons, picturing himself as an ugly rhinoceros tormented by the Cute and Fuzzy Bunnies, cuddly creatures who endlessly deride the hapless rhino's looks and personality. Meanwhile, a strange little girl wreaks violent revenge on anyone who insults her grotesque dog, and in one throwaway shot, we see that the hero's cat lives in a little house adorned with the head of mice mounted on plaques. Rent this one at your own risk.

10 (1979). Blake Edwards's comedy about an aging neurotic was an enormous box-office success, thanks in large measure to its advertising campaign featuring Bo Derek rising out of the sea, an Aphrodite in spandex and cornrows. Edwards publicly denounced the ads, saying they misrepresented the film. He was right. *10* does capitalize—literally as well as figuratively—on Bo as the heterosexual male's ideal sex object, but Edwards's point of view toward the obsessive desire of his protagonist, George Webber (Dudley Moore), is far from uncritical. When he encounters Bo at a Mexican beach resort, our hero scalds himself—first on the hot sand, and later in bed with her. To the constantly interrupted tune of Ravel's *Bolero,* George succeeds only in finding out what an idiot he is.

CHERRY, HARRY, AND RAQUEL (1969). Russ Meyer, the director the French film journal *Cahiers du Cinéma* has called *"le Walt Disney du porno,"* collaborated with Tom Wolfe to spin this radically disconnected tale of raunch, drugs, and gigantic breasts. *Cherry, Harry, and Raquel* is a western, sort of. It has a sheriff (Harry), an Apache (Geronimo), many dusty landscapes, and an unbelievably built woman (Soul) who dances around the desert wearing nothing but a full Indian headdress and who, at one point, attempts to mount a butte. Also on hand are the buxom and sexually insatiable Cherry and Raquel, who bring the eponymous ménage à trois full circle with a torrid lesbian sex scene, which Meyer weirdly intercuts with a bloody gunfight between Harry and Geronimo. As the film's hilarious epilogue says, *Cherry, Harry, and Raquel* is a comment on modern times; what it actually says is anyone's guess.

GOOD AND EVIL

—•—

BY MASON WILEY

Here's a collection of movies on video that will frighten, bewitch, and enchant. First, some films about witches who cast their spells on unsuspecting humans for their own diabolical pleasure. Second, movies about retributions, wherein the villainy is so monstrous that God Himself must step in to clean up the muck made by wanton mortals. Finally, as a chaser to all this horror, as a ray of hope for all mankind, as proof that there is one among us who can triumph over sin and sorcery, we present four films starring Doris Day.

WITCHCRAFT

THAT OLD BLACK MAGIC

———•———

The premier witch in cinema has to be Margaret Hamilton in *The Wizard of Oz;* she comes complete with broom, black hat, and green skin. Hamilton notwithstanding, movie witches are often alluring creatures who bedevil men with their supernaturally sexy desires. And while the two films below by Roman Polanski feature some serious sorcery and devil worship, the other two ably prove that nothin' says lovin' like someone from a coven.

I MARRIED A WITCH (1942). René Clair's antic screwball comedy concerns a witch burned in colonial New England who hexes her accuser by condemning him and all his male descendants to unhappy marriages. When her evil spirit is freed by a bolt of lightning 260 years later, she sees that the current scion of the accused family, Fredric March, is about to follow form by marrying a shrew, Susan Hayward. Mischievously, the witch assumes the shape of Veronica Lake, peekaboo bangs and all, and attempts to seduce March with a potion that will make him "a slave to love's captivity." Her plan backfires when she accidentally drinks her own brew and falls for him. Complicating matters further is her warlock father, Cecil Kellaway, a prankish sprite who invented the hangover but is inclined to come out soused every time his spirit hides in a bottle of booze. Director Clair spikes this fluffy concoction with a few barbs at man's eternal cruelty, whether it's witch burning or the electric chair, all the while maintaining a lightweight, romantic-comedy flavor in the grand old Hollywood tradition.

ROSEMARY'S BABY (1968). You can view it either as a warning not to marry a self-obsessed actor (John Cassavetes) or as a gentrification night-mare, in which a young housewife (Mia Farrow) discovers that her neighbors in a crumbling Upper West Side apartment house are Satan's helpers, out to find him a mate. Even Mia's gynecologist is of no help; he's played by Charles Grodin, who, as usual, is an unreliable wimp. No wonder she settled for Woody Allen; next to this crowd—Ruth Gordon, Patsy Kelly, Elisha Cook, Jr.—he's normal. Director Roman Polanski never resorts to hackneyed haunted-house techniques; instead he keeps the strange events as eerily ambiguous to the audience as they are to Farrow. Like *Repulsion* and *The Tenant,* this is a subjective Polanski probe of urban madness.

MACBETH (1971). Polanski's first movie after the murder of his wife, Sharon Tate, is an unsparing portrayal of how primitive life must have been in the Middle Ages. Shakespeare's three witches are incarnated here as a young hippie, a mean-looking nun, and an old crone who looks like the Grim Reaper in drag. This trio is first glimpsed burying a dismembered hand holding a dagger, in a ritual that involves chanting and spitting. After the opening credits, which are punc-tuated with the sounds of medieval combat, we see Macbeth, played by handsome young Jon Finch, as he turns away from the routine hanging of enemy prisoners. Clearly, this is a time of daily violence and death. Thus, Macbeth and Lady Macbeth's misinterpretation of the witches' prophecy makes sense, since murder is the basis for any exchange of politi-cal power. Beautifully photographed on the beaches of Wales, and co-scripted by Polanski and critic Ken-neth Tynan, this is a powerful version of the tragedy of ambition.

THE WITCHES OF EASTWICK (1987). Cher, Susan Sarandon, and Michelle Pfeiffer are three friends in a small present-day New England town who have been widowed, divorced, and deserted, respectively, by their hus-bands. Because they're so lonely, they fail to notice that they're capable of witchcraft, such as causing a sudden thunderstorm. They spend one eve-ning over several martinis conjuring

---

MOVIE GHOULS
WHAT'S IT ALL ABOUT?

●

HALLOWEEN (1978)
Dr. Sam Loomis *(Donald Pleasence)* to Sheriff Brackett *(Charles Cyphers)*:
I met this six-year-old child with this blank, pale, emotionless face and the blackest eyes—the Devil's eyes. I spent eight years trying to reach him and then another seven trying to keep him locked up, be-cause I realized that what was liv-ing behind that boy's eyes was purely and simply—Evil.

A NIGHTMARE ON ELM STREET (1984)
Marge Thompson *(Ronee Blakley)* to her daughter, Nancy *(Heather Langenkamp)*:
You want to know who Freddy Krueger was? He was a filthy child murderer who killed at least twenty kids in the neighborhood. . . . We found him in an old abandoned boiler room where he used to take his kids. We took gasoline, poured it all around the place, made a trail out the door. Then we lit the whole thing up and watched it burn. He can't get you now. He's dead, honey, be-cause Mommy killed him.

forts to avoid Nicholson result in his diabolical wrath, and the witches are forced to fight hellfire with hellfire. Of the three, the repressed Sarandon is the funniest, and Veronica Cartwright is a howl as a prude who suffers one indignity after another. George Miller *(The Road Warrior)* directs with his customary kinetic flair.

MOVIE GHOULS
WHAT'S IT ALL ABOUT?

INVASION OF THE BODY SNATCHERS (1956)
Dr. Dan Kauffmann *(Larry Gates)* to Miles Bennel *(Kevin McCarthy)* and Becky Driscoll *(Dana Wynter)*:

Less than a month ago, Santa Mira was like any other town—people with nothing but problems. Then, out of the sky, came a solution. Seeds drifting through space for years took root in a farmer's field. From the seeds came pods, which have the power to reproduce themselves in the exact likeness of any form of life.˙ . . . There's no pain. Suddenly, while you're asleep, they'll absorb your minds, your memories, and you'll be reborn into an untroubled world.

ALIENS (1986)
Young Newt *(Carrie Henn)* to Ripley *(Sigourney Weaver)*:

My mommy always said there were no monsters—no real ones —but there are.
Ripley:
Yes, there are, aren't there.
Newt:
Why do they tell little kids that?
Ripley:
Most of the time it's true.

GOD'LL GET YOU
HAPPY JUDGMENT DAY

"**B**etter him than me" is not one of man's nobler sentiments, but it does carry a certain entertainment value. Watching others get their just deserts is a perfect diversion, particularly after a bad day. The more heathen or hedonistic the doomed characters, the more fun it is to see them pay an awful price. These movies pose as cautionary tales, but don't believe it; they're the cinematic equivalent of the Romans throwing Christians to the lions. After all, the Colosseum is where the whole "thumbs down" business began in the first place.

SAMSON AND DELILAH (1949). It takes place B.C., or, more specifically, C.B., as in De Mille, the director with a sensibility slightly less sophisticated than that of a child's book of illustrated Bible stories, which this hilarious epic resembles. George Sanders is the chief Philistine, whose bad idea it is to throw a party to humiliate the blinded Samson in a temple with lots of columns. The supposedly muscle-bound Victor Mature plays Samson, a casting choice that purportedly inspired Groucho Marx

up their ideal man, and that very night, Jack Nicholson, a mysterious millionaire, arrives in town. As luck would have it, they have willed a visit from the Devil himself; after he has bedded the three of them, both individually and collectively, they find themselves being snubbed by the townspeople for being sluts. Their efto quip, "I never see movies where the man's tits are bigger than the woman's." Playing Delilah is the smaller-busted Hedy Lamarr, who had this to say about movie-star acting: "Any girl can look glamorous; all she has to do is stand still and look stupid." The only star left alive at the end is little Russ Tamblyn, who asks, "He was so strong, why did he have to die?" Because that's the way it happened in the book, kid.

THE BIRDS (1963). Alfred Hitchcock first saw Tippi Hedren while watching the *Today* show; she appeared in a commercial for a diet soft drink, walking and turning to smile when a little boy whistled at her. This seminal moment is recreated at the start of *The Birds,* which begins like a sex comedy. Hedren, a spoiled heiress, meets and banters with hunky Rod Taylor in a San Francisco pet shop and impulsively decides to surprise him by delivering a pair of lovebirds to his home in a nearby coastal town. With voyeuristic satisfaction, she sits in a boat and watches him discover her practical joke and then race his car to meet her at the dock. Just as it seems she's charmed him, a gull swooshes down as if to warn her to leave, but Hedren is determined to stay, even if it means the destruction of the entire town. It does. The birds don't quit until Hitchcock lets them have a go at ripping Tippi's pea-green Edith Head suit in the final showdown, which took an entire week to shoot. In initial viewing, *The Birds* works as a horror movie, but in later screenings it becomes an indelible melodrama about fear of abandonment, with the bird attacks underlining the characters' sense of emotional isolation.

THE MASQUE OF THE RED DEATH (1964). Ingmar Bergman meets Sam-

---

MOVIE GHOULS
WHAT'S IT ALL ABOUT?

───────●───────

NIGHT OF THE LIVING DEAD (1968)
TV Announcer:
The level of the mysterious radiation continues to increase steadily. So long as this situation remains, government spokesmen warn that dead bodies will continue to be transformed into the flesh-eating ghouls. All persons who die in this crisis, from whatever cause, will come back to life to seek human victims unless their bodies are first disposed of by cremation. Officials are quoted as saying [that] since the brain of a ghoul has been activated by the radiation, the plan is: Kill the brain and you kill the ghoul.

ALTERED STATES (1980)
Eddie Jessup *(William Hurt)* to his wife, Emily *(Blair Brown)*:
You saved me. You redeemed me from the pit I was in, and Emily, I was in that ultimate moment of terror that is the beginning of life. It is nothing. Simple, hideous nothing. The final truth of all things is that there is no final truth. Truth is what's transitory —it's human life that is real. I don't want to frighten you, Emily, but what I'm trying to tell you is that that moment of terror is a real and living horror living and growing within me now. And the only thing that keeps it from devouring me is you.

---

uel Z. Arkoff in this Roger Corman adaptation of two Edgar Allan Poe stories, the title one and "Hop-Frog." Corman's Red Death is clearly modeled on Bergman's black-and-white

Death from *The Seventh Seal,* only Corman's character has a host of "brothers," each having his own color scheme. Vincent Price strolls around in gold lamé as the evil Prince Prospero, who runs his medieval castle as a members-only club for neighboring nobles, while outside the great unwashed wither away from a terrible plague. In true Arkoff fashion, every female member of the cast is groomed as if seeking employment as a Playboy bunny, including Paul McCartney's then girlfriend, Jane Asher, who spends the movie arguing theology with Price. The screenplay, by R. Wright Campbell and *The Twilight Zone's* Charles Beaumont, pads out Poe's short tales—throwing in heroic serfs and a lascivious lady who drinks a potion and hallucinates a satanic floor show—before climaxing at the masquerade ball, where Red Death violates the dress code and ruins everything.

THE TOWERING INFERNO (1974). In this all-star barbecue, producer Irwin Allen's version of Red Death is fire, which consumes the revelers at a party celebrating the opening of the world's tallest building. Thanks to the chintzy electrical contractor, played by Richard Chamberlain, who wears a brown tux to the black-tie gala, the ugly tower proves to be as cheaply made as it looks. Paul Newman, as the suede-clad architect, feels so guilty that he was out of town when the edifice was erected, he tries to rescue each occupant personally; he consequently does so much climbing about that there are as many shots of his derriere as of his baby blues. Faye Dunaway, as his girlfriend, starts out like her driven character in *Network,* but as soon as the fire erupts, she turns into a gracious hostess calming down her guests. The first star to be roasted is Robert Wagner, as an adulterer whose love becomes a funeral pyre; he makes his exit looking once again like Prince Valiant, this time with wet towels as his armor. Look also for Dabney Coleman, as the fire fighter who says of a passing fireball, "Jesus, it's one of our men!" and for Sheila Mathews—Mrs. Irwin Allen—as the mayor's wife, who, fretting over their daughter, says, "She's such a child, she doesn't even know where I keep the key to the safety deposit box." Obviously, a Republican mayor's wife.

HEAVENLY DORIS

A SUNNY DAY

———————●———————

In these troubled times, those seeking unblemished (if freckled) virtue should look no further than the films of Doris Day. Not one to play an ax murderer—she turned down the role of Mrs. Robinson in *The Graduate* because "it offended my sense of values"—the actress chose parts that allowed her natural optimism to shine through. Born Doris von Kappelhoff, she picked her new surname from the song "Day by Day," which certainly reflects her sunny on-screen disposition, but as far as her real life is concerned, she should have chosen "Blues in the Night." With three bad marriages, the final one to a guy who embezzled her out of her $20 million savings, Doris hasn't had it easy, but she never shortchanged her audience. Any Doris Day performance is a combination of zest, cheer, and intelligence that remains fresh today even if the movie itself has become as dated as the bird that inspired her nickname —Dodo.

CALAMITY JANE (1953). Day's performance in this movie is usually described as "bouncy," and she literally *is* bouncing all over the place as the eponymous tomboy. Her musical-comedy talents are amply evident here; it's a pity this is such a sexist, racist film. Native Americans are treated as either jokes or trouble-makers, and the film's message boils down to: No woman is complete until she makes herself attractive to men. The nadir is a scene in which Day and Allyn McLerie happily clean up a cabin, singing, "A woman and a whisk broom can accomplish so darn much / So never underestimate a woman's touch." While the overt moral is distasteful, the movie's frequent sexual-identity confusions provide a wonderfully subversive subtext. First there is a drag act before an audience of horny cowpokes who like what they see until the man's identity is revealed. Then Day goes to Chicago in her buckskin pants, causing a prostitute to wink leeringly at her and a startled McLerie to exclaim (after Day has told her, "You're the prettiest thing I ever seen"), "You're a woman?" Even virile Howard Keel, as Wild Bill Hickok, spends one scene garbed as a squaw. He gets into a dress before Day does; pretty strange for a movie that scolds her for looking like a frontier Joan of Arc.

THE MAN WHO KNEW TOO MUCH

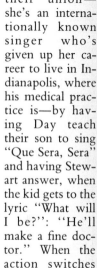

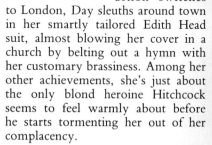

JOSEPH SALINA

(1956). Day's finest dramatic performance is in this Alfred Hitchcock puzzler about a vacationing American couple in Marrakech whose son is kidnapped when they stumble across the path of spies plotting a political assassination. Even before the intrigue begins, the scenes from the marriage of Day and James Stewart are fascinating: she's always one step ahead of her too-trusting husband. Hitchcock subtly delineates the tension of their union— she's an internationally known singer who's given up her career to live in Indianapolis, where his medical practice is—by having Day teach their son to sing "Que Sera, Sera" and having Stewart answer, when the kid gets to the lyric "What will I be?": "He'll make a fine doctor." When the action switches to London, Day sleuths around town in her smartly tailored Edith Head suit, almost blowing her cover in a church by belting out a hymn with her customary brassiness. Among her other achievements, she's just about the only blond heroine Hitchcock seems to feel warmly about before he starts tormenting her out of her complacency.

TEACHER'S PET (1958). Day plays a college journalism teacher—back in the days when students wore coats and ties to class—who invites a hard-boiled city editor to be a guest lecturer. He's played by Clark Gable, here an older version of his cynical reporter in *It Happened One Night*. Alas, director George Seaton is no Frank Capra, and this romantic comedy is not the snappily paced romp it should be. But Gable and Day spar entertainingly as "the old pro and the egghead" with different ideas about reporting. Gable gives Day her sexiest on-screen kiss, to which she reacts with classic indignation before going weak in the knees. Mamie Van Doren makes an all-too-brief appearance as Gable's girlfriend, but she's on long enough to perform "The Girl Who Invented Rock and Roll," which Day reprises later, with her own va-va-va-voom.

PILLOW TALK (1959). Day received her only Oscar nomination for this role, and she certainly deserved it, if only for the scene in which she rides in a convertible with Rock Hudson to a weekend tryst in Connecticut. "I feel so guilty," we hear her thinking. "I practically tricked him into taking me." She goes on to sing "Possess Me" to herself while pulling various ruses, such as checking her makeup in the rearview mirror, in order to cuddle next to Rock. Of course, it's he who has tricked her, and she finds out before they get to the bedroom, necessitating her storming out and telling him, "Bedroom problems! At least mine can be solved in one bedroom; you couldn't solve yours in a thousand!" You see, to get Doris to go with him to Connecticut, Rock has pretended to be a wealthy Texan named Rex Stetson. In fact, he's a playboy songwriter, who tells each of his girlfriends—including commercial spokeswoman Julia Meade—that he wrote his new song just for her; Doris has heard his constant duplicity on their party line and become disgusted. Not connecting the voice with Rex in the flesh, she's hooked, even when the songwriter casts aspersions about the Texan over the phone: "There are some men who are very devoted to their mothers, you know, the type that likes to collect cooking recipes, exchange bits of gossip." "What a vicious thing to say!" snaps Doris. This Ross Hunter movie lays on the production values: Every New York apartment has a well-stocked bar, every date includes dinner and dancing, and many scenes begin with Doris primping before a mirror in a new outfit with matching muff. Like Paul Newman in *Hud,* she has a maid named Alma, only this one is a comic drunk played by Thelma Ritter, who advises her, "Six feet six inches of opportunity doesn't come along every day, you know." Amen, Thelma.

POLITICS

●

By J. Hoberman

here's no business like it, except
show business—maybe that's
why it's such a great movie subject.
American politics have always inspired American movies, and vice
versa. You might say they provide
mutual R&D (who came first, Jimmy
Carter or Rocky?).

WASHINGTON

THE DISTRICT OF CORRUPTION

●

istrust of the federal government, particularly Congress, is
as American as apple pie. Except for
brief periods during the New Deal
and the Eisenhower administration,
the notion of Washington as the
graveyard of good intentions has
never gone out of style.

MR. SMITH GOES TO WASHINGTON
(1939). Frank Capra's late-Depression
flag waver is Hollywood's archetypal
political movie—an elaborate (and entertaining) civics lesson. From the
opening "Yankee Doodle" theme and
monuments-of-Washington montage
to the heroic-filibuster closer, Capra
makes shameless use of patriotic symbols (not to mention cute kids and
feisty old-timers). The greatest icon,
however, is James Stewart's Jefferson
Smith, who personifies the innate innocence of the American people. Ap-

pointed to the Senate, the gee-whiz
scout leader manages to be cornball
yet Lincolnesque. We can feel superior
to his naïveté even as we're stirred by
his idealism. When Mr. Smith takes
on the Washington press corps or the
entire Senate, it has the quality of a
popular uprising. Jean Arthur is his
fast-talking assistant; Claude Rains is
memorable as the silver-haired epitome of corruption. And while you
watch Capra's army of pungent supporting players, you may find yourself recalling the real-life pols who
have used *Mr. Smith* as a recipe for
success.

THE SEDUCTION OF JOE TYNAN
(1979). Forty years after Mr. Smith
went to Washington, Alan Alda took
it upon himself to play Stewart's suc-
cessor as the most sincere man in the
Senate—only now the bloom is definitely off the rose. Alda's Senator Joe
Tynan, a caring liberal from New
York, may be anointed "the most
trustworthy politician in America" by
Merv Griffin (as himself), but he's
also a workaholic careerist and a harried family man, saddled with an unhappy wife (Barbara Harris) and a
rebellious daughter. Tynan lives and
breathes politics—he makes a pass at
a labor lawyer (Meryl Streep) by telling her she reminds him of J.F.K. *The
Seduction of Joe Tynan* puts out the familiar message that power corrupts,
but as directed by Jerry Schatzberg

from Alda's script, the movie has its comic side—especially when the star's banal normality plays off the more flamboyant performances of Streep, Harris, and the redoubtable Rip Torn, as a Wilbur Mills–type roué.

No Way Out (1987) This recent D.C. exposé, Roger Donaldson's remake of 1948's *The Big Clock,* opens with an image of the Washington Monument, a totem soon to be invested with explicitly priapic powers. *No Way Out* sets out to illustrate Henry Kissinger's maxim that power is the best aphrodisiac, and it features the most memorable meet-cute of the sexual counterrevolution: Kevin Costner and Sean Young at a high-octane Washington bash, making eyes at each other during "Hail to the Chief" before making love in a limo as it drives around the Mall. (Mr. Smith, eat your heart out.) This glitzy Washington is mainly an arena for macho one-upmanship. Civilization is barely skin-deep—it's appropriate that the action climaxes in a bloody scuffle in the corridors of the Pentagon.

DEMAGOGUES

Big Daddies from Down Home

———————●———————

Since the dirtiness of the political game is a given, the American public has been intermittently titillated by an unscrupulous charismatic leader. While the divinely inspired President of the 1933 nuthouse classic *Gabriel Over the White House* took his cues from Benito Mussolini, more frequently Governor Huey Long, Senator Joseph McCarthy, and King Elvis Presley have provided the models for corn-fed Führers.

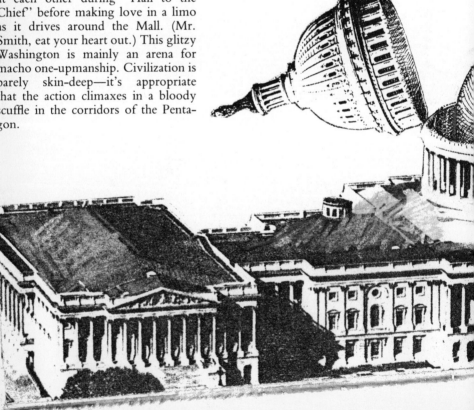

ALL THE KING'S MEN (1949). Robert Rossen's Oscar-winning adaptation of Robert Penn Warren's novel is the best known of the Huey Long–inspired films. Massive, menacing Broderick Crawford plays an honest but ambitious country lawyer who is duped by the local political machine (personified by the conniving Mercedes McCambridge) into running for governor as a bogus reformer. Crawford is totally ineffectual until he throws away his prepared speech and gets funky—"Listen to me, you hicks!" Bucking the machine, he wins the governorship on his second try by promising free medical care and education, then transforms into a dictatorial builder-showman with hypnotic power over women, mainly Joanne Dru. Crawford's brusque, cold-eyed pugnacity was supposedly modeled after Columbia studio boss Harry Cohn.

A FACE IN THE CROWD (1957). A more entertaining and hysterical version of the Huey Long story, made in the wake of television and Elvis, Elia Kazan's *A Face in the Crowd* charts the dramatic rise of a raucous hayseed named Lonesome Rhodes (Andy Griffith) from itinerant Ozark guitar picker to local media rabble-rouser to TV superstar and political kingmaker. Screenwriter Budd Schulberg's satire isn't exactly understated, but then neither is Kazan's direction—he slams his message across with a crazed fervor. Classy Patricia Neal plays the innocent Sarah Lawrence girl who discovers the great man in a back-country jail and is the first to fall under his spell. But the movie belongs to Grif-

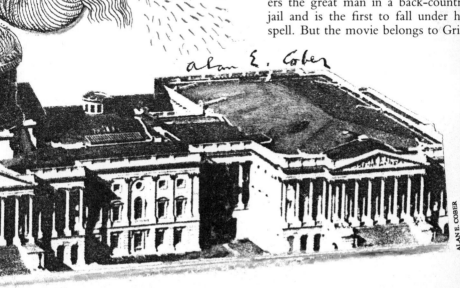

ALAN E. COBER

fith, and Kazan gets him to deliver the performance of a lifetime. If Griffith's intensity didn't scare the American people, it must at least have frightened *him*—Andy hasn't passed within a country mile of it again.

WILD IN THE STREETS (1968). This hilarious drive-in classic picks up where *A Face in the Crowd* leaves off —with rock star Max Frost (Christopher Jones) bidding to take over the country. Hal Holbrook plays a sleazy California liberal who runs for the Senate and is duped by Max into lowering the voting age to fourteen, thus ushering in the apocalypse. Few '60s images compare with the sequence in which Max's acid-burning concubine tells her fellow senators, "America's greatest contribution has been to teach the world that getting old is such a drag." Nothing if not a product of its time, *Wild in the Streets* forecasts Woodstock and Kent State (as well as concentration camps for everyone over thirty). Incidentally, Max runs for president as a Republican, because, as he explains, "Nixon would look dumb with long hair, and Ronald Reagan would look worse."

CAMPAIGNING

VOTE FOR ME

●————————————

L ike a sporting event, an election supplies its own drama—both are among the most intrinsically absorbing of public spectacles. Perhaps that's why the campaign film, like the sports movie, has a hard time competing with the real thing.

STATE OF THE UNION (1948). Frank Capra's intervention into the 1948 election is something of a curiosity— a movie about politics that uses actual names in an imaginary campaign. This time Capra's white knight is Spencer Tracy, a crusty but idealistic industrialist who, egged on by Angela Lansbury, his ambitious mistress (herself a newspaper magnate), decides to run against Dewey, Taft, and MacArthur for the Republican presidential nomination. The skeleton in Tracy's closet is his estranged wife, Katharine Hepburn, and the movie picks up considerably once she arrives on the scene. Half earnest talkathon, half screwball comedy, *State of the Union* is best when Kate starts running off at the mouth. As Tracy's conscience, she encourages him to come out for world government ("with or without Russia") even as Lansbury—anticipating her role in *The Manchurian Candidate*—and arch-fixer Adolphe Menjou persuade the old guy to cut back-room deals with assorted sleazebags.

THE LAST HURRAH (1958). Tracy is a good deal more sympathetic in this atmospheric John Ford paean to the old-fashioned urban political machine, particularly Boston's (although the actual city is never named). As the incumbent Irish mayor, Tracy plays a grand old manipulator gearing up for one final campaign. Sentimental and pessimistic, *The Last Hurrah* is one of Hollywood's few political movies to acknowledge class conflict—a key scene has the irrepressible Tracy crashing some exclusively Wasp preserve to confront his newspaper-mogul nemesis (the sepulchral John Carradine). Although Tracy calls politics "the greatest spectator sport in the country," *The Last Hurrah* takes an extremely dim view of TV. In contrast to Tracy's torch-lit parades and compassionate ward-heeling, his modern opponent mounts an idiotic television campaign—and wins.

THE CANDIDATE (1972). Television rules in Michael Ritchie's bitter, '60s-inflected satire. A rad-lib California lawyer running for the Senate, Robert Redford is initially too pure for politics—his father (Melvyn Douglas) is a corrupt former governor—but he's lured into the race by a Mephistophelian media consultant (Peter Boyle). Unlike most political films, *The Candidate* is issue-explicit: Redford campaigns against the incumbent as a pro-busing, pro-welfare, pro-abortion, anti-Vietnam eco-freak who doesn't know what to do about property taxes and isn't afraid to say so. But to his media handlers, the campaign is simply a matter of youth versus age. In a sense, *The Candidate* is a liberal response to *Wild in the Streets*—it's totally geriophobic. Not only is Redford humiliated by his dad, but during one shopping-center speech, he's punched out by an old crock. After watching this comedy, you'll wonder why anyone would ever run for office —an impression that, ultimately, may have as much to do with Redford's ambivalence toward his own stardom as it does with American politics.

CONSPIRACIES

WE, THE PARANOID

———————●———————

Elections are all well and good, but there's always the suspicion that the nation is controlled by some shadowy, usually right-wing, cabal. Before November 22, 1963, movies tended to see this antidemocratic takeover as a nightmarish possibility; after the Kennedy assassination (and Watergate), it was more often taken as a given.

THE MANCHURIAN CANDIDATE (1962). John Frankenheimer's dark comedy of brainwashing and political assassination perfectly captures the absurdist hipster tone of Richard Condon's novel, with JFK buddy Frank Sinatra as the harried existential hero. (Sinatra helped finance the movie, and one suspects he also wrote his own ridiculously jazzy dialogue: "I've been having this nightmare—a real swinger of a nightmare.") The movie is packed with sinister commies and crypto-Birchers, but the most memorable monster is played by Angela Lansbury—the mother of a fake Korean War hero (Laurence Harvey) and the controlling wife of a dim, McCarthyesque senator, she dreams of "rallying a nation of television viewers to sweep us into the White House with powers that make martial law look like anarchy."

SEVEN DAYS IN MAY (1964). Following *The Manchurian Candidate,* Frankenheimer teamed with Rod Serling to make this somewhat more sober scare film. As in *The Twilight Zone,* the mode is clipped and economical, paranoid yet idealistic: the opening sequence has right-wing pickets scuffling with ban-the-bomb-ers outside the White House, while inside, President Fredric March signs a nuclear disarmament treaty. At the same time, General Burt Lancaster, the crazed Goldwaterite Chairman of the Joint Chiefs of Staff, is planning a military coup. (Lancaster reprised this role from the left in *Twilight's Last Gleaming.*) Serling's script mixes liberal bromides with would-be racy repartee. Kirk Douglas, a more staid hero than Ol' Blue Eyes, has to play Mata Hari to a fading Ava Gardner.

THE PARALLAX VIEW (1974). Five minutes into the movie, the youthful

Senator Carroll—a potential President who describes himself as "too independent for my own good"—is shot down at a Fourth of July fiesta atop the Space Needle in Seattle. From there on it's all Warren Beatty, as a reporter investigating the mysterious deaths of those who witnessed the assassination: before long, everybody's trying to kill him, too. Alan J. Pakula expertly underdirected this low-key elliptical thriller to create mild surreality in a dehumanizing sci-fi-scape.

STAR POLITICS
OFFICE HOLDERS

●

RONALD REAGAN
Governor of California, 1967–75
President of the U.S., 1981–89

GEORGE MURPHY
U.S. senator from California,
1965–71

SHIRLEY TEMPLE BLACK
U.S. representative to the U.N.,
1969
U.S. ambassador to Ghana,
1974–76
U.S. chief of protocol, 1976–77
U.S. ambassador to Czechoslovakia,
1989–

CLINT EASTWOOD
Mayor of Carmel, California,
1986–88

SONNY BONO
Mayor of Palm Springs, California,
1988–

JOHN GAVIN
U.S. ambassador to Mexico,
1981–86

FRED GRANDY
U.S. representative from Iowa,
1987–

WINTER KILLS (1979). Jeff Bridges stars in his specialty role, the likable dope—here the scion of the Kennedy-clone Kegan clan who is earnestly attempting to solve the mystery of his President-brother's murder. William Richert's fast-moving and outrageous cult film is as packed with black humor, sexual insolence, and visual wit as any political thriller since *The Manchurian Candidate* (and once again the source is a Richard Condon novel). We've all been taught that America is the land where anything is possible: *Winter Kills* proposes that this potential is entirely negative. Well, almost entirely—although he made the movie on a shoestring, Richert managed to enlist half the hambones in Hollywood: Richard Boone, Sterling Hayden, John Huston, Dorothy Malone, Eli Wallach, and (an uncredited) Elizabeth Taylor.

TRICKY DICK

NIXON'S THE ONE!

●

Ronald Reagan has his *Cattle Queen of Montana* and JFK has his *PT-109*, but Richard Milhous Nixon is the only living ex-President to have inspired his own subgenre. We eagerly await a video version of John Adams's *Nixon in China*, or perhaps someone will bring out the even more deliriously operatic miniseries *Washington Behind Closed Doors*.

MILLHOUSE: A WHITE COMEDY (1971). Emile de Antonio uses newsreels and TV broadcasts to recount the high points of the then President's career, crisis by crisis. Here again the Checkers speech, the trips to Venezuela, the joust with Khrushchev, and the fabulous "You won't have Dick

Nixon to kick around" press conference that followed his defeat in the 1962 California gubernatorial race. What's least familiar now was most topical then—the antics of the so-called "new Nixon" in 1968. Savor the comeback candidate plagiarizing the recently assassinated Martin Luther King, Jr., for his "I see a day" speech, threatening lawbreakers that he'll "sock it to 'em," and proposing that we "win this one for Ike!"—here the never subtle de Antonio cuts to an image from *Knute Rockne, All American* of the dead Gipper, a youthful, comatose Ronald Reagan.

SECRET HONOR (1984). Perhaps the greatest of Nixon movies, as well as a worthy knockoff of Samuel Beckett's *Krapp's Last Tape,* Robert Altman's film version of Donald Freed and Arnold M. Stone's one-character play is a self-proclaimed "political myth." Surrounded by monitors and hitting the Chivas, the post-Watergate Nixon (Philip Baker Hall) engages in a frantic, free-associative monologue—a ranting recapitulation of his entire career, addressed to a portrait of Henry Kissinger. "They gave you the Nobel Peace Price, and me they called the Mad Bomber." The film is basically one long expletive. Hall, who has the best bebop delivery this side of Joan Rivers, gives a bravura performance —a laughing, babbling, snarling, railing tour de force of incomplete sentences and bursts of inarticulate rage that winds up in conspiracy wonderland: "We're all small-fry nothings compared to the big guys at Bohemian Grove."

ARTISTS

•

By Mitch Tuchman

Fact and fiction attract as if magnetic. On-screen, the lives of real artists and their fictional counterparts are practically indistinguishable; the conventions of plot are too powerful for filmmakers to resist. Take, for example, *Rembrandt* and *The Horse's Mouth;* one is based on fact, one on fiction, but both depict the "timeless" struggle between artist and philistine. In all films about artists, it seems, there's a friend who intones admiringly, "It's your best work, Basil, the best thing you've ever done," and a practical wife who handles the business end. Puccini gets a lot of play, and everyone is poor but no one starving.

FACT

AIN'T IT THE TRUTH?

————•————

A problem with biographies of great artists is what to do about the art. A thousand actors daubing oils will not create a van Gogh. With real van Goghs fetching $50 million and more at auction, owners won't lend. What to do? Turn the easel coyly from the camera? Zoom in on the hand holding the brush? Forge it, or forget it?

REMBRANDT (1936). Of the filmed biographies here, the earliest is the most majestic. Framed by the deaths of Saskia, the artist's first wife, and Hendrickje, his second, Rembrandt's life in the film runs steadily downhill, past disasters stubbornly borne: the rejection of *The Night Watch,* bankruptcy, denunciation, and eclipse. Playing a beleaguered soul and a valorous scamp, a sophisticate of peasant stock given to avuncular wisdom and antisocial defiance—"I can't behave properly, I can't paint properly, but I can live my life properly"—Charles Laughton, with mighty cadences, makes poetry of Rembrandt's every line. Like the name Rembrandt itself, Laughton's characterization became a font of clichés. Director Alexander Korda avoided the obvious pitfall—the art itself—by averting the easel and arranging the actors and extras in tableaux, reproducing the etchings under the credits, and, in what amounts to a coda, picturing Rembrandt painting himself: rumpled and serene in the beret he contributed to the inconography of art, northern light streaming through a window nearer heaven.

THE AGONY AND THE ECSTASY (1965). If Rembrandt was "the greatest painter that ever lived" (as the credits of *Rembrandt* claim), the Sistine Chapel frescoes must be the greatest paintings ever painted and, as such, demand an epic for themselves. Anything less would be sacrilege. Yet lurking behind the pageantry of *The Agony and the Ecstasy* is a simple duet for painter and patron, Michelangelo and Pope Julius II—the artist whose genius was divinely inspired and the prelate whose kingdom was defended with blood. "I planned a ceiling," mocks the Pope (Rex Harrison), "he plans a miracle." Of the act of creation we see false beginnings, fresh designs, rough outlines, fine details; Charlton Heston on his knees, on his back, brush in hand. Regarding the artist's homosexuality, there is a certain tortured resignation but no lisp. Michelangelo's Adam is ultimately innocent, unneedful of salvation, while Julius's reign is compromised by debt, warfare, and the realization that the Divine Mr. M "would make a better priest than I do."

WOLF AT THE DOOR (1987). When Kirk Douglas and Anthony Quinn played Vincent van Gogh and Paul Gauguin in *Lust for Life,* they forever stamped the style of tumultuous emotional highs and lows as a figment of the 1950s, fashionable then but déclassé now. Donald Sutherland depicts a more rational, less emotional Gauguin, in keeping with director Henning Carlsen's astringent tone— Gauguin, deciding on a country outing to abandon his family for an artist's life, simply steps off the wagon and walks down the road. *The Wolf at the Door* primarily concerns Gauguin's bitterly disappointing return to Paris in 1893, his first Tahitian sojourn behind him. When he departs again for Tahiti two years later, Gauguin's expatriation seems less a consequence of his failure to persuade Paris of the superiority of Polynesia than of the fearfulness of his friends to follow any dream at all. Sutherland's Gauguin— with only justifiable madness—is the very picture of twentieth-century sanity in a world of nineteenth-century repression.

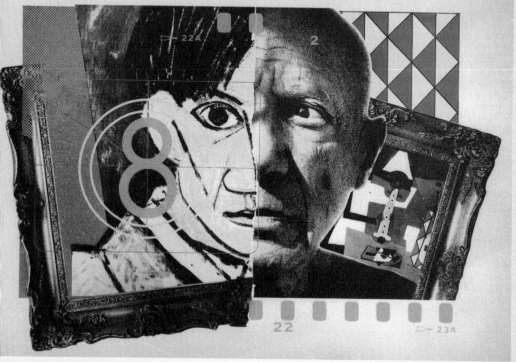

FRANK MILLER

ARTISTS
STARS WHO HAVE HAD THEIR ART EXHIBITED

———●———

LIONEL BARRYMORE

CANDICE BERGEN
(photographs)

RICHARD CHAMBERLAIN

TONY CURTIS

DAN DURYEA

HENRY FONDA

DIANE KEATON
(photographs)

GYPSY ROSE LEE

GINA LOLLOBRIGIDA
(photographs)

GEORGE MONTGOMERY

MARTIN MULL

ANTHONY QUINN

DINAH SHORE

RED SKELTON

ELKE SOMMER

SYLVESTER STALLONE

JONATHAN WINTERS

MARY WORONOV

CARAVAGGIO (1986). Caravaggio, known for his indecorous realism (he reputedly used the bedraggled corpse of a drowned whore as his model for the dying Virgin) and for his satanically violent lifestyle (he stabbed a man in a brawl in Rome and spent the rest of his short life on the lam) is played with near-catatonic lethargy by Nigel Terry, the ecclesiastical high life and profane low life of Rome swirling about him. Director Derek Jarman, like *The Wolf at the Door*'s Carlsen, offers glimpses of works in progress with the actor at his easel but settles chiefly for the by now common strategy of staging the paintings as tableaux, which serves to evoke familiar images for filmgoers but doesn't say much for the imagination of artists, as if painters were merely photographers —or cinematographers—taking pictures rather than making them. Still, Jarman's sly references to contemporary patronage, the beauty of his shadows, and his resourcefulness in the face of a tight budget make all the poetic chaos worthwhile.

A BIGGER SPLASH (1974). Fact or fiction? The presence of David Hockney does not qualify this as a documentary. Clearly, it's a work cobbled together on the Steenbeck, as if director Jack Hazan had set about making a fictionalized biography of an artist and then cast Hockney in the leading role, transposing him to film in much the way that Hockney is shown transposing his intimate associates to canvas. An interior monologue by Mo McDermott, a major character in the film who's in the process of becoming a minor character in Hockney's life, accompanies a stream of unrelated events, more often impenetrable than genuinely mysterious, culminating in the artist's brief disappearance in New York City. He was later found.

THE ADVENTURES OF PICASSO (1980). If biography teeters on the brink of fiction, why not of farce? Nothing about Tage Danielsson's *The Adventures of Picasso* can be wholly believed or comfortably dismissed. This Swedish film rings true even when we suspect it must be false. If cubism did not develop when a starving Picasso fixed his eye on an apple being eaten on the run, is it not so nevertheless that cubism represents a diary of the eye, a compendium of views? If those ubiquitous Picasso ceramics of the late years were not cranked out in a factory called Picasso, Inc., might they not just as well have been? If "art is a lie that reveals reality," then the compounding of a thousand lies, as the film's prologue promises, is bound to tell a great deal—if nothing else, how outrageously artful is the mime of Gösta Ekman, who plays Picasso.

THE MYSTERY OF PICASSO (1956). The real Picasso sits behind a translucent panel, doodling. It's rather charming but unimportant, and were he not Picasso, we wouldn't watch. An artist and his model, a seductress and her admirers, a sleeping woman, a matador thrown: with each new doodle a technique is added from an old hand's repertoire. Picasso begins the seventh drawing by scattering details in a provocative game of connect-the-dots, leaving us to wonder if when alone in his studio he plays with suspense this way. Almost imperceptibly, director Henri-Georges Clouzot masterfully plays his own hand, and the raison d'être of this collaboration is revealed. We become aware that tiny cuts conceal lapses in time; soon a greater part of each drawing is completed between takes; we are informed that the actual time it took to create drawing number twelve is five hours. This is no longer doodling; out of a run-of-the-mill documentary arises a genuine stop-motion animated feature. *Vive* Clouzot!

PAINTERS PAINTING (1973). Gertrude Stein once said that everybody writes autobiography, so she would write her own by writing everybody else's. A similar paradox operates in *Painters Painting,* a film about film-making secreted within a film about art. Emile de Antonio was a figure in the New York art world long before making his early documentaries *Point of Order* (1964) and *In the Year of the Pig* (1969); *Painters Painting* is his recollection of that world. Here are the titans of abstraction and pop—critics and curators, a couple of collectors,

---

ARTISTS

ARTISTS AND PHOTOGRAPHERS WHO HAVE MADE FILMS

———————●———————

JEAN COCTEAU
Beauty and the Beast, Orpheus

BRUCE CONNER
A Movie, Crossroads, Valse triste

JOSEPH CORNELL
Rose Hobart

**SALVADOR DALI
(WITH LUIS BUÑUEL)**
Un Chien andalou, L'Age d'or

MARCEL DUCHAMP
Anemic Cinema

ROBERT FRANK
Pull My Daisy (with Alfred Leslie), *Candy Mountain* (with Rudy Wurlitzer)

NANCY GRAVES
Izy Boukir

RED GROOMS
Tappy Toes, Fat Feet

FERNAND LÉGER
Le Ballet mécanique

CHARLES SHEELER AND PAUL STRAND
Manhatta

ANDY WARHOL
Empire, Chelsea Girls

and a dealer—twenty-four characters who don't entirely agree on either the plot or the parts they played. What emerges is a redefinition of painting, from the mere application of oil (or acrylic) on canvas to the entire complex of production, distribution, and the establishment of the parameters of taste.

ARTISTS
ART MADE FOR THE MOVIES

———●———

L'INHUMAINE (1924)
Some sets by Fernand Léger

THE SCARLET EMPRESS (1934)
Sculptures by Peter Ballbusch

SPELLBOUND (1945)
Design of dream sequence by Salvador Dali

SCARLET STREET (1945)
Paintings by John Decker

PORTRAIT OF JENNIE (1948)
Jennie's portrait by Robert Brackman

3 WOMEN (1977)
Janice Rule's murals by Bodhi Wind

IN THE KING OF PRUSSIA (1982)
Titles by Futura 2000

AFTER HOURS (1985)
Papier-mâché sculpture by Nora Chavooshian

SOME KIND OF WONDERFUL (1987)
Portrait of Lea Thompson by Han Xin

BAGDAD CAFE (1988)
Jack Palance's paintings by Bob Hickson

FICTION
ART FOR ART'S SAKE

———●———

To dramatize the lives of real artists, the art must be faked; for the lives of fake artists, the art must be real. That's the bottom line. A beret does not an artist make.

THE PICTURE OF DORIAN GRAY (1945). When Albert Lewin adapted Oscar Wilde's classic novel to the screen, he hired Ivan Albright to paint Dorian's infamous portrait at its most decrepit. True to his style, Albright, who insisted on daubing his model with fresh chicken blood, produced an image that was puckered and debauched. Lewin hired Ivan's twin brother, Malvin, to paint the portrait unbesmirched. The latter Dorian (pseudonymously signed Henrique Medina) is imperious and lacking all sensuousness, rather like Hurd Hatfield, the movie's star. Today, when agelessness can be had for the price of cosmetic surgery, the edge of Wilde's tale may have been blunted, but his aphorisms remain as sharp as ever. Note: When Lewin was preparing 1947's *The Private Affairs of Bel Ami* (not available on videocassette), he actually sponsored a competition among prominent surrealists—Salvador Dali, Paul Delvaux, and Dorothea Tanning among them—for a painting of the Temptation of St. Anthony to use in the film. A jury that included Marcel Duchamp awarded Max Ernst's painting the $2,500 prize; all eleven entries were circulated in an exhibition nationwide.

AN AMERICAN IN PARIS (1951) and **THE SANDPIPER** (1965). That they are painters is the least interesting aspect of Gene Kelly's character in *An American in Paris* and Elizabeth Taylor's in *The Sandpiper,* both directed by Vincente Minnelli. Kelly's unremarkable Paris street scenes (by an uncredited artist) are practically irrelevant; Taylor's monochromatic nature studies (painted by Elizabeth Duquette) are pleasantly unprepossessing. No, both films are really sallies into the realm of superstardom: *An American in Paris* is about Kelly's charm and grace; *The Sandpiper,* about Taylor's beauty gone blowsy. In its day, the latter film's brassy talk of atheism and abortion may have been hot stuff, but now it reads like an old issue of *Cosmo* washed up on the beach. For all Minnelli's visual sophistication, his conception of artists was rather naive: "artist" for him was shorthand for a license to behave unconventionally within the context of conventional genres. Still, you can't beat the concluding ballet in *An American in Paris,* with sets inspired by Utrillo, Toulouse-Lautrec, and Dufy, or Taylor's posing nude for sculptor Charles Bronson—that's what used to be called "arty."

THE HORSE'S MOUTH (1958). Gully Jimson, the English eccentric played to the hilt by Alec Guinness (he also wrote the screenplay, based on the comic novel by Joyce Cary), is the most convincing artist in a fiction film. Jimson is a transcendent realist; he paints "not any old tub or woman, but the tub of tubs and the woman of women." Like him, his work (painted by John Bratby) is uncompromisingly candid, larger than life, and menacing. Directed by Ronald Neame, *The Horse's Mouth* succeeds where other fictions fail: The art and the artist are so believably true to each other, and the story true to them both. Jimson is seeking the site and the wherewithal to realize his grandest vision: a Last Judgment as memorable as Michelangelo's. His mural ultimately topples, but the movie lives on and on.

AN UNMARRIED WOMAN (1978). Erica Benton (Jill Clayburgh), newly abandoned by her philandering husband, has resolved to take a chance once more on men. Saul Kaplan (Alan Bates) is the man chanced. An artist, Kaplan, like Jimson in *The Horse's Mouth,* is the perfect embodiment of his work (painted by Paul Jenkins). Both are soothing and decorative; both are about chance, about acceptance, about sensuousness. If Erica is the essence of woman, Saul is the ideal of man: humorous, handsome, chivalrous, and compassionate. If in the end his commitment to art is the undoing of Erica's feminist paradise, at least director Paul Mazursky makes no moral judgments.

A SUNDAY IN THE COUNTRY (1984). The tragedy of seventy-year-old turn-of-the-century artist Monsieur Ladmiral (Louis Ducreux) is to have witnessed the dawn of European modernism and declined to take part. Now he rues his choice but paints on in his genteel and passionless manner, hoping yet to discover in the redness of a cushion some secret so far denied him. A Sunday spent with his stolid, respectful, but unloved son and his daring, unstable, but cherished daughter represents the horns of his dilemma: to begin anew at seventy and perhaps fail, or to learn to cherish his conservative values and never know what risk might have profited him. The screenplay, by director Bertrand Tavernier and his then wife, Colo, is a bit too much like the son, but happily, the cinematography, by Bruno de Keyzer, is just like the daughter.

THE MODERNS (1988). Alan Rudolph *(Welcome to L.A., Choose Me)* wrote the book on phonies, and his own poetics are suspiciously fake. Take the closing of *Trouble in Mind:* Geneviève Bujold, musing on her decision to open an early-morning restaurant, concludes that it's "the best time to see the dawn." Deep! Who better than Rudolph to limn the lives of the factual and fictional fakes of Gay Paree? Gertrude Stein's epigrams have never seemed more opaque nor Hemingway more addled. Bujold here plays a dealer of early moderns who is as full of bull as a candidate in November. She promotes Keith Carradine as a forger (with forgeries by David Stein) of Cézanne, Matisse, and Modigliani to a soon-to-be-widowed collector (Geraldine Chaplin), whose grief is something less than genuine as well. Announcing that "Paris has been taken over by imitators of people who were imitators themselves," these fictional fakes embark for Hollywood.

MUSICALS

—•—

BY HOWARD GENSLER

The uniquely American movie musical, which has been clinging to the genre-life-support system since the Eisenhower administration, got no help from the '50s-redux presidency of movie star Ronald Reagan. Fortunately, you can perform some mouth-to-mouth with home video. The selection below is not comprehensive—there's no Berlin *(Top Hat)*, Gershwin *(An American in Paris)*, or Porter *(Kiss Me Kate)*—but included is a sampling of classics and personal favorites that provide an overview of different styles from different eras.

Before World War II, Busby Berkeley was at Warner Bros., and Fred Astaire and Ginger Rogers were at RKO. Berkeley was big and brash, and his dancers talked just like Warner's gangsters; Astaire and Rogers were graceful, witty, and oh-so-elegant; and the beautiful black-and-white gems provided by both studios took a bit of the sting out of the Great Depression.

DAMES (1934). It's not the best of the Berkeley extravaganzas, but this tale of greed and hypocrisy has remained refreshingly and religiously relevant. Superrich Ezra Ounce (Hugh Herbert) offers $10 million (not bad for 1934) to his middle-class relatives if they prove to be morally pure—no smoking, no drinking, and *no* show business—and help him ruin, er, *run* the Ounce Foundation for the Elevation of American Morals. Along the way there's the corny kissin'-cousin romancing of the overexuberant Ruby Keeler and the human Dr. Seuss character Dick Powell; the vamping of Joan Blondell; great dance concoctions, like the sexist, sapphic title tune; and dandy dialogue as well: "It's a great show. It's a musical show. Got some of the swellest songs in it you ever heard in your life."

SWING TIME (1936). George Stevens directed. Astaire and Rogers danced. And Jerome Kern and Dorothy Fields wrote the songs. Better than Berlin's *Top Hat?* At this level, who cares? The plot—and I use the term loosely—concerns gambler Fred's coming to New York to win enough money to marry his hometown sweetie (Betty Furness) but falling for dance instructor Rogers instead. The standout songs are beautifully woven into the story; highlights are the froth of "Pick Yourself Up" and the drama of "Never Gonna Dance." Warning: The ending is dumb, but everything else glistens.

STORMY WEATHER (1943). Even if this film didn't have Lena Horne, Bill "Bojangles" Robinson, and Cab Calloway, and even if it weren't the perfect showcase for all the black musical talent that Hollywood otherwise refused to hire, *Stormy Weather* would be worth watching if only for its final few minutes. That's when the fabulous Nicholas Brothers appear, spinning and splitting and leaping around like a pair of rubber-limbed puppets. (If you've never seen the astonishing Nicholases—other options on video are *The Pirate* and *That's Dancing*—then you'll be glad to hear that the movies' best male dance team are not only still walking, they're still tapping.) The pairing of twenty-five-year-old Horne and sixty-four-year-old Robinson is a little silly, and the vaudeville bits and racial stereotypes are seriously outdated, but talent wins out, and this fast-paced film, which features Horne's stunning version of the Harold Arlen–Ted Koehler title tune, is highly entertaining.

MEET ME IN ST. LOUIS (1944). Picture-postcard Americana from Vincente Minnelli. More of a family love story than a boy-meets-girl movie, this turn-of-the-century period piece is shamelessly sentimental but never clench-your-teeth cloying. The wooing of Judy Garland by Tom Drake ("The Boy Next Door") gives the film its corset-and-parasol sex appeal, and Garland gets the best solos, including "Have Yourself a Merry Little Christmas." But the real film-stoppers are the rousing "Trolley Song" and Garland's duet with the adorably bratty scene stealer Margaret O'Brien. The whole thing is so cornball, it's a miracle that it's still watchable in our *sophisticated* times, but sincerity is evident in every fame, and you can't help being charmed and uplifted by the film's old-fashioned down-home virtues.

The war ended, MGM was king, Gene Kelly was the crown prince, and all the years of military madness merely became an excuse for musicals to get more cheerful and Technicolorful. Original scores began to give way to compilations of songs from yesteryear (a bad sign), and by 1958, with the release of the danceless Oscar winner *Gigi,* all the air had gone out of the MGM era.

SUMMER STOCK (1950). The last of the Kelly-Garland teamings, *Summer Stock* is a throwback to the Garland–Mickey Rooney "Let's get Dad's barn and put on a show" subgenre popular a decade earlier. Here, Garland plays a plucky country girl whose starry-eyed sister (Gloria De Haven) promises their farm to a troupe of New York actors so they can try out their new show. Miffed, Garland makes the city slickers pitch in with the chores. That's the comedy part. The songs, except for the tacked-on "Get Happy," are nothing special, but the screenplay is pleasantly punchy, and Kelly has a few nice dances. De Haven, Phil Silvers, Eddie Bracken, Hans Conried, and Marjorie Main also make a top supporting cast. *Summer Stock* is so campy, it's probably fresher now than it was in 1950.

SINGIN' IN THE RAIN (1952). The pinnacle, the apex, the zenith of studio-system musical moviemaking. A spoof of the birth of sound and its effect on a silent-screen star (Jean Hagen, at her funniest), *Singin' in the Rain* is a tour de force of joy for star Gene Kelly; his co-director, Stanley Donen; and writers Betty Comden and Adolph Green. Kelly is the stuntman who becomes a star, Donald O'Connor is his sidekick, and Debbie Reynolds is the "serious" actress working as a flapper who helps dub a sword flick into a musical. There's also Cyd Charisse at her most eye-catching. The film's tone is beautifully set up by the pratfalls and biting humor of the opening "Dignity" montage, and from start to finish there are witty, dazzling dances performed to the hummable tunes of Nacio Herb Brown and Arthur Freed. For years, I've been telling anyone who'd listen that *Singin' in the Rain* is the best movie ever made. They think I'm kidding.

OKLAHOMA! (1955). The best of the Rodgers and Hammerstein adaptations—and yes, I've seen *The Sound of Music*—*Oklahoma!* succeeds, in large part, because director Fred Zinnemann recaptures the essence of the stage show and maintains a certain rugged, rarefied air of realism while relocating in the great outdoors. The storybook songs and Agnes de Mille's dances, 'ceptin' maybe "Pore Jud Is Daid," are seamlessly woven into the film's fabric, so when Gordon MacRae croons in front of a cornfield, it seems perfectly natural. Shirley Jones, in her film debut, is tantalizingly coy, and Gloria Grahame is jus' darlin'. Beefy Rod Steiger provides a sense of menace rarely seen in musicals, and his runaway carriage ride with Jones would do any western proud.

After Woodstock and America's loss of innocence, the best years of the movies' most innocent genre were finished. The end of the studio system had drained the musical talent pool, and the demise of the original Technicolor process (with *The Godfather,* in 1972) brought a pallid, more natural look to this unnatural, once vibrant art form. All the great Tin Pan Alley composers were either retired or deceased; a questionable war and political scandal turned a generation of filmgoers into cynics; and wholesomeness, once a song-and-dance staple, became decidedly unhip.

CABARET (1972). Based on the smash Broadway show about Germany on the verge of Nazism, Bob Fosse's *Singin' in the Reich* set a whole new standard for musicals. It no longer being credible to have fresh-faced youngsters burst into song, *Cabaret* uses the sleazy dance numbers of Berlin's Kit Kat Klub to counterpoint its smarmy narrative of prostitution, bisexuality, transvestism, abortion, and anti-Semitism. Sure, it's all tasteless—especially Joel Grey's brilliant performance as master of ceremonies—but in a tasteful kind of way. Liza Minnelli wonderfully alternates between tough and childlike, and Fosse's direction and choreography paint a vivid picture of a decaying society. Highlights from John Kander and Fred Ebb's score are "Two Ladies," "The Money Song," and the nightmarish "Tomorrow Belongs to Me." Divine decadence.

HAIR (1979). Twyla Tharp's dance sequences are stagy yet suitably slapdash and the often crude Galt MacDermot–Gerome Ragni–James Rado score works better in support of director Milos Forman's musical memorial to the Vietnam era than it ever did as a main attraction on Broadway. The film's plot is a Woodstock-era version of *On the Town* in which John Savage's straitlaced hick comes to New York to join the Army, falls in with a tribe of flower children (led by Treat Williams), and romances a pseudo-snooty debutante (Beverly D'Angelo). Highlights: "I Got Life," "Black Boys/White Boys"—watch for Ellen Foley and Nell Carter cameos—and "Let the Sunshine In."

THE TEN MOST UNDERRATED MOVIES OF THE '80s

BY MICHAEL McWILLIAMS

Picking the ten most underrated movies of the '80s is like taking off all your clothes in a Macy's window—you show more of yourself than of what you're supposed to be selling. If I were to say, for example, that *Mommie Dearest* is the most underrated movie of the decade (which it is), I'd be telling much more about my tastes than about the movie. In fact, the only reason *Mommie Dearest* isn't on the list below is that I grew hard of hearing listening to the chorus of groans every time I mentioned it. Even so, the following ten movies should be disreputable enough to make any groaner hoarse. The order is alphabetical.

EYE OF THE NEEDLE (1981). Donald Sutherland, Nazi spy, washes up on a Scottish island and is taken in by Kate Nelligan and her crippled husband. But what promises to be a cloak-and-dagger melodrama soon becomes an emotionally complex love story. The hubby is no gem, Sutherland isn't entirely scum, and Nelligan . . . well, Greer Garson never had such problems. Eventually, Kate gets to blow off steam like Dustin Hoffman in *Straw Dogs* (even at this, she is magnificent). Directed by the late Richard Marquand, who charged Ken Follett's plotting with movie-movie electricity and let the great Miklos Rozsa burn up the soundtrack.

THE HIDDEN (1987). Like *Scanners* and *The Howling,* a skid-row grossout with brains, and humor. But this one is special—it has a heart, too. Kyle MacLachlan, always an alien (and always a delight), comes to Earth posing as an FBI agent out to solve a series of grisly murders. The cop he helps, in more ways than one, is Michael Nouri. The special effects are spectacular, but director Jack Sholder doesn't lose sight of the jokes and the heart tugs—more important, he doesn't tug too hard. It's *E.T.* for grown-ups.

JUST TELL ME WHAT YOU WANT (1980). Maybe the only romantic comedy of the decade that revels in its viciousness without seeming reactionary or stupid. Alan King, who's like a vaudevillian Lear, is zillionaire industrialist Max Herschel, and Ali MacGraw, who's *good* (really), is his mistress, Bones. Their sparring has much of the wit of *All About Eve* and all of its rottenness. When told to phone MacGraw, King snaps, "I wouldn't call that bitch a taxi to take her to hell." Written by Jay Presson Allen, directed by Sidney Lumet, and buoyed by a sterling crew: Dina Merrill, Keenan Wynn, Myrna Loy.

THE MAN WITH TWO BRAINS (1983). This third collaboration between Steve Martin and director Carl Reiner (just before *All of Me*) is the funniest of the bunch. It's supposed to be a send-up of mad-scientist movies, but its anything-for-a-laugh farcicality makes it closer to *Airplane!* Martin is so much more exciting here than in the pastel, upscale *Roxanne,* it's like seeing him in underground porno. And Kathleen Turner gives the performance of her life as his sex-crazed-sadist wife. Time-capsule moment: Martin grabs Turner by the scruff of the neck and screams, "Into the mud, scum queen!"

MASS APPEAL (1984). The cornball Broadway play reaches the screen with husks intact. Jack Lemmon is Father Farley, a backslapping priest who has sold out to his upper-crust congregation. Zeljko Ivanek is Mark Dolan, a "fiery" seminarian. Guess what? *They learn from each other.* Lemmon is more Lemmon than ever—this is his *Mommie Dearest.* And Ivanek is superb in a let's-get-it-to-the-back-balcony sort of way. The only modern element is the explicit gay theme, but even this is enjoyably sweet. It's the most satisfying mix of Catholicism and homoeroticism since Patsy pawed Sister Benedict in *The Bells of St. Mary's.*

THE MIRROR CRACK'D (1980). What might have been a rehearsal for *Murder, She Wrote*—with Angela Lansbury as Miss Marple sleuthing among the rich and famous—becomes a more subversive pleasure when two Hollywood divas, Elizabeth Taylor and Kim Novak, square off *as* Hollywood divas. They're making *Mary, Queen of Scots* in England—Taylor is Mary, Novak is the real Queen Elizabeth. While Taylor has the meeker role, in and out of corsets, Novak breaks twenty-five years of sleepwalking on-screen. Clashing with her director, she snarls, "I could eat a can of Kodak and *puke* a better movie." With Rock Hudson and a sleazily funny Tony Curtis.

MY FAVORITE YEAR (1982). Peter O'Toole—who has for years looked like an extra in a George A. Romero movie—came through in the '80s with one robust performance after another, especially in this pastrami-on-wry comedy about TV's golden age. As Alan Swann, the Errol Flynn–type profligate who must appear on a Sid Caesar–type show, O'Toole embodies the spiritual ironies of Hollywood, particularly when, realizing that the

TV show is live, he bellows, "I am not an actor—I'm a *movie star!*" Expert support from Joseph Bologna as King Kaiser.

RADIO DAYS (1987). Woody Allen's childhood reminiscence is his masterpiece, because it plays to all his strengths—one-liners, nostalgic sentiment, a near-fetish for design detail—and avoids the fact that he has less in common with Chekhov the playwright than with Chekov the guy on *Star Trek*. Mia Farrow (talk about underrated!) heads a hearty cast of cultural stereotypes, who are never less than enchanting because they're like dream figures in a child's play. And when these apparitions themselves start to reminisce, it's like a trip to the Emerald City set to the beat of the Andrews Sisters.

THE STEPFATHER (1987). This lip-smacking thriller—all about a "family values" man who marries widows with children, gets disappointed real fast, and then slices them up—is the perfect kiss-off to the Reagan era. Terry O'Quinn (Mark Harmon crossed with Ichabod Crane) does the niftiest mad-slasher turn since Jessica Walter's in *Play Misty for Me,* and the director, Joseph Ruben, keeps everything bright, fleet-footed, funny. His most memorable set piece—involving O'Quinn, a two-by-four, and one hapless soul—evokes genuine pity and terror.

SWEET DREAMS (1985). Jessica Lange is such a voluptuous Patsy Cline, she makes that other Patsy-mad lang—k.d.—look like Lily Tomlin's Tommy Velour (what's great about k.d. has much more to do with Elvis). Lange not only gets down Cline's big-hipped swagger and lava-lamp grin, she gets at the woman behind the Bronco Billy facade. Ed Harris, as husband Charlie Dick, supplies the beef, and it's USDA prime. When he hauls Lange into the rain and forces her to say that she'll always love him, it's a dramatic mirror of Cline's intoxicating S&M songs ("sweetened" for the soundtrack and lip-synched to perfection). Directed by Karel Reisz.

SCI-FI

•

BY PETER BISKIND

The stuff that passes for sci-fi these days—the teen space epics, the cutesy, feel-good, inspirational fantasies, the endless drecky Trekkie junk —isn't worth the celluloid it's shot on. Real sci-fi, the genuine article, the pods and blobs, big bugs, little green men, fifty-foot women, and fantastic voyagers, was spawned in the '50s, when, for reasons best known to students of popular culture (the bomb's as good an explanation as any), the genre finally came into its own. By the decade's end, sci-fi had virtually disappeared, only to re-emerge in the late '60s in more bizarre and ambitious, if less interesting, forms: *Barbarella*, Jane Fonda's exercise in kitsch; *2001: A Space Odyssey*, Stanley Kubrick's psychedelic pudding; the campy *Planet of the Apes* cycle; and John Boorman's mannered *Zardoz*. Then in 1977 came *Star Wars*, and the rest, as they say, is history. The following selection is weighted toward the '50s, sci-fi's golden age, a time when real monsters didn't eat quiche.

THE THING (1951). James Arness played the bloodthirsty "carrot" that slurps up the boys at the base in this pioneering flying-saucer thriller, which scared the pants off '50s audiences. Following quickly on the heels of *Destination Moon* and *Rocketship X-M*, *The Thing*, was one of the first '50s sci-fi movies to feature a nasty monster from outer space. In the early drafts of the zingy script (by Charles Lederer), the visitor was to have been considerably more outré, but apparently the special effects folks weren't up to the job, and it turned out to be nothing more unusual than an oversized human. Given the primitive nature of the effects, it's testimony to the skill of producer Howard Hawks and director Christian Nyby that the film holds up as well as it does. (Sci-fi does not live by effects alone—witness the fate of the dumb 1982 remake, by John Carpenter.) When they're not busy devising ways of getting rid of the alien, the soldiers and scientists fight over who's going to run the show—the movie's real theme. The no-nonsense soldiers are led by Kenneth Tobey (whose role here ensured him endless cameos from homage-mad movie-brat directors of the future), while the scientists are led by a soft-on-aliens Thing-symp egghead (Robert Cornthwaite). Needless to say, the film's allegiances are clear. Don't miss the classic paranoid injunction—"Watch the skies!"—at the end.

THE DAY THE EARTH STOOD STILL (1951). "Klaatu barada nikto" are the unforgettable (at least to trivia pursuers) words Patricia Neal uses to discourage the robot Gort (played by Lock Martin, doorman at Grauman's Chinese Theater and one of the tallest men in Hollywood) from incinerating Washington, D.C., with its laser eye.

Robert Wise's thinly disguised attack on the arms race, with Michael Rennie as Klaatu, the emissary from outer space who warns quarreling humans to shape up or ship out, proves that messages don't have to be sent by Western Union. The film has a you-are-there documentary flavor that makes it surprisingly convincing and goes a long way toward normalizing some of the loonier aspects of the script (such as Klaatu's Christ-like return from the dead). Klaatu's stylish flying saucer served as a prototype for spaceships to come, particularly Steven Spielberg's dolled-up, rhinestone version in *Close Encounters of the Third Kind.* Look for vintage howlers: Walter Reed Army Medical Center doctors smoking, and '50s newscasters Gabriel Heater, H. V. Kaltenborn, Drew Pearson, and Elmer Davis casting with their hats on.

WAR OF THE WORLDS (1953). A suspiciously shaped meteor sets Geiger counters aflutter when it lands in California. Unlike the soldier in *The Day the Earth Stood Still,* who shoots Klaatu the moment he sets foot on terra firma, the locals in this film are friendly, only to be vaporized by ill-intentioned Martians who want Earth for themselves. Miraculously, the special effects in producer George Pal's harrowing classic of interplanetary carnage, based on the H. G. Wells novel and Orson Welles's legendary 1938 radio hoax (Welles convinced a goodly number of Americans that Martians had landed in Grovers Mill, New Jersey), still chill. Thrill to the spectacle of the U.S. Army's most advanced weapons fizzling in the face of an alien invasion! Rejoice as Los Angeles is burned to a cinder by spidery beings flitting about in airborne goose-neck lamps topped with throbbing parking lights whose humming

green beams fry anything that moves! When all seems lost, the Martians are laid low by "the littlest things that God in his wisdom had put upon the Earth": bacteria.

THIS ISLAND EARTH (1955). Big-domed Metalunans snatch some Earth scientists to enlist their help in a losing battle with the planet Zahgon. There are wonderfully sticklike performances by Rex Reason (watch him laboriously construct a TV-like "interociter" from circuit diagrams obtained through a suspiciously advanced mail-order catalog) and Faith Domergue (a lesser-known Howard Hughes girlfriend) in this triumph of vintage sci-fi kitsch. It has great special effects, too, including the spectacularly granulated surface of ravished Metaluna and the ugliest alien ever, a truly repulsive gray-matter slime ball covered with veins like ropes. Why the high-IQ Metalunans think they can expect help from the low-IQ Reason and Domergue is known only to the screenwriter.

FORBIDDEN PLANET (1956). A Freudianized sci-fi version of *The Tempest,* directed by Fred M. Wilcox, who was famous for his Lassie movies, and featuring Walter Pidgeon as Dr. Morbius, a lost-in-space Prospero, and Anne Francis as his comely daughter. The two live together in Electra-fied bliss on Altair-4, the sole beneficiaries of the powers of the Krell, an advanced civilization that mysteriously vanished. Enter some rescuers from Earth, and up pops the dread "planetary force" that had torn the rest of Morbius's expedition limb from limb; it is nothing less than the "monster of [Morbius's] Id." Don't miss cute Robby the Robot, the R2D2 of the '50s who recently reappeared in *Earth Girls Are Easy.*

INVASION OF THE BODY SNATCH- ERS (1956, 1978). "At first glance, everything looked the same. It wasn't. Something had taken over the town." The "something" was the celebrated pods that transform the good people of Santa Mira into identical peas. Watch Kevin McCarthy and Dana Wynter futilely struggle against them in Don Siegel's paranoid McCarthyite (Joe, not Kevin) classic. Phil Kaufman's baroque remake, with Donald Sutherland in the McCarthy (Kevin, not Joe) role (but catch Kevin's cameo), is just as good in its own way.

THE INCREDIBLE SHRINKING MAN (1957). Sci-fi-meister Jack Arnold's greatest movie, based on a novel by Richard Matheson, follows the adventures of poor Grant Williams as he gradually shrinks to the size of an ant after being showered with radioactive fallout while boating. His encounters with the family cat and then a spider (particularly the scene in which he impales the unfortunate arachnid on a needle) are extremely well done, but the emotional core of the film is his oddly compelling relationship with the female circus dwarf who befriends him on his way down. Beware of Lily Tomlin's 1981 rip-off, *The Incredible Shrinking Woman.*

THE FLY (1958, 1986). What do you say about a film in which, thanks to a "teleportation" experiment gone awry, the head of a man ends up on the body of a fly? Do a remake! The original was a surprisingly taut little number starring Vincent Price. The remake is a wonderfully clever (without being campy) David Cronenberg special, with all the really disgusting F/X we've come to expect from the director of *Scanners* and *Videodrome*. It is also the most persuasive abortion-on-demand film this side of *Rosemary's Baby*. Cronenberg succeeds where others have failed, coming close to making a star out of Jeff Goldblum and at the same time showcasing the considerable talents of Geena Davis, who makes the most of a script that confines her to saying "Yeah."

ALIEN (1979) and **ALIENS** (1986). Ridley *(Blade Runner)* Scott's original follows a simple and-then-there-were-none formula, but how well he does it. Great scenes: the alien splattering blood all over the crew when it explodes out of John Hurt's chest; the decapitation of science officer Ash, whose head goes on to deliver several key plot points; and the lovely Sigourney Weaver, stripped down to her Jockey panties (actually, there's no label showing; the product-placement person on this film was probably executed), playing cat and mouse with the alien. You'd think it would have been hard to catch any winks after such a gut-wrenching tussle, but the sequel opens with Weaver, in deep "hyper-sleep," returning to Earth, where she's actually persuaded to go back for more (much, much more). Director James *(The Terminator)* Cameron's mucous monsters are better than ever, and he dresses down the high-tech look of the original with a veneer of it's-a-dirty-job-but-somebody-has-to-do-it shabbiness. The spaceship looks like an old shoe.

FAME

●

By Owen Gleiberman

Has fame ever been cheaper than it is right now? In our "people"-addicted culture, the line between real stardom and Dweezil Zappa stardom grows thinner every day. Yet fame is (or should be) more than just a matter of Being Famous. The public has a powerful need to believe that the famous have earned their place in the heavens and that stars are born because they were meant to be stars, just as we were meant to bask in their light. The movies below flesh out some of our fantasies and nightmares about the people we dream we'd like to be. Following those films, in the cause of democracy, are some movies about fans, our on-screen representatives, the ones who act out the love affair—or love-hate affair—we carry on from afar.

THE FAMOUS

WE LIKE YOU, WE LIKE YOU

●

Is it actually lonely at the top, or is that just a rumor spread by celebrities so we don't get too jealous? Probably both. The movies presented here are about people who followed their dream and found it. Most of them are cautionary tales: we're invited, for a while at least, to share in the glamour and then to thank God we don't have to pay the price.

THE HARDER THEY COME (1973). The first words you hear are the jaunty lyrics of "You Can Get It If You Really Want," which could be a sentiment out of *Flashdance*. But this crudely enthralling cult movie from Jamaica is about how badly you have to want it—in this case, bad enough to kill. Jimmy Cliff plays Ivan, a bad-ass optimist who comes to Kingston with dreams of cutting a hit record. Confronted with institutionalized pov-

erty and a fascistic record producer, he turns outlaw, hitting the top of the charts even as his WANTED poster appears throughout the nation. The story sprawls a bit, but *The Harder They Come* is an infectious piece of pop mythmaking, and Cliff offers one of the rare rise-of-a-pop-star portrayals with real anger in it. He also wrote and performed much of the reggae score himself, and it's one of the most exhilarating musical soundtracks ever done; it spins you right past the rough spots. Directed by Perry Henzell.

A FACE IN THE CROWD (1957). If you know Andy Griffith only from his Mayberry days, you owe it to yourself to see this. He plays Lonesome

Rhodes, a self-styled "country boy" recruited to do an early-morning show on a hick-town radio station. His homespun charm catches on. Soon, he's moved to a television station in Nashville, then national TV, then superstardom, then super-duperstardom. . . . You get the picture. This over-the-top Budd Schulberg–Elia Kazan collaboration was the *Network* of its day, though it's much easier to take; it's less a snobbish putdown à la Paddy Chayefsky than it is a prophetic satire of celebrity in a spanking-new media age (this was, after all, 1957). The image of Lonesome Rhodes carries eerie echoes of a lot of familiar folks: Elvis Presley, Jerry Falwell, Jim Jones, Ronald Rea-

ELWOOD SMITH

gan. And Griffith is simply amazing. Beaming a smile as wide as the Grand Canyon, he's like a demonic, sex-crazed Jeff Bridges, a cracker-barrel demagogue who won't rest till he's pleased everybody all of the time.

THE ROSE (1979). "Where am I?" asks rock singer Rose (Bette Midler), her private plane heading for the next concert date. "I never know where the fuck I am!" The way her face crumples into tears, it's clear she really doesn't. Back when *The Rose* was first released, it seemed to be little more than an exhaustingly commercial rock 'n' roll fable, a kind of Vegas-ized version of the Janis Joplin story. It looks better now. The blandly mainstream musical score is forgivable; rather than selling out, it renders the movie a late-'70s period piece. And for anyone who knows Midler only from her high-camp high jinks in such Touchstone hits as *Ruthless People* and *Big Business,* her performance will come as a revelation. As Rose, she's a drunken, disheveled counterculture diva, hooked on the very stardom that's sucking her dry. Midler conveys her character's adrenaline-charged talent and drive, her astonishingly fragile core, and everything in between. Memorable supporting work by Alan Bates (as Rose's Mephistophelian manager) and Frederic Forrest (as the good ol' boy who's too late to save her) make this a thrilling actor's showcase. Directed by Mark Rydell and shot by Vilmos Zsigmond, *The Rose* is not a great film, but it is a powerful one.

A STAR IS BORN (1954). A star also dies, and that's the fun part. In this splendidly masochistic George Cukor musical drama, James Mason plays a movie idol who latches on to obscure nightclub singer Judy Garland, makes her a star (and his wife), and then watches, horrified, as her career eclipses his. The movie really starts when Mason loses his grip; suddenly, a '50s-Technicolor musical is poised on the edge of the abyss. Garland is at her moody best singing "The Man That Got Away," but even that can't hold a candle to Mason's antics at the Academy Awards. When he drunkenly slaps her in the face, it's such a campy-ghastly moment, you may think you're watching the outtakes.

CIAO! MANHATTAN (1973). Part documentary, part amateur fiction, this fascinatingly horrendous movie is like a poisoned valentine to its star, Edie Sedgwick, pedigreed member of Andy Warhol's Factory crowd. It isn't about Sedgwick's fifteen minutes of fame, exactly; it's about the degradation after the fame. She spends most of the movie lolling around topless in her makeshift bedroom (actually, it's the awning-covered deep end of a mansion's empty swimming pool) while a couple of hostile hippies tend to her needs and try to get the rest of her clothes off. Interspersed are bits from her '60s fashion spreads and her appearances in Warhol's films. With her lithe beauty and clipped, silver-dyed hair, Sedgwick prefigured the cocky androgyny of the punk era; she had the true star's knack for self-invention. Mostly, though, the film shows the drugged, silicone-enlarged, out-of-it Sedgwick dropping such mind-numbing pronouncements as "I got hooked on speed at the Factory. Then I became a heroin addict to get off speed." There's considerable doubt she even knew what she was saying, which makes *Ciao! Manhattan* both the definition of an exploitation film and a testament to how stiff the price of popularity can be.

THE IDOLMAKER (1980). Ray Sharkey plays a would-be rock star in late-'50s Brooklyn who's got talent, moves, attitude—everything but looks. So he becomes a pop Svengali instead, turning a couple of handsome young kids into rock idols by teaching them how to sing, how to dress, how to *be*. Evidently inspired by the life of Bob Marcucci, the Philadelphia hotshot who "created" Frankie Avalon and Fabian, this is one of the only rock movies about the much-scorned post-Elvis/pre-Beatles era, and it's amazingly free of condescension. In his first outing as a director, Taylor Hackford captures what made these original bubble-gum stars appealing. (The songs—all of them new—are so catchy, they may send you scurrying back to your Fabian singles.) And Sharkey gives a powerhouse performance. Standing off-stage as his prize creations drive the teenyboppers wild, he's both rapturous and jealous, doomed to spend his career a step away from the spotlight he craves.

FUNNY GIRL (1968). Barbra Streisand's incandescence here doesn't begin with her voice, nor does it begin with her perfect, whiplash line readings. It begins with musical comedienne Fanny Brice's desire—her need —to become a star, which is really Streisand's need poking through and transforming the character she's playing. This is arguably the last great gasp of studio-system moviemaking (directed by William Wyler; scored by Bob Merrill and Jule Styne). Perhaps that's why it remains Streisand's best film: Her larger-than-life talent belongs not to an era of realism (as, say, Cher's does) but to an era of larger-than-life stars. *Funny Girl* has one obvious weakness—that "dashing" stick Omar Sharif—yet this somehow bolsters Streisand's performance. If her

Fanny Brice finds it lonely at the top, that's because no one could ever really match her aura.

THE FANS

LOVE IS A MANY-SPLENDORED THING

————————●————————

It isn't lonely at the bottom: There are far too many others to keep you company. The trouble with being a fan is that we often want to be the thing we love. Then again, sometimes we want to kill it.

A HARD DAY'S NIGHT (1964). It captured Beatlemania as it was happening, and more than two decades later, it remains a peerlessly zesty rock 'n' roll fable. Director Richard Lester's jump cuts now seem as exhilarating as Godard's, John Lennon's wisecracks as well-timed as Groucho's. Yet this original Fab Four movie is innocent in a way no later rock film could be, and much of the credit must go to the thousands of screaming teenage girls in the audience—the ones whose lips form such magical words as "George!" and "Paul!" and "Ringo!" while tears stream down their cheeks. When Len and Mac shake their mop tops in unison after the line "She loves you, and you know you should be glad!" it sends the audience into hyperspace. No Guns N' Roses concert ever generated as much sexual hysteria. Watching these British bobby-soxers get their first taste of audience frenzy, you understand why the '60s had to happen.

THE KING OF COMEDY (1983). Unlike other Robert De Niro antiheroes, Rupert Pupkin isn't meant to be a three-dimensional character. A polyester nebbish who pesters and finally kidnaps his talk-show-host idol (Jerry Lewis) for the chance to perform a five-minute monologue, Rupert is a figment of our national neurosis; he's John Hinckley gone Vegas. Martin Scorsese's dazzlingly cynical satire is almost too acidic for its own good (the movie has its mind made up about what an idiot Rupert is even before he opens his dum-dum mouth), yet its relentlessness holds you. Sandra Bernhard's high-decibel groupie grows tiresome pretty quickly, and no wonder: When the movie works, it's not about berserk fan worship; it's about a kind of obsessive idolatry that on the surface remains as cool and bland as a television screen.

Outrageous! (1977). In this shaggy, enjoyable cult film, female impersonator Craig Russell plays a Toronto hairdresser who comes to New York and becomes the featured attraction at a drag-queen cabaret. The movie is about how he summons the courage to leave his day job and become a star, but Russell isn't really a star here: He's the ultimate fan. His witty impressions of Mae West, Carol Channing, Barbra Streisand, and Judy Garland, among others, are the gay movie maniac's equivalent of playing air guitar —they're an adolescent fantasy of worshiping your idols until you merge with them. When Russell merges, he's almost better than the real thing. Directed by Richard Benner.

Play It Again, Sam (1972). In *Annie Hall,* Woody Allen goes on dates and gets nervous. Here, he goes on dates, gets nervous, and receives on-the-spot advice from fairy godfather Humphrey Bogart (played by professional Bogie clone Jerry Lacy), who is the last word in coolheaded Hollywood macho. *Play It Again, Sam*

was directed by Herbert Ross and not by Allen himself, which is the main reason it's often underrated. In fact, the blind date with Jennifer Salt is perhaps the most hilariously nerdy sequence of Allen's career. What gives this movie its soul is Woody's longing to be just like his idol, a desire that's treated with a sly blend of satire and affection.

Woodstock (1970). A rock-concert epic in which the audience upstages and transcends the stars. Watching Michael Wadleigh's surging documentary, you're almost convinced the legendary three-day festival was set up in order to be filmed, like the Nuremberg rally in Leni Riefenstahl's *Triumph of the Will.* The hippies swim nude, do rain chants, take mucho drugs, slide in the mud, and make peace signs into the camera. They're so blissed-out (and so self-satisfied), it's easy to see why this was both the apotheosis of '60s communalism and its swan song. Some of the musical acts have aged badly, but the performances of Jimi Hendrix, the Who, and Sly and the Family Stone have lost none of their power, and neither has the mesmerizing multiscreen imagery, which a young editor named Martin Scorsese helped to put together.

Nashville (1975). It was Robert Altman's genius to realize that making a movie with twenty-four lead characters might be the truest way to capture the soul of America. Beneath its gleeful pokes at presidential politics and C&W music, *Nashville* is probably the most loving vision of American life ever filmed; Altman's affection for this country's diversity— for its *democracy*—is built into the film's very form. The musical performances give the movie its afterglow, and we see them through the eyes of all the fans who have flocked to Nashville like religious cultists. (At one point, Altman even puts Shriners in the audience.) Years after you've seen it, you'll remember the adoring/demanding crowds at the Grand Ole Opry, Keith Carradine serenading his female admirers with "I'm Easy," and Kenny, the mysterious mama's boy, staring raptly at country queen Barbara Jean as he reaches for the key to his violin case. . . . In the remarkable cast are Henry Gibson, Lily Tomlin, Geraldine Chaplin, Ronee Blakley, Karen Black, Shelley Duvall, and Keenan Wynn.

STAR 80 (1983). In Bob Fosse's criminally underrated film about the murder of *Playboy* centerfold Dorothy Stratten (Mariel Hemingway), the main character isn't Stratten but her sleazy husband and killer, Paul Snider, who worshiped at the altar of the *Playboy* mystique. Eric Roberts plays Snider as both clammy and soulful; he makes this greasy hustler's reverence for the Hefner domain so palpable it recalls Brando's desire to be a contender. Snider wants people to "treat us that special way, the way they treat *stars!*" and when Stratten tries to shake him off her coattails, he explodes. Some critics complained the movie was an example of the very exploitation it was condemning, but that's just what's powerful about it. Fosse doesn't moralize; he puts you inside Snider's skin-glitter dreams.

VIRGINS

•

BY MICHAEL ZIMBALIST

Virgin births are reputed to be quite rare, yet every birth is the birth of a virgin. Virginity is a condition we've all shared; its loss, an eventuality for all but the few. Not surprisingly, stories about deflowering have formed the basis of a wide variety of movies. The following guide to virginity on video is divided into three sections. "Breaking Away" features meddlesome parents trying to influence their children's first love. In "Paradise Lost," naive initiates discover encroaching responsibilities and uncomfortable freedoms just outside the gates of Eden. And finally, "Love and Death" explores the unsettling connection between the end of virginity and the end, period.

BREAKING AWAY

MOTHER, PLEASE, I CAN DO IT MYSELF

———————•———————

Cruel fathers withhold their daughters; jealous mothers hide their sons. Even Venus, the goddess of love, couldn't help interfering when her darling son Cupid was smitten by beautiful Psyche. The four movies below give proof that parents, whether matchmaking or match-breaking, would do best to butt out.

SPLENDOR IN THE GRASS (1961). This ballad of teenage woe begins with one of the cinema's most celebrated French kisses. Breathlessly, Bud (Warren Beatty) and Deannie (Natalie Wood) swallow each other, their hormones rushing with the same inexorable fury as the waterfall beside which Bud's convertible is parked. Then Deannie suddenly shoves him aside. "No," she says. "We mustn't." Deannie's modesty is imposed by a frigid mother who connives to keep her unspoiled until the wealthy Bud proposes marriage. But all Bud's father's dreams are pinned on his son. He refuses to let Bud marry young, advising him instead to find "a different kind of girl" to service those dawning sensations. How hopeless for Bud and Deannie! Strained by parental pressure, their love ends as abruptly as their opening kiss. Bud is overcome by malaise, while Deannie descends into madness—proving that prolonged virginity may be hazardous to one's mental health. Screenplay by William Inge; directed by Elia Kazan.

YOU'RE A BIG BOY NOW (1966). Bernard Chanticleer's father gives him two simple words of advice: "Grow up." Bernard (Peter Kastner) knows that his first step is to find a girl who's "willing," but like many a rookie in search of nookie, he passes up the sure thing for a more elusive goal. She is Barbara Darling (Elizabeth Hartman), an inscrutable go-go dancer. More than a few obstacles keep Bernard from his dream: There's his doting mother, who mails him locks of her hair and weeps at the thought of her baby as a man; there's a malicious rooster, trained to attack pretty girls, patrolling the halls of his rooming house; and most of all, there's Barbara herself. She turns out to be a man hater, psychically scarred by the lecherous wooden-legged hypnotherapist who "counseled" her in high school. Writer-director Francis Ford Coppola *(You're a Big Boy Now* was his M.F.A. thesis for UCLA) sketches this improbable universe with a calculated clumsiness designed to evoke Bernard's confusing coming-of-age. And where would you expect such a twisted tale to reach its salty climax? Inside a pretzel factory, of course.

THE GRADUATE (1967). Wouldn't it be nice if Benjamin Braddock asked Elaine Robinson out on a date? His parents think so. So does her dad. The only one who objects is Elaine's mother, Mrs. Robinson, because she'd like to have Ben all to herself. Mike Nichols nabbed nearly every conceivable directorial honor for this box-office smash, and the critics all raved, seizing the story of Ben and Mrs. Robinson as emblematic of the generational schisms wrought by the Vietnam War. Viewed twenty-two years later, however, the film is remarkable for the virtual absence of any cultural references to the late '60s. As Ben, Dustin Hoffman is awkward, overly polite, and always well-dressed; he's hardly a hippie. The seductive Mrs. Robinson (Anne Bancroft), on the other hand, is a champion of deflower power. When she and Ben finally rendezvous in a hotel room, he becomes afraid. "Do you find me undesirable?" Mrs. Robinson asks. "Oh, no," he answers. "I think you're the most attractive of all my parents' friends." Sensing an opening,

she confronts him with her suspicion that this is going to be his first time. He says nothing. "It *is*," she says with cold delight. The accusation is as effective as ice on a burn, and—coo coo ca choo, Mrs. Robinson—their affair begins.

PRETTY BABY (1978). After gestating for twelve years in the opulent womb of a sumptuous New Orleans bordello, Violet (Brooke Shields) is ready to become one of the girls. On the eve of her initiation, her mother (Susan Sarandon) offers the following piece of advice: "Don't act like you know it

---

VIRGINS
ACTORS' FEATURE-FILM DEBUTS

MEMORABLE
Timothy Hutton, at 20
Ordinary People (1980)

Warren Beatty, at 24
Splendor in the Grass (1961)

David Bowie, at 29
The Man Who Fell to Earth (1976)

NO BIG DEAL
Tom Cruise, at 19
Endless Love (1981)

Sidney Poitier, at 26
No Way Out (1950)

Robert Duvall, at 32
To Kill a Mockingbird (1963)

AWKWARD
Robert Blake, at 9
Mokey (1942)

Michael J. Fox, at 19
Midnight Madness (1980)

Rock Hudson, at 23
Fighter Squadron (1948)

VIRGINS

ACTRESSES' FEATURE-FILM DEBUTS

———⬤———

MEMORABLE
Kathleen Turner, at 27
Body Heat (1981)

Julie Andrews, at 29
Mary Poppins (1964)

Glenn Close, at 35
The World According to Garp
(1982)

NO BIG DEAL
Jodie Foster, at 9
Napoleon and Samantha (1972)

Susan Sarandon, at 24
Joe (1970)

Diane Keaton, at 24
Lovers and Other Strangers (1970)

AWKWARD
Daryl Hannah, at 18
The Fury (1978)

Debra Winger at 22
Slumber Party '57 (1977)

Goldie Hawn, at 23
*The One and Only, Genuine,
Original Family Band* (1968)

---

all. You won't get a tip that way."
The "cherry bustin' " is celebrated
with unabashed grandeur. To a flour-
ish of trumpets, baby Brooke, spar-
klers in each hand, is carried aloft on a
pallet of red velvet as Madame Nell
(Frances Faye) presents her to the
high-class clientele. "A virgin," she
proudly announces. "And it's her
wish that one of you gentlemen be the
first." Until they were shut down by
the Navy during World War I, brothels like this thrived in the Storyville
section of New Orleans. Louis Malle's
sensitive portrait of this bygone lifestyle is so intimate, so richly detailed,
that the whorehouse begins to feel like
our house. Soon after receiving critical
acclaim for *Pretty Baby,* Shields,
America's favorite virgin, went on to
lose it again on-screen in *The Blue Lagoon.*

PARADISE LOST

THOSE WEREN'T THE DAYS

———⬤———

As time goes by, we all tend to
idealize the innocence of our
youth, forgetting how terrifying and
uncomfortable adolescence really is.
The following six films clearly affirm
that nostalgia begins only after virginity ends.

LITTLE DARLINGS (1980). Dense
concentrations of horny adolescents
and the relative absence of adult supervision combine to make summer
camp one of the time-honored devir-
ginizing institutions. On the bus to
the all-girl Camp Little Wolf, Angel
(Kristy McNichol) and Ferris (Tatum
O'Neal) make a bet: Whoever loses
her virginity first wins. Ferris targets
Gary (Armand Assante), the athletic
instructor. He appears to be the only
grown-up within miles—a convenient situation for the none-too-cau-
tious campers, who commandeer a
bus to go buy rubbers at the local gas
station. There, Angel meets Randy
(Matt Dillon), AWOL himself from
the all-boy camp down the road, and
a rebellious, tough-talking smoker
just like her. When they finally tryst
in an old boat house, director Ronald
F. Maxwell takes the movie beyond
the often satirical script, vividly ex-
posing the psychic pain of teenage
sexuality. Tears take the place of a

cigarette for Angel in the aftermath of her first time. "God," she says, "I feel so lonesome."

BILOXI BLUES (1988). Neil Simon's memoir of childhood's end (directed by Mike Nichols) begins with an aerial shot of a train crossing a bridge. Chugging toward adulthood aboard this penetrating symbol of passage is Simon's alter ego, Eugene (Matthew Broderick). He and his Army buddies are going to Mississippi for a basic-training regimen that will include riflery, calisthenics, and Rowena (Park Overall)—a lady in the business of helping soldiers earn their stripes. When Eugene reports to her bedroom, Rowena instantly realizes that it's his first tour of duty and tries to make the experience seem special. "Don't be offended," he responds with polite candor. "This really doesn't have to be the greatest experience of my life. I just want to get it over with." And in exactly twenty-five seconds, he does.

THE MIRACLE OF MORGAN'S CREEK (1944). While dancing wildly at a send-off party for soldiers, Trudy Kockenlocker gets banged in the head. She wakes up the next morning to discover that sometime during the night she got married—and you know what *else* that means. . . . Sure enough, she's pregnant. But who could the father be? Poor Trudy has only the dimmest recollection of a name: something like "Ratskywatsky." As Trudy dreams up scheme after scheme to cope with her impossible situation, this Preston Sturges comedy whizzes forward like a bullet, piercing the conventional moral armor of its time. Betty Hutton, wily and beguiling from beginning to end, displays a limitless reserve of Yankee ingenuity as the indefatigable Trudy,

a character as fertile as the great American plains. Her pregnancy's surprising outcome is a portent of our nation's ascendancy in world affairs. World War II, after all, was when America lost her innocence and emerged with global responsibilities and commitments.

GEORGY GIRL (1966). Lynn Redgrave stars as Georgy, a charming, chubby-cheeked virgin whose self-doubts and frumpy attire restrain an otherwise magnificent personality. Far more sophisticated than her parents—the servants of a millionaire called Mr. James (James Mason)—Georgy shares a London flat with her friend Meredith (Charlotte Rampling), a fashionably svelte gamine. Playful flirtations from Meredith's boyfriend, Jos (Alan Bates), only add to Georgy's insecurities, and an offer from Mr. James to become his mistress is far too businesslike to kindle her passion. Georgy's story debunks the myth of virginity that holds purity to be somehow preferable to the knowledge of earthly delights. Only after sleeping with Jos does our heroine discover the other Georgy, deep inside, and gain the confidence to shed her dowdy feathers and fly.

SUMMER OF '42 (1971). On the rustic island where their families spend the summer of 1942, Hermie (Gary Grimes) and his best friend, Oscy (Jerry Houser), use a purloined medical textbook as their guide to the subtleties of physical love. While Oscy dabbles with girls his age, Hermie develops a painful crush on a more mature woman, Dorothy (Jennifer O'Neill), whose husband has left for the war. Through Hermie's quest, director Robert Mulligan conveys the heroism with which young men overcome their virginity: the daring caresses in darkened theaters, the humiliation of buying condoms for the first time. And just as summer's greenery inevitably yields to the burnished browns of fall, awkward Hermie stumbles into Dorothy's arms.

SMOOTH TALK (1985). Life at home is practically unbearable for Connie (Laura Dern): her mother (Mary Kay Place) constantly harps that she's uncooperative; her father (Levon Helm) thinks only of himself; and her sister (Elizabeth Berridge) is an obnoxious goody-two-shoes. So Connie and her friends spend every free moment cruising for boys. Decked out in a halter and made up like a vamp, Connie is clearly more alluring than she realizes. And one night at a hot-dog joint, she's spotted by the psychopathic Arnold Friend (Treat Williams), who won't be satisfied until he's the one who has her first. Arnold captures his prey using nothing but "smooth talk" —mesmerizing, maniacal patter that glides back and forth between violent threats and calm, reassuring sweetness. Reworking a short story by Joyce Carol Oates, director Joyce Chopra bends the virginal rite of passage into an emotional U-turn that sends Connie back to the nest she sought so desperately to leave.

LOVE AND DEATH

OUT, OUT! BRIEF VIRGIN

───────●───────

When the first petal falls from the blossom of youth, it's a reminder that the flower itself will eventually turn to dust. Here are four films in which the loss of virginity is linked with the loss of life.

TESS (1980). Perhaps death's whisper

VIRGINS
DIRECTORS' FEATURE-FILM DEBUTS

───────●───────

MEMORABLE
Orson Welles, at 26
Citizen Kane (1941)

Dennis Hopper, at 33
Easy Rider (1969)

Robert Redford, at 43
Ordinary People (1980)

NO BIG DEAL
Ron Howard, at 23
Grand Theft Auto (1977)

Martin Scorsese, at 26
Who's That Knocking at My Door? (1968)

George Lucas, at 26
THX-1138 (1971)

AWKWARD
Francis Ford Coppola, at 23
Tonight for Sure (1962)

Oliver Stone, at 28
Seizure (1974)

Nancy Walker, at 59
Can't Stop the Music (1980)

---

seems to haunt every frame of this Roman Polanski masterpiece because Geoffrey Unsworth, the director of photography, died during its filming. His evanescent renderings of English country life, seamlessly brought to completion by Ghislain Cloquet, earned a Best Cinematography Oscar. As the maiden Tess, seventeen-year-old Nastassja Kinski leaves her destitute family for the estate of the noble d'Urberville clan, believing them to be distant relations. She quickly becomes the object of solicitation by her "cousin" Alec (Leigh Lawson), and her desecration of her virtue resonates throughout the remainder of Tess's misfortune-plagued life. Polanski's adaptation of Thomas Hardy's classic Victorian novel (poignantly dedicated to his wife Sharon Tate, who was brutally murdered by the Manson family) is a searing indictment of man's inhumanity to woman.

BADLANDS (1973). Kit (Martin Sheen) is the most gorgeous boy that young Holly (Sissy Spacek) has ever seen. She thinks he looks just like James Dean. And though she can't understand why, Kit is infatuated with her, too. When Holly's pet fish dies, she turns to Kit for comfort, knowing that he's familiar with death from his work in the stockyards. That familiarity soon becomes much more vivid when Kit murders Holly's father, a cruel disciplinarian who refuses to sanction their love. The swooning duo escape to the forest, where they hide out in a thatched tree house. Immune to all civilizing forces, they leave their destiny to nature, killing whenever they need to and living with no aims other than enjoying each other and evading capture. Terrence Malick wrote, produced, and directed this hypnotic fairy tale of doomed first love. To Holly, and to nearly everyone Kit meets on his murderous romp through life, he's a hell-bent American hero, as compelling, as beautiful, and as violent as an exploding star.

ANDY WARHOL'S DRACULA (1974). A pale, sickly Count Dracula cannot survive without the blood of virgins, or, in the Transylvanian vernacular, *wirgins*. With his coffin strapped to the top of a car, Dracula (Udo Kier) and his assistant, Anton (Arno Juerging), travel to Italy, where, they think, people are very religious and keep their daughters pure. The count is taken in by the effete, aristocratic Di Fiore family, one of whose daughters must surely be a . . . *wirgin*. Little does he suspect that the Di Fiores' servant Mario, played by Warhol regular Joe Dallesandro (in deadpan Brooklynese), has been tending to more than just the fields. When Dracula taps into the juicy jugulars of the two most marriageable daughters, the effect of their "impure blood" on his digestive system results in some of the all-time greatest Grand Guignol ever thrown up on the screen. Eventually, Joe figures out that the "creep from Rumania" is a vampire and spares the youngest Di Fiore virgin from the count's sacrificial bite by removing her authenticity. You've got to hand it to Andy Warhol and writer-director Paul Morrissey—their vision of the traditionally virile Dracula as a frail cherry-picker is positively batty.

HAIL MARY (1985). In this irreverent updating of the Virgin Birth, Joseph is a cabby and Mary works in a gas station. Mary's explanation for her pregnancy invites skepticism from all quarters. "Some song and dance," her gynecologist declares. She refuses to let Joseph touch her, fearing retribution from her baby's *real* father. Small wonder that the faithful flocked to the picket lines when this movie bowed at the New York Film Festival. Mary is less a bearer of God's child than the mouthpiece for director Jean-Luc Godard's metaphysical musings.

FAMILY TROUBLES

BY ED SIKOV

In divorce-ridden, domestically perturbed 1990s' America, the term "family values" has strangely come to signify the renaissance of hearth and home that comes from one's financial contributions to the politician or televangelist of choice. Confident dads will once again carve moms' exquisite roast chicken while packs of breathless, ruddy children rush in from games of touch football. Until this happy vision is realized, however, we'll have to make do with the current mess, which is more than adequately represented in movies available on videocassette. So, kids, wash your hands, turn on the VCR, and get ready for dinner, and make sure that the carving knife in Dad's hand is aimed at the chicken and not at you.

MEAN MOTHERS

DON'T FOOL WITH 'EM

In our distrusting and generally misogynistic post-Freudian age, a fine target of contempt and rage can be found in the figure of Mother. Such noble, sacrificial matriarchs as Stella Dallas and Mildred Pierce find their opposite in the silver screen's many vicious, lousy mommies who conveniently sop up all the blame for their children's ruined lives. These women suggest an updated variation on that wonderful old Victorian song: *"M is for the many ways we hate them / O is for the odious things they do. . . ."*

THE BROOD (1979). Nola Carveth (Samantha Eggar) has a problem. She bears grudges—literally. A patient at the Somafree Institute of Psychoplasmics, an experimental asylum run by the peculiar Dr. Raglan (Oliver Reed), Nola is the daughter of an abusive alcoholic mother and a weak-willed father and thus has more than her share of "issues." Dr. Raglan encourages her to express her rage physically, so she gives birth to it, or rather *them*—hideous, color-blind babies ("They see things only in black and white") who have humplike feeding sacs and commit gruesome murders to avenge their mom. David Cronenberg directs with a keen eye for unsettling images, the most devastating of which may be the traumatized face of Nola's normal daughter, Candy, as she tries to cope with an unusual childhood.

NOTORIOUS (1946). Alfred Hitchcock's films are rife with rotten, domineering mothers whose pernicious influence emanates even from beyond the grave. In *Notorious,* Alex Sebastian (Claude Rains) is stuck with one of the worst. A gentle, good-natured man living in Rio de Janeiro (never mind that he's a Nazi plotting to build an atom bomb), Alex is seduced by Alicia (Ingrid Bergman) an American who is herself a Nazi's daughter. They marry. But when Alex discovers that he's made the mistake of his life, he goes straight to Mother (Leopoldine Konstantin), who whips out a cigarette, drags deeply in concentration, and utters one of the most horrifying lines ever offered from mother to son: "We are protected by the enormity of your stupidity." Then, as Eric Rohmer and Claude Chabrol once put it, "following his mother's advice, he decides to poison the woman he was careless enough to marry."

BLOODY MAMA (1970). There's more to this Roger Corman cheapie than rampant violence, sick humor, drug abuse, Shelley Winters, prison rape, and incest (as if anyone would *need* more). A wildly exaggerated account of the Barker gang's notorious crime spree, the film sardonically treats Ma (Ms. Winters) and her boys as a degenerate Depression-era Partridge Family, traveling through the countryside and providing cheap entertainment to a bored nation. Why, those madcap Barkers get into one fix after another! First they rape some white-trash slut, then they choke an inconvenient witness, and the next thing you know, two of them are in jail and Mama has to rob a bank to pay for a lawyer. Like so many young Americans, the Barker boys just want to make a better world for themselves; sadly, they end up machine-gunned to death while their far more blameworthy mother raves idiotically about animals digging up their junkie brother's

---

FAMILIES

———●———

Henry Jaynes Fonda, actor (1905–82)

Married actress *Margaret Sullavan* in 1931; divorced in 1933

Married *Frances Seymour Brokaw* in 1936; she died in 1950
Daughter, *Jane,* an actress, born in 1937
Son, *Peter,* an actor-director-producer, born in 1940

Jane married director *Roger Vadim* in 1965; divorced in 1970
Daughter, *Vanessa,* born in 1969
Married political activist *Tom Hayden* in 1973
Son, *Troy,* born in 1973

Peter married *Susan Brewer* in 1961; divorced in 1973
Daughter, *Bridget,* an actress, born in 1964
Son, *Justin,* born in 1966
Married *Portia Rebecca Crockett* in 1975

Henry married *Susan Blanchard,* stepdaughter of *Oscar Hammerstein II,* in 1950; divorced in 1956
Daughter, *Amy,* adopted in 1953

Married *Countess Afdera Franchetti* in 1957; divorced in 1962

Married *Shirlee Adams* in 1965

---

grave. (Skinny, youthful Robert De Niro is a standout as the junkie brother.)

ORDINARY PEOPLE (1980). With her spectacular performance as a Waspy mother from hell (by way of Lake Forest, Illinois), Mary Tyler Moore makes it impossible to look at her perky television persona without seeing something cold and nefarious underneath. In Robert Redford's profoundly male-oriented film, she plays Beth Jarrett, a woman whose elder son's death by drowning has turned her into a selfish, uncaring, and supremely heartless bitch, especially to her suicidal son, Conrad (Timothy Hutton). As husband Calvin (Donald Sutherland) finally comes to realize, Beth can't stand messes of any kind. (We already know this, having seen her interrupt one of the only conversations she has with Conrad to adjust a vase to its precise and proper place.) How difficult it is, then, for Beth to countenance Conrad's chain-smoking, coffee-guzzling, and suspiciously Jewish-sounding psychotherapist (Judd Hirsch). Thank heaven she never sees how dingy and unkempt his office is.

CREEPY KIDS

THE DEVIL'S PLAYGROUND

For a culture that dotes on mewling little babies in cribs, we've certainly produced a large number of movies about heinous children. Besides the films recommended here, there's the archetypal *Bad Seed* (murderous child), *Mildred Pierce* (grasping, adulterous child), *Carrie* (disturbed telekinetic child), *Night of the Living Dead* (zombie child), *Rosemary's Baby* (Satan's child), the *Omen* series (Satan *himself* as child), and lots of others. Prospective parents are advised to skip this section and move on to something more reassuring.

IMITATION OF LIFE (1959). One of the classic "women's weepies" of the late '50s, this dazzling Douglas Sirk tearjerker is, as its title suggests, a pure simulacrum. Lana Turner is brilliantly unbelievable as Lora Meredith, an aspiring actress who meets a homeless black woman, Annie Johnson (Juanita Moore), at Coney Island. Each woman has an intolerable daughter, though Annie's little girl, Sarah Jane (Karen Dicker and, later, Susan Kohner), is by far the worse. Neurotic and obnoxious, Sarah Jane doesn't like being half-black (her father is white); since she's very light-skinned, she spends the rest of the film passing as white, much to her mother's heartache and shame. Lora, meanwhile, virtually ignores her own daughter (Terry Burnham and then Sandra Dee) in a single-minded quest for stardom; just listen to the mad, triumphant way Lora blurts "Amerigo Fellucci!"—the name of the director who offers her the lead in his next Italian art film. Sirk may have loved his characters, as the late Rainer Werner Fassbinder once claimed, but he doesn't really trust any of them, except maybe Mahalia Jackson, who appears at the end to sing "Trouble of the World."

THE PARENT TRAP (1961). As the credits put it, it's "Hayley Mills and Hayley Mills" starring in this Disney comedy about bratty identical twins. The girls, separated in infancy by divorced parents (Maureen O'Hara and Brian Keith), finally meet each other at a girls' camp and plot to reunite the family. Walt Disney's tyranny of happiness forces a cozy resolution, but not before the film's oddly corrosive premise has had a chance to sink in. The parents, rich and selfish, have each utterly abandoned one of their children without so much as a yearly Christmas card. And when the tough-to-take little missies finally bring their folks together (by switching identities, then revealing the ruse), the two abrasive adults do nothing but launch into one screaming match after another. By the time the whole sick business is over, the domestic stage is set for the two Hayleys to grow up into the female answer to *Dead Ringers*.

MEET ME IN ST. LOUIS (1944). One of the great MGM musicals, Vincente Minnelli's *Meet Me in St. Louis* is suffused with a lovely, nostalgic glow. Sure to please anyone who wants nothing more than great songs, costumes, and sets (not to mention a superb Judy Garland performance), the film tracks the sweetly domestic life of a St. Louis family in the year leading up to the 1904 World's Fair. But lurking under the cheerful surface is a dark little horror story in the form of the family's youngest daughter, Tootie (Margaret O'Brien). Morbid and subversive, tiny Tootie runs around committing ghastly pranks—gleefully planning her doll's funeral ("She has four fatal diseases!"), throwing flour in a neighbor's face on Halloween ("I'm the most horrible!"), telling a nasty lie about her sister's boyfriend ("He tried to kill me!"). Later, after a lot of happy songs are sung, Father (Leon Ames) suddenly threatens to ruin everyone's life by moving the family to New York. Mom (Mary Astor), the maid (Marjorie Main), and the girls are all upset by the news, but only Tootie takes action. She decapitates Father in effigy. He changes his mind.

KING LEAR (1971). This is, after all, the tragedy that gave us the expression "How sharper than a serpent's tooth it is to have a thankless child." Of course, Lear has not one but *two* ungrateful children, and it's especially galling because he's turned over his entire kingdom to them. In this stark film version (the first since the silent era), directed by Peter Brook, Paul

Scofield is an ancient, imposing shell of a Lear tormented by his too-long life as well as by daughters he calls "unnatural hags." Having written the play before the days when everything got blamed on Mother, Shakespeare mentions Lear's children's other parent only once (and even then it's offhanded), leaving the maddened king no one but himself and the human condition to thank for the miserable state of his family. In one particularly disturbing scene, the old man looks his eldest daughter, Goneril (Irene

---

FAMILIES

———●———

Sir Michael Redgrave, actor
(1908–85)

Married actress *Rachel Kempson,*
in 1935
Daughter, *Vanessa,* an actress,
born in 1937
Son, *Corin,* an actor, born in
1939
Daughter, *Lynn,* an actress, born
in 1943

Vanessa married director *Tony
Richardson* in 1962; divorced in
1967
Daughter, *Natasha,* an actress,
born in 1963
Daughter, *Joely,* an actress, born
in 1965
Vanessa had a son, *Carlo,* with
actor *Franco Nero* in 1969

Lynn married actor-
photographer-manager *John
Clark* in 1967
Son, *Benjamin,* born in 1968
Daughter, *Kelly,* born in 1970
Daughter, *Annabel Lucy,* born in
1981

**COMPILED BY ELIZABETH
FINKELSTEIN**

FAMILIES

———●———

Walter Huston (né Houghston),
actor (1884–1950)

Married journalist *Rhea Gore* in
1905; divorced in 1913
Son, *John,* a director-
screenwriter-actor, born in 1906;
died in 1987

John married *Dorothy Harvey* in
1927; divorced in 1933

Married *Leslie Black* in 1937;
divorced in 1945

Married actress *Evelyn Keyes* in
1946; divorced in 1950
Son, *Pablo,* adopted in 1947

Married dancer *Enrica Soma,* in
1950; she died in 1969
Soma's daughter, *Allegra,*
adopted by *John*
Son, *Walter Anthony (Tony),* a
screenwriter, born in 1950
Daughter, *Anjelica,* an actress,
born in 1952

John had a son, *Danny,* a director,
with actress *Zoë Sallis* in 1962

Married *Celeste Shane* in 1972;
divorced in 1975

Worth), straight in the eye and declares, "Thou art a boil, a plague-
sore, or embossèd carbuncle in my
corrupted blood." These are troubles
not even the best-trained family therapist could ever hope to resolve.

FEMALE TROUBLE (1974). Dawn
Davenport: a name that lives in in-
famy. A juvenile delinquent turned
abusive parent turned success-crazed
desperado, Dawn (played by Divine)
is the kind of offspring every parent
dreads, even those who don't live
in Baltimore. Director-sleazemeister
John Waters revels in the dreadful
Dawn's downhill slide. First, the big,
ugly, fat girl is crushed by deprivation: at Christmastime, Mr. and Mrs.
Davenport fail to give their daughter
the cha-cha heels she desperately cov-
ets, so the shallow, materialistic teenager knocks her mother down with
the Christmas tree and leaves home.
Dawn is then subjected to far greater
indignities, such as being raped by a
man (also played by Divine) who
drives an Edsel, having acid thrown
in her face by someone named Ida
(Edith Massey), and witnessing the
final, terrible conversion of her repellent daughter, Taffy (Mink Stole),
into a Hare Krishna—just as Waters
himself put it) "to get on her mother's
nerves." Thus the torch is passed to
the next generation.

NUCLEAR EXPLOSIONS

THERE'S NO PLACE LIKE HOME

———●———

When it comes to domestic dis-
cord, sometimes nobody is
really at fault. Instead, it's just the
way things are; it's this permissive society; it's the nature of the patriarchal
system; it's human nature. Whatever
it is, it's beyond repair.

THE HILLS HAVE EYES (1977) and
THE HILLS HAVE EYES II (1985). As
the sequel's prologue helpfully reminds us, "In the mid-1970s, a family
of tourists from Cleveland unwisely
left the paved highway and drove off
across the desert on an unmarked dirt
road. Soon lost, they wandered onto
a vast deserted bomb range inhabited
only by tarantulas, rattlesnakes, and a
wild family of cannibals unknown to
the civilized world." Living as they do

on a bomb site, this family—daddy Jupiter, sons Mars and Pluto, and daughter Ruby—is nuclear in every sense of the word. But just like ordinary people, they, too, have their internal discontents. In the first of these two Wes Craven films, Ruby saves the life of one of the tourists by siccing a rattler on Mars; she returns as one of the good guys in the sequel, in which the patriarchal role, vacated by the now-dead Jupiter, is taken over by a nefarious uncle named Reaper.

REBEL WITHOUT A CAUSE (1955). Filmed in CinemaScope, this Nicholas Ray masterpiece loses something (a good chunk of the image) on videocassette, but the magnitude of James Dean's performance as the tormented Jim Stark comes through intact. The deeper one gets into the film, the more ironic its title becomes; by the end, it's tough to imagine what *isn't* wrong with Jim's world. Jim, Judy (Natalie Wood), and John (Sal Mineo) meet one night at a police station; Jim's drunk, Judy's left home, and John's been shooting puppies for kicks. All three are products of quietly hellish homes, Jim's being the worst only because we see it in the most detail. His father (Jim Backus) is an emasculated worm, his mother a castrating shrew, and as for Grandma (as Jim tells it), "somebody oughta put poison in her Epsom salts." Lacking decent bonds at home, the three kids form their own family, with Jim and Judy as the parents and John as their son. The scene inside the planetarium, when the kids learn how minuscule they are compared to the universe, is always unnerving.

SISTERS (1973). Orphaned twins, raised by nuns and malevolent-looking doctors, are finally separated after a lifetime of togetherness. One's nice, the other isn't. An attractive young advertising rep meets the good one, Danielle (Margot Kidder), on a Manhattan game show; later, when he offers to escort her home, she tells him she lives on Staten Island. It's a bad sign. If you get beyond Margot Kidder's unintentionally Clouseau-like French-Canadian accent, *Sisters* is an engaging suspense movie. Director Brian De Palma, always the misanthropic showman, orchestrates a vision of disintegrating family life that extends beyond that of his poor, freakish heroines. Take the young reporter (Jennifer Salt) who gets involved in some of evil twin Dominique's unpleasantness. In classic imitation-Hitchcock fashion, she has a mother you'd just like to stuff.

MARTIN (1976). A teenage vampire tale set in a depressed mill town outside Pittsburgh, George A. Romero's *Martin* is also the story of an immigrant family (Romanian, of course, given the legend) falling apart under the doubly appalling strain of old-world custom and western Pennsylvania anomie. The eponymous bloodsucker (John Amplas), an orphan, is sent by distressed relatives to live with his elderly cousin Cuda (Lincoln Maazel) and Cuda's granddaughter, Christina (Christine Forrest). Cuda believes that the boy is Nosferatu; Christina thinks he's just the messed-up product of their morbid family; Romero leaves the diagnosis ambiguous. Yes, Martin does have an odd taste for other people's vital fluids. But given the hopelessness of his family situation, the poor boy's need for new blood is simply a matter of survival.

THE '70S

BY JACK BARTH

Future students of '70s-ology won't be seeking cultural insight from such trendsetting "statement" films as *Saturday Night Fever* and *Smokey and the Bandit*. No, they'll be analyzing movies that simply tried to cash in on the zeitgeist and unintentionally left a cinematic Rosetta stone (or rather, Anderson tape). With the following movies on videocassette, you can discover—just as those future students will—the *real* '70s, Hollywood-style.

THE PEOPLE!!

"YOU LIGHT UP MY LIFE . . ."

Topping the mountain of appellations for this era was white-disco-suit wearer Tom Wolfe's "Me Decade." (Fortunately, selfishness and greed were abolished in the '80s). Despite such cynicism, some '70s people, especially the three in the films below, really "made a difference."

VIVA KNIEVEL! (1977). Unlike in the 1971 movie *Evel Knievel,* which top-lined the criminally underrated George Hamilton, here Kneivel plays himself, "a freewheeling superbiker" (according to the liner notes). Gene *(Xanadu)* Kelly is "a rummy bike mechanic," and pantsuited Lauren Hutton is "an intrepid photographer who

trades barbs—and hearts—with the wily Knievel." The wily (and tender-hearted) Knievel distributes Evel Knievel toys in an orphanage. A saucer-eyed tot casts aside his crutches and limps across the dorm: "When I saw you walk away from that crash in England, I figured I could do it, too. You're the reason I'm walking, Evel *—you're the reason!*" Says Evel to Hutton: "I'm just a man doing his own thing. Are you a woman or a Ms.?" Mobsters lure him to Mexico for a fatal crash so they can smuggle drugs back on the international day of mourning: After all, who would in-

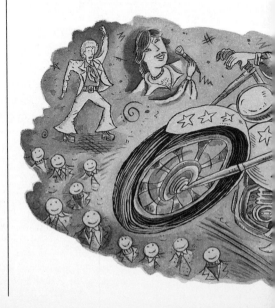

spect *Evel Knievel's* funeral procession? Good plan—*not!*

CAN YOU HEAR THE LAUGHTER?
(1979). Ira Angustain (no, not Tony Orlando) plays Freddie Prinze—Mr. "Looooking good!"—in this made-for-television biopic. Freddie earns his comic's stripes when his pal Nat teaches him the Hollywood Screenwriter's Comedy Imperative: Use your own life for material. The hilarious cockroach jokes and lazy-Hispanic gibes commence. Figuratively overnight, Freddie gets his break on Carson and stars in the TV megahit *Chico and the Man.* But does he heed Nat? "Fred needs to slow down . . . down . . . down." Nope. It's full throttle, '70s-style, and one day he "can't hear the laughter anymore." Instead of getting his ears cleaned, he goes gaga for guns; gobbles drugs, drugs, drugs; dons shiny shirts of the Devil's own Qiana . . . *blam!* Joe Piscopo, don't let this happen to you. We need you too much, man.

RICHARD SALA

THE HAPPY HOOKER (1975). The most erotically charged image of the 1980s had to be that of Lynn Redgrave, at the climax of any Weight Watchers frozen-food commercial, as she tossed off her bulky outer clothing and spun fetchingly to reveal her sexy, svelte body. Well, fellow Redgrave gazers, think of this as *Weight Watchers: The Movie.* La Lynn's performance as Xaviera Hollander, the Dutch madam, memoirist, and *Penthouse* columnist, gives new meaning to the term "women's movement." William *(Winter Kills)* Richert scripted this enlightened romp. Watch for the scene in which Lynn dons a Louise Brooks wig; she looks just like—gasp! —that other dream girl, Kaye Ballard!

THE LIFESTYLES!!

"THAT'S THE WAY / UH-HUH UH-HUH . . ."

———————⚫———————

In the '70s, you didn't need to be rich and famous to have a lifestyle. All you needed was "the right stuff": the right look, the right attitude, the right drugs, and the right tunes thumping from your quadriphonic eight-track tape player. (But mostly, you needed the right drugs.)

FRITZ THE CAT (1972). "It's X-rated . . . and animated!" Ho-ho-ho, I'll say! Ralph Bakshi's anthropomorphic, racially aware critters (based on the Robert Crumb comic) cavort in Greenwich Village, taking drugs and manning the sexual revolution: "Ever done it with an aardvark?" Fritz ventures uptown for a Harlem adventure that becomes a gory riot. He has to "bug out" when the pigs (literally—right on!) chase him, but the cat ends up rolling in clover. The raunchy situations and rockin' soundtrack will make you bug out, too—but first, put the kids to bed.

PLAYERS (1979). The powdery fingerprints of energetic '70s party guy–producer Robert Evans are all over this kilo of glam. During his Wimbledon finals match against Guillermo "Señor Boogie" Vilas, Dean-Paul Martin flashes back on the torrid affair he had with Ali MacGraw. ("I don't answer questions," says the enigmatic Ali, responding to a pry into her past. "I'm allergic to them; they make me break out.") Pancho Gonzalez blows the "real actors" off the screen as Dino's gruff coach. Other pros, including John McEnroe and Ilie Nastase, are scattered about the mise-en-scène like rolled-up C notes on a mirror, and smiley guy Steve Guttenberg is on hand as Dino's buddy. Young hustler woos stiff but attractive older woman? It's the rich man's *Moment by Moment.*

THE FISH THAT SAVED PITTS-BURGH (1979). Okay, any movie sounds funny with "fish" in the title. *Sophie's Choice*—sad. *Sophie's Fish*—funny. *Ordinary People*—poignant. *Ordinary Fish*—my ribs are cracking! But this zany bouncefest is the catch of the day, indeed. A bumbling, dissension-ridden pro basketball squad, on the advice of an astrologer, is traded (with the exception of leader Julius "Dr. J." Erving) for a team of compatible Pisces. With the stars now in conjunction, the Pisces proceed to tear up the league. Jonathan Winters, as the team's owner, is as funny as Larry Bird is cute, but *Modern Romance*'s Meadowlark Lemon and *Airplane!*'s Kareem Abdul-Jabbar help

make the hoops action more believable than a Charlotte Hornets–Miami Heat tilt. And Steve Guttenberg is *nowhere in sight!*

CAN'T STOP THE MUSIC (1980). It was the death knell *(bonggg!)* of an era *(bonggg!),* a termination that came with the surprising alacrity of a Bounty towel soaking up a spill. Allan Carr, the Midas of cheesy entertainment, hired Nancy Walker, the shrimpy Rosie of "quicker-picker-upper" fame, to direct *un film à clef* portraying the rise of America's disco darlings, the Village People. Their guru is played by—oh, happy day!—Steve Guttenberg, who roller-skates with a demented grin through Manhattan traffic. Fun, right? "Relax . . . boogie . . . have a good time," says Jack Weston. But that's not what this movie's about at all. *CSTM* is about the *death of fun,* about the ineluctable advent of an avaricious new decade. Valerie Perrine enunciates the theme: "The '70s are dead and gone," she screeches ominously. Bruce Jenner symbolizes the future: He's a tax lawyer who falls for Perrine like a ton of pure Tropicana orange juice. The message? Dress normal. Listen to music you can't dance to. Go to sleep early. After all, as Perrine, the shapely harbinger of disco doom, intones, "The '80s are gonna be something wonderfully new and different."

THE REVENGE!!

"ONE TIN SOLDIER RIDES AWAY . . ."

———————●———————

Okay, so we lost some dumb war in the '70s. That doesn't mean we have to take stuff lying down. It's payback time on the home front: Peace is over if you want it to be!

Convoy (1978). Truck drivers were the cowboys of the '70s, just as investment bankers were in the '80s. The chart-busting smash-hit anthem that tapped this trend, C. W. McCall's "Convoy," vented our frustrations with gas "shortages" and the fifty-five-mile-per-hour speed limit; Sam Peckinpah's movie adaptation drives the theme home. With truckers' de-lite Ali MacGraw by his side, Kris Kristofferson defiantly leads a pedal-to-the-metal interstate caravan; vengeful smokey Ernest Borgnine rides his tail. "Wow, men with foliant sideburns making raunchy CB patter —movie magic!" you might exclaim. Add a heaping helping of Peckinpah's patented slo-mo crashes and the kittenish MacGraw's distinctive emoting, and you've got the '70s all wrapped up in one handy cassette.

Billy Jack (1971). Billy's a war hero, a Rambo-esque mayhem machine who hated the war and now protects a "freedom school" on an Indian reservation. The vile townsfolk —a typical civic leader is seen socking his pregnant daughter in the eye— mistrust the weirdos: Billy's lethal limbs are the only thing preventing Wounded Knee II. Agonizingly long touchy-feely scenes alternate with spectacular karate. Scan forward for signs of Billy's "slow burn": he rubs his head methodically ("They tell me I'm supposed to control my bad temper . . ."), touches his index finger to the tip of his nose ("But when I see what you done here . . ."), uh-oh ("I . . . just . . . go . . . ber- . . . ZERK!")! KAPOW!!!

Final Chapter—Walking Tall (1977). Buford Pusser's a war hero, a Rambo-esque et cetera who, in part one, returned to Tennessee to become a sheriff. He earned respect for

his big stick and for his resentment of upside-down laws protecting criminals. Gangsters killed his wife and maimed him, but he retained his height. In the talky, sluggish *Part 2, Walking Tall*—picture *Cries and Whispers* with Liv Ullmann brandishing a big stick—he got some revenge but couldn't nail the evil mastermind. In *Final Chapter*, bleeding hearts unseat

Buford as sheriff for his civil-rights infractions. Bleakness. Then things get *weird*. A Hollywood producer buys Buford's story and shoots *Walking Tall,* starring Joe Don Baker (who played Buford in part one but was replaced by Bo Svenson in parts two and three). Svenson, the "real" Buford, is asked to play "himself" in the sequel, but his car is sabotaged and he dies. The end?

HARPER VALLEY P.T.A. (1978). If you think only J.R. found life after *I Dream of Jeannie,* you missed Barbara Eden in this adaptation of Jeannie (!) C. Riley's chart-busting smash-hit ballad. Captain Nelson's Jeannie tells off the PTA board with the song's lyrics, which, while peppy and sassy on vinyl, seem nasty and brutal on celluloid: "This is just a little Peyton Place, and you're all Harper Valley hypocrites!" Swinish locals toilet-paper her house—and Jeannie . . . just . . . goes . . . ber- . . . ZERK! She makes one hag's hair fall out, marches pink elephants through the house of alcoholic Pat Paulsen, dumps a ton of manure on another crone, and—oh-ho, a waterbed joke! Throughout, the song resounds: a Muzak version, an "action" version, a minor-key "sad" version, a determined march. It makes you long for adaptations of other chart-busting smash-hit '70s songs: *Piano Man*—a lounge pianist stalks unappreciative patrons; *American Pie* —what *really* happened at the levee; *Tie a Yellow Ribbon*—a Rambo-esque war hero returns home to a bare oak tree and just goes berserk. . . .

THE '70S
WHERE ARE THEY NOW?

—————●—————

JOHN BELUSHI
Abel's Hill Cemetery, Chilmark, Massachusetts

GODFREY CAMBRIDGE
Forest Lawn Memorial Park, Glendale, California

KAREN CARPENTER
Forest Lawn Memorial Park, Cypress, California

BILLY CARTER
Lebanon Cemetery, Plains, Georgia

PETER FINCH
Hollywood Memorial Park Cemetery, Los Angeles

ANDY GIBB
Forest Lawn Memorial Park, Hollywood Hills, California

JETHROMANIA!!

"THANK GOD I'M A COUNTRY
BOY . . ."

—————●—————

Who was the quintessential '70s auteur? Coppola? Scorsese? Nah! While nobody was looking, Mr. Max Baer, Jr., beat the beardos at their own game.

HOMETOWN USA (1979). According to the liner copy, "If you loved *American Graffiti,* you'll adore *Hometown USA,*" and this is probable indeed, particularly if you're seeking a *Cracked* magazine parody *(American Grafrooti?)* of *Graffiti*'s Terry the Tiger subplot. A nerdy, John Candy-ish '50s guy, nicknamed Rodent, gets a cool car for one night. A genuine cool guy joins him; in a sidesplitting sequence our nutty protags blackmail a girl into having sex with them, but— uh-oh!—her father is police commissioner. Of all the luck! The girl of Rodent's dreams is no Suzanne Somers in a T-Bird: she's a hooker— and an ugly one at that. Ha!

MACON COUNTY LINE (1974). Jethro produced, co-wrote, and stars in this fact-based tragi-sit, set in 1954 Dixie. Two likable young petty-thief brothers and a Spacekian hitchhiker break down in Jethro's town.

Jeth, the bigoted sheriff, is no Andy of Mayberry; he hassles their Yankee keisters. Meanwhile, two mean, ugly, oily, greasy bad guys, sweaty and horrible, come to town and commit heinous mischief that Jethro attributes to our heroes. Jethro's teddy-bear smile makes his malevolence all the malevolenter; he gives the performance of his life, eclipsing even the "double-naught spy" episodes of *The Beverly Hillbillies.*

ODE TO BILLY JOE (1976). Jethro returns to the '50s South for an altogether ooky coming-of-ager based on Bobbie "the Thinking Man's Elly May" Gentry's chart-busting 1967 smash, in which Billy Joe McAllister mysteriously jumps off the Tallahatchie bridge. And just as the tape package promises, "Now this classic ballad gives up its secret." Glynnis O'Connor and Robbie Benson play the song-crossed young lovers; the problem is, poor Robbie, abetted by a stringy Michel Legrand score, is just too "romantic"—he's horny. And when they finally try to push, push in the bush, he can't, because, he confesses, "I have been with a man, which is a sin against nature." So he throws himself off the bridge. Now you know—enjoy the film!

And so ends our hustle through the 1970s. Let us not forget the landmark films that are unavailable on video: *Roller Boogie* (Linda Blair on wheels), *Kansas City Bomber* (Raquel Welch on wheels), *The Trial of Billy Jack* (170 pulse-pounding minutes), and *Billy Jack Goes to Washington* (155 taut, edge-of-your-seat minutes). When I see all the drab, *black-and-white* snoozefests gathering dust at video stores and think of these *classics* that may be *lost forever* . . . I . . . just . . . go . . . ber- . . . ZERK!

SMALL TOWNS

●

By John Clark

People (well, politicians) like to say that we live in a global village. This is a nice sentiment, but it doesn't take into account a crucial fact about small towns: Nothing ever happens in them. Nothing except births and deaths and the stuff in between. In the movies, the miserably insignificant lives of townsfolk have only occasionally been captured in a realistic way; more often, locals are killed off or used to dramatize the filmmakers' own obsessions (hypocrisy, man's inhumanity to man). In fact, the events and issues in some of these movies get so big and the people so small that the place on the screen might as well *be* a global village.

LOCALS

OUR KIND OF PEOPLE

●

It's hard to make a compelling movie about the minutiae of small-town life. Blown up on the big screen, they look even more boring than they actually are. Filmmakers deal with this difficulty by introducing traumatic events—from the Great Depression to the new Benetton store —that highlight how people cope in a day-to-day way.

THE SHOP ON MAIN STREET (1965). "I'm your Aryan and you're my Jew-

RAUL COLON

ess. . . . Understand?" Imagine saying this to the old lady who runs your local button shop. Tono the carpenter (Josef Kroner), a fundamentally decent man, has been appointed the "Aryan comptroller" of Rosalie (Ida Kaminska) by his Nazi-sympathizer brother-in-law, who himself has been commissioned by the Germans occupying their Eastern European village. Her shop, ironically, turns out to be worthless, but the Jewish community, which has been supporting her, secretly pays Tono to leave her alone. This setup has all the character and simplicity of a folktale (say, by Kafka). Directors Ján Kadár and Elmar Klos linger too long over Tono's dilemma as each new measure against the Jews places him and Rosalie in greater jeopardy; still, this Oscar-winning Czech film delivers. "What can I do?" cries Tono as the Jews are finally being rounded up. "What? I'm nobody. A zero." Not exactly—his anguish alone is worth something.

BACK TO THE FUTURE (1985). Crispin Glover was separated at birth. In the beginning of this Robert Zemeckis–directed, Steven Spielberg–approved high-concept fantasy, he plays Michael J. Fox's wimpy dad—the oily, browbeaten head of a white-trash family—and he looks and sounds exactly like George Bush did before he ran for President. But by the end, after Fox tinkers with the past, Glover has become a charmless, statesmanlike sci-fi writer, resembling the dubious man of the people created by Bush's image makers during the campaign. The startling parallelism of Glover's performance spills over into the town itself. In the present, its seedy downtown has been abandoned in favor of the suburbs and a mall. We can infer that people like Glover have

let Main Street decay because of a lack of self-respect. However, when Fox returns from the past to find the new, improved Dad, along with the material success that accompanies his self-confidence (new cars and tennis outfits), the town is *still* a dump. So much for the trickle-down theory.

BLUE VELVET (1986). While *Back to the Future* ambivalently embraces Reagan-era values, *Blue Velvet* gives them a big kiss-off. As if to symbolize the point, the hilariously vulgar villain (Dennis Hopper, who says things like "You are *so* fuckin' suave") puts on lipstick and gives our straight hero (Kyle MacLachlan) a big, red smooch. You think he'll do more to the helpless MacLachlan, but director David Lynch pulls back. It's just as well. *Blue Velvet* works because of its suggestiveness, even if what it suggests isn't entirely clear: the enormous man walking the little dog; the droll, effeminate impresario (Dean Stockwell) of a harem of dumpy women; the detective standing stock-still with part of his brain shot out. And the dialogue! When MacLachlan finds a moldy ear and brings it to the police, a cop says, "Yes, that's a human ear all right." A family cookout celebrates a return to order—a marvelously demented order, in which burgers fry to the strains of Isabella Rossellini's rendition of the title song.

RETURNEES

You Can't Go Home Again

———●———

Filmmakers have taken Thomas Wolfe's celebrated dictum to heart, though doubtless few have read the book. No matter: It makes perfect dramatic sense. What better way to stir up a placid town than bring back a local boy who's seen the world?

THE RETURN OF MARTIN GUERRE (1982). Based on a true story, this absorbing French film by Daniel Vigne has a terrific premise: Suppose a worthless, wandering native son returns home vastly improved, only he's an imposter. In a sixteenth-century village, teenage Martin Guerre marries Bertrande but is unable to consummate the union until he's been flogged with a feather duster by the priest. He's not much of a provider either, and eventually he takes off. Years later Martin (Gérard Depardieu) returns. This grown man is an ox and a charmer, but his encounters with neighbors and relatives are tentative. Doesn't he know these people, or has he simply forgotten them? His wife (Nathalie Baye) just seems grateful (and a few other things besides). Then, when passing vagabonds question his identity, Martin finds himself with a rope around his neck. Throughout we are treated to the harsh realities of medieval life—pigs are worth more than people in a place like this.

THE CHASE (1966). Texas sports the ugliest town on the list. It's full of abominations: adultery, greed, hate, the whole nine yards. There's more cleavage here than in Las Vegas, and every man packs a pistol, making *The Chase* as uplifting (and as entertaining) as a particularly garish episode of *Dynasty*. The madness comes to a head when Bubber (Robert Redford) escapes from prison and heads home to his wife (Jane Fonda), who is sleeping with his best friend (James Fox), who is married and the son of the richest man in town (E. G. Marshall), who appointed Marlon Brando sheriff, who has integrity because he wants

to be a farmer. Lillian Hellman "adapted" this from, of all things, a novel and play by gentle Horton Foote. Nobody's exempt from the blight, even the teenagers: They join their parents at a junkyard where Redford has been cornered—an outing that would look like a tailgate party if it weren't for the Molotov cocktails.

THE DEER HUNTER (1978). Main street meets the Ho Chi Minh Trail—young, rawboned Americans are sent overseas to fight in steamy jungles against cruel Asians. *The Deer Hunter* is saved from the predictability of its premise by director Michael Cimino's bleak yet affectionate vision of the place our boys left behind. Robert De Niro, Christopher Walken, and John Savage play the western-Pennsylvania steelworkers who swap blowtorches for M-16s. They live in an industrial wasteland, their immigrant values fast becoming irrelevant. Cimino devotes long stretches (some have said too long) to their horseplay—shaking up beer cans and throwing lunch meat at each other. But that's exactly what young working-class guys would do. These same guys went to Vietnam and, if they came back, were unable to articulate what happened to them. Says De Niro, showing John Cazale a bullet, "You see this? This is this. This ain't something else. This is this."

VISITORS

STRANGERS IN A STRANGE LAND

———————●———————

In some small towns it's still the case that if strangers buy, say, George Bailey's house, it'll always be the Bailey house, regardless of how long they live there. People are slow

RAUL COLON

to change. Well, that may be human nature, but it won't sell tickets. But suppose the outsiders pose a real threat. . . .

HIGH PLAINS DRIFTER (1973). Shane goes straight to Hell. The situation is familiar—a town of quaking shopkeepers, pitted against three killers, hires a long gunfighter (Clint Eastwood, who also directed). Their savior is less a knight than a spaghetti-western sociopath; in his first few minutes in town, he commits three murders and a rape. Sign him up! In exchange for Eastwood's help, the townspeople promise him anything he wants, so, among other things, he makes a babbling dwarf both sheriff and mayor and has the town painted red and renamed Hell. We're in for a civics lesson, all right, but it's a deliriously crude one. The outlaws are so mean they put out a wounded man's eye with a stick ("Dog," says one,

"he sure had a lot of blood left in him, didn't he?"). And the townspeople are so contemptible they stand idly by while their marshal is bullwhipped to death on Main Street. One vestige of the traditional western: the barkeep (Paul Brinegar), who played Wishbone on Eastwood's TV show, *Rawhide.*

THE MUSIC MAN (1962). Yes, my friends, we got trouble. Right here in River City. Professor Harold Hill (the *sensational* Robert Preston) has come to sell musical instruments and uniforms and lessons, only he doesn't know one note from another. So what does he do? He makes trouble. Right here in River City. He makes trouble for the mayor (Paul Ford) by urging the townspeople to boycott his pool hall. He makes trouble for the school board by urging them to sing like a barbershop quartet (only on video, the fourth guy is *always* cut off). He makes trouble for Winthrop (yes, it's *Ronny* Howard) by urging him to sing songs with *s*'s in them (he's got a *terrible* lithp). He makes trouble for the boy's sister, Marian the librarian (Shirley Jones), by urging her to—well, as she tells her mother, "you'll find it in Balzac." Now the professor's got trouble . . . but to look at the lovely Miss Jones, it's really no trouble at all.

JEAN DE FLORETTE (1986). A farmer is being buried with his favorite shotgun. During the procession to the grave, the men following the casket begin to realize that the gun may still be loaded and that the slightest jog could set it off. In other words, they're being held at gunpoint by a dead man. After watching *Jean de Florette,* you may wish that gun had let fly. These guys are no good at all. When a hunchbacked Gérard Depardieu, a stranger from the city, moves with his family to the land he inherited from the gun-toting farmer (his uncle), the neighbors let his crops bake rather than tell him there is a spring on the farm—it's none of their business. One unscrupulous local (Yves Montand) and his nephew (Daniel Auteuil) have plugged up the spring so that Depardieu will be ruined and sell the land to them cheap. It's reminiscent of Salieri's slow murder of Mozart in *Amadeus,* except that Depardieu doesn't have Wolfie's music to redeem his foolishness. (That makes him more like you and me.) Redemption comes instead from his stunning progeny: Emmanuelle Béart, who plays his avenging-angel daughter in the conclusion of this two-part saga, *Manon of the Spring.*

THE STRANGER (1946). Although relatively svelte here, Orson Welles is too big for this—or any other—town.

Besides directing, he plays a Nazi superman hiding out in a Connecticut village, teaching history to "the sons of America's first families" and marrying the daughter (Loretta Young) of a Supreme Court justice. And there's more. Working late one night, Welles offers to walk his wife home, and she says, "In Harper there is nothing to be afraid of"—a statement she might reconsider if she knew that he'd strangled a crucial link to his past and buried the corpse on their wedding day. Says a local when the body is found, "I knew darn well it was the same fella. 'Course, he's changed some. Being buried in the earth does it." Well, these New Englanders are flinty, but—not to push the point—they represent the same people the Nazi duped or subdued during his years in power. All the more reason to be grateful for Nazi hunter Edward G. Robinson, who says to Young, after her husband has been impaled by the town clock, "Pleasant dreams."

BAD DAY AT BLACK ROCK (1954). Bad, *bad* day at Black Rock—a one-horse town in the most spectacularly desolate country imaginable (augmented by director John Sturges and the vibrant color cinematography of William C. Melor). Stranger Spencer Tracy wears a black hat and a black suit, and his left sleeve is stuffed uselessly in his left jacket pocket. And Tracy's the hero. Arrayed against him are a host of familiar faces: Robert Ryan, Ernest Borgnine, Walter Brennan, Dean Jagger, Lee Marvin, John Ericson, and—the only woman in town—Anne Francis (this apparently was her specialty, since she later appeared as the only woman on an entire *planet* in *Forbidden Planet*). These noirish-neighbors silently watch Tracy get off the train, rebut his efforts to hire a car, and generally try to run him out of town. "You look like you need a hand," says Marvin sarcastically. Tracy is in quest of a man named Komoko, who clearly has met with foul play. Brennan, the town's doctor and mortician ("I get 'em comin' and goin' "), is the first to break ranks and give Tracy that sorely needed hand: He loans him his hearse.

IN THE HEAT OF THE NIGHT (1967). Virgil Tibbs (Sidney Poitier) is that Hollywood rarity, a three-dimensional black character. It's shocking enough to see him on film, let alone in a small southern town. The local police don't know what to make of him either, so they throw him in jail on a murder charge. It turns out that Tibbs is a Yankee homicide detective, visiting his mother. Irony number two is that the town's bigoted chief of police, Gillespie (Rod Steiger), needs his help to crack the case. These two don't get along. Not surprisingly, they begin to respect each other, although it's hard won (Gillespie's leather holster seems to groan with the effort) and neither man really changes. With all due respect to Howard Rollins and Carrol O'Connor, who play this pair on the NBC television series, they can't approach Poitier and Steiger's hostility and mutual dependency.

AN ELEGANT HOLLYWOOD THREESOME

•

BY MASON WILEY

George Cukor, Mary Astor, and Fred Astaire were three of the classiest acts in Hollywood. Here's a selection of their best films—many of them triumphs over public scandal, off-screen squabbles, and old age.

COLORFUL CUKOR

A CIVILIZED MAN

•

Theater was George Cukor's life. He started at twenty as a stage manager; at twenty-six, he was directing Ethel Barrymore and Jeanne Eagles on Broadway. When it became clear that talking pictures weren't a passing fad, Cukor left for Hollywood and got a job as the dialogue director on Universal's antiwar epic *All Quiet on the Western Front*. Within three years, Cukor was directing pictures, and his career took off when David O. Selznick became his producer: *Dinner at Eight* and *Little Women* were their 1933 crop. After Cukor was fired from *Gone With the*

Wind, he stopped working for Selznick, but continued to direct for the next forty years. Cukor saw life as a theatrical event, and his characters are always playing actors' games, even if they're not in the business. His actors usually do the best work of their careers in his films and have the Oscars to prove it.

DAVID COPPERFIELD (1935). Selznick took Spielbergian glee in adapting his favorite childhood books into movies, and this Dickens novel was a million-dollar dream project. Cukor and Selznick researched England for months before lovingly recreating it at MGM's Culver City lot. The picture is impeccably cast, starting with W. C. Fields as Micawber; this is Fields's only dramatic performance, and not only is he perfectly Dickensian, he's as funny here as in his rowdy Paramount romps. Equally lovable are Edna May Oliver as feisty Aunt Betsey and Lennox Pawle as her companion, Mr. Dick. Basil Rathbone plays an evil stepfather, and Freddie Bartholomew, the ten-year-old newcomer found by Selznick and Cukor in Britain, was so good that MGM signed him immediately and gave him top billing over Spencer Tracy two years later. Cukor doesn't treat the material quaintly but gives Dickens's melodramatic passages an exciting intensity, and the ensemble of character actors makes every moment count.

HOLIDAY (1938). Katharine Hepburn had wanted to do Philip Barry's romantic comedy ever since she had understudied it on Broadway in 1928. When RKO offered her a screen test four years later, she played a scene from it as her acting sample. Six years later, she finally persuaded Columbia's Harry Cohn to let her star in the movie. Her friend Cukor, who had directed her first picture at RKO *(A Bill of Divorcement),* was in charge of juggling the elements of drama, comedy, and romance in this story about a rich girl who doesn't share her sister's values but falls for the sister's lower-class boyfriend, Cary Grant. This charming, rueful comedy has more resonance than the later Cukor-Hepburn-Barry-Grant effort, *The Philadelphia Story.*

GONE WITH THE WIND (1939). Big deal if Victor Fleming got the directing credit and the Oscar; it was George who did all the research, designing, and casting before he got sacked midproduction because of scaredey-cat Clark Gable, who felt uncomfortable whenever Cukor added "Darling" or "Dear" to his directorial requests. Gable got his hunting buddy Fleming as Cukor's replacement, but Fleming proved to be not man enough to take on Vivien Leigh. Once, when Leigh refused to alter her interpretation of Scarlett, Fleming screamed, "You can shove this script up your royal British ass," and stormed off the set. To Leigh's and Olivia de Havilland's minds, Cukor was still their director, and they sneaked away to confer with him for the rest of filming. So, in a way, Cukor never left the movie.

ANTHONY RUSSO

GEORGE CUKOR

———————●———————

"People say Hollywood is vulgar, not cultivated. Yet Hollywood has touched the imagination and emotions and affections of the world, for better or worse. I'm very grateful to it, and I think there's a lot of envy in the people who knock it."

"I remember watching the camera come in close on Joan Crawford's face once, and when it got to its closest, she *shone!* And I thought, No husband or lover ever saw anything quite like that intimate thing she just did with the camera."

"In his very first film, *It Should Happen to You,* Jack Lemmon was so intense, I had to keep telling him, 'A little less, Jack.' Finally, he said, 'I'm doing it *so* much less that now I'm down to nothing at all.' I said, 'That's the *idea,* Jack.' "

ANGELA LANSBURY

"He introduced me to style."

JOAN FONTAINE

"I learned more about acting from one sentence of George Cukor's than from all my years of acting lessons."

SHELLEY WINTERS

"I don't know if George is a feminist, but he treated women equally years before it was fashionable."

MAUREEN O'SULLIVAN

On her death scene in David Copperfield:
"They raved about my agonized look and the tears in my eyes, but it was all because George was twisting my feet off camera. I couldn't get it right."

A DOUBLE LIFE (1947). Ruth Gordon and Garson Kanin's script afforded Cukor a chance to create a theatrical film noir about an actor (played by the elegant Ronald Colman), who has a disturbing habit of staying in character off-stage. As his actress ex-wife in the movie puts it, "We were engaged during Oscar Wilde, broke it off during O'Neill, married during Kaufman and Hart, and divorced during Chekhov." No wonder she's worried when he considers their co-starring in *Othello.* Edmond O'Brien plays a press agent who's too Iago-like, at least in Colman's demented estimation, and Shelley Winters is a waitress who offers herself as dessert but makes the mistake of asking Colman to "Put out the light, will ya?" Colman got an Oscar for this part, which first-choice Cary Grant turned down because he didn't feel he could pull off the Shakespearean scenes.

A STAR IS BORN (1954). Judy Garland stars, which means heartbreak has to follow the fun. This was Cukor's first wide-screen movie, and many of his beautifully composed shots are ruined on video. But then, the movie has been so historically mutilated, its fragmented condition is now part of its legend. The version "restored" by film historian Ron Haver, now available on cassette, only adds to the Brechtian distancing, because we are asked, at one point, to watch a series of still photographs from a lost scene while listening to the rediscovered dialogue track. The movie was dated even back in 1954, but that doesn't make it any less fascinating. Garland sings "The Man That Got Away" and the "Born in a Trunk" number that climaxes with "Swanee." James Mason, as the dissolute Norman Maine, keeps up with and complements Garland; they're a good-looking and believable couple. Moss Hart's screenplay contains many astringent observations about Hollywood, Jack Carson gives a wonderfully loathsome performance as a publicist, and George Hoyningen-Huené's color design makes Los Angeles a combination paradise and hell.

RICH AND FAMOUS (1981). In Cukor's last film, made at age eighty, he was still capable of such raunchy sex scenes that Pauline Kael was offended, arguing that "they don't seem like what a woman would get into." *Rich and Famous* is an updated version of the Bette Davis–Miriam Hopkins drama *Old Acquaintance* (1943), here starring Jacqueline Bisset and Candice Bergen as college chums who go on to become writers: Bisset is the "serious" novelist who finds writing difficult and draining, and Bergen is a Danielle Steel type who effortlessly cranks out best-selling crap. Bergen's is a full-blown comic performance, and she's not afraid to make a fool of herself. Bisset acts with an absurd gravity that Cukor debunks through her love scenes: getting it on with a stranger in the restroom of an airplane during landing and watching Matt Lattanzi slip out of his skintight blue jeans with the precision of Gypsy Rose Lee. In an interview during the filming, Cukor summed up the appeal of the movie: "We take these two bitches over a period of twenty years, and it's done as a sophisticated comedy, with lots of beautiful sets and clothes." A major drawback is the movie's terrible sound quality; you can't always understand what the actors are saying—especially Bisset, a graduate of the Oliver Reed school of unintelligible acting.

ASTONISHING ASTOR

SHE'S A LADY

————●————

Mary Astor was a great actress, a great beauty, and a great lay. In her scandalous diary, which was made public in 1936 during a custody battle with her second husband, she described her fling with celebrated playwright George S. Kaufman thusly: "Once George lays down his glasses, he is quite a different man. . . .We shared our fourth climax at dawn." On screen, her sexual passion rages beneath a lovely, patrician mask that is always composed and ladylike. Since Hollywood specialized in madonna/whore scenarios, Astor got plenty of work, and the diaries only confirmed what audiences already knew: Mary Astor was hot to trot.

RED DUST (1932). Suffice it to say that Astor's competition for Gable's attention is the formidable Jean Harlow, and yet she holds her own. There's no question whom Gable will pick in the end, but the mutual seduction scene between him and Astor during a rainstorm on an Indochina rubber plantation is as much fun as his banter with Harlow, who acts as if she's in just another of her snappy

MARY ASTOR

———●———

"I could have been a bigger actress if I'd had more ambition. But whenever I think back about it all, I end up believing that perhaps the fact that I wasn't too ambitious is the secret of my career longevity. I never burned myself out and never worked so much the public got tired of me. Instead they just got used to me."

From the infamous diary:
"Why the hell I keep writing things down in this book I don't know."

JOHN HUSTON

"Together we worked out her characterization of the amoral Brigid O'Shaughnessy: her voice hesitant, tremulous, and pleading, her eyes full of candor. She was the enchanting murderess to my idea of perfection."

JOHN BARRYMORE
To Astor:
"You are so goddamned beautiful, you make me feel faint."

GEORGE S. KAUFMAN
"There is only one thing I resent about the case. Some newspaper writer referred to me as a middle-aged playwright. The reason I resent it so much is because it's true."

MRS. GEORGE S. KAUFMAN
"I am not going to divorce Mr. Kaufman. Young actresses are an occupational hazard for any man working in the theater."

comedies. Director Victor Fleming and screenwriter John Lee Mahin keep the entertainment coming, like hosts at a bachelor party.

DODSWORTH (1936). A successful car magnate retires and fulfills his promise to take his wife on a trip to Europe. Guess whom he meets on the boat going over? This swanky Samuel Goldwyn production is a deluxe package—the sets got an Oscar—and Sinclair Lewis's novel provides adult drama for Sidney Howard's trenchant script. Walter Huston and Ruth Chatterton are a lively Mr. and Mrs. Dodsworth; the suspense hangs on whether Huston will drop the vain Chatterton for the mature Astor, who has a swell

villa in Naples. David Niven and Paul Lukas play two of Chatterton's smooth European suitors. Director William Wyler makes it all go down nice and easy.

THE HURRICANE (1937, 1979). Even Astor can't compete with Dorothy Lamour's sarong in this disaster movie set in a Pacific island paradise. Yes, there was a disaster-movie craze in the '30s just like in the '70s, thanks to MGM's *San Francisco* in 1936. Sam Goldwyn had the wit to hire John Ford to pull off this elaborate tug-of-war between Jon Hall's idealized native and Raymond Massey's cruel imperialist, a struggle that climaxes with the eponymous tempest. Astor is

Massey's kind-hearted wife, and La-mour is Hall's island girl. In the sexy and colorful 1979 Dino De Laurentiis remake, the imperialist has a daughter (Mia Farrow) who falls for the hunky native chief. Party idea: Show both versions, serve mai-tais, and compare.

THE MALTESE FALCON (1941). Astor fits right into John Huston's amoral universe, and she's a match for Humphrey Bogart's Sam Spade, a duplicitous private dick who cuckolds his partner and takes his name off their agency the moment he's rubbed out. Astor is the worst client any detective ever had, but when she asks him, "What else is there I can buy you with?" Bogie can't resist and takes her to bed. Though it's classified as film noir, *The Maltese Falcon* today seems more like Huston's 1985 spoof *Prizzi's Honor,* except that Astor doesn't try to play a good girl, the way Kathleen Turner does. When Astor confesses, "I haven't lived a good life—I've been bad," she means it. Her tour de force is lovingly wrapped in Warner Bros. realism, with Huston's stylish camera prowling around the characters as they try to outcon each other. Only an idiot would add color to the mix.

HUSH . . . HUSH, SWEET CHARLOTTE (1965). Robert Aldrich's entertaining gothic melodrama set on a run-down Louisiana estate is Astor's swan song. Like Aldrich's *What Ever Happened to Baby Jane?,* this picture stars Bette Davis and starts in a flashback. In the late '20s, someone polished off Bruce Dern with a butcher knife. Jump to the mid-'60s, when the surviving suspects have one last go at one another. Astor is Dern's widow, and Davis is the belle he was about to run off with, now a neglected hag after years of being blamed for the murder. Olivia de Havilland shows up as Davis's cousin and turns out to be a lot less nice to Bette than Melanie was to Scarlett. Joseph Cotten lends his ghostly presence, and Agnes Moorehead is a howl as a redneck Thelma Ritter. Astor's screen time is brief, but she makes her character a vivid participant in the ghastly goings-on.

DEBONAIR ASTAIRE

DANCE WITH ME

———————●———————

Fred Astaire came to Hollywood at the age of thirty-four, after a quarter-century of show-biz experience spent dancing with his sister Adele, who left their act to marry a British lord named Cavendish. Since Astaire's romantic steps require a feminine dancing partner, his films are a quest for the perfect woman, one who can move with the natural ease of his long-lost sibling. A Pirandellian pattern runs through Astaire's musicals, as their plots comment, albeit lightheartedly, on his relationships with the partner in his life. Astaire himself is always dapper and down-to-earth, never a snob or an aesthete. He usually portrays a dancer, and in his movies, at least, it appears to be a steady line of work. But then, Astaire makes all of life seem like a lark when he dances.

YOU WERE NEVER LOVELIER (1942). After nine movies together, Ginger Rogers left her partnership with Astaire to play dramatic parts, nabbing an Oscar for her first try, *Kitty Foyle,* in 1940. He ended up two years later at Columbia, matched with its biggest star, Rita Hayworth, who makes up for what she lacks in lip-syncing ability in her dancing. Sleekly gowned by Irene, Hayworth provides no fluffy obstacles for Astaire, and her backless outfits show that her shoulder blades are as beautiful as her smile. The pair dances to two Jerome Kern–Johnny Mercer songs and one jazz number, "The Shorty George," played by Xavier Cugat and His Orchestra and arranged by Lyle "Spud" Murphy. The plot resembles *The Taming of the Shrew* in that Hayworth has two younger sisters who can't marry until she does; Adolphe Menjou is believable as the sort of father who could follow such a stupid tradition.

EASTER PARADE (1948). When Gene Kelly began to rise at MGM in the '40s, Astaire thought it was time to quit, so he retired in 1946. Two years later, Kelly broke an ankle before starting this musical with Judy Garland, and MGM offered the job to Astaire. He never retired again. Ginger Rogers (in *Top Hat*) is hilariously lampooned by Ann Miller as Astaire's feathery partner who dumps him when she's offered an opportunity to star as a headliner. Astaire gets even by taking the unknown Garland and trying to turn her into a facsimile of Miller, feathers and all, but their ballroom act is so clumsy it turns into burlesque. They change their style to vaudeville, become a big success, fall in love, and sing the title song at the end. Astaire's outstanding solo here is "Stepping

ANTHONY RUSSO

Out With My Baby," part of which is in slow motion, and the Irving Berlin score gives Miller a chance to tap and spin to her heart's content in a snazzy number entitled "Shaking the Blues Away."

THE BARKLEYS OF BROADWAY (1949). After *Easter Parade,* Astaire's future at MGM was secure, but things weren't so rosy for Judy Garland. Betty Comden and Adolph Green wrote a script about a married Broadway dance team who bicker, separate, and finally reunite, but Garland's chemical dependency caught up with her. Enter Ginger Rogers, eager to prove that she could still keep up with Astaire in the dancing department and lending a ring of truth to the feuding scenes. When Fred sings the great "They Can't Take That Away From Me" to Ginger, she stands there grimacing. Their last dance together on film is "Manhattan Downbeat," which, with its swirl of glorious Technicolor, is a spectacular finale for all their black-and-white triumphs.

ROYAL WEDDING (1951). By this time, MGM had had its fill of Judy Garland and her recurring illnesses during production. Jane Powell replaced her in this musical created to cash in on the wedding of Elizabeth II to Prince Philip. Astaire and Powell play a brother-sister dancing act visiting London during the wedding who

FRED ASTAIRE

On dancing:

"I have no desire to prove anything by it. I have never used it as an outlet or as a means of expressing myself. I just dance."

"On the set lots of times in those dance sequences, I'd work very, very hard. Then I would see the rushes the next day, and on film it would look like I'd been standing still. It's an athletic business, dancing, even though it may look like just waltzing from here to there."

ADELE ASTAIRE

"Fred is clothes-mad. He's always been. He tries on ten ties before he chooses the one he likes well enough to wear. When he goes to his tailor, he studies clothes and mulls over them for hours, weighing the merits of this plaid against that check, and yet, damn it, he always looks so casually gotten together, so offhand, as if he never gave it a thought."

GINGER ROGERS

"He is a charming, wonderful man. I hope that he enjoys the attention and love and respect that everyone has for him. I hope he just swims in it."

CYD CHARISSE

"Every time I want to smile, I think of Fred Astaire."

MIKHAIL BARYSHNIKOV

"It's no secret. We hate him. He gives us complexes, because he's too perfect."

JOHN O'HARA

"He is endowed with the physical equipment of a decathlon champion, the imagination of an artist, the perseverance of an expert in dressage, the determination of a gyrene drill sergeant, the self-confidence of a lion tamer, the self-criticism of a neophyte in holy orders, the pride of a man who has created his own tradition—and the ability to go home when he has done his job."

---

end up marrying Britons themselves —he a commoner and she a title. The joke in the casting is that Astaire's beloved is played by Winston Churchill's upper-crust daughter Sarah, and Powell's lord is the lumpy Peter Lawford. Astaire and Powell have one cute number, "I Left My Hat in Haiti," by Alan Jay Lerner and Burton Lane, but he's better off dancing with inanimate objects: a metronome, a hat rack, and, in one solo in a gymnasium, parallel bars, as well as the famous dance up the walls and across the ceiling that director Stanley Donen recreated thirty-five years' later for a Lionel Richie video. Another routine, a shipboard duet with Astaire and Powell, prefigures *The Poseidon Adventure*. Anglophiles will enjoy the color footage of the Queen's wedding recession.

FUNNY FACE (1957). Astaire is a photographer modeled after Richard Avedon, who was in fact the photographic consultant on this fantasy set in the world of haute couture. Audrey

Hepburn, as the Greenwich Village beatnik Astaire transforms into a Paris model, wears clothes by Hubert de Givenchy. Kay Thompson, as a butch magazine editor surrounded by a retinue of young women, makes do with clothes by Edith Head, but she doesn't seem to mind as she belts out "Think Pink." Most of the songs are by George Gershwin, and director Stanley Donen sustains a giddy Gershwinesque spirit throughout. The Paris locations are lovely, and Astaire walking jauntily before the Arc de Triomphe is a beautiful sight.

SILK STOCKINGS (1957). Essentially the end of Astaire's film-musical career (although he appeared in MGM's *That's Entertainment* anthologies and Francis Coppola's *Finian's Rainbow*), this *Ninotchka* with songs—by Cole Porter, superbly orchestrated by André Previn—shows that Astaire, at fifty-six, was keeping up with new trends in popular music. The first number, "Too Bad," turns into a cha-cha free-for-all, while Fred's dynamite finale, "The Ritz Roll 'n' Rock," is the black-tie flip side to the masterful Elvis Presley title number in *Jailhouse Rock*. Janis Paige executes a brassy turn in a spoof of Esther Williams, and she and Astaire satirize the film industry of the '50s with a sassy song called "Stereophonic Sound." As the movie's title suggests, this is a feast for lingerie fetishists: Paige sings a strip-tease number called "Satin and Silk," while Cyd Charisse, as Ninotchka, undresses to the title theme, changing from her drab serge into a sexy Merry Widow. Charisse also has an outstanding number with her clothes on, the jazzy "Red Blues." Director Rouben Mamoulian makes sure everything looks great, and, to top it all off, Peter Lorre shows up, deservedly getting the last laugh.

SLOW MOVIES/ FAST FILMS

•

By Owen Gleiberman

Movies, like drugs, can be uppers or downers, and more often than not, the difference is how quickly they move. You may be in the mood for something kinetic and racy, the cinematic equivalent of an amphetamine rush. Then again, there's much to be said for a slow-moving film that seduces you into its snail's-pace world. Selected below are movies you can use as mood enhancers—slow films and fast films you can synchronize to your pulse.

SLOW MOVIES

THE LEISURE CLASS

————•————

Whoever said "slow" had to mean "boring"? At its best, an unhurried tempo is something to luxuriate in. It can lead us to a quieter age, mimic our contemporary ennui, even take us into the world of dreams. Think of each of the movies that follow as part hallucination, part bubble bath.

BARRY LYNDON (1975). Stanley Kubrick's eighteenth-century extrava-

ganza was lambasted for being a static series of pretty pictures, yet the film's rigorous pace is actually what makes it dramatic. Kubrick made the first movie about the eighteenth century that looks and feels and *moves* like the eighteenth century. In a way, it's just as sci-fi as his *2001: A Space Odyssey* —both are epic studies of an alien world where people hide their souls behind a thicket of manners; in *Barry Lyndon,* the very lack of technology (and the speed that comes with it) is as mysterious and enthralling as the most highly developed space colony. Ryan O'Neal plays the cad of a hero, and his Irish-brogued guilelessness works well. The more roguishly he behaves, the more we see the shocking selfishness of an ordinary man. The climactic duel between Barry and his stepson plays like the longest staredown in history, and it's one of the most suspenseful scenes ever filmed.

ERASERHEAD (1977). David Lynch's apocalyptic nightmare probably comes closer to capturing the precise atmosphere and texture of a dream than any other movie. Juxtaposing the horrid and the banal with more purely surreal relish than he did in *Blue Vel-*

vet, Lynch tells the story of a geeky Everyman (John Nance, sporting the titular hairdo) who gets his girlfriend pregnant and sees his worst anxieties incarnated in the newborn infant: a

---

SLOW MOTION

THE SCENES BELOW ARE ESPECIALLY INTERESTING WHEN SLOWED DOWN ON YOUR VCR.

───────●───────

GUILTY PLEASURES
Rebecca De Mornay turns and faces Tom Cruise during their first close encounter in *Risky Business.*

Dennis Quaid gets undressed with Ellen Barkin in *The Big Easy.*

Olivia Hussey, alone with Leonard Whiting the morning after, hears a knock at the door in *Romeo and Juliet.*

METAMORPHOSIS
In Walt Disney's *Cinderella,* the Fairy Godmother gives Cinderella and her animal friends the royal treatment.

HI, GUY
A parapsychologist rips off his face in *Poltergeist.*

PECKING ORDER
Tippi Hedren gets attacked in an upstairs room by *The Birds.*

ADVENTURES IN BULIMIA
A contestant cuts loose in *Stand By Me*'s blueberry-pie-eating contest.

The fattest man alive eats one "wafer-thin" mint too many in *Monty Python's The Meaning of Life.*

---

mewling monster baby (surely the inspiration for Ridley Scott's *Alien*) with a head like that of a jellied calf fetus. The movie is *so* slow that the pace becomes funny; everything happens with an absurdly threatening clarity, as though the world were about to collapse in on itself. *Eraserhead* is best for late-night viewing, when it's astonishing black-and-white imagery can melt into your unconscious.

L'AVVENTURA (1960). The death of romance—before it became a cliché. Michelangelo Antonioni's art-house landmark takes the form of a deconstructed mystery. A woman disappears during a cruise, and her lover (Gabriele Ferzetti) and best friend (Monica Vitti) team up to find her. They never do, and when they commence an affair and begin to hope (in shame) that she'll never show up, the romance is doomed to be every bit as unfulfilled as the search. *L'avventura* finds Antonioni, rhapsodist of alienation, at the most concrete and despairing. His poetically depressed style— it's like Hitchcock underwater—perfectly expresses the burning longings of his characters. Great, but not exactly a popcorn movie.

THE NATURAL (1984). A baseball film as slow and reverent as the game itself. Roy Hobbs (Robert Redford) has it in him to be the best player there ever was. Unfortunately, Fate intervenes, in the form of a murderous groupie (Barbara Hershey) who puts a bullet in Roy that ends up sidelining him for fifteen years. When he returns, he's not just a man, he's an apparition: a fallen angel in search of redemption (and a league batting title). Freely adapted from Bernard Malamud's novel, *The Natural* is nothing less than a morality play in pinstripes. Director Barry Levinson brings to the story such craftsmanship and detail that every frame seems to quiver with his love for the game. And Redford's performance is the most underrated of his career. The acting is all in his face; he has a Zen dynamism here, and the stature of a truly mythic hero. Fine supporting work as well, from Glenn Close, Darren McGavin, Robert Duvall, and Wilford Brimley.

IVAN THE TERRIBLE, PART I (1942). Twisty castle corridors bathed in murk; actors slinking through them like overgrown puppets; magnificently brooding music by Prokofiev. Sergei Eisenstein's elaborate black-and-white spectacle turns the life of Czar Ivan IV into a gothic Shakespearean nightmare; the movie is so languorous and deliberate it's like some Byzantine Russian version of Kabuki. Yet if you give this oddball epic a chance, it can be a tantalizing experience. Eisenstein's visuals have a larger-than-life grandeur, and Nikolai Cherkassov turns Ivan into a splendid icon of ambition and woe.

STRANGER THAN PARADISE (1984). It's the most deadpan comedy ever made, but *Stranger Than Paradise* will keep you thoroughly entertained. In a series of rambling blackout sketches, director Jim Jarmusch eavesdrops on the lives of a hostile Lower East Side hipster (John Lurie), his cloddish best friend (Richard Edson), and the hipster's rather savvy teenage cousin (Eszter Balint), who's visiting from Hungary. The three are utterly indifferent to just about everything (not least of all each other); the movie's triumph is that their cool, monosyllabic torpor comes off not as a put-on but as an honest expression of jadedness—grace under pressure in

a garbagy world. Jarmusch's style redefines the word "sly." In this up-from-Warhol wasteland, the most nondescript comment can leave you in a fit of giggles.

THE GOOD, THE BAD, AND THE UGLY (1967). They're called spaghetti westerns, but a better term might be peyote westerns. This is the best of them, the one in which Sergio Leone perfected his brand of hallucinatory action spectacle. Ennio Morricone's famous Marlboro-Man-on-acid theme song (doodle-doodle-doo . . . wah-wah-wah) ushers us into the story of three desperadoes—Clint Eastwood (Good), Lee Van Cleef (Bad), and Eli Wallach (Ugly)—in search of Confederate treasure. Fans of the later Clint will be surprised to see his James Dean pompadour; he has a laconic, youthful sexiness. And whenever things threaten to slow down *too* much, Wallach injects a note of ripsnorting energy. The final shoot-out is probably the best thing Leone ever filmed. Time itself seems to stretch to infinity as the music, the cactus-flower vistas, and the ultra-close-ups of eyes, guns and souls cohere into a full-blown visual.

VERTIGO (1958). To say that this movie is about a guy with fear of heights is like saying that *Psycho* is about a motel with lousy room service. For James Stewart, the retired San Francisco cop, acrophobia is really the fear of life itself. *Vertigo* is a meditation on the idea of plunging, which is exactly what Stewart must do when he, uh, falls for Kim Novak, the mysterious woman he has been hired to follow. Is Novak really the reincarnation of her great-grandmother? And after Stewart loses her, is the woman he meets in the second half (also played by Novak) the reincarnation of the first one? The film is about terror, lust, and (above all) mystery, which the mathematically exacting Alfred Hitchcock at once feared and longed for. Hitchcock buffs celebrate the movie for its thematic dimensions, yet what really puts *Vertigo* over is that the entire film seems to unfold in a trance state. It's as if Hitchcock had slowed down the mechanics of his earlier films, peeked through the cracks, and seen the abyss.

FAST FILMS

THE GREAT RACE

———————●———————

Okay, now you're good and relaxed. There are times, however, when you want entertainment that keeps you in high gear, as surely as you crave that seventh cup of coffee. So if you feel that need—the need for speed—the following movies should provide a good fix.

HIS GIRL FRIDAY (1940). Howard Hawks directed this masterpiece of lickety-split verbal Ping-Pong. Charles Lederer's script, adapted from Ben Hecht and Charles MacArthur's play *The Front Page,* is a great machine, but it's Hawks who gets the actors to step on one another's lines. Cary Grant is the deliriously ruthless editor Walter Burns, and Rosalind Russell is his ex–wife and ex–star reporter, Hildy Johnson, whom he goads into covering one last big story because he knows it's the way to her heart. Although they spend the entire movie squabbling, these two were obviously meant for each other. That's because they share the thrill—the breakneck rhythm—of big-city yellow journalism, which the film portrays as the newspaper equivalent of the Indy 500.

MAD MAX (1979). George Miller's original slash-and-burn thriller makes you feel as if you're right there in the car, pressing down on the accelerator. (Relax, dude, it's only the fast-forward button.) Miller's breakneck style isn't just a matter of making the highway face-offs speedier than in any previous film. In his crumbling, futuristic Australia, speed and existentialism are one: When you're moving this quickly (and without seat belts), no God is going to save you. Mel Gibson, still sporting a bit of baby fat, is the idealistic young family-man cop who goes on a rampage when terrorist bikers kill his comrade and then his wife and child. A comic-book plot, to be sure, but no Hollywood revenge thriller ever had a villain as grand as the Toecutter. Played by Hugh Keays-Byrne, he's like one of Shakespeare's lyrical villains reborn as a homicidal Hell's Angel.

NORTH BY NORTHWEST (1959). Hitchcock again, this time putting us aboard a runaway train of a movie. Cary Grant plays a New York advertising executive, Roger O. Thornhill, who is mistaken for a spy. As Grant spins from one danger to the next, Hitchcock keeps upping the ante and bounding all over the country; the film's underlying atmosphere is one of jet-age exhilaration. You'll want to see it for the justly famous set pieces (Grant getting crop-dusted in the cornfield, the Mount Rushmore climax), and also because it remains the spiritual prototype of the James Bond series—even if Hitchcock's genius wasn't so much for making reality outlandish as for making the outlandish seem real.

INDIANA JONES AND THE TEMPLE OF DOOM (1984). For Indy's second outing, Steven Spielberg plays it straighter than he did in the (intentionally) campy *Raiders of the Lost Ark* and, paradoxically, winds the thrills even tighter. (You won't find it easy to say "It's only a movie.") The bravura opening may be the densest piece of slapstick ever staged. After that, the film sputters for about half an hour until Indy (Harrison Ford), his new paramour (Kate Capshaw), and his faithful young assistant (Ke Huy Quan) encounter the cult of Kali, which practices blood rituals in an orangy underground temple—at which point the film hits overdrive and never lets up. Spielberg leapfrogs from one elaborate setup to another: Indy drinking an evil potion and turning into a mean guy, a roller-coaster escape on coal carts, a heart-in-the-throat climax on a suspended rope bridge. Some found the film exhausting, but Spielberg's whole impulse is to make relentlessness itself a gas. He does.

THE COTTON CLUB (1984). If it went by any slower, it probably wouldn't work, but Francis Coppola keeps the subplots whirring; he's like that plate spinner on *The Ed Sullivan Show.* This is the closest anyone has come to doing in cinematic terms what E. L. Doctorow did in the novel *Ragtime.* Using his dazzling re-creation of the legendary Harlem club as a larger-than-life stage set, Coppola combines fictional melodrama with actual historical figures, tossing them all in the air like so much confetti. The movie is far from Coppola at his best, but it is greater than the sum of its parts—a raw chunk of vibrant Americana. The cast includes Richard Gere as the trumpet player Dixie Dwyer, James Remar as the gnomish mobster Dutch

---

FAST FORWARD

GET A NEW PERSPECTIVE ON THESE FAMILIAR SCENES BY SCANNING AT A HIGHER SPEED.

———●———

SMASH HIT
Jonathan Winters single-handedly destroys a gas station in *It's a Mad, Mad, Mad, Mad World.*

HIS MIGHTY SWORD
Errol Flynn duels with Basil Rathbone in *The Adventures of Robin Hood.*

MARRIAGE COUNSELING
All of *Who's Afraid of Virginia Woolf?*

IF I HAD A HAMMER
Robert De Niro, as Jake LaMotta in *Raging Bull,* bangs his head against the wall of his Miami jail cell.

ANTIQUE AEROBICS
Jane Russell sings "Ain't There Anyone Here for Love" to a gym full of semiclad musclemen in *Gentlemen Prefer Blondes.*

DANCE, LITTLE SISTER
The nuns at the abbey sing "Maria," about the irrepressible Julie Andrews, in *The Sound of Music.*

SHOUT, SHOUT, LET IT ALL OUT
Marilyn Burns screams through the entire dinner at the *Texas Chainsaw Massacre* clan.

Schultz, Diane Lane as Schultz's kept girlfriend (with whom Gere, hired as her escort, falls in love), Bob Hoskins as the charming-rascal proprietor

Owney Madden, Gregory and Maurice Hines as tap-dancing brothers, and Lonette McKee as one of the club's "high-yaller" chorus girls.

ROBOCOP (1987). A smashingly nihilistic thriller. Dutch director Paul Verhoeven's film is set in 1990s Detroit, a world of terrorist criminals, trashed dreams, and unrestrained corporate malevolence. Its rhythm, though, is pure 1980s punk. Verhoeven keeps things racing with a kind of fast-track fury, and it's this witty, headlong rush that makes the film so much more pungent than *The Terminator*. Peter Weller plays RoboCop, the lumbering metallic enforcer who's been fashioned out of a dead cop but who remains just a wee bit human—he's an unexpectedly touching hero. The film also features a terrific villain (Kurtwood Smith), a wonderfully ruthless yuppie (Miguel

Ferrer), and stupendous special effects by Rob Bottin, who provides images as disparate as RoboCop's ghostly high-tech face and the awesomely gross aftermath of a man's being dunked in toxic waste.

TOP GUN (1985). Sure, it's sleazy, pseudo-patriotic, rock-video dreck, but you can eat it like candy. It's also a first-rate action movie. What makes the flight scenes so tense isn't just their astonishing speed and technical excellence (though on that level they surpass anything else to date) but the fact that there's a real dread in them; in its packaged way, *Top Gun* acknowledges the dark side of *The Right Stuff*. As for Tom Cruise—well, the truth is that he could be charming in a movie about the Hitler Youth. Which, when you come right down to it, this practically is.

———————●———————

TRIANGLES

●

BY JOE W. SMITH

Boy-meets-girl is a formula as old as Hollywood itself: a kiss on the lips and black ink in the books. But what about the other old formula, in which a third party slithers in to upset the applecart? Where would Adam and Eve have been without the serpent to put a stop to all that boring bliss? In the movies selected here, the parallel straight lines of a couple are twisted into the more intriguing form of a triangle. What these films all seem to say is that love is never easy, and that when you try to get more than two to tango, someone's going to get his or her feet stepped on.

BOY-GIRL-BOY

AND MAY THE BEST MAN WIN

————●————

A peculiar sexual dynamic often appears in triangles where two men share a woman. Usually, the men are also tied in some other way —they're either buddies, brothers, or colleagues—and jealousy mingles with that old male-bonding issue. Boys will be boys, after all, and having a mutual object of desire can be just another painfully pleasurable sporting event.

JULES AND JIM (1961). With a burst of glee, two best friends (Henri Serre and Oskar Werner), *artistes* in pre-

World War I Paris, take up with a magnetic woman (Jeanne Moreau) who reminds them of a mysterious sculpture. Their idyllic triangle topples years later when they discover such ugly adult things as security and responsibility. François Truffaut delicately orchestrates his characters' emotions, bringing insight to all sides of the story; there's probably never been a more rounded and complex consideration of the joys and sorrows of a three-cornered love affair. Raoul Coutard's shimmering black-and-white photography and Georges Delerue's lilting score flesh out the lyricism of Henri-Pierre Roche's novel, and Moreau's magnificent performance is an inspiration to bohemian-leaning young women everywhere.

SABRINA (1954). When it comes to your high-society triangles, you can keep *The Philadelphia Story*—I'll take that other Hepburn gal in this suave Billy Wilder romantic comedy. Audrey, looking unspeakably beautiful, has her pick of two millionaire brothers. She loves William Holden, the cad with the bad blond dye job, but she's blind to Humphrey Bogart, what with his hangdog mug, sourpuss manner, and unspoken love for her. There's never much doubt about who'll end up in which corner, but the steps are so much fun you won't mind. *Sabrina*'s visual elegance is on a

TRIANGLES

GEOMETRY, HOLLYWOOD STYLE

●

Robert Wagner
Natalie Wood
Warren Beatty

Peter Hall
Leslie Caron
Warren Beatty

Debbie Reynolds
Eddie Fisher
Elizabeth Taylor

Eddie Fisher
Elizabeth Taylor
Richard Burton

Amy Irving
Steven Spielberg
Kate Capshaw

Simone Signoret
Yves Montand
Marilyn Monroe

Victor Mature
Rita Hayworth
Orson Welles

Luise Rainer
Clifford Odets
Frances Farmer

par with its verbal wit, further evidence that writer-director Wilder is one of the last of the Renaissance men. It also evokes an era when people took ocean liners to Paris to find their souls, and plastic was a neat invention instead of a standard condition. All to the continuing strains of "Isn't It Romantic?" and "La Vie en rose." See it and swoon.

ROXANNE (1987). Writer-producer-actor Steve Martin plants himself firmly in the center of this bouncy re-working of Edmond Rostand's classic play, *Cyrano de Bergerac.* Cursed with an outsize shnoz, Martin helps hunky fellow fireman Rick Rossovich woo blonde astronomer Daryl Hannah, the woman he himself adores. As the unrequited lover, Martin taps a deep well of pathos and aw-shucks romance in a performance that begs comparison with the greats of comedy. Australian director Fred Schepisi, usually a gloomy Gus (*The Russia House, A Cry in the Dark,* etc.), shows an unexpectedly nimble touch, and he's aided enormously by the breathtaking light and space of the film's British Columbia location (not done full justice on a VCR). *Roxanne* allows you the dignity of love's pain with a minimum of Sturm und Drang. Perfect for a heartbroken evening when you need cheering up.

LAST SUMMER (1969). Woody Allen calls her the Pheromone Queen, and Barbara Hershey's pheromones are prominently displayed in this item, where much of the action centers on whether or not she's going to shuck her bikini top. Hershey plays a libidinous teenage tart on Fire Island who engineers an erotic threesome with two blond boys, played by Bruce Davison and a pre-*Waltons* Richard Thomas. The fleshy brunette holds the lithe, sun-kissed lads in sexual thrall, instigating a heavy-petting session at the movies and a drug-induced shampoo orgy that must be seen to be believed. Enter Catherine Burns, as a pale ugly duckling from Cleveland named Rhoda. The triangle turns into a sharp-edged square and comes to a very bad end. Frank Perry's film is a relic of the post-*Graduate* youth-film era, but it has moments of truth, most of them generated by Burns's performance, which can't help striking a chord in anyone who ever felt as if he had cooties.

CAUGHT (1949). A carhop betters herself at the Dorothy Dale School of Charm, then goes bananas, trapped between the loony tycoon who married and impregnated her and the dreamboat pediatrician who loves her. The great Max Ophuls *(Letter From an Unknown Woman, La Ronde, Lola Montès)*, a German émigré, directed this potboiler for MGM. The clash between a courtly European filmmaker and a plot that's soapy enough to give Danielle Steel pause makes for one of those blissful occasions when Camp meets Art and lightning strikes; out of this triangular sow's ear, Ophuls and screenwriter Arthur Laurents have made a silk purse. Solid performances by Barbara Bel Geddes, James Mason, and Robert Ryan, and as an added bonus, cameos by *Gilligan's Island*–er Lovey Howell (Natalie Schafer) and Beaver's mom, June Cleaver (Barbara Billingsley). Unaccountably neglected, *Caught* is a real find.

GIRL-BOY-GIRL

LADIES AND GENTLEMEN

———————●———————

Women don't exactly cotton to three-way arrangements. Sharing a man typically brings out not female bonding but rather a desire to duke it out with the other woman or to plunge into a pit of masochistic suffering.

MOGAMBO (1953). There are creatures galore in this African hunting saga, but the real prey is the Great White Hunter played by Clark Gable. Sleepwalking through a role he played twenty years earlier in *Red Dust*, Gable still gives off enough sex appeal to turn up the jungle heat as he's stalked by wildcat Ava Gardner and wolf-in-sheep's-clothing Grace Kelly. The young Kelly gives off a trembling, neurotic sexuality, which may be due to the reported real-life crush she had on Gable during filming. Gardner, however, is in total, hilarious control as the hard-drinking, wisecracking Broadway showgirl who has no problem communicating with the animal kingdom. The battle between the lady and the tramp is great fun, and since both beauties actually seem to deserve Gable, the narrative tension is in high gear. Director John Ford's devout Catholicism comes shining through when Gardner, the fallen woman, makes a confession behind a bamboo curtain.

BACK STREET (1961). Susan Hayward gets the hell out of Lincoln, Nebraska ("You call this living?" she scoffs at the local USO), and whambam, she's a famous fashion designer jetting between New York, Paris, Rome, and London. But the redhead's life is no bowl of cherries. You see, there's this rich guy she fell for in Lincoln who's got an alcoholic witch of a wife. Hayward suffers and suffers as the odd woman out, all the way up to the tragedy-laced happy ending. Vera Miles has some fun playing the witch, and her fashion-salon showdown with Hayward is a hoot. John Gavin plays the object of it all, looking and acting more like a Ken doll than one might have thought humanly possible. (The fact that he's ten years younger than Hayward—which makes for some weird chemistry—is ignored.) Fannie Hurst's durable, tear-jerking novel (also adapted to film in 1932 and 1941) is given lots of Kennedy-era gloss by producer Ross Hunter and director David Miller.

X, Y AND ZEE (1972). Before she discovered the Betty Ford Center, Elizabeth Taylor chomped on the scenery in this woolly British drama. As Zee, Taylor screams like a banshee and gets tied up, slapped around, and called a "bloody slut" by Michael Caine, who plays her husband—their matches of physical and verbal abuse are vicious fun to watch. A triangle forms when drab Laura Ashley–type Susannah York stumbles between them, and Liz sets out to make mincemeat of her. Things might have gone better without Brian G. Hutton's dull direction, which neutralizes the sick sexual frissons of Edna O'Brien's screenplay. Even so, the two dizzying party scenes make a superb anthropological record of the period's nadir in taste, and Liz's wardrobe could only have looked better on Divine.

STARTING OVER (1979). James L. Brooks cut his big-screen teeth writing and co-producing this romantic comedy years before all the huzzahs over *Terms of Endearment* and that other triangle, *Broadcast News*. Nobody sleeps with anybody in *News*—a very late-'80s concept—but in *Starting Over,* the characters are thoroughly at the mercy of their hearts and loins. Jill Clayburgh is the insecure, dowdy Boston schoolteacher in love with sensitive, divorce-shocked Burt Reynolds. Candice Bergen is Reynolds's dumb, glitzy ex-wife, who unintentionally makes Clayburgh cower and sends Reynolds into a tailspin. With his usual humanism, Brooks etches another seriocomic portrait of modern men and women whose emotional lives have run amok. Director Alan J. Pakula matches Brooks's ear for dialogue with an observant eye and gets endearing performances from the leads (Clayburgh and Bergen were Oscar-nominated). This is the movie that was supposed to change Burt Reynolds's image, but those northeastern tweeds just didn't take.

TRIANGLES
GEOMETRY, HOLLYWOOD-STYLE

———————●———————

Douglas Fairbanks, Jr.
Joan Crawford
Clark Gable

Polly Platt
Peter Bogdanovich
Cybill Shepherd

Paul Snider
Dorothy Stratten
Peter Bogdanovich

Flora Carabella
Marcello Mastrioanni
Catherine Deneuve

Rose Kennedy
Joseph Kennedy
Gloria Swanson

Robert Evans
Ali MacGraw
Steve McQueen

Louise Treadwell
Spencer Tracy
Katharine Hepburn

Glenne Headly
John Malkovich
Michelle Pfeiffer

KINKIER COMBOS
THREE FOR THE SEESAW

———————●———————

Here, we move out of the heterosexual zone and into the twilight world of sexual ambiguity and gay love. As they swerve away from the straight and narrow, these triangles generate ever more complicated geometry.

GILDA (1946). This is ostensibly the story of two men who are all hot and bothered over a feisty sexpot (Rita Hayworth). But hey, wait a minute. What does creamy young Glenn Ford *mean* when he tells leering old George Macready, "I was born last night when you met me in that alley"? And how about that toast to Macready's, um, walking stick? There's more where that came from—*Gilda* is truly one of the most perverse movies ever to sneak out of Hollywood. Rudolph Maté's lush photography and Hayworth's feverish performance will make your head spin as you try to keep tabs on the double entendres. Charles Vidor directed from Marion Parsonnet's script, and you'll wonder how they ever got away with it.

THE SERVANT (1963). A piece of dank, dark kink featuring not one but two triple combos. At the center of both is the title character, a snake named Hugo Barrett, chillingly played by Dirk Bogarde. Barrett vies with his master's twit of a girlfriend (Wendy Craig) for power over the aristocratic wimp himself (James Fox). And for a bit of share and share alike, Barrett brings along his slutty "sister" (Sarah Miles). *The Servant's* stylized presentation of psychological collapse amid a haze of nicotine and alcohol in a frosty London town house is guaranteed to give you the willies. Sprung from the minds of novelist Robin Maugham, scenarist Harold Pinter, and director Joseph Losey, this was a shocker when it was first released, and even today the sexual territory it pushes into might seem best left unexplored.

THE KILLING OF SISTER GEORGE (1968). Dragging around in baby-doll pajamas and lacy black underwear, delectable Susannah York is the target of two aging bitches, expertly played by Beryl Reid and Coral Browne. When she's not molesting nuns in the back of a taxi, Reid is home pelting York with freshly baked scones or making the poor dear chow down on dead cigar butts. Browne is a sleek, chic TV exec out to halt this bulldozer and give York a proper home. Director Robert Aldrich, continuing in the full-throttle tradition of *What Ever Happened to Baby Jane?*, makes this a clash of the gorgons in which such lines as "You're a dreary, inadequate, drunken old bag" are spit out with the utmost conviction. If you're expecting sensitivity and restraint, forget it.

SUNDAY BLOODY SUNDAY (1971). Peter Finch and Murray Head's lingering kiss can still draw a gasp from an audience, but sex isn't what director John Schlesinger and screenwriter Penelope Gilliatt are after. A callow young artist (Head) is shared by a deceptively serene doctor (Finch) and a deceptively brittle employment agent (Glenda Jackson). With its jangling telephones and colliding schedules, the movie is a painfully accurate portrait of the difficulty of true devotion in the modern world. Peggy Ashcroft, speaking to Jackson in a brilliant cameo, sums it up: "There is no whole thing. You have to make it work." Store the Seconals on the top shelf before you watch this one.

PARTING GLANCES (1986). Michael's lover is a handsome, intelligent, slightly boring bureaucrat. His ex is a funny-looking, rude, slightly dangerous musician who still has a hold on Michael's heart. Bill Sherwood's film examines what happens when these two classically opposed ends of a tri-angle are about to leave Michael's life. The site is specific—gay Manhattan at the dawn of the AIDS epidemic—but the feelings are universal: confusion, loss, and imperfectly balanced affec-tions. This shoestring effort with an impressive cast of little-known actors (Steve Buscemi as the ex-lover and Kathy Kinney as the boys' jolly friend are standouts) is funny and poignant and richer with insight than practi-cally anything coming from the main-stream.

———————●———————

UNDERDOGS

●

BY ROB MEDICH

It's 1980, Syracuse University. I'm in an auditorium full of snotty college kids, many from comfortable families, watching my first movie on campus, *Breaking Away*. We cheer a lot (college kids do this at campus movies). But do we cheer for the rich, attractive, snotty college kids in the film, who vaguely resemble us? No way! We root for the lower-class, out-of-school locals: the underdogs. They are our soul mates. Underdogs are everyone's soul mates. So when you feel oppressed, when the odds are against you, when you need a victory, don't despair. You can gather inspiration from underdogs in the movies.

MAN VS. MAN

DAVIDS AND THEIR GOLIATHS

———————●———————

We have seen the enemy, and they have the odds and the upper hand. Only a fool would bet against them. Aside from that, it's a perfectly fair fight. Now let's cream 'em, like these people did!

WAIT UNTIL DARK (1967). Two ex-con con men and a cold-blooded killer prey on a sweet young woman who unknowingly possesses a doll stuffed with heroin. And she's blind. Gosh, think she's vulnerable enough? She does have a few aces in the hole, though. First off, she's played by Au-drey Hepburn. Audrey tends to bounce back in situations like this. Plus, she's going to "blind school," determined to become "the world's champion blind lady." Finally, because her husband's a photographer, their Greenwich Village basement apartment doubles as a darkroom (this works to her advantage later on). As far as thrillers go, this one includes moments of total darkness as well as unnerving off-key piano and guitar plunking. In other words, hold on to those seat cushions. Avoid this film if you're a claustrophobic achluophobic.

ROCKY (1976). Many called this John G. Avildsen Best Picture Oscar winner a Cinderella story. Actually, it's much closer to "The Tortoise and the Hare" (Rocky even has two turtles—Cuff and Link). Heavyweight champ Apollo Creed (Carl Weathers) chooses to fight unknown Rocky Balboa (Sylvester Stallone) because he has a marketable ring name—"The Italian Stallion." This "stallion" has the potential but lacks the fire. He lives a lonely, uninspired life in a Philadelphia ghetto working as "a leg-breaker to a cheap, second-rate loan shark," which he does poorly, since he lectures one delinquent instead of breaking his bones. With the chance at the boxing title, he learns he has people to win for, especially his nerdette girlfriend (Talia Shire). And so while Creed sashays around in three-piece suits, full of glitz and gimmicks,

Rocky trains furiously, beating up sides of beef. The clichéd sequels don't approach the freshness and honesty of the original. Stallone also wrote it, and you know what? He's pretty good.

SIXTEEN CANDLES (1984). Molly Ringwald is the queen of the suburban teenage sneer—a condition forcing one side of the upper lip perpetually to ride higher than the other. Still, she wins us over in this love story of the John Hughes persuasion. Samantha Baker (Ringwald) yearns for Jake Ryan (Michael Schoeffling), a wealthy, preppie high school senior with good bone structure. He, however, hangs with Caroline (Haviland Morris), the prettiest, most popular, most stacked blond in the senior class ("I could name twenty guys that would kill to love me," she reminds Jake). The only guy who would kill to love Samantha is "Farmer" Ted (Anthony Michael Hall)—a freshman nerd with delusions of coolness. Samantha, a mere sophomore suffering from a boob inferiority complex and a family that's forgotten her sixteenth birthday, can't imagine Jake dropping the bombshell for her. In the end, he does, but we know she'll soon realize how dull and shallow he really is. It's classic Hughes: You'll relate, you'll laugh, you'll cringe.

RETURN OF THE JEDI (1983). Darth Vader's pretty darn mean. But when it comes to pure, perfect evil, even the big, black-masked one himself concedes, "The emperor is not as forgiving as I am." In *Jedi,* we finally meet this wicked emperor (Ian McDiarmid), a hooded, ancient man with bad skin. Besides him, our band of galactic rebels must also defeat Jabba the Hutt—an oversize, slime-oozing slug—and a new and improved Death Star in this, the finale of George Lucas's (first?) *Star Wars* trilogy. By the end, *Jedi* confirms that better guns don't guarantee better armies and that the oppressed, armed with good intentions and determination, can topple powerful oppressors. This installment is the most satisfying of the three, fleshing out relationships (can Darth really be Luke's dad?) and concluding the saga. Do, however, see the others first if somehow you haven't. Aside from underdog inspiration, they prove once and for all that blood is thicker than empires.

MAN VS. SOCIETY

SHALL THE MEEK INHERIT THE EARTH?

————•————

We have seen the enemy, and the enemy is everyone but us (and they're real shmucks, and the odds against us are overwhelming). But then, that didn't stop these folks.

BREAKING AWAY (1979). For the climactic bicycle race that caps off this fine sleeper, the clique of spoiled, snobby college brats gets assigned the team number 1. The townie-boy heroes get stuck with number 34. Such is the social status of our band of underdogs—a quartet of young Bloomington, Indiana natives (Dennis Christopher, Dennis Quaid, Jackie Earle Haley, and Daniel Stern) with class-inferiority complexes who are just trying to find their place in society. Stern's Cyril is the worst case of the four, comfortably identifying with failure. ("It was somewhere about here," he says, pointing to a spot at the local swimming hole, "that I lost all interest in life.") Christopher's Dave, on the other hand, still dreams of success as he simulates the lifestyle of his heroes, an Italian bicycle racing team. And for Dave and his friends, bicycling is the way they choose to prove themselves. Like its characters, Peter Yates's tender, low-budget film triumphed over many flashier competitors, winning a Best Original Screenplay Oscar, nabbing a Best Picture nomination, and featuring the best serenade scene you'll ever see.

THE OUT-OF-TOWNERS (1970). They come from the land of common decency—Twin Oaks, Ohio. They're visiting the city "where people have to live on top of each other, and they don't have enough room to walk or to breathe or to smile at each other," and what's worse, you "have to give away watches in your sleep to men in black capes." Yes, amid the lost luggage, transit and garbage strikes, muggings, robberies, vicious dogs, and gas-main explosions, you'll realize that naive George and Gwen Kellerman never stood a chance in badass New York City. (Snaps George to a car that won't stop to rescue them in Central Park, "I hope you get in trouble someday!") Sandy Dennis and Jack Lemmon shine in this paranoid Neil Simon classic, directed by Arthur Hiller, that smoothly blends one nightmare into the next on a roller coaster of running gags. (Lemmon played another tortured Manhattanite in the film adaptation of Simon's *The Prisoner of Second Avenue*.) With its *Wizard of Oz*–like moral, *The Out of Towners* joins the league of films that put the fear of New York in the hearts of all Middle Americans.

WORKING GIRL (1988). Tess McGill belongs to Wall Street's bridge-and-tunnel (or in her case, ferry) secretarial pool. In *Working Girl,* they wear rainbow eye shadow and too much jewelry and believe that "success" equals an engagement ring. But Tess (Melanie Griffith) wants more. As she says, "I've got a mind for business and a bod for sin." Unfortunately, her bod attracts creeps while her ambitious, night-school-educated mind must compete with "brains" from Wharton and Stanford. Her boyfriend and peers don't understand her. Her best friend, Cyn (Joan Cusack, in a grade-A performance), asks, "What do ya need speech lessons faw? Ya tawk fine." So when her blue-blooded barracuda boss (Sigourney Weaver) gets laid up, Tess takes her place, teams up with Harrison Ford, and makes her move. This Mike Nichols vision of the American dream builds a metaphorical bridge of guts, smarts, and determination from pink-collar Staten Island to Wall Street. And don't miss

---

UNDERDOGS
LITTLE MEN

●

Mickey Rooney

Al Pacino

Dustin Hoffman

Alan Ladd

Edward G. Robinson

Noriyuki "Pat" Morita

Michael J. Fox

Irving "Swifty" Lazar

Spike Lee

Buster Keaton

Charlie Chaplin

Irving G. Thalberg

Dudley Moore

UNDERDOGS

LITTLE WOMEN

———●———

Nancy Walker

Zelda Rubinstein

Holly Hunter

Linda Hunt

Judy Garland

Janet Gaynor

Pia Zadora

Bette Midler

Mary Pickford

Marion Davies

Dolly Parton

those inspirational Statue of Liberty shots.

MR. SMITH GOES TO WASHINGTON (1939). Frank Capra gave us this loving portrait of an American patriot back when America already had a real hero in FDR. Where was Capra when all we had were Nixon and Reagan? Anyway, here James Stewart, as Jefferson Smith, recites Washington and Lincoln and puts out forest fires. So when he's appointed to the corrupt, snake-infested U.S. Senate, it's clear that, as his secretary (Jean Arthur) tells him, "This is no place for you. You're halfway decent." Smith angers the crooked politicians by championing a good cause detrimental to their bad cause, and nearly the entire Senate and nation turn against him. What to do? Stage a twenty-three-hour filibuster (without, apparently, a trip to the john) in that uniquely passionate, down-to-earth Stewart style. Says he,

"I suppose when one man goes up against a large organization like that, one man can't get very far, can he?" Guess again, Mr. Smith.

THE COLOR PURPLE (1985). Listen, Whoopi: I know good roles for black actresses are as common as a McDonald's on Rodeo Drive, but you should really see this one again before choosing your next project. Remember how good it felt getting that Oscar nomination, and how carefree it felt to act without a holster? You were so good in this, too. The way you gave those innocent little glances that hinted, "I may be oppressed, sweet, and quiet, but the wheels are turning, and I'll get my way without anyone even knowing it." And we really felt for you. I mean, even forty years after the slaves were freed, your husband, Danny Glover, still treated you like one. Forbidding you to see your sister. Telling you, "You're black, you're poor, you're ugly, you're a woman. You're nothin' at all!" Even your father was no damn good, giving away your baby. But you finally showed them (and helped your friend Oprah bounce back, too). Yes, I know, maybe the ending was just a bit *too* optimistic. But then, we accept that director Spielberg sometimes wears glasses, not of the color purple, but of the color rose.

MAN VS. HIMSELF

DR. JEKYLL BEATS HIS OWN HYDE

———●———

We have seen the enemy, and the enemy is us (and we're real shmucks, and we make our own odds). The people in the movies below are their own worst enemies, and boy, do they make tough opponents.

RUTHLESS PEOPLE (1986). Kidnapping sounds ruthless. But kidnappers Ken and Sandy (Judge Reinhold and Helen Slater) wear Huey and Dewey masks, and Ken accidentally chloroforms himself. Unlike all the other stereo salesmen, Ken can't even lie to his customers. Sandy's upset that their kidnappee, the nouveau riche Barbara Stone (Bette Midler), hates them; she jumps when Barbara yells "Boo!" In other words . . . they're too nice, okay? They're wimps. Wusses. Weaklings. They're their own biggest obstacle. It was their lack of business savvy that allowed Barbara's husband, Sam (Danny DeVito), to steal Sandy's priceless spandex-miniskirt designs in the first place. Now Sam wants them to go ahead and kill Barbara. So Ken and Sandy actually have two battles: Good vs. Slimy (DeVito) and Good vs. Goody-Two-Shoes (themselves). But regardless of the outcome, they could never really lose. After all, this is the Touchstone comedy formula at its finest.

RAGING BULL (1980). When a man steps into a boxing ring and obliterates his opponent, he's a prizefighter. When he treats his family and friends the same way, he's 1940s boxing champ Jake LaMotta, portrayed in this Martin Scorsese movie by Robert De Niro. Though LaMotta wants his family's love, something always seems to come between them. Perhaps it's his violent bouts of paranoia and jealousy. This kind of rage helped make him champ, but in real life, he winds up in the ring alone. Incidentally, if you never thought boxing cinematography could be breathtaking, check out Michael Chapman's handiwork.

SHAMPOO (1975). How, you ask, can Warren Beatty be an underdog in a film in which he beds four babes in two days? Keep an open mind. In this "period piece" (Election Day 1968), Beatty plays George, a hairstylist whose uncontrolled libido stands between him and his ambitions. He wants the security of a relationship. He wants to be a hairdressing "star" and open his own salon. But the fact that he sleeps with the wife (Lee Grant), daughter (Carrie Fisher), and mistress (Julie Christie) of a potential backer (Jack Warden) doesn't help. It also does little for his relationship with Goldie Hawn, who thinks she's his main squeeze. As this tongue-in-cheek look at the sexual revolution rolls on, the babe juggling, stress, and lies all wear George down. He wants so much. But a hungry kid loose in a candy shop easily gets sick.

THE LOST WEEKEND (1945). Any good writer would rather do anything than write. Putting a word on that blank page could drive him to triumph . . . or to mediocrity. In the case of Don Birnam (Ray Milland), it drives him to drink. What begins as 100-proof write-aid degenerates into a total write-off, or as Birnam himself puts it, "Don the drunk versus Don the writer." Don the drunk lies, steals, and nearly hocks Don the writer's most valued possession—his typewriter. Billy Wilder's nightmarish classic drags us through the conflict, right into boozer's hell. Can Birnam possibly defeat the disease, write that first novel, and find happiness with his sweet, uppercrust girlfriend (Jane Wyman)? Probably not, since she eventually became the matriarch of a TV vineyard.

JOURNALISTS

●

BY JAMIE MALANOWSKI

Thanks to the founding fathers and the Bill of Rights, the American people enjoy the benefits of a free press. And thanks to that free press, American moviemakers have at their disposal a convenient occupation—journalism—through which to tell stories about politics, war, crime, scandal, and even show business. Journalists in particular love these movies, if for no other reason than that in them they are treated as serious, important people and only seldom as nuisances, which is the reception often accorded them in real life.

NEWSPAPERS

BLACK AND WHITE AND TREAD ALL OVER

———————●———————

In general, newspaper movies mythologize reporters, making them seem savvy and interesting, if not existentially heroic. (There are exceptions—in *Manhunter,* the highly annoying reporter for a *National Enquirer*–like paper gets immolated by a madman.) In truth, some reporters *are* existential heroes, but most are just pretty good at asking questions.

JOSH GOSFIELD

166

ALL THE PRESIDENT'S MEN (1976). Virtually the whole movie consists of Bob Woodward and Carl Bernstein (Robert Redford and Dustin Hoffman) doing legwork. Director Alan J. Pakula and screenwriter William Goldman pulled off a number of not-so-easy tricks: They made an event that had already been saturated with coverage seem suspenseful, and they fashioned a story that had a beginning, middle, and end, even though the actual Watergate saga continued for more than a year after the Woodward-Bernstein part ended. The film had impact outside the theaters, helping to promote the late-'70s and '80s phenomenon of journalist-as-celebrity (which explains why Jack Nicholson plays the Bernstein-inspired role in *Heartburn*).

THE PARALLAX VIEW (1974). Pakula directed this film two years before *All the President's Men,* and his darker, more pessimistic mood is very much in evidence. Warren Beatty plays Joseph Frady, an ex-alcoholic reporter with a history of seeing things that aren't really there; as providence would have it, he's the one who uncovers a monstrous assassination bureau. Pakula, as if he were shooting a documentary, lets the viewer hunt for details amid big vistas, heightening the sense of mystery, confusion, and paranoia. Beatty gets to show off many of the reportorial techniques taught at our nation's finest J-schools: disarming a killer, engaging in high-speed car chases, hitting up the boss for petty cash. The late Walter McGinn is marvelously creepy as the lizardly corporate killer who recruits Beatty to join the bad guys.

BETWEEN THE LINES (1977). It's *twentysomething—the movie.* Attractive people with interesting jobs at a rag-tag underground Boston newspaper experience alienation, confusion, and unnamed yet powerful yearnings as they attempt to grow up. Lindsay Crouse stands out as someone whose act is more together than her peers'; so does Jeff Goldblum as a rock critic whose act isn't even under construction. Not much journalism is revealed here, but Goldblum does offer one strikingly authentic line, telling his publisher, "It's not that I'm unhappy here, I'm fucking broke."

THE KILLING FIELDS (1984). Roland Joffé's outstanding film about two heroic men, one of whom recklessly endangers the other. Sydney Schanberg (Sam Waterston) is a reporter for *The New York Times* in Cambodia in 1973, a man dedicated to "getting the story"; Dith Pran (Haing S. Ngor) is the local assistant who worships him. As the American-backed government begins to topple, Schanberg consciously ignores Pran's peril and passively allows his devoted aide to convince himself to stay. Both men are placed in grave danger, but whereas Schanberg's status as a Westerner eventually rescues him, Pran is left to face the murderous Khmer Rouge. There are many compelling scenes and memorable performances, among them John Malkovich's as a *Times* photographer who chooses a Pulitzer prize–like ceremony to remind the award-winning Schanberg that he has probably cost Pran his life. (Monologuist Spalding Gray also has a teeny part, which he leveraged into a film of his own—*Swimming to Cambodia,* an interesting bottom bill to this epic.)

FOREIGN CORRESPONDENT (1940). From its opening dedication ("To the intrepid ones who went overseas to be the eyes and ears of America"), it's clear this Alfred Hitchcock thriller is going to be turgid, melodramatic, and a lot of fun. Some of the heartiest (if unintended) laughs are delivered early on, when a publisher, dissatisfied with the reports being filed from about-to-be-war-torn Europe ("I want some facts—any kind of facts!" he snaps), sends a crime reporter, Johnny Jones (Joel McCrea), to cover the situation abroad. Jones is appropriately disrespectful—"Give me an expense account and I'll cover anything"—except when the publisher requires him to change his name to the ridiculous Huntley Haverstock, to which he acquiesces rather easily. Jones's pliability earns him a spot in some of Hitchcock's most memorable sequences—chasing an assassin through a sea of umbrellas, losing his obligatory trench coat in a windmill, going down in an airliner over the Atlantic —which fortify a movie that otherwise goes adrift when dealing with a cloying romance or the relationship between the villain and his daughter.

SWEET SMELL OF SUCCESS (1957). One of the best measures of this atmospheric movie's appeal is that a character in Barry Levinson's sharply observed *Diner* does nothing but recite its lines. Burt Lancaster is appropriately tyrannical as J. J. Hunsecker, a Winchellesque columnist for the *New York Globe* (coincidentally, the employer of *Foreign Correspondent*'s Haverstock) who rules his demimonde with the press's power to create or destroy, and Tony Curtis is magnificent as Sidney Falco, the hustling publicist who is consumed by desperate ambition and hates himself because of it (the sting on Curtis's face is visible, even when he explains his philosophy: "My experience, in brief, is dog eat dog"). The film was shot in black and white by James Wong Howe, giving it a grittiness that underscores the hierarchies among the characters. In the script by Clifford Odets and Ernest Lehman, Falco's early prediction—"Every dog has its day"—comes crashingly true.

WOMAN OF THE YEAR (1942). Virtually the definition of a romantic comedy, *Woman of the Year* rests comfortably on a few strong set pieces held together by the wit, intelligence, and rapport of its stars, Spencer Tracy and the dazzling Katharine Hepburn. Sam is a sports reporter; Tess is a political columnist. His initial skepticism toward her turns into enchantment, while she goes nuts over the big lug. The film doesn't shy away from showing us Hepburn's cold and manipulative side, but it rather easily succumbs to happy ending–itis: she gives up her career and heads for the kitchen, and Sam, moved by the gesture, allows her to keep on working, now that she has promised to treat him right. By today's standards, this is close to a politically correct compromise, grounded totally in fantasy.

ALL ABOUT EVE (1950). How nice to have the entertainment pages represented. *All About Eve* is Bette Davis's picture, true, but it is also George Sanders's, and he fully deserved the Oscar for his supporting role as the charming, cynical, and condescending-but-witty theater critic, Addison DeWitt. Sanders gets to do all the things journalists do best: stand off to the side acidly commenting on the poor mortals who populate his beat, and in the end, reveal the villain of the piece. That person, regrettably, is himself, but his admission has such verve, he gets away with it.

BROADCASTING

FLOATING ON AIR

———————●———————

Movies haven't quite gotten around to creating a cinematic archetype of the broadcast journalist, though based on the films that have been released to date, it seems fair to say these reporters are presented as more vapid than their counterparts in print. Where would anyone get such an idea?

BROADCAST NEWS (1987). This film is really two movies, a big American satire that is trying to walk down the street with a sensitive, personal, Eric Rohmer–type movie hanging on to one leg. The way James L. Brooks ribs the news business is right on. The way he captures the emotional inarticulateness of young network news professionals (played by William Hurt, Albert Brooks, and Holly Hunter) is pretty right on, too, but he is kinder to his characters than they deserve. You're expected to admire them, excuse their failings, and join them in making fun of their jobs, to which, of course, they nonetheless remain staunchly dedicated. In other words, it's all a lot like life, and as in life, you wish these people would just stop whining and make some happy endings for themselves. Jack Nicholson is only perfect in an uncredited cameo as the network's celebrity anchorman.

THE YEAR OF LIVING DANGEROUSLY (1982). Mel Gibson is Guy Hamilton, a green foreign correspondent for an Australian broadcasting network who is trying to make sense of the strange, confusing, and horrifying events leading up to the attempted Communist coup in Indonesia in 1965. Gibson and Sigourney Weaver, who plays a British diplomat, have a memorable courtship featuring a couple of particularly vivid scenes—the two of them falling for each other during a sudden tropical downpour and, soon after, recklessly necking in an automobile as they run a roadblock. Everyone was so astonished to discover that it was Linda Hunt playing the male role of Billy Kwan, Gibson's Chinese-Australian cameraman, that they gave her an Oscar.

MAGAZINES

INVESTIGATIONS ABOVE SUSPICION

———————●———————

Magazine writers in movies seem like a glamorous lot, if only because they usually appear to have generous expense accounts and are often presented in scenes where groups of them eat and drink with great humor and gusto. Well, that's it exactly.

JOURNALISTS

GREAT *VARIETY* HEADLINES

———————●———————

BALLYHOOED HULLABALOO
(July 15, 1925)
Enormous publicity surrounds the Scopes "monkey" trial.

WALL ST. LAYS AN EGG
(October 30, 1929)
Black Tuesday.

BULL MARKET GONE WITH THE WIND
(October 28, 1987)
Black Monday.

FOOD CRISIS SOURS RADIO GRAVY
(November 5, 1947)
Fears are stirred by Standard Brands' cancellation of Fred Allen's radio show.

SALARY WITH FRINGE ON TOP
(November 28, 1962)
Producers balk at the stars' high salary demands.

Magazine journalism—nothing but money, food, booze, and laughter, just like in the movies.

SALVADOR (1986). Richard Boyle is a freelance photographer, a man so selfish, undisciplined, and disreputable that you wouldn't ask him to watch the sidewalk for five minutes for fear that he would pawn or donate or just plain lose the concrete. Yet he becomes our Virgil, taking us on a tour of the hell that is El Salvador, and suddenly we are relieved to find ourselves in the company of a man in his milieu. Among the ways Boyle finds redemption for his wayward past is by showing some journalistic dedication and making sure a colleague's photos reach his magazine in New York. James Woods is terrific as Boyle, and Jim Belushi is equally good as his drug-fried sidekick.

UNDER FIRE (1983). In another film about Central America, Nick Nolte, a photographer for *Time* magazine, commits a reprehensible violation of ethics—helping Nicaraguan rebels with disinformation—but gets away with it because his heart was in the right place and because in that duplicitous land, he's only a pawn in a much bigger conspiracy. Though the picture is long and muddy, it does have a moment of curious interest when Gene Hackman takes a seat at the piano and sings "Spring Can Really Hang You Up the Most."

THE PHILADELPHIA STORY (1940). This film is one of a select few—the others include *Gone With the Wind* and *The Scarlet Pimpernel*—that are somewhat concerned with the class struggle and yet pretty much side with the rich. The only remotely unattractive wealthy person in *The Philadelphia Story* is the terrifically attractive Tracy

Lord (Katharine Hepburn), who, during the course of the film, is taught to overcome her personal flaw of judgmentalism (she being one of those rare, occasionally chilly, judgmental rich people who give all the warm, commonsensical, levelheaded, salt-of-the-earth rich a bad name). One of her tutors turns out to be Mike Connor (James Stewart), a sour, sardonic reporter for *Spy* magazine (its first incarnation) who, while infiltrating her society wedding, loses his prejudice against the rich at almost the same moment Tracy recognizes his finer, sensitive side. Though it's surprisingly toothless, the movie is full of breezy barking.

STREET SMART (1986). Christopher Reeve, who, of course, was reporter Clark Kent in the *Superman* movies, shows up here as a drowning writer at a slick weekly magazine who fakes a story about an unnamed pimp in order to get back in favor. The scheme backfires when the cops conclude that the fictional pimp is, in fact, someone they suspect of murder. *Street Smart* is notorious because screenwriter David Freeman based it in part on his experience faking a story for *New York* magazine. Fortunately, all this profiteering from unethical behavior did not lead to box office success, although the performances of Morgan Freeman, Kathy Baker, and Andre Gregory, as the odious editor, make it worth taking a look at.

THE FLY (1987). Remember, Geena Davis gets to meet the Fly only because she's a freelance writer for a science magazine, one of the many cinematic journalists who appear to be quite comfortable sleeping with their subjects. Besides playing a writer in *The Fly,* Davis was Chevy Chase's researcher in *Fletch;* Jeff Goldblum, her real-life husband and, in this film, the insect of her dreams, also played a reporter for *People* magazine in *The Big Chill,* as well as a rock critic in the aforementioned *Between the Lines.* Perhaps Davis and Goldblum got these roles because they are intelligent and funny and attractive and tall, characteristics shared by virtually every journalist in the country.

CENSORSHIP

●

BY MASON WILEY

Moral guardians have always been waiting at the gates of Hollywood, eager to expurgate what they do not like to see. The notorious Production Code, begun in the early '30s, when Mae West tried to tell it like it is, was so strict that movies retreated into fantasy—it was all that was left. The Code finally crumbled in 1968, and we got the alphabet soup–style rating system we have today, but studios still find it necessary to launder movies for the impressionable public. Herewith, we present the real dirt—films that meet the censor's wrath.

CUT UP

SINS OF OMISSION

———————●———————

You can't keep a good movie down, though censors of all sorts have tried a variety of ways to suppress some of the best films ever made. Scenes have been cut up, releases have been held up, seals of approval have been denied—moviemakers have suffered innumerable indignities when bringing an original vision to the screen. Thanks to video, however, we can sometimes see in our homes what we couldn't see in American cinemas.

SCARFACE (1932). Eleven days after director Howard Hawks commis-sioned a screenplay about gangland violence, he had a final draft. Loosely based on news accounts of Al Capone, Ben Hecht's script has the frenetic tabloid spirit of *The Front Page;* one motif, an *X* found at the scenes of the film's frequent murders, was inspired by *X*-marks-the-spot newspaper captions for lurid crime photos. Various state censors delayed the film's release for nearly a year, and all sorts of stupid scenes had to be added to appease them, such as an ending in which the Capone-like Scarface is hanged. Many of these cumbersome interruptions to Hawks's machine gun–paced melodrama remain in the video version, including the opening title: "This picture is an indictment of gang rule in America and of the callous indifference of the government to this constantly increasing menace to our safety and our liberty." After two more similarly stern messages, Hawks's narrative begins, and so does the fun: Scarface's first murder. Paul Muni plays the title role with almost simian energy, and the archetypal plot propels him through a joyride of noise and mayhem. The censor-appeasing scenes stick out like a sore thumb; in one, a newspaper editor and a bunch of stuffy concerned citizens who look as if they wandered out of a Three Stooges comedy take on the subject of violence. In another, a police chief snarls that gangsters are worse than "our old western bad men" because they shoot people in the back and not "in the middle of the street at high noon." The chief concludes, "When I think what goes on in the minds of these lice, I want to vomit!" Evidently, the censors never insisted on subtlety.

KING KONG (1933). The great monster didn't have any problems when he premiered in 1933, because the Production Code was not yet being strictly applied, but by the time of his 1938 rerelease, the Hays Office was ruling Hollywood with an iron fist. The censors decided that the popular Kong was too violent for Americans.

rector Vittorio De Sica interested David O. Selznick in a script about a poor young father in war-ravaged Rome who finally finds work putting up Rita Hayworth posters around town, only to have his precious bicycle stolen the first day on the job. Selznick wanted Cary Grant to play the lead, but De Sica, stressing the lifelike simplicity of the story, argued for Henry Fonda, who Selznick felt wouldn't sell tickets. Instead, De Sica raised his own money and cast the Grant/Fonda role with a handsome electrician who had never acted before. Lamberto Maggiorani's heart-

BRIAN CRONIN

Scenes featuring his tendency to step on people and to chew on them were removed, making him much better behaved during his appearances on Outer Skull Island and in Manhattan. Saddest of all, Kong was not allowed to make gentle love to his leading lady, the legendary Fay Wray, by ripping off her clothes in the jungle. Not to worry: The original cut has been restored for video, so you can thrill to all of this most primal of movie nightmares.

THE BICYCLE THIEF (1948). After his international hit *Shoeshine* in 1946, di-

breaking performance is just one of the miracles of this timeless drama rooted in the stark beauty of post-war Rome. The Hays Office was not sufficiently impressed by the movie's humanity to bless it with its Seal of Approval—precluding wide distribution in the United States—because two scenes violated standards. The first is a light moment that happens as the father and his young son chase after the thief: The kid attempts to relieve himself against a wall, and Dad lets him know they don't have time for that. The other is a scene in which the father tracks the thief into the kitchen of a brothel. De Sica refused to make the cuts, and the movie played without the seal. Hollywood apologized to De Sica a year later by giving the movie a special Oscar.

THE WILD BUNCH (1969). Director Sam Peckinpah's brutal, beautiful western is about a gang of veteran outlaws who realize their glory days are over. Says leader William Holden, "I'd like to make one good score and back off." Retorts partner Ernest Borgnine, "Back off to what?" In Peckinpah's view, their beloved Wild West has already been domesticated by railroad barons and temperance marchers, both of whom seem a lot less appealing than the titular fun-lovers. Ben Johnson and Warren Oates are the rowdiest members of the gang,

ready to unwind at a moment's notice by drinking and whoring; in the latter department, Peckinpah has the strictest mammary standards for actresses this side of Russ Meyer. When Peckinpah sprang his violent, adult version of the traditional western on the year-old Classification and Rating Administration (CARA), it responded with an X rating; cuts were then made to procure the more financially desirable R. The uncut 145-minute European release is now available on video. The edited footage explains why Holden is being pursued so vehemently by Robert Ryan (something that happened in a brothel, natch) and shows a shootout between the Mexican militia and a rebel force. Other scenes—Edmond O'Brien's confession about his grandson's death, the bunch's idyll in a Mexican village—were removed just to make the film shorter, but these details about life on the Texas-Mexico border in 1913 are what make *The Wild Bunch,* with its choreographed bloodbaths, so serenely elegiac. The restored video shows what Peckinpah was after: a genuine horse opera.

CRIMES OF PASSION (1984). "You can be as violent as you want in this country," groused director Ken Russell, "but you talk about sex and everyone reaches for their chastity belts." The belt came to Russell in the form of the dreaded X rating that CARA threatened to give this provocative sexual melodrama until deletions were made. Producer-writer Barry Sandler's script brings sexual frustration and fulfillment to the fore in the very first scene, a group-therapy session in which we meet our hero (John Laughlin). He's stuck in a marriage with his high school sweetheart (Annie Potts), who doesn't like sex and puts off his advances with "Stop it, we just got cable." Who can blame him when he falls for Kathleen Turner? A true two-faced woman, Turner is by day Joanna Crane, a driven careerist, but by night she's the sultry, cheap prostitute China Blue, who cynically helps men get their rocks off and makes them pay for it. When Laughlin asks Turner, "Who are you?" just before they first make love, she snaps, "It's not a prom date, sweetie. I'm a hooker, you're a trick. Why ruin a perfect relationship?" They go on to have the greatest sex of all time, which Russell renders artfully by their shadows on a window shade—a depiction that proved too titillating for the censors, who insisted on its removal, along with a scene in which Turner takes on a cop with his nightstick. This sadomasochistic moment is followed by an unexpectedly poignant one, in which Turner is hired by a wife to service her terminally ill husband. The unedited video version restores the movie's dramatic balance, as well as the arty shots of Aubrey Beardsley illustrations and Japanese erotic prints that the philistine raters demanded be snipped for being too "pornographic." Oh, brother.

CLEANED UP

ABRIDGED TOO FAR

———————●———————

Sometimes you wonder why Hollywood even bothers with a controversial property, especially when producers purge everything in the original that made it controversial in the first place. Plays and novels go into the studio washer and come out sanitized; the filmmakers can then either try to imply what's missing or just grind out the usual "wholesome entertainment."

A STREETCAR NAMED DESIRE (1951). No one gave Hollywood's Hays Office more headaches than Tennessee Williams, who couldn't help writing about the subjects the Code had clearly labeled taboo. The film's opening title brags about "the Pulitzer Prize and New York Critics Award play" it's based on, but Joseph Breen, the Hays Office chief, begged producer Charles K. Feldman not to make the movie, citing in a memo Code violations by three characters: Blanche DuBois's deceased husband ("There seems little doubt that this young man was a homosexual"); Blanche herself ("Her peculiar and

---

FINAL CUT
TALES OF PRERELEASE MADNESS

———————●———————

BULL DURHAM
The scene in which Tim Robbins tells Kevin Costner that he's heading to the big leagues was originally shot in a whorehouse. "The whorehouse was clearly tonally wrong, and people were very antsy about it," says writer-director Ron Shelton. So about two months after the film had wrapped, "I reshot the same scene in the pool hall and didn't change a line of dialogue. I think it helped the movie a lot. In fact, Kevin told me he thought his work in the pool hall was among the best work he'd ever done, because by that time he really knew who the character was."

FINAL CUT
TALES OF PRERELEASE MADNESS

●

BIG

Audiences at test screenings for the film lobbied for a "happy" ending, in which Elizabeth Perkins would join Tom Hanks in childhood. "The ending that was always written in the script was that he went back and she didn't," says the film's director, Penny Marshall. "At one point, the studio wanted her to go back. We talked about it, but [co-producer] Jim Brooks and I didn't want to change it. It wasn't a battle or anything. It was logic conversations: What's she going to tell *her* parents? Are they going to be doing it in junior high? Also, this was the script the studio bought, and if they were worried about the ending being bittersweet, they should have worried about it a few years earlier."

neurotic attitude toward sex, and particularly to sex attraction for young boys, has about it an erotic flavor that seems to verge on perversion of a sort"); and, of course, Stanley Kowalski (whose rape of Blanche is "both justified and unpunished"). Thus, in the film, Blanche no longer recounts walking in on her husband and "an older man who had been his friend for years," and instead of confronting him with the truth—"I saw! I know! You disgust me"—she just gives him that old taunt "You're weak!" and he blows his brains out; she has also learned not to say to the newspaper boy, "It would be nice to keep you,

but I've got to be good—and keep my hands off children." As for Stanley, he now protests, "I never once touched her!" and, as punishment, he loses his wife, who runs upstairs with the baby, vowing, "I'm never going back, never!" Despite these setbacks, director Elia Kazan and the actors bring the force of the play to life; when Marlon Brando bellows "Stella!" at the end of the movie, there's no question that she'll come back to the comfort of his arms, no matter what the Hays Office has made her say.

THE BAD SEED (1956). Here is the rare case when the inane morality of the Production Code actually *helped* a property. Maxwell Anderson's stage thriller about a genetically evil homicidal brat is so absurd to begin with, the censors inadvertently turned it into a riotous dark comedy. Except for a new ending, which upholds the Code's edict that "crime shall never be presented in such a way as to throw sympathy with the crime as against law and justice, or to inspire others with a desire for imitation," the screenplay is faithful to the play, preserving such pearls of dialogue as "'What would you give me for a basketful of kisses?' 'A basketful of hugs!'" Shooting most of the movie on what appears to be a leftover stage set and blocking members of the original Broadway cast as if they were still acting before a live audience, director Mervyn LeRoy created his most fantastic film since producing *The Wizard of Oz*. Evelyn Varden enters as she did on Broadway, announcing her role: "Here's your effusive neighbor from upstairs." Eileen Heckart, wearing Joan Crawford ankle-strap shoes, has not one but two drunk scenes as the distraught Mrs. Daigle, and Nancy Kelly, as the little murderer's nice mother, spends the whole movie wailing. As Rhoda Penmark, the young recipient of the eponymous gene, Patty McCormack rates up there with Boris Karloff and Bela Lugosi as one of the most memorable screen monsters, and her ultimate demise—added by Hollywood—fits her character perfectly. Don't miss the final bows for "our wonderful cast" and the closing request not to divulge "the unusual climax" of this "motion picture whose theme dares to be startlingly different."

CAT ON A HOT TIN ROOF (1958). Once again, a gay male in Tennessee Williams becomes simply "weak." As *Variety* reported when the film was made, "Change of motivation will have the leading character [Brick], played by Paul Newman, merely morally weakened by prolonged adolescence and refusal to assume adult responsibilities, rather than by AC/DC problems." George Cukor refused to direct the film without the homosexuality, so director–co-writer Richard Brooks took over and gave Big Daddy a chance to attack youth in general: "You and Skipper and millions like you living in a kid's world, playing games, touchdowns, no responsibilities!" Gone are Jack Straw and Peter Ochello, the gay couple who took in Big Daddy when he was starting out. Maggie (Elizabeth Taylor) sleeps with Skipper in this version not to prove that he's gay, but to show Brick what a louse Skipper is for sleeping with his friend's wife. (And she pleads that "nothing happened.") Brooks caps it off with a happy ending for Brick and Maggie and for Big Daddy and Big Mama, too. In spite of all this tidying up, the movie is plenty erotic, with Taylor in her slip and Newman in his pajamas. Brooks moves the action out of the bedroom and takes it all over the house, throwing in a thunderstorm for good measure. Yet his best directorial touch is his simplest—the wonderfully sexy moment when Newman avoids Taylor by shutting the bathroom door and, faced by her hanging nightgown, grabs it lustfully. Oh, baby, baby!

BREAKFAST AT TIFFANY'S (1961). Perhaps the best single image to sum up the difference between the movie and the Truman Capote novella it's based on is the close-up of a stuffed parrot in a birdcage in Holly Golightly's apartment; Capote's Holly would never have tolerated a cage in her dwelling. The rueful reminiscence of New York City during World War II in the book is replaced by the movie's romantic-comedy view of swinging-'60s Manhattan. Holly's cocktail party, a "stag party" in the novella, is now a coed shindig that gives director Blake Edwards a chance to demonstrate his trademark party gags. Audrey Hepburn's Holly is more a harmless kook than the wistful but wise woman of Capote's memoir. Holly's involvement with an imprisoned Mafia don, which results in her desperate flight from town in the novella, is here played for laughs. Even worse, she's subjected to a climactic tongue-lashing from the leading man, George Peppard, who scolds, "You're afraid to stick out your chin and say, 'Okay, life's a fact!'" Peppard's character is no longer Capote's autobiographical neophyte writer; in George Axelrod's screenplay, he's become a typical movie hunk for Holly to win over in a happily-ever-after ending. With Henry Mancini's music and a fine cast, the movie is irresistibly romantic and satisfying, but Capote's haunting and disturbing tale is lost along the way.

Less Than Zero (1987). The Production Code was twenty years dead when Twentieth Century Fox adapted Bret Easton Ellis's novel about the nihilistic lives of rich Los Angeles teenagers, but the studio got cold feet nevertheless. Ellis's amoral characters, drug-taking bisexuals who find entertainment value in a snuff film or an unattended corpse, didn't jive with Nancy Reagan's "Just Say No" ideal or the post-AIDS climate of sexual fear, so the studio turned the two leads into respectable role models. Clay, the book's passive hero, a casual cocaine user who becomes alienated from his aimless old friends, is transformed into a spotless white knight, played by Andrew McCarthy, who never snorts but instead strives valiantly to rescue his friends from their decadent habits. In short, he's a bore. Jami Gertz plays his girlfriend with perfect Valley-girl vacuousness, but the film makes the mistake of asking us to root for her when, suddenly and unbelievably, she dumps her cocaine down the drain. The character of Julian, a fugitive figure in the novel, becomes the movie's sacrificial victim, dying for his generation's hedonistic sins. Ironically, as played by the engaging Robert Downey, Jr. (an excellent performance), Julian is the only interesting person in the movie—at least he has a sense of humor. Director Marek Kanievska must have realized that nothing would contrast better with the movie's empty characters than its glittering settings and perfume-ad-gorgeous cinematography.

THE TWELVE DAYS OF CHRISTMAS

By Beth Lapides and Gregory Miller

Numbers count. Ask anyone who has a lucky number. Or who plays the numbers. Or the next person who says "I've got your number." We depend on numbers to organize, launch, and locate us, but they also stand for things. One isn't just a number, it's the loneliest. Ten isn't just the first two-digit integer, it's the ultimate object of desire (at least according to Blake Edwards).

But why twelve days of Christ-

TIM LEWIS

CHRISTMAS

YULETIDE GIFTS IN THE MOVIES

———— ● ————

Lady in *Lady and the Tramp*

The little mogwai that would give birth to *Gremlins*

Four penguins and a live octopus for Monty Woolley from admirers in *The Man Who Came to Dinner*

A toy fire hydrant for Asta in *The Thin Man*

Long pants for Rosalind Russell's nephew from his *Auntie Mame;* he gives her a not-quite-diamond bracelet

A pink bunny suit for the young hero of *A Christmas Story*

A doll for Helen Mirren's daughter from an Irish lad named *Cal*

mas? Maybe it's because Jesus had twelve apostles, who, according to numerologists, correlate with the twelve signs of the zodiac, the Twelve Tribes of Israel, and the twelve attributes of the soul, representing nothing less than the entire spectrum of human experience! Then again, maybe twelve is just all the gifts the lyricist's "true love" could afford.

So whether you're looking to compute the entire spectrum of human experience, to escape the accursed holiday spirit, or just to count cassettes till you fall asleep, we hope this numerological Christmas Video Guide will help you add it all up.

ONE FLEW OVER THE CUCKOO'S NEST (1975). Out of the void comes the seminal number one. And out of the rugged mountains of Ken Kesey country comes rebel yangmeister Randle McMurphy (Jack Nicholson). Imprisoned in the cuckoo's nest because "I fight and fuck too much," the mischievous rake single-handedly stiffens the spirits of wimpy mental ward–mates Charlie "I am not a child" Cheswick (Sydney Lassick), sniveling Martini (Danny DeVito), and stuttering Billy Bibbit (a potent performance by the thinking man's Don Knotts, Brad Dourif). McMurphy locks horns with castrating bitch Nurse Ratched (Louise Fletcher) winning battles with basketball, blackjack, and the World Series but losing the war. This first-class production was awarded the top three Oscars (as well as Best Director and Best Adapted Screenplay), but the story itself is just a bad boy's redemptive fantasy. Think *your* holidays are insane? Nurse Ratched's ward will make any family reunion seem tame.

TWO WOMEN (1961). Proving it takes two to tango, Best Actress Oscar winner Sophia Loren matches Jack's yang with a double dose of yin as a young Italian widow trying to dominate/liberate her virginal daughter (Eleanora Brown). They play out their duet against the backdrop of World War II, which is appropriate numerically and otherwise: duality, after all, is a double-edged sword, a precondition for war as well as for love. And both are the subject here, as the conflict between armies makes refugees of Loren and Brown. Tragically, it's the war, not love, that turns this pair from a mother and daughter into two women.

THREE DAYS OF THE CONDOR (1975). A bookish CIA researcher (Robert Redford), code-named Condor, still trusts a few people, but he gets cynical fast when he, along with most of mid-'70s America, is forced to move beyond the dichotomy of good guys and bad guys. It's Christmastime in New York City (itself a three-way street), and the three days (condensed from the six days of the source novel, by James Grady) begin with a bang—all of Condor's coworkers are efficiently massacred while he's out at the local deli. Unable to tell who's on his side, or if *anyone*'s on his side, or what his side is, or if he even *has* one, Redford kidnaps A Total Stranger (Faye Dunaway) who understands (and even empathizes with) his alienation. But ultimately Condor has to fly solo. Or does he? Feel as if everyone's turning against you this holiday season? Maybe they are.

THE 4TH MAN (1979). The fourth operation in alchemy is *sublimatio,* the distillation of Flesh into Spirit. Here, director Paul *(RoboCop)* Verhoeven distills celluloid into a reverie on Catholicism that's also a funny, gory, homoerotic four-star thriller. He gives no quarter as he spirits icons (crosses, Madonnas, etc.) away from the Church and makes them his own. For Gerard, his protagonist, "being Catholic means having imagination." And imagination is both his salvation and his torment in an affair with a scissors-wielding widow who appears to have killed her three previous husbands. As he tries to avoid becoming her next victim, it is the fourth dimension—time—that pins him to the cross of his lust.

FIVE CORNERS (1988). A pictograph (⌂) of a home has five sides. Home is where the heart is. Humans have five senses. Coincidence? Blue-collar bard John Patrick Shanley

doesn't seem to think so. His Five Corners is a fictional Bronx neighborhood in 1964 that's home to an ensemble of quirky characters. Tim Robbins is a son-of-a-dead-hero-cop turned nonviolent peace activist with a dog named Buddha; his beliefs are challenged by John Turturro, a returning bad seed, who'd rather go out in a blaze of glory than be a fifth wheel. And (count 'em) *five* Shanley-syncratic story lines are tied up in the rooftop damsel-in-distress climax, with the damsel (Jodie Foster) standing for home, animal rights, and maybe, just maybe, that elusive sixth sense.

CHRISTMAS

YULETIDE GIFTS IN THE MOVIES

———●———

Money—lots of it—for James Stewart and family, because *It's a Wonderful Life*

A hollow-ended bullet for Danny Glover from Mel Gibson in *Lethal Weapon*

One hundred dollars, to Shirley MacLaine from Fred MacMurray, in *The Apartment*

A watch for Cybill Shepherd (which stops after she takes a quick skinny-dip in the pool) from Jeff Bridges in *The Last Picture Show*

A Rolex watch (which later proves to be a lifesaver) for Bonnie Bedelia from her employers in *Die Hard*

The shoes for Divine that unfortunately were not cha-cha heels in *Female Trouble*

SEXTETTE (1978). Six is a love number. It corresponds in astrology to the planet Venus, in tarot cards to the Lovers, and in our video guide to the sex goddess Mae West's last movie. This kitsch classic is a mishmash of musical production numbers and cameos (including lunatic Keith Moon as Mae's costumer) with a reverse-*Lysistrata* plot that finds Mae lubricating the way to world peace by West-

TIM LEWIS

ing around with lots of handsome guys, including Timothy Dalton (as her sixth husband), Tony Curtis, and an entire U.S. gymnastics team. This is the only star vehicle we've ever seen without even one star close-up, and no wonder: Mae was eighty-six, her eyes are closed, and she looks propped up. But she can still reprise many of her best lines. Our favorite: "I'm the girl who works at Paramount all day and Fox all night."

THE SEVEN SAMURAI (1954). God created the world in six days (or so the story goes), and on the seventh day he rested, but the beleaguered Japanese farmers in this movie are working eight days a week, and an attack by marauding brigands is the last straw. Who they gonna call? Brigandbusters! Seven Asian cowboys, each of whom, like the seven days, dwarfs, and deadly sins, has his own charm: manic insanity, silent grace, boyish innocence, etc. These defenders of the helpless do the heroic thing and look great doing it in their pre-Miyake skirts, but farmer-turned-samurai Toshiro Mifune steals the show in his show-all loincloth. Other movies *(The Magnificent Seven, ¡Three Amigos!)* have reworked the action-packed plot, but director Akira Kurosawa, fusing glowing black-and-white photography, indelible performances, and his particular brand of tragicomedy, has created a world that can never be duplicated.

EIGHT MEN OUT (1988). Lay an eight on its side and you get an infinity sign, a curveball of a doodle that goes on forever. And in 1919 (a year vividly recalled by writer-director John Sayles and his team), America's optimism seemed infinite. That's why the Chicago "Black Sox" scandal was such a foul ball. Only eight White Sox struck out for the bucks at the World Series, but their errors flew out of the ballpark, affecting fans, club owners, gamblers, and several One-Scene Wives (relegated to the bull pen as the boys take the field). As in other Sayles films, it's the group that stars, not just one player, but look for the director himself as the muckraking sportswriter Ring Lardner, who isn't afraid to dig his cleats into the mud as he calls the rigged game.

8½ (1963). Just in case one movie a day isn't enough, there's Federico Fellini's eighth-and-a-half film (counting collaborations as halves), which stars Marcello Mastroianni as Guido, a Felliniesque film director who wants to collaborate with everybody (except maybe the audience). Guido's Felliniesque life keeps getting mixed up with his Felliniesque art. Poor man, he wants all the girls but can have only one. Well, maybe one and a half.

9 TO 5 (1980). This movie *could* be considered an eight—the number of hours between nine and five (infinite though they seem), during which office workers Dolly Parton, Lily Tomlin, and Jane Fonda toil under their "sexist, egotistical, lying hypocritical bigot" of a boss, Dabney Coleman. But according to numerology, people with a "nine vibration" work to make the world a better place, and that seems an apt description of this lively trio, who pool their resources to free themselves and their fellow female wage slaves and humanize (with perhaps a little coercion) their inhuman taskmaster. And they have a good time doing it. A better world is a lot to ask from Santa, so if that's what you've got in mind, you may have to follow this movie's prescription and take matters into your own hands.

THE TEN COMMANDMENTS (1956). On a scale of one to ten, Cecil B. De Mille's lavish biblical epic ("The story of the birth of freedom") is, well, a ten. But how can you measure the suffering of the Hebrews in the "never-ending valley of toil and agony"? The treachery of Dathan (Edward G. Robinson), pimping his people out of the brick pits of Goshen? The lust of Nefretiri, the "sharp-clawed, treacherous little peacock," crying, "Oh, Moses, Moses, you stubborn, splendid, adorable fool!"? The earnest overacting of (goyish) Chuck Heston as Moses, the Rod of God himself, who leads the unending streams of men and beasts of burden through the burning crucible of desert toward the Promised Land? How do you judge the finest matte painting this side of *Indiana Jones?* Or the first on-screen surrogate-motherhood debate between Moses' two moms ("I gave him life"—"I gave him love")? Yes, we admit that the burning bush and Passover pestilence do look a little washed-out, but the parting of the Red Sea—how can you put a tape measure on that? "So let it be written, so let it be done."

11 HARROWHOUSE (1974). The eleventh card in the tarot is Justice, and it *may* just be a coincidence, but this caper comedy is about the poetic justice of beating the system—the Consolidated Selling System, that is, which is run by ultra-Brit John Gielgud and has $12 billion worth of diamonds hidden behind four-inch armor, electric eyes, and all that other stuff you always have to avoid in a heist movie. Deadpan actor extraordinaire Charles Grodin is a diamond merchant who teams up with thrill-seeking divorcée Candice Bergen and disgruntled employee James Mason to beat the System. Lucky for them they don't hear the goofy '60s score, or they wouldn't have a chance.

THE DIRTY DOZEN (1967). The hanged man, the twelfth card of the tarot, symbolizes the world turned upside down, and this classic wartime-mission movie begins with a hanging. In the Nazi-inverted world of 1944, it's up to Lee Marvin and his dozen dirty, murdering, raping, sociopathic apostles to make the world safe for democracy. Marvin forges his twelve angry men into one happy family, and by the last supper they're hanging together, playing it by the numbers, all the way to "Sixteen—we all come out like it's Halloween."

SCREWBALL COMEDIES

◆

BY ED SIKOV

In 1934, forced by the newly instituted Production Code to stop suggesting sexual combat on-screen, the best comedy writers and directors began to see that they could ditch the sex and still keep the combat, and screwball comedy was born. Contentious, anarchic, and more than a little nervous, screwball comedies are not just funny films about crazy people. Some are lavish, others are hysterical, but they're all about the intractable, indelicate condition of love. The Marx Brothers may be screwy, but they aren't screwballs; that distinction belongs instead to the idealized men and women—Cary Grant, Carole Lombard, William Powell, Myrna Loy, Henry Fonda, Irene Dunne, and others—who are reduced (and elevated) to insanity in the pursuit of something resembling happiness.

TWENTIETH CENTURY (1934). The financial success of Frank Capra's 1934 *It Happened One Night* prompted dollar-eyed Tinseltown to go screwball. But the nastier, more raucous *Twentieth Century,* Howard Hawks's adaptation of the hit Hecht-MacArthur play, was in many ways the genre's first full-blown venture into the world of romantic insanity. John Barrymore is Oscar Jaffe, the ego-

maniacal impresario who molds unknown actress Mildred Plotka (Carole Lombard) into a star, changes her name to Lily Garland, and tortures her into a sick love affair, only to recoil in hammy horror when she matches him in both fame and gargantuan self-absorption. A comic masterpiece, *Twentieth Century* fared badly at the box office; America's heartland wasn't yet ready to see big, glamorous stars brutalize each other for laughs.

THE THIN MAN (1934). Made in less than three weeks and released without much fanfare, MGM's screen version of Dashiell Hammett's detective novel turned into such a big hit that it spawned five sequels and countless imitations. William Powell and Myrna Loy are Hammett's Nick and Nora Charles, a pair of rich, witty drunks who know enough not only to accept an element of irrationality in their lives but also to exacerbate it. Style incarnate, the Charleses—accompanied by their fabulous fox terrier, Asta—float through the film on a cloud of martinis and money. Plot specifics hardly matter; the *Thin Man* films are about their own aura—two swell people trapped in a dark, stupid, murderous world. Listen to some dialogue: Nick (reading a newspaper account of his exploits): "I was shot twice in the *Tribune*." Nora: "I read you were shot five times in the tabloids." Nick: "It's not true. He didn't come anywhere near my tabloids."

THE MOON'S OUR HOME (1936). An underrated gem of the studio era, *The Moon's Our Home* was directed by William A. Seiter, a director to whom little critical attention has ever been paid. Dorothy Parker and Alan Campbell contributed that magnificent Hollywood bonus called "additional dialogue," but the film's authorship doesn't much matter. Look instead at its schizoid treatment of romance: a violently temperamental Hollywood actress named Cherry Chester, who's really an heiress named Sarah Brown (Margaret Sullavan), falls in love with best-selling travel writer Anthony Amberton, whose real name is John Smith (Henry Fonda). With a total of four different identities between the two protagonists, it's no wonder Fonda resolves things by forcing Sullavan into a straitjacket for the final clinch. The bizarre irony of the casting is that the stars had already suffered through their own riotous, fight-filled marriage in real life, a period described in *Fonda: My Life* as "like living with lightning."

THE AWFUL TRUTH (1937). The most elegant of screwball comedies, Leo McCarey's *The Awful Truth* rests on a charming, wry premise. It's the story of how a failed marriage can become a romantic success, provided the players are ironic enough to appreciate the humor. Dashing Jerry Warriner (Cary Grant) and his lovely wife, Lucy (Irene Dunne), are both enjoying vague, Production Code–sanctioned affairs, and their marriage quickly evaporates in a cloud of distrust. Hus-

tled into divorce court, where they battle furiously over custody of their dog (played by Asta, who'd become a screwball star in his own right), the Warriners find themselves faced with a drab, humorless future apart, though it takes the rest of the film for them to overcome their pride enough to admit it. Besides, they find they can't squabble when they're separated, so they learn—as only the most profound lovers can—that they're the only ones who can give each other a fair fight.

NOTHING SACRED (1937). Even in an era of tough, backbony comedies, *Nothing Sacred* stands out as unusually cynical and unforgiving. Bilious beyond words, Ben Hecht's tale of journalistic fraud and personal perfidy (directed by William Wellman) tells what happens when a New York newspaper wantonly uses the story of a dying young woman to boost its circulation. In an effort to restore his drooping career, reporter Wally Cook (Fredric March) tracks down innocent young Hazel Flagg (Carole Lombard), who's said to be slowly succumbing to radium poisoning. Cook's cheesy paper, run by the tyrannical Oliver Stone (Walter Connolly), quickly makes Hazel the toast of the city; all over New York, crowds are moved to tears by the tragic woman's heroic struggle. The catch: Hazel's a lying little schemer who's got about as much radium in her system as Wally has integrity in his. Like other screwball couples, they're made for each other.

BRINGING UP BABY (1938). The quintessential screwball comedy, in which Katharine Hepburn's harrowingly self-assured heiress succeeds in breaking down Cary Grant's repressed, bespectacled paleontologist to the point of love, Howard Hawks's *Bringing Up Baby* was a flop at the box office and added fuel to Hepburn's then-flaming unpopularity. One critic went so far as to say that the comedy had been designed to torture the actress, though in fact the damage to Grant seems more extensive. *Baby* is no less painful today; modern audiences simply aren't used to seeing controlling Bryn Mawr types destroy the lives of weak-willed men—especially in comedies. (If it happens at all, it's pitched as pure tragedy, as in *Body Heat*.) Quick, sharp, and breezy, this is still one very dark film; most of the second half takes place at night and in jail, and it ends in an inevitable collapse.

MY FAVORITE WIFE (1940). Three years after *The Awful Truth,* Leo McCarey brought Irene Dunne and Cary Grant back together for another disintegrated-marriage comedy. (This time McCarey produced and Garson Kanin directed.) The new twist was unintentional bigamy, the Code era's answer to promiscuity. Once someone discovers he or she has two spouses, *nobody* can have sex, which is precisely what happens when Dunne, in a gender-switched update of *Enoch Arden,* returns from seven years on a deserted isle on the very day that Grant has had her declared legally dead and married supervixen Gail Patrick. Cross-dressing adds to the confusion; Dunne appears as a merchant marine, and Grant models several great dresses under the fascinated gaze of a stock psychiatrist. Randolph Scott co-stars as Dunne's muscular island boyfriend. She calls him Adam, he calls her Eve, and Grant, his mind reeling with possibilities, is made a jealous wreck.

THE LADY EVE (1941). Preston Sturges wrote this sublime comedy of female deceit and male ineptitude while in Reno, the popular divorce resort. The story of Charles "Hopsie" Pike (Henry Fonda), the maladjusted, snake-obsessed heir to an ale fortune, and his salvation at the dazzling hands of con artist Jean Harrington (Barbara Stanwyck), *The Lady Eve* is full of twists. Jean is something of a Depression Cinderella—the worthy girl suddenly elevated into wealth—but she's also a crook. The marriage crumbles, but that's what the bride wanted all along. And though the unrepentant Jean has transformed herself into phony nobility ("the Lady Eve Sidgewick," thank you), Sturges uses her multiple roles not to question the role player's real identity but to further humiliate poor Hopsie, who's just dumb enough never to figure out what's going on.

MRS. AND MRS. SMITH (1941). Given the anxiety that runs through the screwball genre, it's not surprising that Alfred Hitchcock was drawn to it. But *Mr. and Mrs. Smith,* Hitchcock's third American film, hasn't fared well in the annals of film history; critics expecting suspense haven't known what to do with this (apparently) light comedy about a couple (Robert Montgomery and Carole Lombard) who discover that they aren't legally married. Hitchcock himself later denied interest in the film, though at the time he was more enthusiastic—especially, one imagines, once it became a commercial hit. Lombard is particularly charming in the role of the society wife forced by both romance and fate to demand that her husband prove his love anew. He does, in a perfect blend of screwball sensibility and Hitchcock's personal vision: He simply gets her in a headlock.

CRIME

●

BY PETER BLAUNER

Recently, a young man from Queens, New York, named Thomas Mickens paid the ultimate fan's tribute to his favorite movie, the 1983 remake of *Scarface*. Not only did he take his nickname, Tony Montana, from the film's lead character, he gave several of his properties around the neighborhood the same name, including Montana Dry Cleaners, Montana Grocery, and Montana Sporting Goods. In fact, Mickens was so entranced by the movie that when the cops moved in to bust his multimillion-dollar crack empire, they found the *Scarface* video hooked up to TV screens in the front and back of his Rolls-Royce Silver Spur.

The connection between real-life criminals and the movies goes back at least as far as the time Al Capone's henchmen went to question co-screenwriter Ben Hecht about the script for the original *Scarface* (1932). And it's no secret that some recent major films have had mob backing. But filmmakers who try to tell the story from the criminal's point of view run two risks. If they are too true to the vile, stupid, petty, boring, and squalid nature of most crime, they can turn off an audience. But if they put on too much gloss and glamour, they lose all credibility.

Here, then, are ten good movies that cover the criminal spectrum.

STRAIGHT TIME (1978). Dustin Hoffman plays a small-time thief struggling to make his way in the world after doing a stretch in a California state prison. Along the way, he runs into M. Emmet Walsh, as a manipulative parole officer; Theresa Russell, as a not-very-bright young woman who becomes his girlfriend; and Harry Dean Stanton, as another worn-down thief who joins him for a jewel heist, with disastrous results. What gives the film, which was directed by Ulu Grosbard, its drive and poignancy is Hoffman's character's need to connect and succeed in the outside world and the absolute certainty that no matter what he does, he cannot.

ACROSS 110TH STREET (1972). If anything, the three black thieves who set this plot in motion stand even less of a chance than Hoffman's ex-con. They begin by ripping off $300,000 from a Mafia "bank" in Harlem. After that, they never have a moment's peace; they are hunted down relentlessly by the mob and a corrupt cop, played by Anthony Quinn. Taut, intense, and extraordinarily violent, this film was underrated when it came out, but it holds up remarkably well —not only because it is a rare realistic view of inner-city crime, but because it refuses to judge its sordid characters as they crawl over corpses and one another in their struggle to survive. "It pumped so much pressure into the world of the new black movies that it blew that world apart," wrote Greil

Marcus. Directed by Barry Shear, who earlier did *Wild in the Streets*.

IN COLD BLOOD (1967). Truman Capote's "nonfictional novel" told of the slaughter of the Clutter family in Holcomb, Kansas, and the subsequent capture and execution of the two murderers, Dick Hickock and Perry Smith. Richard Brooks's film adaptation has a cool visual style, almost like a documentary, which matches the deliberate pace of Capote's prose. But Brooks's script and Conrad Hall's black-and-white photography have their own eerie quality, suggesting the strangeness of the victims as well as the killers. What's most striking about the film today, though, is young Robert Blake (eight years before his television series *Baretta*) giving a frightening and utterly convincing performance as the murderous Smith.

THE HONEYMOON KILLERS (1970). Watching this movie is like being locked in a car on a dark night with someone you don't completely trust behind the wheel. Tony LoBianco and Shirley Stoler play a couple of American grotesques—doomed, mismatched lovers. He is weedy, feral, and untrustworthy; she is enormous, compulsive, and needy. Together, they play out a horrifying scheme in which he lures lonely women out on dates and proposes marriage to them, with Stoler's character pretending to be his sister. They take the women's savings and then murder them remorselessly. Dank, claustrophobic, and weirdly engrossing, this movie, based on a true story and directed by Leonard Kastle, never quite gives in to the comforts of conventional narrative. Truffaut named it one of his favorite films.

DOUBLE INDEMNITY (1944). Though Raymond Chandler couldn't stand James M. Cain's books and couldn't get along with director Billy Wilder, who worked with him on this script based on Cain's 1936 novel, he nevertheless helped put together one of the most entertaining of all films noirs. Fred MacMurray plays the hapless insurance agent who is seduced by Barbara Stanwyck into coming up with a plot to kill her husband and collect his insurance money. Edward G. Robinson plays MacMurray's best friend, the investigator who begins to unravel the scheme. Elements of the suspenseful and often grimly funny *Double Indemnity* have been used in such modern films as *Body Heat,* but without the same emotional impact.

TAXI DRIVER (1976). This movie seems to have been shot through a psychotic's eyes. "A person should not devote himself to morbid self-attention," intones Travis Bickle (played by Robert De Niro) as he goes about the business of talking to himself, pursuing unattainable blond women, shaving his head, popping pills, and plotting to assassinate a presidential candidate. The obsessive characters in the back of his cab (including one played by director Martin Scorsese) and the glimpses of hell outside his window are like monstrous figments of his imagination made real. They incite him to heights of rage and, toward the end, cathartic violence. Bernard Herrmann's haunting score and Michael Chapman's bleary-eyed cinematography add to the New York atmosphere. Paul Schrader wrote the screenplay—his best.

HIGH SIERRA (1941). Humphrey Bogart could summon up a hard, scarred quality that made him persuasive as a hood in his earlier movies. It also gave weight to some of the more sentimental scenes in this Raoul Walsh film, based on a W. R. Burnett novel (Burnett and John Huston wrote the screenplay). Bogart plays "Mad Dog" Roy Earle, an ex-convict planning a big hotel robbery. He is sidetracked by a crippled young girl he meets and loses his heart to. He gives her money for corrective surgery, but she refuses his love. After bungling the hotel job, Bogart winds up on the run again in the Sierra Nevada Mountains of California. Many later films would take the search for freedom in America's wide-open spaces as a theme, but few would do it as movingly.

WHITE HEAT (1949). Even by contemporary standards, this is a shockingly brutal movie, but with one great scene following another, it builds tremendous momentum. James Cagney plays Cody Jarrett, a sociopathic train robber who gets terrible headaches, kills blithely, and loves his mother (who's also in his gang). While he is in prison, another member of the gang steals his wife and murders his mother, which tears him completely off his hinges. Cagney's "Ma's dead!" breakdown in the prison dining room is a classic of Oedipal dementia. Edmond O'Brien gives a subtle performance as the dislikable heel of an undercover agent who helps Cagney break out of prison to avenge his mother's death. His creepy blandness somehow makes Cagney's righteous madness seem noble by contrast. The tension builds inexorably down the stretch, and when Cagney explodes—literally—at the end, it is not just fitting, it is the only logical conclusion.

SCARFACE (1932). Not so long ago, Paul Muni's performance as mobster Tony Camonte was called too primitive, and this film was treated as a period piece. But some of today's

gangsters make Camonte and the style of urban warfare in *Scarface* seem quite modern. Other movies have cribbed the most basic, obvious parts, including the incest subtext, the punchy dialogue, and the way George Raft, as Muni's sidekick, keeps tossing a coin in the air. What's most effective and powerful about the film, though, is the way director Howard Hawks moves the camera along the periphery of violence. In one scene, Boris Karloff, playing an Irish gangster, is seen throwing a bowling ball down a lane. As he moves out of the frame, we hear a burst of machine-gun fire. But instead of lingering on his death, the camera keeps moving down the lane. The ball knocks down nine pins and leaves one standing, which wobbles and gyrates for a moment . . . and then falls among the others.

THE THIN BLUE LINE (1988). The first time I saw this documentary—which restages the murder of a Dallas cop, retraces the investigation that followed, and re-examines the conviction of drifter Randall Adams—its artful, elusive quality made me suspicious. I wanted to know more of the facts before I agreed with filmmaker Errol Morris's conclusion that the wrong man was sitting on death row. But by the time I saw it again, on a small screen, Morris had been proven right, and I was able to relax and sink into it. The film has a dense, shifting texture, unlike any other documentary. Time is suspended, and every moment becomes meaningful. The cast of real-life characters (including the lawyers, cops, and witnesses) who set themselves before Morris's camera is even more remarkable. Randall Adams is like a desperate ghost, clinging to his memories before they drift away. David Harris (on death row for a different murder) has a sweet smile and a laconic, unnerving presence, and admits to being present at the cop's killing—but stops just short of saying he pulled the trigger. Largely because of this film, the higher courts in Texas recently set aside Adams's conviction and freed him after twelve years in prison. Ironically, vindication and freedom weren't enough for Adams, who sued Morris for the rights to his life story.

———————●———————

RELIGION IN EXTREMIS

BY ELLEN HOPKINS

The fact that saints, sinners, and assorted religious loons have always been particular pets of the movie industry has less to do with West Coast piety than it does with the Joe Bob Briggs take on cinema (more buckets of blood = more reviewer stars; the Texas "critic" follows a similar equation for numbers of bosoms exposed). Those who'd dismiss this analysis as cynical should try and rustle up a showier concept than martyrdom or casting out devil babies. Cecil B. De Mille, in fact, was quite forthright about his reason for using stories from the Bible: What better way of getting sex scenes past the censors?

MIRACLES

"HOW CAN THESE THINGS BE?"
JOHN 3:9

Bona fide miracle movies inspire awe or helpless shrieks of laughter—there's precious little middle

ANITA KUNZ

ground. They do not, under any circumstances, make anyone feel all warm and fuzzy inside. No one ever told John the Baptist, "You're a good man, John. Some day folks 'round here will 'preciate all this baptizing you been up to." Thus, *It's a Wonderful Life* is a little too *nice* to qualify as an MM (ditto *Heaven Can Wait* and some other looking-good-feeling-good-just-got-back-from-the-dead films). A few of the more genuine article follow.

THE SONG OF BERNADETTE (1943). In 1858, a schoolgirl in a French village claimed she saw a "beautiful lady" appear out of nowhere in a nearby grotto. Soon the village—Lourdes—was inundated by the blind, the sick, and the lame, looking to be cured. What this refreshingly stark movie details are the lesser known, less rosy aspects of the making of a holy place and a saint—Bernadette was reviled as a liar, retarded, or plain old nuts for claiming the Virgin Mary would visit what had till then been the town dump. Jennifer Jones is a tad too gorgeous to be a peasant schoolgirl, but she's faithful to the filmmakers' vision of the saint as simpleton. And Vincent Price is deliciously silky as the town prosecutor, twitching with glee at the prospect of locking up this troublemaker. Equally satsifying are stodgy church officials who dismiss a grubby child's regaining the use of his legs as *not the sort of cure God would care to be known for.*

THE TEN COMMANDMENTS (1956). The Red Sea isn't all that's parted in De Mille's camp, steamy epic. Three hours and thirty-nine minutes are but an instant when the sights include Yul Brynner (Rameses) in what appears to be a Mary McFadden line of field hockey skirts. (Poor Rameses: His rival, Moses, played by Charlton Hes-

ton, is saddled with only one handicap —poor-quality bronzing gel.) Then there's the passel of Jewish mamas packing for the Promised Land ("Benja-min, don't forget the oil!") But the standout hoot is Anne Baxter as the trashy princess Nefretiri, one minute purring "You old crocodile" to the pharaoh, the next snarling at Heston, "You call yourself a prophet, a man of God, but *I* know better." Miracles come by the bushel. Staffs turn to asps. Water turns to blood. And, of course, there's the Miracle of the Makeover. When Moses returns from the burning-bush jaunt, his once matted, greasy locks have been washed, Tenaxed, and blown dry. His wife instantly understands: "He has seen God."

THE SEVENTH SEAL (1956). A large, dark bird hovers over a northern sea. A gleaming chess set perches on the rocky shore. What does this *mean?* It's time for a look at life and death the Ingmar Bergman way. Max von Sydow is the heartsick knight, back from the Crusades and seeking to understand "what will become of those of us who want to believe but cannot" as he plays a game of chess with Death (who has agreed to a brief reprieve for his marked man). Plague reigns in this land. Pretty young girls are served up for rape or the stake. Flagellation upstages more conventional forms of entertainment. A woman gives birth to the head of a cow. Ask a snoozing loafer for directions, and odds are you're questioning a dead man no one bothered to bury. And the miracle is that in the midst of all these memento mori, a juggler given to improbable visions and his lovely wife and laughing babe can live on strawberries and milk, can make their way through the dark and savage forest and emerge unscathed.

AGNES OF GOD (1985). There's a coyness to this did-she-or-didn't-she story of a nun (Meg Tilly) who mysteriously conceives, then gives birth to a baby found strangled minutes after delivery. Miracles abound—or, more accurately, possible miracles—but the one miracle the audience longs for never happens: Jane Fonda (as Sister Agnes's court-appointed psychiatrist) giving up smoking. Whatever the focus of the scene—confrontation, catharsis, or stigmata (Agnes gets those too)—Fonda's first reaction is to fumble for her Lucky Strikes. Much in this movie annoys, in particular a mother superior (Anne Bancroft) so hip she makes Freudian jokes. See *Agnes* instead for the light that streams through Sven Nykvist's golden lens and for the translucent Tilly, who can utter such lines as "Bad babies come from when a fallen angel squeezes in down there" without eliciting a snicker.

FAKERS

"BEWARE OF FALSE PROPHETS"
MATTHEW 7:15

————●————

The essence of the faker is small-time. Even when the faux religious are trafficking in souls (as opposed to mere money or notoriety), they just don't get the same results the saints or the Antichrists do.

WISE BLOOD (1979). The world Hazel Motes (Brad Dourif) wants to grace with his Church of Christ Without Christ is littered with highway graffiti promising WOE TO THE BLASPHEMERS and graves embellished with 3-D phones and signs informing you that JESUS CALLED. Every last misfit in town wants a piece of the redemption

RELIGION
BLESS THE BEASTS AND CHILDREN: GREAT RELIGIOUS CEREMONIES AND RITUALS IN THE MOVIES

————●————

Move over, Margaret Mead: there's almost as much anthropology in movie weddings as there is in a Jackie Mason routine. Take, for example, the marriage of Julie Andrews and Christopher Plummer in *The Sound of Music;* it's the ultimate Aryan fantasy—and anti-Nazi too. There's also *The Deer Hunter,* with its western Pennsylvania/Eastern Orthodox nuptial bash: a showcase of quaint customs and omens of death. And who can forget the "Sunrise, Sunset" wedding in *Fiddler on the Roof?*

Other bridal exotica: the drugged bride *(Sixteen Candles),* the fainting bride *(Mystic Pizza),* and, most memorable of all, the stolen bride—Katharine Ross in *The Graduate,* whose escape from church with Dustin Hoffman is made possible by a well-placed cross that locks the congregation inside.

The wedding in *The Godfather* is eclipsed, in measures of heavenly outrage, by the christening of Michael Corleone's godson: Francis Coppola artfully crosscuts the ceremony with the slaughter of Michael's enemies. The horrors of baptism Protestant-style are evoked via flashback in *Midnight Cowboy* when Jon Voight confronts a religious nut case.

action—"Goddamn Jesus hog," hisses the wanna-be blind preacher (Harry Dean Stanton) when Motes tries to muscle in on his territory. Even Motes's pared-down vision of a church "where the blind don't see and the lame don't walk and what's dead stays that way" seems to be just another scam when a guitar-playing hustler (Ned Beatty) informs him, "Listen, friend, you got some good ideas. . . . All we gotta do is promote." Directed with bleak humor by John Huston; based on the novel by Flannery O'Connor.

ANITA KUNZ

MONTY PYTHON'S LIFE OF BRIAN

(1979). A star hurtles across the sky and three wise men make their way to a humble stable, where they announce to a startled new mother that they wish to pay homage to her babe. " 'Omage?" she shrieks. "You're drunk—it's disgusting." This is Monty Python at its finest, a romp through ancient Palestine guaranteed to offend just about everyone. Brian (the late Graham Chapman) is the unluckiest of men—an unwilling con, born to be mistaken for the Son of God in a salvation-hungry land abounding with false prophets ("There shall in that time . . . be a great confusion as to where things really are," raves one, "and nobody will really know where lieth those little things with the sort of raffia-work base that has an attachment"). Pilate has a speech impediment; lepers bitch about being cured and thus deprived of their begging potential "without so much as a by-your-leave." And when a capacity crowd can't make out what the real Jesus is preaching, a confused onlooker explains that "Blessed are the cheese makers" is "not meant to be taken *literally*. It refers to any manufacturers of dairy products."

ELMER GANTRY

(1960). "Like it or not, we're in competition with the entertainment business," says one minister to another in this raucous look at the underbelly of the evangelist m o v e m e n t, based on the Sinclair Lewis novel. Burt Lancaster is Elmer, a coarse drifter on the make, and Jean Simmons the more complex Sister Sharon Falconer, a refined evangelist in partnership with a man who talks about "scoring touchdowns for Jesus." They make quite a pair—"like two cops working over a criminal," says Sister Sharon's manager after one of their tent revivals causes a man to bark with great urgency. Subtlety is not one of the movie's virtues. When Sister Sharon takes Elmer for a peek at her larger-than-life revolving crucifix, she demands, "What have you got to match that?" and his leering answer is to jump her—but in light of more recent evangelical history, it now seems frighteningly prescient.

MARJOE (1972). Marjoe Gortner, whose given name is a combination of Mary and Joseph, started preaching at the tender age of three. This odd documentary intercuts home movies of "the world's youngest evangelist" (his mother/coach would call out "Oh, Jesus!" if he wasn't whipping folks into a frenzy fast enough) with footage of the grown-up Marjoe, who's looking for a way out of the preaching racket (during off-hours, Gortner wears tie-dyed shirts and love beads). He finds it by confessing on film that he doesn't believe in God and never has. To thoroughly seal his fate, Gortner shows the film crew the backstage tricks of his trade—how to talk in tongues, fake a healing, or get your very own stigmata. There's a repellent smugness to the message, but much is forgiven when Gortner lays hands on a dog for the benefit of his giggling girlfriend: "This *dog* wasn't walking like this before. . . . This *dog* was in a wheelchair. . . . Brothers and sisters, open your hearts and your purses, behold *this dog*. It's a miracle!"

THE MIRACLE OF THE BELLS (1948). Yes, it's contrived; yes, it can be silly and sentimental. But who cares when you get to hear Lee J. Cobb as a muckety-muck film director sourly discounting the PR value of the titular miracle with the observation, "Do you think for one moment that *God* is interested in selling movies for me?" But that, in fact, seems exactly His design. Or at least that of a fast-talking Hollywood agent. Fred MacMurray plays a man who isn't above a little hocus-pocus when it comes to promoting the first (and last) movie of a dead starlet he once loved. Cobb is reluctant to release a picture that fea-

tures a literal has-been and is unimpressed by the press agent's classy argument against shelving it: "Kind of mean for a girl to have two funerals—one for her body, one for her soul." So MacMurray (with the aid of an astonishingly fresh-faced Frank Sinatra as a small-town priest) sets out to stage a press event to rival that of the greatest promoters of all—the Apostles.

ANTICHRISTS

"O GENERATION OF VIPERS"
MATTHEW 3:7

———————●———————

These people mean business, and they aren't much good for laughs. What they are good for is nightmares. By my lights, devil movies are far more terrifying than anything Hitchcock ever did.

THE NIGHT OF THE HUNTER (1955). Robert Mitchum carries a proverb on his tongue and a switchblade in his pocket as Harry Powell, the man who marries rich widows, then slits their throats in God's name—"the religion the Almighty worked out betwixt Him and me." Shelley Winters is the gullible widow whose son and daughter are reluctant to come clean and tell nice Mr. Powell where their real daddy hid the $10,000 he'd stolen. Movies don't come much scarier than this. "Don't he never sleep?" the boy asks when the killer's shadow won't go away. Seen through the eyes of the children, it's a voyage down memory lane, back to a time when the bogeyman could be living in your very own home.

THE RULING CLASS (1972). "I am the absolute unknowable righteous

RELIGION

BLESS THE BEASTS AND CHILDREN: GREAT RELIGIOUS CEREMONIES AND RITUALS IN THE MOVIES

———●———

In *The Apprenticeship of Duddy Kravitz,* Richard Dreyfuss hires a British film director to record the bar mitzvah of a wealthy relative. Instead of a sentimental home movie, the Brit comes up with an ethnographic documentary, juxtaposing shots of the bar mitzvah with a graphically detailed circumcision and African tribal dances.

Luis Buñuel's *The Discreet Charm of the Bourgeoisie* gives the ritual of last rites a new twist. A dying gardener confesses to a monsignor that in his youth he killed his employers, and he points to a photo of the victims, a young couple. The monsignor suddenly realizes that he has stumbled upon the murderer of his parents. He blesses the peasant, then takes a rifle and shoots him.

Funerals on film run from the sacred to the profane. Few images are as lyrical as that of the dead, naked Indonesian child, surrounded by flowers, being ritually washed by his disconsolate mother in *The Year of Living Dangerously.* The New Orleans French Quarter procession that starts off *Live and Let Die* is a little jazzier. The coffin, we soon discover, is empty—that is, until a freshly murdered body fills it.

BY HOWARD KARREN

eternal lord of hosts, king of kings, lord of lords," chants Peter O'Toole as Jack, the fourteenth Earl of Gurney. "His lordship," counters his shrink, "is a paranoid schizophrenic." England ("this teeming womb of privilege," Jack's father calls it) and its aristocrats are mercilessly lampooned in this story of what happens when a sweet-tempered madman who hangs from his crucifix before tea comes into his inheritance. What happens, of course, is that everyone is terribly polite. "Yes, he's a nut case," admits Jack's manservant. "Most of these titled fleabags are." The joke quickly turns nasty, however, when Jack is "cured"—turned into his namesake, the Ripper. His friends and family think that this newly vicious fruitcake, given to bussing women's hands before stabbing them and to delivering long tirades about a God who "flays, stabs, and mutilates," is, at long last, one of them.

CARRIE (1976). This gothic confection brought new meaning to that horrid expression "the curse." Poor Carrie (Sissy Spacek)—becoming a woman *and* the Devil's tool on the very same day couldn't have been easy. Imagine the PMS the telekinetic teen would have had to look forward to if prom night hadn't come along. From Carrie's sex-craved, Bible-toting mom (Piper Laurie) to the seniors with the bitchinest bods (Nancy Allen and Amy Irving), almost everyone in Brian De Palma's world has at least a touch of evil, and so, naturally, they burn for it. The only clear-cut exception, the nice gym teacher (Betty Buckley), gets sliced in two for her decency.

THE EXORCIST (1973). After years of second-rate devil spawn, it's surprising to go back and see just how good this, the mother of them all, actually is. And how creepy. Even if you laugh at the by-now-clichéd green vomit, it's impossible to munch popcorn with an entirely light heart. Especially since this Devil bears no resemblance whatsoever to the elegant period piece from kinder, gentler movies—the gentleman who made neat and tidy bets for souls and didn't seem all that formidable an adversary. Instead, this Lucifer is he who can cause a twelve-year old to pee on the floor, call priests "cocksucker," and masturbate with a crucifix—the biggest gross-out king of all.

———————⬤———————

DIRECTORS' CHOICE II

BY HOWARD KARREN AND SCOTT IMMERGUT

PETER BOGDANOVICH

———●———

The man who made the 1971 documentary *Directed by John Ford,* who angrily defended his idol Orson Welles from the questions of authorship in Pauline Kael's essay "Raising Kane," and who in *The Last Picture Show* heralded the death of American innocence by showing a clip from Howard Hawks's *Red River* is a man who knows the work of great directors intimately. Here are three outstanding examples he suggests for home viewing.

RIO BRAVO (1959). Before dying out in the late '60s, the western genre reached levels of consummate purity, and this is a fine example. Far more morally complex and more thoughtfully shot than Fred Zinnemann's flashy art-of-the-cinema primer *High Noon* (which it is said to be a response to), this tense Howard Hawks drama has two surprises: a young Ricky Nelson, with riveting blue eyes, contentedly strumming his guitar, and Dean Martin giving a subtle, accomplished performance. Nelson's gunslinger and Martin's drunk deputy join the inde-

scribable Walter Brennan in helping sheriff John Wayne (in top form) uphold the principle of The Law against a band of thugs who are terrorizing the townsfolk. Though the color is glorious, this is a microcosmic western without grand landscapes, and in many ways, it's perfect for home video—the choreography of the fights and the dramatic precision of the character conflicts will have you watching scenes over and over.

THE QUIET MAN (1952). During this movie's climactic, epic fistfight—between Sean Thornton (John Wayne), a former boxer who has returned to his birthplace in Ireland to live a peaceful, domestic life, and "Red" Will Danaher (Victor McLaglen), a powerful local bully—an old man being given last rites hears the ruckus outside, gets out of bed, and hurries off to catch the excitement firsthand. (The old man is played by director John Ford's brother Francis, who, ironically enough, died soon after the movie was released.) Though *The Quiet Man* is a nostalgic vision of Ireland in the 1920s, it's rich with details that transcend its sentimental theme. Filmed in lustrous color, it features a radiant Maureen O'Hara as Mary

Kate Danaher, McLaglen's feisty sister and Wayne's heartthrob.

GRAND ILLUSION (1937). The films made by Jean Renoir in France during the 1930s *(Grand Illusion, La Chienne, Boudu Saved From Drowning, The Crime of Monsieur Lange, The Rules of the Game)* are collectively one of the high points in movie history, and *Grand Illusion,* the story of prisoners of war, is the sweetest and the saddest of the group. The time is World War I, and the theme is the decline of aristocracy, with its gentlemanly code of honor, and the rise of the democratic spirit. On one side is Erich von Stroheim, as the German officer who heads the POW camp, a heroic soldier who detests the pettiness of his role as administrator; on the other side is Jean Gabin, as a French lieutenant with humble roots, a strong sense of camaraderie, and a mission: to escape. The two stars are ineffably good, and the various acting styles of the cast mix together to casual perfection.

SPIKE LEE

———————●———————

The maverick Spike Lee here does the right thing by his devoted audience, and recommends three dramatic representations of urban life and strife.

PIXOTE (1981). Before Hector Babenco made *Kiss of the Spider Woman* (and then shuffled up to Albany to make *Ironweed*), he co-wrote and directed this unforgettable Brazilian story about an amoral ten-year-old urchin, Pixote (pronounced pee-*shote*), who learns to survive on the streets of São Paulo and Rio de Janeiro. The movie has been compared to Italian neorealist masterworks and Luis Buñuel's *Los Olvidados,* yet Babenco's film has less deliberate pathos than the former and fewer self-conscious flourishes than the latter—it takes a levelheaded approach to its explosive subject. Pixote (Fernando Ramos da Silva), younger than most juvenile delinquents, quickly graduates from the horrors of reform school to drug-dealing to a strange relationship with a prostitute (Marília Pera). Da Silva (shot dead by police in 1987 at the age of nineteen) is mesmerizing —his face alternately worldly, childlike, masklike, transparent.

RAGING BULL (1980). If you thought it was impossible for director Martin Scorsese and actor Robert De Niro to exceed the operatic power of *Taxi Driver,* this is proof to the contrary. The hero of *Raging Bull*—former middleweight boxing champion Jake LaMotta—has more complex shadings than *Taxi Driver*'s psychopath, Travis Bickle, yet he's equally obsessed with achieving greatness and redeeming himself. LaMotta's anger and frustration surface episodically— in fights with his wives and in the ring —and build in rhythmic crescendos, intensifying the biographical narrative into an epic of self-destruction and spiritual grace. De Niro trained for the fights and then gained fifty pounds to portray LaMotta as a middle-aged mess. But the key to the movie's greatness is not the technical mastery of either the actor or the director but the poetry they produce with it. De Niro's performance is an emotional roller coaster; Scorsese and cinematographer Michael Chapman's black-and-white images of water and violently flashing lights, '40s nightclubs and stark New York streets, will grab a permanent place in your mind's eye.

WEST SIDE STORY (1961). The *Romeo and Juliet* story of Puerto Ricans and whites in New York's urban jungle is decent enough, but when you add in the electrifying combination of Jerome Robbins's choreography and Leonard Bernstein's score, *West Side Story* rises to the top ranks of musicals. Robert Wise's production is competent, and Natalie Wood and Richard Beymer are a glamorous Maria and Tony. Neither Wood nor Beymer is actually singing, of course, but no matter—the songs ("Maria," "Tonight," "Somewhere") will still exhilarate you. The hiphop generation, however, may not understand just how revolutionary Robbins's mix of athletic prowess, balletic grace, and modern-dance vocabulary was at the time.

NORMAN JEWISON

●

Below are three solid American classics recommended by a director whose diverse output includes prestigious adaptations *(A Soldier's Story, Agnes of God)*, inventive comedies *(The Russians Are Coming, The Russians are Coming, Moonstruck)*, and tense dramas *(The Cincinnati Kid, In the Heat of the Night)*.

THE GRAPES OF WRATH (1940). John Ford's timeless adaptation of the John Steinbeck novel poignantly captures the anguish of one of the most troubled times in American history—the Great Depression. The story follows a family of sharecroppers, the Joads, as they leave their overworked dust-bowl farm in Oklahoma for presumably greener pastures in California. After an arduous journey (two family members die along the way), the Joads discover that the only jobs available in their new home are as migrant farm workers—the absolute lowest rung on the social ladder. Henry Fonda, as Tom Joad, gives one of the best performances of his career; Jane Darwell, as Ma Joad, the emotional anchor of the family, won the Best Supporting Actress Oscar; and John Carradine, as Casey, the former preacher who calls for better working conditions, sets a great example for his three actor sons (David, Keith, and Robert). The stark, beautiful cinematography is by *Citizen Kane*'s Gregg Toland.

THE TREASURE OF THE SIERRA MADRE (1948). Although it was a box office bomb when it was released, John Huston's examination of fear and greed among Americans stranded in Mexico during a prospecting expedition is without doubt one of his finest films. The eclectic cast includes Humphrey Bogart as the born-loser-turned-psychopath Fred C. Dobbs (a marked departure from his *Casablanca* stereotype, which for some explained the movie's commercial failure), Walter Huston as the prospector Howard (he was reportedly forced to play the role sans dentures by his son), and Tim Holt as the boyish, naive Curtin. Max Steiner's overwhelming score sounds as if it belongs with a spaghetti western, but see *The Treasure of the Sierra Madre* if for no other reason than to hear Alfonso Bedoya utter the now classic line "Badges? . . . I don't have to show you no stinkin' badges!" Both Hustons won Oscars.

IT'S A WONDERFUL LIFE (1946). This Frank Capra classic, even in its colorized form (which you should avoid—the black-and-white is far lovelier), never fails to tug at the heartstrings. James Stewart stars as

George Bailey ("Do you want the moon, Mary?"), the man who is given a chance to see what the world would be like without him and thereby realizes the impact every individual makes on those around him. "I thought it was the greatest film I ever made," says Capra in his autobiography, *Frank Capra: The Name Above the Title.* "Better yet, I thought it was the greatest film *anybody* ever made." Capra's modesty notwithstanding, by the end of 1947 *It's a Wonderful Life* had largely been forgotten, but thanks to repeated yuletide airings on television, it has gained a following that has grown into nothing short of a cultural phenomenon.

JOHN SAYLES

Novelist-filmmaker John Sayles, who established his reputation with such low-budget gabfests as *Return of the Secaucus Seven* and *Lianna,* surprised us by recommending three action-oriented Asian classics. Two other films mentioned by Sayles, Ermanno Olmi's *Il posto* and Mario Monicelli's *I campagni,* are unavailable on cassette.

YOJIMBO (1961). The legendary Toshiro Mifune, as a wandering samurai in early-nineteenth-century Japan, arrives at a village in which two feuding merchants live. Each is willing to pay him to take his side, but the samurai, forever aloof, instead incites an orgy of violence that annihilates both parties, while he walks away unscathed. This spirited Akira Kurosawa adventure so brilliantly adapted the themes and style of the American western that it was inevitable it would end up reincarnated—as Sergio Leone's *A Fistful of Dollars,* starring Clint Eastwood

(Kurosawa's *The Seven Samurai* had already been copied by *The Magnificent Seven*). For those who know Kurosawa only for the majesty of his later epics *Kagemusha* and *Ran,* the lively satire of *Yojimbo* is a must.

RED BEARD (1965). How to be a good doctor, Japanese style: Akira Kurosawa once again places his favorite lead, Toshiro Mifune, in Japanese history; here he plays an experienced doctor in a public clinic in the early 1800s who teaches a young intern the nonmedical skills and sacrifices required by their chosen profession. The three-hour-plus running time is tough going for some, but master storyteller Kurosawa weaves together the several subplots with plenty of action and pathos.

ENTER THE DRAGON (1973). Martial arts wizard Bruce Lee (who played Kato on television's *The Green Hornet*) died weeks before this showcase of his remarkable talent reached the screen. An American co-production, *Enter the Dragon* is the best kung fu picture of its day. Lee plays a secret agent who attends a martial arts contest in an island fortress. His aim: to nab the contest's sponsor, the evil Han, and to avenge his sister, who killed herself when threatened with rape by Han's right-hand man. Lee's English is embarrassing, but his action scenes will impress die-hard skeptics, the flying bodies creating an effect that's perilously close to screwball comedy.

BARRY LEVINSON

The writer-director of *Diner, Tin Men,* and *Avalon,* and director of *Good Morning, Vietnam* and *Rain Man,*

Barry Levinson has always been a keen interpreter of the futility—and the humor—of his characters' ambitions.

PATHS OF GLORY (1962). Many years before Peter Weir made *Gallipoli,* Stanley Kubrick dramatized how French soldiers on the front lines in World War I were ordered forth by their upper-class superiors to certain and pointless slaughter, and *Paths of Glory* (which was once banned in France) still has the power to shock today, even in the post–*Full Metal Jacket* era. In fact, *Jacket*'s long tracking shots of boot camp Marines standing at attention are the direct descendants of Kubrick's experimentation with long dolly shots through the trenches in *Paths of Glory.* Complementing Kubrick's direction is a magnificent performance by Kirk Douglas, as the colonel ordered to lead his men into a battle he knows they cannot win.

RAISING ARIZONA (1987). This is a cartoon-inspired fantasy joyride from Joel and Ethan Coen (co-writer–director and co-writer–producer, respectively), the stylishly warped minds behind *Miller's Crossing.* Nicolas Cage and a then unknown Holly Hunter star as newlyweds H.I. and Edwina McDonnough; he's a convicted convenience-store klepto, she's a cop, and they get chummy over the course of H.I.'s arrests. Edwina desperately wants a child, and after several unsuccessful (and hilarious) attempts at conception, she talks H.I. into kidnapping one of the famous Arizona quintuplets, figuring that since there are so many of them, the parents won't notice. Great supporting performances from former boxer Randall "Tex" Cobb, as the apocalyptic biker, and John Goodman and William Forsythe as H.I.'s prison buddies.

THE PRODUCERS (1968). Mel Brooks's first feature is arguably his best. Zero Mostel plays Max Bialystock, a has-been theater producer desperately hoping to revive his career. When his meek accountant, Leo Bloom (Gene Wilder), offhandedly points out that by overcollecting from investors and then producing a flop he'd never have to pay back the surplus cash, Bialystock jumps at the idea and convinces Bloom to be his co-producer. After an exhaustive search for the worst play ever written, the two finally settle on *Springtime for Hitler,* a cheerful musical celebration of Der Führer, featuring aerial views of dancing swastikas and a drug-crazed Dick Shawn in the title role. But as Max and Leo watch in horror, their surefire flop turns into a comedy smash. "It has a very good balance of story and character," says Mel Brooks today of *The Producers'* enduring popularity. "Leo Bloom, who leads a prosaic, plebeian, run-of-the-mill life, lives with a glimmer, a dream of glory. I think it is a very common dream."

An offer he couldn't refuse: Francis Coppola was unable to come up with a definitive list, so instead he recommended *any* movie directed by Akira Kurosawa, Preston Sturges, Alfred Hitchcock, Lewis Milestone, or Raoul Walsh.

CONTRIBUTORS

JACK BARTH is the author of *American Quest* and *Roadside Hollywood*.

SHEILA BENSON is the film critic of the *Los Angeles Times*.

PETER BISKIND is an executive editor of PREMIERE and the author of *The Godfather Companion* and *Seeing Is Believing: How Hollywood Taught Us to Stop Worrying and Love the Fifties*.

PETER BLAUNER is the author of *Slow Motion Riot*, to be published in May by William Morrow.

JOHN CLARK is the copy editor of PREMIERE.

CHRISTOPHER CONNELLY is a senior editor of PREMIERE and the host of MTV's *The Big Picture*.

DAVID DENBY is the film critic of *New York* magazine and a columnist at PREMIERE.

HOWARD GENSLER is a freelance writer living in Philadelphia.

OWEN GLEIBERMAN is the film critic of *Entertainment Weekly*.

J. HOBERMAN is the film critic of *The Village Voice* and a columnist at PREMIERE.

ELLEN HOPKINS is a freelance writer living in New York.

SCOTT IMMERGUT, formerly an associate editor of PREMIERE, is a creative executive at Hollywood Pictures.

HOWARD KARREN is a senior editor of PREMIERE.

BETH LAPIDES AND GREGORY MILLER live and work together in Los Angeles; Lapides is a comedian/performance artist and Miller is a screenwriter.

MICHAEL McWILLIAMS is the television critic of *The Detroit News* and author of *TV Sirens: A Tantalizing Look at Prime Time's Fabulous Females*.

JAMIE MALANOWSKI is the national editor of *Spy* magazine and a frequent contributor to PREMIERE.

ROB MEDICH is an associate editor of PREMIERE.

TERRI MINSKY is PREMIERE's contributing editor.

MARJORIE ROSEN is a senior writer at *People* and the author of *Popcorn Venus: Women, Movies, and the American Dream*.

LUC SANTE is the author of *Low Life*.

ED SIKOV is the author of *Screwball: Hollywood's Madcap Romantic Comedies*.

JOE W. SMITH is a story analyst at Twentieth Century Fox.

MITCH TUCHMAN is the managing editor of the Los Angeles County Museum of Art and co-author of *Painters Painting*, a book based on the documentary film.

MASON WILEY is a syndicated video columnist and co-author of *Inside Oscar: The Unofficial History of the Academy Awards*.

MICHAEL ZIMBALIST is a writer-producer based in Los Angeles.

THE
GREATEST
MOVIES
OF THE
'80s

THE VOTES

—————•—————

At the end of 1989, PREMIERE magazine asked a group of film world notables (in tandem with the magazine's top editors) to pick the ten best movies of the '80s. The lists below (with one exception) are in descending order; the top choice was awarded ten points, the next nine points, and so on, down to the last, with one point. Except for titles followed by an asterisk (★), all films were released commercially in New York City or Los Angeles between January 1, 1980, and August 31, 1989.

DAVID DENBY
New York/PREMIERE
Wings of Desire
The Night of the Shooting Stars
E.T. The Extra-Terrestrial
Shoah
Ran
Hannah and Her Sisters
Salvador
Melvin and Howard
Local Hero
Dressed to Kill

J. HOBERMAN
The Village Voice/PREMIERE
Shoah
Raging Bull
Sans Soleil
Blue Velvet
The '80s
From the Pole to the Equator
Danton
Wings of Desire
Dust in the Wind
Diary for My Children

ROGER EBERT
Siskel & Ebert
Raging Bull
The Right Stuff
E.T. The Extra-Terrestrial
Do the Right Thing
My Dinner With Andre
Raiders of the Lost Ark
Ran
Mississippi Burning
Platoon
House of Games

GENE SISKEL
Siskel & Ebert
Raging Bull
Shoah
The Right Stuff
My Dinner With Andre
Who Framed Roger Rabbit
Do the Right Thing
Once Upon a Time in America
Moonlighting
Sid & Nancy
Kagemusha

SHEILA BENSON
Los Angeles Times
Fanny and Alexander
Blue Velvet
Heimat
Wings of Desire
Hannah and Her Sisters
Little Dorrit
Tucker: The Man and His Dream
Raging Bull
E.T. The Extra-Terrestrial
Down by Law

ANDREW SARRIS
New York Observer
Berlin Alexanderplatz
Boyfriends and Girlfriends
The Singing Detective
After the Rehearsal
A Nos Amours
Thérèse
L'Argent
Empire of the Sun
Housekeeping
Full Metal Jacket

DAVID ANSEN
Newsweek
The Night of the Shooting Stars
Atlantic City
Fanny and Alexander
Terms of Endearment
Hope and Glory
Hannah and Her Sisters
E.T. The Extra-Terrestrial
My Beautiful Laundrette
Entre Nous
Dreamchild

LAWRENCE COHN
Motion picture editor, *Variety*
Fanny and Alexander
Kagemusha
E.T. The Extra-Terrestrial
Das Boot
A Room With a View
Tess
Man of Iron
Wings of Desire
Fitzcarraldo
Breaker Morant

JIM JARMUSCH
Writer/director
Raging Bull
Love Streams
On Top of the Whale★
Dead Ringers
The Road Warrior
Toute une nuit
Do the Right Thing
The Hit

The Evil Dead
The State of Things

JOHN PATRICK SHANLEY
Writer/director
When Father Was Away on Business
Do the Right Thing
My Life as a Dog
Blue Velvet
Babette's Feast
Dangerous Liaisons
Paris, Texas
My Dinner With Andre
Tess
Brazil

LAWRENCE KASDAN
Writer/director
(in alphabetical order; one point each)
Babette's Feast
Back to the Future
Das Boot
Diner
Hope and Glory
Lawrence of Arabia (director's cut)
Local Hero
The Long Good Friday
Platoon
The Road Warrior

RICHARD PRICE
Writer
Raging Bull
Wings of Desire
Stranger Than Paradise
Danton
The Thin Blue Line
Blue Velvet
Death of a Soldier
Carmen
True Confessions
The Untouchables

MIKE MEDAVOY
Chairman,
Tri-Star Pictures
Amadeus
Platoon
The Killing Fields

Witness
Hannah and Her Sisters
E.T. The Extra-Terrestrial
Risky Business
Mississippi Burning
Dead Poets Society
The Unbearable Lightness of Being

DON SIMPSON
Producer
Raging Bull
Terms of Endearment
Tootsie
Platoon
Stand By Me
The Big Chill
Mona Lisa
Tin Men
Big
The Road Warrior

STEPHEN HARVEY
Associate curator, Museum of Modern Art, New York
Raging Bull
Three Brothers
Ran
Prizzi's Honor
Wings of Desire
Local Hero
Broadway Danny Rose
Distant Voices, Still Lives
La Nuit de Varennes
Au Revoir les enfants

RICHARD PEÑA
Program director, Film Society of Lincoln Center
L'Argent
Berlin Alexanderplatz
Francisca★
Passion
The Three Crowns of the Sailor★
Blue Velvet
Himatsuri
Yellow Earth★
Memories of Prison
Blade Runner

HELGA STEPHENSON
Executive director, Festival of Festivals, Toronto
Dead Ringers
This Is Spinal Tap
Dangerous Liaisons
Veronika Voss
Wings of Desire
Mephisto
The King of Comedy
Blue Velvet
House of Games
Tangos, the Exile of Gardel

SUSAN LYNE
Editor/publication director, PREMIERE
Raging Bull
Platoon
The Unbearable Lightness of Being
Shoot the Moon
Wings of Desire
Who Framed Roger Rabbit
Diner
Local Hero
The Killing Fields
E.T. The Extra-Terrestrial

PETER BISKIND
Executive editor, PREMIERE
Salvador
RoboCop
The Road Warrior
Who Framed Roger Rabbit
Zelig
Sid & Nancy
Tootsie
Raging Bull
Reds
Once Upon a Time in America

DEBORAH PINES
Executive editor, PREMIERE
E.T. The Extra-Terrestrial
Rain Man
Witness
Sophie's Choice
Au Revoir les enfants
Out of Africa

Dangerous Liaisons
A Soldier's Story
Blue Velvet
Platoon

JILL KEARNEY
West Coast editor, PREMIERE
Raging Bull
Wings of Desire
The Shining
The King of Comedy
Parting Glances
Pixote
Things Change
The Kitchen Toto
The Dead
sex, lies, and videotape

CHRISTOPHER CONNELLY
Senior editor, PREMIERE
Raising Arizona
Local Hero
Who Framed Roger Rabbit

The Big Chill
Matewan
Lili Marleen
Terms of Endearment
48 Hrs.
The Natural
Zelig

HOWARD KARREN
Senior editor, PREMIERE
Raging Bull
Once Upon a Time in America
The Road Warrior
Hannah and Her Sisters
Law of Desire
Prizzi's Honor
Dreamchild
The Terminator
Blue Velvet
Cutter's Way

COMPILED BY KITTY BOWE HEARTY

THE WINNERS

—●—

REVIEWED BY THE EDITORS AND STAFF OF PREMIERE

1.

105 POINTS

RAGING BULL (1980). In *Taxi Driver,* director Martin Scorsese makes a brief appearance as a passenger in Robert De Niro's cab; the man tells De Niro (the near-psychotic Travis Bickle) how women enrage him and directs the cabbie to look at the proof of his wife's infidelity: erotic shadows on an apartment window shade. In *Raging Bull,* there is no proof; boxing champion Jake LaMotta's misogynistic eruptions are groundless—the insane symptoms of raw, untamable desire. The movie, the story of LaMotta's rise and fall (based on his autobiography), is so emotionally extreme, yet so icily controlled, it's hard to imagine how Scorsese and De Niro can ever top their work here; *Raging Bull* is a monument of the American cinema, undoubtedly the finest movie of the '80s. For his performance as La-Motta, De Niro sports a swollen nose and a convincing boxer's physique (he also gained more than fifty pounds to play LaMotta as a middle-aged failure). The intensity of his acting will make you forget the self-conscious Method poses of his work elsewhere,

and it obliterates any possibility of class condescension toward the hopelessly boorish LaMotta. The fight scenes—some of them historic—are apocalyptic battles, punctuated with slow-motion close-ups of battered faces; ballistic sound effects; and the relentless, searing, strobelike flashes of photographers' lights. Framing the fights, and supplying a refreshingly unpsychoanalytic motivation for La-Motta's rage, are his perverse relationships with women (two wives and an underaged siren in Miami). Scorsese directs this episodic tale with the spiritual grace of a half-crazy prophet (a quality less in evidence in his *Last Temptation of Christ*). Michael Chapman's black-and-white cinematography is flawless; the movie's beautiful, painful images perfectly formalize La-Motta's torment—blood splattering the audience at the boxing ring; Cathy Moriarty, as his teenage second wife, kissing his rippled stomach; LaMotta courting her beside a miniature-golf-course church; the aging boxer bellowing and ramming his head against a stone wall in jail. The viewer witnesses these events like a priest listening to a confession. It's only the fragmented, subjective evidence of a man's life, but, as is true in all great works of art, that incomplete reality is all you need to know.

(Howard Karren)

2.

59 POINTS

WINGS OF DESIRE (1988). It's hard to imagine how a foreign art film with angels, a trapeze artist, and Columbo (Peter Falk as himself) could become one of the most popular and acclaimed movies of the decade, but then *Wings of Desire* is unlike any movie you've seen in this decade or any other. Director Wim Wenders fashions the black-and-white cinematography of the renowned Henri Alékan into a vision of Berlin as poetic as the film's cadenced narration. The camera circles the bombed-out skeleton of Kaiser Wilhelm Memorial church and glides alongside unsuspecting straphangers on a subway train, the air abuzz with a symphony of whispers; an old woman frets about her next rent payment while a young man chooses to end his worries with suicide. It's the angels' job to listen to these nameless voices, to "observe, collect, testify and preserve," but one of them, played by Bruno Ganz, is losing interest. Yearning to escape the weightlessness of eternity, he chooses to enter the mortal world of color, gravity, and history. Ganz is a consummate actor; his elegance as an angel is matched by his enthusiasm as a human when he revels in the taste of coffee and is mesmerized by Marion the trapeze artist and the brilliant redness of her lips. In his greatest work since *Kings of the Road* (1976), Wenders finally resolves the alienation and wanderlust of his earlier films as well as his preoccupation with American culture. Transporting the dramatic love story of *Paris, Texas* home to Berlin, he imbues it with a resonance of mythic proportions. As Marion says to Wenders's "fallen" angel: "There is no greater story than ours, that of a man and a woman."

(Caroline Kirk)

3.

46 POINTS

E.T. THE EXTRA-TERRESTRIAL (1982). What is there to say about the cute little feller who was too spaced out to phone home? Three hundred and sixty-eight million dollars (it's the biggest-grossing film ever) can't be all wrong. Steven Spielberg's feel-good fable gave aliens an uplift at a time when Reagan and the Reaganauts were riding high and the only good alien was a documented worker scrubbing Nancy's floors. Spielberg's direct line to the American aorta and Carlo Rambaldi's special effects made the ugly-adorable little extraterrestrial an instant cult hero, who appealed as much to baby boomers as to their children. Henry Thomas is wonderful as the boy who befriends E.T.; ditto Peter Coyote as the only adult over thirty he can trust. Spielberg's fable of suburbia, California-style, can tell grown-ups a lot about America in the '80s, but kids relate directly to the plot and the characters with startling, visceral immediacy. *(Peter Biskind)*

4.

40 POINTS

BLUE VELVET (1986). "It's a strange world," says innocent young Jeffrey Beaumont (Kyle MacLachlan), and he ought to know. When he finds a severed human ear in a field near his house, the polite college kid goes straight to the police—but the detective's strangely blasé reaction and his own childlike curiosity eventually prompt him to get to the bottom of the mystery himself. At the heart of it is "the blue lady," Dorothy Vallens (Isabella Rossellini), a foreign nightclub singer who's being terrorized by a gang of criminals led by the sadistic Frank (Dennis Hopper). One night, Jeffrey sneaks into Dorothy's apartment and hides in her closet; he watches silently as Frank subjects her to fetishistic sexual torture in what appears to be a nightly ritual. Dorothy has to put up with it because Frank has kidnapped her husband and son, but it's clear that she's given in to the cycle of brutality so completely that she thrives on pain. And wholesome Jeffrey, with Dorothy's help, soon surprises himself with his own peculiar capacity for kinkiness. Through the adventures of his clean-cut young hero, director David Lynch uncovers the dark underside of the all-American town of Lumberton, in a film of rare power and poetry. What lies behind the facade is both disturbing and strangely comical (witness heavily pancaked drug dealer Dean Stockwell and his harem of three-hundred-pound lovelies). But it's the hypernormality of the facade itself that gets under your skin—the frighteningly regular moms, the eerily familiar schoolgirls, and the too-red roses that sway in the breeze.

(Christopher Bagley)

5.

29 POINTS

HANNAH AND HER SISTERS (1986). Highbrow they are, Hannah and her brood. A typical exchange: "Do you like Caravaggio?" "Oh, yes. Who doesn't?" Also typical: "It has an organic quality . . . totally interdependent. It breathes." Certainly, that's a highbrow way to describe a building. But really, wouldn't people just be better off dumb as hounds? *Hannah and Her Sisters* reminds us of the pitfalls of human intelligence—the waste products being fear and overanalysis. Mickey (Woody Allen) fears death because he can't confirm the existence of an afterlife; Elliot (Michael Caine), possibly fearing middle age, acts on his lust for Lee (Barbara Hershey), the sister of his selfless wife, Hannah (Mia Farrow); Holly (Dianne Wiest) constantly compares her talent with her relatives' (a Waspy show-business family suffering assorted chemical dependencies) and repeatedly comes up short. Eventually, though, acceptance of self and life (don't worry, be happy) sets these folks straight. What an accomplishment for the Woodman, himself an expert at creating his own problems (but then, few well-adjusted people could craft a film as fine as this). Allen's people—as opposed to mere characters—ring true in every frame, and every frame is meticulously placed. Also priceless: the music (Dixieland jazz, classical, old standards); the "chapter" headings (the most provocative being ". . . Nobody, not even the rain, has such small hands"); and, best of all—so rare in an Allen film—an ending that's thoroughly *happy*. (Rob Medich)

PLATOON (1986). *Platoon* is arguably the best Vietnam movie to come out of Hollywood. It doesn't have the ambition and lunatic epic sweep of *Apocalypse Now* and *The Deer Hunter,* but it fairly crackles with authenticity, the kind of sharply observed detail that can be conferred only by someone who was there. Director Oliver Stone spent a year in Vietnam as a GI, and his film presents a starkly etched picture of what it's like to fight in the jungle. The soundtrack is alive with the hum of insects and drum of rain; Stone's grunts develop bug bites the size of golf balls, blisters on their feet as big as dumplings. And unlike in most war films, instead of fighting the enemy, the soldiers fight each other. One of the best things about *Platoon* (something no other Vietnam film has captured) is the gulf between the Army's druggies—hip, cynical, mostly black—and the boozers, the prowar redneck lifers. *Platoon*'s Army is down, dirty, and stoned, in more ways than one. Nevertheless, the politics of what Stone intended to be an anti-Vietnam War film are ambiguous enough so that there is something for everyone, the Rambos as well as the Ron Kovics. Catch the extraordinary performances of Willem Dafoe, Tom Berenger, and Charlie Sheen.

(Peter Biskind)

6.

28 POINTS

FANNY AND ALEXANDER (1983). Ingmar Bergman draws on the memories of his childhood in turn-of-the-century Sweden for the last and perhaps the greatest film of his illustrious career. In the grand, rich colors of a fairy tale, *Fanny and Alexander* brings to life the world—both magical and horrible—of ten-year-old Alexander. Detailing a mighty struggle between good (the beauty and vigor of Alexander's father's family) and evil (the deformity and sickness of his minister stepfather's), Bergman, in effect, has distilled his own version of Strindberg's *A Dream Play,* in which, as Strindberg wrote, imagination "spins out and weaves new patterns." On one mysterious Christmas Eve, for example, Alexander, sitting in the si-

lence of his family's empty mansion, watches a statue long enough to see it move. Later, when his mother marries the minister who presided over his father's funeral, the dead man watches sadly from the next room. And then, in the fantastic climax, his stepfather's grotesquely obese aunt stumbles from her sickroom in flames and the reverend himself gets burnt to a crisp. Whether or not we believe that these events actually happen, for Bergman, what is imagined is often more powerful and more tangible than what is "real." *(Caroline Kirk)*

7.

26 POINTS

SHOAH (1985). Marcel Ophuls, who directed one Holocaust classic, *The Sorrow and the Pity,* called *Shoah* another—"the greatest documentary about contemporary history ever made." Claude Lanzmann's nine-and-a-half-hour spectacle, which took ten years to complete, documents the nuts and bolts of the Final Solution with interviews of former camp guards—the technicians of extermination, who eagerly describe their work, as if they have only been waiting for someone to ask them. Lanzmann even prevails upon one of them to sing a little ditty called "The Treblinka Song." *Shoah* caused a furor when it came out; it was denounced as anti-Polish for its relentless exposure of Polish anti-Semitism, then and now. And, in fact, the Polish witnesses—peasants, railroad workers—who lived near the camps, watched the boxcars come and go, and occasionally did odd jobs for the Nazis do not come off particularly well. If, as Ophuls remarked, Hitler has always been the fall guy for the German people and their Eastern European allies, *Shoah* restores the balance. Lanzmann has captured the banality of evil with a vengeance.

(Peter Biskind)

WHO FRAMED ROGER RABBIT (1988). It's not often that the year's biggest-grossing movie also turns out to be the best, but it happened in 1988 with *Who Framed Roger Rabbit,* Touchstone's inspired blend of adult animation and live action, which rolled over the competition and, in a crowded field of celebrity rabbits, made a star out of its eponymous hero and household names of his busty wife, Jessica; British actor Bob Hoskins; and an array of loony Toons. Executive-produced by Steven Spielberg, directed by Robert Zemeckis, and animated by a team led by Richard Williams, the noir-ish *Roger* (it's set in '40s Los Angeles and sports a *Chinatown*-type story) copped four Oscars and features cameos by virtually every important cartoon character in movie history, including the incomparable Betty Boop, Bugs Bunny, Dumbo, Tweety Bird, and Mickey. Be sure to catch the brilliant Baby Herman "Maroon Cartoon" at the beginning and the piano duet by Donald and Daffy Duck, and listen for the voice of Kathleen Turner as the sultry Jessica. (Peter Biskind)

8.

25 POINTS

DO THE RIGHT THING (1989). A shapely Puerto Rican woman named Rosie Perez slugs the air in front of her during *Do the Right Thing*'s opening credits. Public Enemy is chanting/yelling "Fight the power! Fight the power!" and explaining why Elvis means nothing to them ("He was a racist / That sucker was simple and plain") while Perez stabs space with her gloved fists. Her skimpy outfits alternate between tight skirts and boxing shorts with bras; her huge earrings swing wildly as she bounces and punches, dances and sweats. Perez is utterly mesmerizing as the seductive and unrelenting warrior. It's an electric beginning to a remarkably powerful film. Spike Lee's *Do the Right Thing* is a virtual explosion of dissatisfaction, faded hope, and strained love in a predominantly black Brooklyn neighborhood. Lee plays Mookie, a deliveryman for a successful pizzeria owned by Danny Aiello, a stubborn Italian. A glistening Korean fruit-and-vegetable market is nearby. But everyone who's black is struggling. When the summer heat grows unbearable and it becomes painfully clear to the black neighbors that they are being beaten into ineffectuality, a riot erupts, bombarding the screen with dazzling scenes of a minirevolution.

(Bruce Bibby)

9.

24 POINTS

THE ROAD WARRIOR (1981). Before there was a "Crocodile" Dundee, girls and boys, Australian director George Miller won the world over by outdoing Hollywood at its own game —the epic action-adventure. *Mad Max,* his movie was called; in it, youthful Mel Gibson led a one-man war of revenge against the sadistic meanies who had killed his family and friends. The sequel, released in the United States as *The Road Warrior,* multiplies the original in almost every way. *Mad Max* was vaguely futuristic; *The Road Warrior* is in postnuclear hell. *Mad Max* was a personal vendetta; *The Road Warrior* is a last-ditch effort to save a civilized community.

Mad Max has motorcycles; *The Road Warrior* had souped-up cars, helicopters, tanklike war machines, and massive trucks. In *Mad Max*, Gibson faced a small squad of goons; in *The Road Warrior*, he battles an army of grotesques in leather wrestling gear. And Miller pulls it off. The script is peppered with snide dialogue and executed with flair, and the wasteland setting is artfully decorated with clever details. *The Road Warrior* is arguably the best B-movie blockbuster ever produced, and the final chase scene, led by Gibson in a semi, is exhilarating. *(Howard Karren)*

10.

20 POINTS

Local Hero (1983). In this comedy written and directed by whimsical Scotsman Bill Forsyth, Peter Riegert is MacIntyre, a young Houston oil executive who is sent to Scotland to buy up an entire coastal village so that it can be replaced with a refinery. Abandoning his one and only love—his sporty car—and his not-so-swinging Texas single life for the lush, green hills of the "old country," Mac is at first bewildered by the village's eccentric inhabitants. But if you're expecting the usual urban vs. rural platitudes, never fear: The humor here is subtly British and refreshingly underplayed. True, the locals marinate Mac's pet bunny, but when they discover his suit pockets are lined with cash, dollar signs flash in their eyes, and they become more than eager to sell out of paradise (as they say, you can't eat the view). The only snag is that Mac, the yuppie, has fallen in love with the place. Burt Lancaster is perfect as his slightly wacko boss, Happer, who's more interested in comets than profits. And besides the great music by Mark Knopfler, there are enough lovely vistas and beautiful beaches to tempt you to bag everything yourself and relocate to the Highlands. *(Jodie Burke)*

Terms of Endearment (1983). Aurora and Emma Greenway have a Krazy Glue kind of mother-daughter bond. While most mothers pray their infants will sleep through the night, Aurora (Shirley MacLaine) awakens baby Emma to make sure she's still breathing. With her only child safely crying, Aurora, relieved, retires to bed. Such are the guts of *Terms of Endearment,* the James L. Brooks film that asks: Does Krazy Glue hold forever? Will loving someone enough let you keep her? Obviously not. As Emma grows up into Debra Winger (who holds her own here), she marries Flap Horton (Jeff Daniels), whose career path takes her away from Mother. The two women use the long-distance phone line like an umbilical cord—right up until the tearjerker ending. MacLaine more than earns her Best Actress Oscar here as she creates her authentic but unique Aurora—a dominating, repressed, and obsessive woman who softens slightly by the end, thanks in no small part to her extroverted, lecherous neighbor (Jack Nicholson). Nicholson, incidentally, again proves that if anyone really deserves the obscene salaries he gets, it is he. Crown this Best Picture winner the king of the "You'll laugh, you'll cry" genre. *(Rob Medich)*

11.

19 POINTS

Berlin Alexanderplatz (1980). Watching this fifteen-and-a-half-hour Rainer Werner Fassbinder saga of prewar Berlin (which was made in one- and two-hour episodes for German television) is like watching an entire season of *Twin Peaks* in one sitting: Some elements might seem overly repetitive, and sequences of prolonged absurdity might start to drag, but the entire effect would be . . . transcendent. No matter how you choose to watch it (and on home video, at least you have some choice), *Berlin Alexanderplatz* is essential viewing for the serious filmgoer. Based on Alfred Döblin's fatalistic novel, it traces the Candide-like journey of Franz Biberkopf, an ex-con who tries to rebuild his life amid the decadence of Weimar Germany. A cinematic poet and showman, Fassbinder weaves a thrillingly complex fabric of unforgettable characters, rhythmic editing, dazzlingly fluid cinematography (by Xaver Schwarzenberger), and haunting music (by Peer Rabin). With Günter Lamprecht, Hanna Schygulla, Barbara Sukowa, and Elisabeth Trissenaar. *(Howard Karren)*

THE NIGHT OF THE SHOOTING STARS (1982). The title refers to the Night of San Lorenzo, during which, Tuscans believe, each shooting star grants a wish. And when, in the opening shot, a shooting star ignites the storybook-blue sky framed by a bedroom window, the movie's narrator makes her wish—to find the right words to tell her sleeping baby about a Night of San Lorenzo that occurred many years ago. Thus she begins, recounting her experience as a six-year-old during the final days of World War II in the town of San Martino. To escape the vengeful and desperate bombings of the occupying Nazis, the town's remaining citizens (old men, women, and children) head off on a journey to meet the advancing Allies. This remembered "night" of San Lor-

enzo is actually several days and encompasses both horrible and pathetic moments: A crazed, sadistic fifteen-year-old Blackshirt lures some peasants to their deaths, then yelps like a terrified puppy when he meets his own; the narrator's mother strikes her and squeals "Bitch! Bitch!" when the little girl sits on the group's precious basket of eggs. There are moments of triumph, too, such as when a friend of the narrator's, dressed in shining Roman armor, slays a vicious Blackshirt with a score of spears. And it is precisely these fantastic yet objective memories, filtered through a six-year-old's point of view, that fulfill the narrator's wish. Directed by Paolo and Vittorio Taviani. *(Caroline Kirk)*

12.

18 POINTS

RAN (1985). According to director Akira Kurosawa, his three-hour epic *Kagemusha* (1980) was just a dress rehearsal for *Ran,* the most expensive Japanese movie ever made and certainly the crowning masterpiece of Kurosawa's legendary cinematic career. Having already led Tatsuya Nakadai through *Kagemusha,* Kurosawa takes the actor to tragic extremes in the role of Lord Hidetora Ichimonji, a Japanese King Lear, who is utterly ruined by his children. "Ran," which means "fury," "revolt," or "madness," refers as much to Hidetora's ultimate state of mind as to a cosmos seemingly indifferent to human suffering. Clouds mushroom silently in the sky and crickets buzz in the heat of summer as Hidetora's illustrious kingdom endures round after bloody round of meaningless carnage. In one breathtaking sequence, Hidetora's castle is attacked on one side by his eldest son's soldiers, bearing red banners, and on the other by a second son's army, advancing in streams of yellow. Soundlessly (save for Toru Takemitsu's haunting score), red and yellow banners swirl and blend as Hidetora's men are slaughtered and his royal concubines commit hara-kiri. By the time this epic film reaches its finale, those left alive can only wonder about their chaotic world, which the gods have apparently abandoned. The mesmerizing Mieko Harada co-stars as Hidetora's evil daughter-in-law, Lady Kaede. *(Caroline Kirk)*

13.

17 POINTS

DANGEROUS LIAISONS (1988). This much we know: The script and costumes are great—both won Academy Awards. The movie itself, which is about a pair of eighteenth-century French aristocrats who amuse themselves with erotic power plays, was nominated too. So the only real issue is what to make of John Malkovich as the Vicomte de Valmont, who seduces virgins (Uma Thurman) and virtuous married women (Michelle Pfeiffer) for sport. The beetle-browed Malkovich speaks with a fey lisp, which apparently has cost him the praise he deserves. He may not be conventionally sexy, but as Valmont he is intensely sexual. His posture, his demeanor, his palpable insolence exude the power that he knows he holds over every woman but one—his partner in decadence, the Marquise de Merteuil (Glenn Close). Directed by Stephen Frears, the film is based on Christopher Hampton's play, which was in turn adapted from the novel *Les Liaisons dangereuses*. The video is letter-boxed—top and bottom black strips preserve the rectangular screen image—so we can appreciate every inch of Frears's lush vision.

(Terri Minsky)

DEAD RINGERS (1988). Don't be put off by the nightmarish scenes you may have heard about in *Dead Ringers* —gynecological surgeons wearing deep scarlet uniforms and using instruments that look like talons. Canadian writer-director David Cronenberg *(The Fly, Videodrome, Scanners)* is a fascinating artist: There's no mistaking his disquietingly beautiful cinematic world, filled as it is with clean, organized, coldly lit spaces and alienated humans spilling their viscera. Here, Jeremy Irons skillfully portrays identical-twin doctors—one suave and sociable, the other hardworking and shy—who can imitate each other well enough to fool the women they share (including the splendid Geneviève Bujold). As a team, the brothers complement each other perfectly; but an aching sense of personal incompleteness leads them to drug addiction and ruin. *Dead Ringers* is yet another disturbing vision from an extraordinary talent.

(Howard Karren)

THE RIGHT STUFF (1983). Director Philip Kaufman's adaptation of Tom Wolfe's frenzied, New Journalistic account of America's entry into the space race is no *Top Gun*. It demythologizes the Mercury astronauts (they're either skirt-chasing publicity hounds or God-fearing publicity hounds) and makes iconoclastic icons out of the anonymous test pilots who preceded them, particularly Chuck Yeager. (It's one of the book's intriguing contentions that airline pilots routinely pay homage to Yeager's cool by imitating his lazy drawl.) The film was not a success when it came out, possibly because it became tangled up in John Glenn's presidential bid and audiences expected a straight-forward piece of American campaign propaganda. Instead they got Ed Harris as John Glenn, hero-nerd; an egotistical "Gordo" Cooper, charmingly played by Dennis Quaid (before he became self-consciously charming); and a panicky Gus Grissom (the splendid Fred Ward), who "screw[ed] the pooch." Of course, the same audiences who rejected this marvelous satire of media-manipulated hero worship re-elected Ronald Reagan.

(John Clark)

14.

16 POINTS

MY DINNER WITH ANDRE (1981). A highly entertaining grown-up version of a college bull session, conducted by two relentless neurotics at a swank New York restaurant. In one corner is Andre (Andre Gregory), an avant-garde theater director who dropped out to find the meaning of life through such activities as eating dirt and being buried alive. He hogs the first half of the film and picks up the check. In the other corner is Wally (Wallace Shawn), a hilarious, chubby sensualist whose worldview can be reduced to a cup of cold morning coffee free of dead insects. Except for a few exteriors, *Andre,* directed by Louis Malle, consists entirely of Andre and Wally's table talk and an occasional intrusion by an elderly waiter with spastic eyebrows. This scenario may seem static and sleep-inducing—Andre's ad nauseam accounts of his arid adventures do make the eyes grow heavy—but Wally debunks the new-age BS with a common sense so welcome that it looks like the highest (and most engaging) form of philosophy imaginable. He's a dumpy George Bernard Shaw (GBS). *(John Clark)*

15.

15 POINTS

WITNESS (1985). With his first film shot in America, director Peter Weir strikes a perfect balance between the weighty mysticism and artiness of his Australian movies *(Picnic at Hanging Rock, The Last Wave)* and the weightless thrills of Hollywood action flicks. Harrison Ford plays John Book, a gruff but honest Philadelphia homocide detective who happens upon pervasive corruption in his own precinct. When a young Amish boy (Lukas Haas) witnesses a vicious murder committed by cops that Book knows, he and the boy seek refuge in the boy's rural home. The streetwise detective somehow manages to blend in with the pious farmers, looking laughably "plain" in their traditional black garb, until his inherently "English" (i.e., violent) nature blows the cover: He punches an obnoxious tourist in the nose. Weir makes the most of the exotic Amish country locations, right up to the suspenseful shoot-out at the end (watch out for the wheat silo). But what makes this action movie *really* exciting is the love story between Book and the boy's widowed mother, Rachel (Kelly McGillis). During a barn raising, Book works and sweats with the men while Rachel and the women tend to their cold lemonades and midday meal; the camera dances leisurely between the two groups, keeping time with the characters' stolen glances. As he did in *The Year of Living Dangerously,* Weir avoids explicit scenes of lovemaking; he relies instead on Maurice Jarre's stirring score and John Seale's sensual imagery —whether of rolling wheat fields or McGillis's naked breasts—to build a sexually charged atmosphere of passion and fear. *(Caroline Kirk)*

16.

14 POINTS

L'ARGENT (Robert Bresson; 1984). *Not available on video*

ONCE UPON A TIME IN AMERICA (1984). This Sergio Leone epic is the perfect gangster film for the '80s. There is no femme fatale, no family honor to defend. Instead, there's confusion and disillusionment, unfulfilled love and betrayed friendships. The story spans more than forty years and is seen via the elastic memory of David "Noodles" Aronson (Robert De Niro), who returns to New York City after a thirty-five-year "vacation" in Buffalo. The trip back triggers a fragmented series of recollections, and these, in the form of flashbacks, cumulatively build to a startling climax. Noodles's memories are of long-lost or dead friends, people he gave up when he went into hiding—a woman, Deborah (Elizabeth McGovern), whom he loved and, more important, his friend and partner Max (James Woods). The sense of mystery and loss is mirrored in Ennio Morricone's exquisite score, which assigns leitmotivs to Noodles and the figures of his past. Running almost four hours long (accept no abridged versions), *Once Upon a Time in America* is a vast and unusual saga that is filled with twists and veiled with the moral ambiguity of memory. Its strength is in its attenuation; you'll feel sad when it's time to leave.
(Elise Mac Adam)

SALVADOR (1986). No question about it: When James Woods shuts his mouth for a second and stops telling everyone within earshot about his grade-point average and his stint at MIT, he's the most interesting actor in America. And his best film is *Salvador,* another Oliver Stone masterpiece from the dark side. The team of Woods and Stone is a potent one—not for weak tummies—and each brings out the worst, which is to say the best, in the other. Here, Woods plays perhaps the most unpleasant character in the rogues' gallery of loonies and psychos that constitutes his gift to film history: a philandering, drug-crazed journalist, down and out in Central America, the land of U.S.-supported death squads and leftist guerrillas. A little on the shapeless side, this underappreciated gem of engagé filmmaking (a lost art in America) enjoyed some celebrity on the coattails of *Platoon,* but it deserves a following of its own. Woods takes his character on the journey from pig to partisan that Jane Fonda has a copyright on, and he makes it believable. With James Belushi in a supporting role.
(Peter Biskind)

17.

12 POINTS

THE BIG CHILL (1983). You might say that this epic '80s ensemble piece from Lawrence Kasdan is all talk and no hope. A group of former '60s radicals (à la John Sayles's *Return of the Secaucus Seven*), now lonely, disillusioned thirtysomethings, reunite at the funeral of a friend who has committed suicide. Though the cast is uniformly excellent, Glenn Close is especially good as Sarah, the hospitable housewife, and so is William Hurt, as Nick, the Porsche-driving, pill-popping, mysteriously impotent loner. Completing the entertaining mix are Kevin Kline as Close's mellow entrepreneur of a husband, Jeff Goldblum as a pesky *People* reporter, Tom Berenger as a tanned TV idol,

Mary Kay Place as an unmarried professional yearning for children, JoBeth Williams as a wife and mother yearning for romance, Meg Tilly as the suicide's flaky young ex, and lots of elegiac, analytical schmoozing, adult game-playing, and old-fashioned flirting. After all is said and said and said, the film has trouble outperforming its soundtrack of Motown classics. But then again, you can't really dance at a funeral.

(*Jodie Burke*)

PRIZZI'S HONOR (1985). There is something undefinable about Jack Nicholson's undying allure. His belly is extended, his hair is thinning, his demeanor is crabby, yet women pant for him. Kathleen Turner and Anjelica Huston in *Prizzi's Honor* are no exception. Huston, in fact, actually describes to her father in the movie the extent of both Nicholson's equipment and his endurance (Pop nearly dies on the spot). She is referring to one evening when Nicholson—a rather feeble hitman—was being shy about his desires. "You wanna do it?" Huston finally proposes, in the brilliant Brooklynese that helped her win an Oscar. "Yeah, but with all the lights on?" asks Nicholson. "Yeah," she says. "Right here. On the Oriental. With all the lights on." *"Mamma mia,"* he mutters as he descends. Turner—another "hitter" —is enthralled by Nicholson as well, and the two assassins marry. But as Nicholson ultimately learns, marrying within the profession can get *very* complicated. Director John Huston is at his funniest and darkest in this slick tale of an imperious Mafia family.

(*Bruce Bibby*)

TOOTSIE (1982). Michael Dorsey: A difficult actor. Masquerades as Dorothy Michaels, a middle-aged woman, for a soap-opera role. Once played a tomato in a commercial. The shoot went half a day over schedule because Michael wouldn't sit down. Tomatoes can't sit, he insisted. . . . Dustin Hoffman: Also a difficult actor. Plays Michael Dorsey and Dorsey playing Dorothy Michaels. Refused to follow *Tootsie*'s script when it called for some jerk to steal a taxi from under Dorothy's nose. "I'm not a woman. If I start to get in a cab as a woman and the other guy beats me to it, I'm going to try to kick the shit out of him," he insisted. . . . You: The viewer. Expected to see a perfect little androgynous farce. You do. But you also see something no other movie gives you: a chance to watch Dustin Hoffman playing a character whose "difficult" acting method mirrors his very own. And it pays off. *Tootsie* scores as a romantic comedy, a parody of the soap-opera business, and a study of gender roles in the '80s—a sex farce with little actual sex. Equal kudos to director Sydney Pollack and co-stars Jessica Lange, Teri Garr, and uncredited Bill Murray.

(*Rob Medich*)

18.

11 POINTS

DANTON (1983). Poland's most accomplished director, Andrzej Wajda, took advantage of the Solidarity-driven thaw of the early '80s to turn his attention to the French Revolution. The Socialist government of François Mitterrand, which initiated this Polish-French co-production, doubtless expected a celebration of the events that led to the decapitation of the French monarchy, but that's not how things turned out. Much to the reported displeasure of Mitterrand, Wajda portrayed Robespierre, Saint-Just, et al., in a less than flattering light, while he made a hero of stop-the-revolution-I-want-to-get-off Danton, who is brilliantly played by Gérard Depardieu. Wajda pits Polish romanticism against the French Enlightenment, sex against politics (in the first scene, a naked young boy in a tub has an erection while he's beaten about the head and shoulders for being too dense to learn the Declaration of the Rights of Man) in a bold drama of ideas. *(Peter Biskind)*

THE KING OF COMEDY (1983). Comedy—whew. Not exactly. This bitingly, blackly, scarily funny film is no Marx Brothers romp; rather, it's a direct descendant of Martin Scorsese's *Taxi Driver*. Robert De Niro—who else?—plays Rupert Pupkin, a thirty-four-year-old would-be comic who wants a spot on *The Jerry Langford Show* (read *The Tonight Show*) in the worst way, which is exactly how he goes about getting it. Pupkin is only one of a score of stage-door jills and johnnies who mob the show's host (played with icy concentration by Jerry Lewis) each night. Langford and his people try to give Pupkin a tactful brush-off, but they don't realize who they're dealing with: a bona fide urban psycho. With his crazed-groupie sidekick, Masha (Sandra Bernhard), the creepy Pupkin gets his air time, and guess what? His monologue is only a bit sicker, and a bit less funny, than the average stand-up comedian's shtick: "Like everybody else, I grew up in large part thanks to my mother. If she were only here today, I'd say, 'Mom, what are you doing here? You've been dead for nine years!'" With his slick suits, slicker hair, and Wayne Newton–style mustache, De Niro is a marvel as a guy whose elaborate politeness covers a wealth of weirdness. Watch for longtime *Tonight Show* producer Fred de Cordova as Bert, the producer of *The Jerry Langford Show,* and cameos by such talk-show regulars as Tony Randall, Victor Borge, Dr. Joyce Brothers, and "li'l ol' me," Ed Herlihy.

(Elizabeth Brevitz)

19.

10 POINTS

AMADEUS (1984). Music is at the center of Miloš Forman's *Amadeus*. The eighteenth-century Viennese society it depicts is one in which music shapes identities, forms the basis of political arguments, creates romances, and destroys lives. At the film's opening, we meet the aging composer Antonio Salieri (Oscar winner F. Murray Abraham). He performs some of his pieces for a priest, his confessor, hoping that the man will recognize his work. With each piece the priest shakes his head in apology until Salieri plays the opening bars of *Eine kleine Nachtmusik*. Suddenly, the priest's face lights up. "Yes, I know that," he says. "That's charming. I didn't know you wrote that." Salieri's reply is at once despairing and furious: "I didn't. *That* is Mozart." And *that* is Salieri's torment: He is a mediocre talent. *Amadeus,* based on the play by Peter Shaffer, fleshes out Salieri's cosmic war with God, who has blessed the infantile, lascivious Mozart with all the genius the older man lacks. Mozart infects every corner of Salieri's world—from the music lessons the prodigy gives in the court of the tone-deaf Emperor Joseph II (Jeffrey Jones) to his game of mocking the works of other composers (such as Bach and, of course, Salieri) to his brilliant opera productions (staged by Twyla Tharp). Salieri's jealousy knows no bounds, and Mozart must pay the price; but Salieri's fate is ultimately ironic—he is the hero of a movie named after his nemesis. *(Elsie Mac Adam)*

KAGEMUSHA (1980). Set in sixteenth-century Japan, Akira Kurosawa's *Kagemusha* opens with the great Shingen, lord of the Takeda clan, declaring that he will do *anything* to keep the country safe from civil war. That has included banishing his father and killing his son, and now he has devised a plan by which his rule will continue even after his death. How can this be? A *kagemusha,* or "shadow warrior"—a man who is the spitting image of Shingen —will replace him. The only drawback is that the would-be imposter happens to be a coward and a petty thief. On the fateful day when Shingen is killed by a sniper, the lowly but loyal Kagemusha struggles with the performance of his life. For an uneasy and awkward three years, his public impersonation of Shingen keeps the soldiers' morale high; at times, even Kagemusha feels Shingen's strength within him. Inevitably, the charade is exposed. Kagemusha is pelted with stones as he stumbles out into the rain with nothing but his former rags to protect him. A pawn of political intrigue, the shadow warrior joins the original Lord Shingen in death without anyone ever even knowing his name. *(Caroline Kirk)*

THE KILLING FIELDS (1984). Roland Joffé's nightmare vision of the devastation of Southeast Asia is told from an unusual, personal point of view. As the United States–backed government crumbles, *New York Times* reporter Sydney Schanberg stays behind to cover the fall of Phnom Penh to the Communist Khmer Rouge. At his side is Dith Pran, his Cambodian assistant and translator, who risks his future by remaining with Schanberg to the end and not fleeing with the rest of his family. Predictably, when the Khmer Rouge come, Schanberg is airlifted away with other foreign nationals, and Pran is left to the sharks. And for the next several years, while Schanberg guiltily paces in New York, Pran observes firsthand the genocidal atrocities of the Khmer Rouge. Starring Sam Waterston as Schanberg, John Malkovich as a photographer, and a remarkable nonprofessional actor, Cambodian refugee Dr. Haing S. Ngor, as Pran (he won the Best Supporting Actor Oscar). *(Kitty Bowe Hearty)*

RAISING ARIZONA (1987). A convenience-store-robbing ex-con named H. I. McDonnough (Nicholas Cage) falls in love with a petite correctional officer named Ed (Holly Hunter). They marry, and being such a happy, loving American couple, it's no surprise that they want to have a baby. But, sad to say, they can't—Ed is sterile. So when the McDonnoughs hear about the newborn quintuplets of Nathan Arizona, local merchant king of unfinished furniture, they make up their minds to kidnap one of the babies and keep him as their own. And naturally, when two dumb old prison pals of H.I.'s (John Goodman and William Forsythe) show up for a surprise visit, they want in on the baby-stealing action, too. Adding to the chaos are the frequent, nightmarish appearances of Randall "Tex" Cobb as "The Fury That Would Be . . . the horrible lone biker of the apocalypse." Who else but two brothers (*Blood Simple*'s Joel and Ethan Coen) could have such a consistently funny and weird creative vision? Joel co-writes and directs, Ethan co-writes and produces, and this time out, they hired Barry Sonnenfeld for his clever cinematography. *(Jodie Burke)*

WHEN FATHER WAS AWAY ON BUSINESS (Emir Kusturica; 1985). *Not available on video*

20.

9 POINTS

ATLANTIC CITY (1981). "On the boardwalk in Atlantic City / Life will be peaches and cream . . ." This sprightly tune reverberates through Louis Malle's film about the American culture of self-reinvention. Rather than peaches and cream, however, the lives of the movie's characters are made up of dreams, disappointments, and meager payoffs. Sally (Susan Sarandon) has come to Atlantic City to learn to be a blackjack dealer so she can work her way to glamorous Monaco, but in the meantime she earns a living shucking shellfish at a casino oyster bar. Lou (Burt Lancaster), her aging secret admirer, is a small-time numbers runner who consoles himself with the fantasy that he was once *almost* in the mob. As he gazes longingly into Sally's kitchen window each night, watching her rub lemon juice on her hands, arms, neck, and breasts to remove the stink of fish, his yearning and his sense of life's diminishing returns are palpable. This was not the first film in which Lancaster, a superb actor, played hidden heartbreak—remember *The Swimmer?*—but it's especially poignant to see the then-sixty-seven-year-old star portraying a man settling into old age. With his eye for such ironic details as an abandoned hotel being blown up, echt lounge singer Robert Goulet spinning a tune in the Atlantic City Medical Center's Frank Sinatra Wing, and *Penthouse* publisher Bob Guccione, Sr., describing his kind of gal ("I adore attractive, well-groomed, educated women"), Malle expertly depicts the garish and crumbling culture of a resort town whose time has passed. *(Elizabeth Brevitz)*

BOYFRIENDS AND GIRLFRIENDS (1988). For the sixth and final installment in his "Comedies and Proverbs" series, French director Eric Rohmer avoids flashy camerawork and exotic locales, removing all potential distractions so that his characters are free to do what Rohmerian heroes and heroines do best: talk. The yapping sessions take place in the drab, modern Parisian suburb of Cergy-Pontoise, where Blanche, who's klutzy, nervous, and quick to blush, works at the Ministry of Culture. She doesn't have a boyfriend ("Not at the moment," she says, although it's been a couple of years). Soon she befriends Léa, a freewheeling student who lies blithely and bounces guiltlessly from bedmate to bedmate. Léa introduces Blanche to two men: Alexandre (elegant, charming, but ultimately shallow) and Fabien (honest, caring, but ultimately living with Léa). At first, Blanche falls for Alexandre, but eventually she has to confront the moral dilemmas engendered by her attraction to Fabien. It sounds mundane, and it is—but Rohmer has a gift for illuminating the higher truths that lie dormant in even the most banal situations. The cast of unknowns, which numbers only five, sustains the action skillfully, all the way through to the playfully ironic ending in which everyone's problems are definitively (and farcically) resolved. *(Christopher Bagley)*

LOVE STREAMS (1984). Watching a film by John Cassavetes is like being a fly on the wall in your crazy aunt's house. The camera hovers outside of rooms and peeks around corners with the tentative air of a young child wandering down the hall in the middle of the night to overhear an argument. Cassavetes's next-to-last film, *Love Streams* reunited him on-screen with his wife, Gena Rowlands. She plays Sarah, an obsessive woman whose main fault is loving too much. Recently divorced, Sarah returns from a disastrous trip to Europe and takes a taxi straight to the house of her alcoholic, womanizing brother, a popular writer (Cassavetes). The two are opposites. She believes that love is continuous and eternal (the eponymous streams); he hardly acknowledges that it exists. Despite their differences, they are able to take care of each other as no one else can, sustained by the delicate balance between her obsessiveness and his nonchalance. *Love Streams* is alternately painful, childlike, and funny. Cassavetes was an eccentric and original filmmaker—he will be missed. (*Elise Mac Adam*)

RAIN MAN (1988). Meet the Babbitt brothers. Neither connects with people. But then Raymond (Dustin Hoffman) is autistic. Charlie (Tom Cruise) has no excuse. Raymond does math at lightning speed and memorizes a phone book up to *G* (in clinical terms, he's an autistic savant). Charlie communicates and deals with people—he even has an Italian girlfriend (Valeria Golino)—but mostly in a crude, self-absorbed, distant manner (in clinical terms, he's a jerk). Put the two together and you get several Oscars. The plot has it that Charlie doesn't know Raymond exists until Raymond inherits their father's $3 million estate. Charlie then kidnaps Raymond and takes him cross-country. But aside from the plot's revelations and Hoffman's meticulous performance, what really stands out under Barry Levinson's direction is *Rain Man*'s beautiful cinematography, sharp editing, and imaginative score. And it's the film

that had Americans chanting, "Uh-oh —fifteen minutes to Wapner."
(*Rob Medich*)

ROBOCOP (1987). One of the best action films of the '80s—up there with *The Road Warrior*—*RoboCop* is blessed with a clever premise, a cleverer script, really nasty bad guys, and spectacular special effects. Directed by Paul Verhoeven, the movie is set in the near future, when the privatization-of-everything madness unleashed in the Reagan era has gotten so extreme, Detroit's hapless police department has been turned over to a ruthless corporation. Enter RoboCop (Peter Weller), a sort of robotic Bernhard Goetz on steroids, to take on a gang of meanies led by scuzzy Kurtwood Smith, not to mention a rival robot in the climactic battle of the hardware heavies. Like *Die Hard*, this is an action movie for grown-ups as well as kids, one that doesn't insult the intelligence. (*Peter Biskind*)

THIS IS SPINAL TAP (1984). So you say you like classic films? They don't come much more classic than this, Rob Reiner's hilarious mockumentary of "Britain's now-legendary" heavymetal band Spinal Tap. As filmmaker and Tap fan Martin Di Bergi, Reiner turns an unrelenting lens on band members David St. Hubbins (Michael McKean), Nigel Tufnel (Christopher Guest), Derek Smalls (Harry Shearer), their keyboardist, and their doomed drummer as they embark on an American tour to promote their latest album, *Smell the Glove*. Unfortunately, Spinal Tap's stateside appeal seems to have crested, and they wind up playing Air Force–base rec rooms and being billed below the puppet show at a Stockton, California amusement park—all this despite their energetic renditions of such tasteful, bass-heavy tunes as "Sex Farm" and "Big Bottom" ("The bigger the cushion, the better the pushin'. . . / Big bottom drives me out of my mind / How could I leave this behind?"). The screenplay, by the film's fab four leads (yes, they wrote the songs, too), punctures the band's idiotic pretensions and self-absorption: When Di Bergi points out that one reviewer described a previous Tap album, *Intravenous de Milo,* as "a sea of retarded sexuality and bad poetry," Nigel responds, "That's nit-picking, isn't it?" In the rock world, Nigel later so aptly perceives, "It's such a fine line between stupid and clever," and *This Is Spinal Tap* is both: It's stupid-clever.

(Elizabeth Brevitz)

THREE BROTHERS (1982). Director Francesco Rosi is known for his resolute social consciousness; many of his films explore the hardships wrought by the rapid pace of economic and political change in modern Italy. In *Three Brothers,* however, Rosi's direction is suffused with such a depth of feeling that the film is more remarkable for its emotional impact than for its political relevance. The story concerns three very different middle-aged brothers (an accomplished judge, a morose teacher, and a seditious factory worker) who return to their ancestral home in southern Italy years after moving north to find work in the cities. They have come back for their mother's simple country funeral, but they bring their own modern problems with them; their anxious dreams and fervent arguments reveal the degree to which their lives are haunted by crime, terrorism, and, most of all, loneliness. And that, sadly, is all that unifies them. Rosi sets up a powerful contrast between the brothers and their aging father, whose languid movements and quiet manner belie the inner strength with which he bears his grief. The brothers, baffled by the complexity of the urban worlds they inhabit, can only wallow in confusion. But their father, whose loss is more profound, brings to his mourning the understanding of a wise man whose long life in the country has prepared him to accept, and even appreciate, the inevitability of death.

(Christopher Bagley)

THE UNBEARABLE LIGHTNESS OF BEING (1988). Director Philip Kaufman accomplishes what film adaptations of books seldom do: He tells a story. Milan Kundera's acclaimed novel managed to escape the usual Hollywood approach, in which scenes are "opened up" in a way that has more to do with cameras than with ideas. Here, the screenplay, by Kaufman and Jean-Claude Carrière, is blissfully literate, unfolding gracefully and with measure. It is the story of Tomas (Daniel Day-Lewis), a Czechoslovakian doctor living in Prague, who is an adept seducer of women. His favorite, perhaps, is the fiercely independent, bohemian Sabina (Lena Olin), the only one who truly understands his wanderlust. But Tomas instead marries Tereza (Juliette Binoche), a virginal country girl who is both excited and disturbed by his unquenchable lust. Though Tomas wants to remain faithful to his wife, he can't—or won't—change his ways. The 1968 Soviet invasion brings to a halt everyone's charmed, almost quaint, existence. Tomas, Tereza, and Sabina flee to Geneva. The married pair return demoralized to Prague; Sabina ends up in Northern California. They all endure, finally realizing what is light—and so excruciating—about being alive.   *(Bruce Bibby)*

21.

8 POINTS

DAS BOOT (1982). Imagine spending forty-five days in a New York City subway car under the East River with fifty people and one toilet. That will give you some idea of the hell endured by German sailors serving on U-boats during World War II (admittedly, they didn't have to share these confined quarters with New Yorkers). Although victims of Hitler may have a hard time sympathizing with their plight, and others may feel that, like *Anna Christie* (GARBO TALKS!) and *Ninotchka* (GARBO LAUGHS!) *Das Boot* is selling a novelty (GERMAN SOLDIERS WHO LAUGH AND CRY AND SING!), this film, directed by Wolfgang Petersen, goes beyond ideology and stereotypes. The men hate what they're doing and why they're doing it as much as any Vietnam grunt. And there is a fascinating procedural aspect to *Das Boot* as well. Bolts blow and ricochet like bullets when the ship descends to great depths. Sausages are strung every which way, as if in a meat locker. Aside from claustrophobia and Allied surface ships, the worst enemy the men face is boredom, which they deal with by singing Irish folk songs and writing letters to their pregnant French girlfriends and staring morosely into space (what there is of it)—yet another New York subway analogy!   (*John Clark*)

FRANCISCA (Manoel de Oliveira; 1982). *Not available on video*

HEIMAT (Edgar Reitz; 1986). *Not available on video*

MY LIFE AS A DOG (1987). Here in the United States, when suffering strikes people who don't deserve it, we say "It shouldn't happen to a dog." That expression finds its Swedish equivalent in this bittersweet film about a boy growing up in the '50s. Ingmar is a dreamy but resilient kid who muses about bizarre tragedies—Laika, the Soviet astro-dog, running out of kibble in space; a man swinging from a live power line after watching a Tarzan film—in order to put his own losses in perspective. Director Lasse Hallström is expert at providing a child's-eye view of families, friendship, and sex, but the humor and heartbreak of this film are aimed at adults, not children. If you half-remember the comfort of childhood retreats into fantasy, you'll understand *My Life as a Dog*—and marvel to think how much courage and endurance we all needed just to grow up.

(*Elizabeth Brevitz*)

ON TOP OF THE WHALE (Raúl Ruiz; 1984). *Not available on video*

SANS SOLEIL (Chris Marker; 1983). *Not available on video*

THE SHINING (1980). It's not one of Stanley Kubrick's best movies, but even second-rate Kubrick is better than the finest work of most other directors, so get ready for a lush and clever horror movie. The film suffers from being overproduced and underconceived, but it's rescued by occasional flashes of Kubrick's genius and great performances by Jack Nicholson and Shelley Duvall. Nicholson plays a neurotic, blocked writer who takes a job caretaking a deserted, sprawling, down-at-the-heels, and, most important for this story, isolated hotel somewhere in the mountains of Colorado, thinking it will help him work. But when he arrives with his family (Duvall and child), they find out that they're not the only inhabitants of the hotel. . . . Best known for two memorable scenes: Nicholson pounding away at his typewriter, only to have written: "All work and no play makes Jack a dull boy" thousands of times; and later, when Nicholson, frothing at the mouth and rolling his eyes, flails about with an ax and shouts, "*Heeeere's* Johnny!" Featuring a nice supporting turn by Scatman Crothers.

(Peter Biskind)

THE SINGING DETECTIVE (Jon Amiel; 1988). *Not available on video*

STRANGER THAN PARADISE (1984). This offbeat film quickly earned a sizable cult following for director Jim Jarmusch. Some critics dismissed the movie as little more than a hip exercise in stylistics, but today it's still notable for its striking originality and stark beauty. And besides, it's funny. John Lurie plays Willie, a sullen, hyper-Americanized Hungarian immigrant who reluctantly allows his sixteen-year-old cousin from the old country, Eva (Eszter Balint), to spend a few days in his grimy New York apartment. When she arrives, they immediately begin to bicker; he doesn't appreciate her incisive commentaries on his laughable existence ("Where does that meat come from?" she asks as he wolfs down a TV dinner). But soon Willie and his goofball buddy, Eddie (Richard Edson), develop an oddly affectionate rapport with Eva. A year after she leaves, the two men steal a car and drive to Cleveland to visit her; the threesome then travel together to Florida. Not much of a plot, to be sure, but what makes it all so appealing is Jarmusch's wry, bleak vision. Everything's impossibly barren—the characters' lives, the landscapes they inhabit, and even the minimalistic camera techniques Jarmusch uses to capture the desola-tion. But all the emptiness actually does add up to something. Most enjoyable are the odd, seemingly peripheral moments that other filmmakers would pass over but that Jarmusch sees as the most important. In one scene, Willie stumbles through a dumb joke that he's forgotten how to tell. Finally, after a few false starts, he gives up. "I can't remember this joke," he says to Eva. "But it's good." *(Christopher Bagley)*

22.

7 POINTS

AFTER THE REHEARSAL (1984). Although it was released theatrically in the United States, Ingmar Bergman made his semiautobiographical *After the Rehearsal* for Swedish television, and thus it's perfectly suited for home video. All the action takes place on a single set, the theater stage where an aging director (Erland Josephson) is resting after the rehearsal of his fifth production of Strindberg's *A Dream Play*. Two actresses visit him: a young, beautiful one (Lena Olin), with whom he discusses a hypothetical affair, and an older, worn-looking one (Ingrid Thulin), with whom he once actually had an affair and then abandoned. The confined setting underlines the sense that these three characters, especially the director, are somehow trapped, bound to their unchanging destiny. "Listen to the silence, to all the hate, the laughter," says Josephson. "The passion played out here in the past is still here, living its secret, continuous life."

(Caroline Kirk)

AU REVOIR LES ENFANTS (1988). For most of us, childhood is not dominated by Good (as in, say, *Mary Poppins)* or Evil *(Lord of the Flies),* but

230

rather vacillates somewhere in between, as we stumble our way through the lessons of early life. Those lessons have not been lost on Louis Malle, who, having returned to his native France, demonstrates once again his ability to convey a child's sense of boredom, mischief, and guilt. *An Revoir les enfants* is the World War II story of two young friends in a Catholic boarding school, one a Parisian bourgeois and the other a Jew hiding from the Gestapo. With studious neutrality, Malle observes their prepubescent relationship as it evolves. From the movie's beginning, in which the Gentile boy hugs his mother goodbye as if he were her lover, to its tragic end, in which a half-conscious turn of the eye becomes an act of total betrayal. Malle wastes no time with cuteness or melodrama, and instead watches, without blinking, the casual joys and horrors of survival. *(Howard Karren)*

BABETTE'S FEAST (1987). As true as its turtle soup, *Babette's Feast* verges on the spiritually inspired. Gabriel Axel's Oscar-winning film imbues Isak Dinesen's short story with the resonance of a biblical parable. The eponymous event takes place in a remote coastal village in nineteenth-century Denmark when a congregation of devout Lutherans gathers to honor the one-hundredth birthday of its late pastor. A mysterious Frenchwoman named Babette (Stéphane Audran) prepares the dinner, and the townsfolk, suspicious of her foreign menu, solemnly agree to ignore what might be a witch's brew. "Like a wedding at Cana," says one, "the food is of no importance." Yet as they piously munch Babette's spectacular creations and sip delicious "lemonade" (actually Veuve Clicquot champagne), old memories are recounted and lifelong grudges are miraculously resolved. Axel, orchestrating the superb ensemble, never loses sight of the story's humor and simplicity; he shares with Babette the artist's gift of reconciling heavenly and earthly delights.

(Caroline Kirk)

HOPE AND GLORY (1987). Nominated for five Oscars, *Hope and Glory* shows the exhilaration of World War II for a boy living on the outskirts of London. Director John Boorman *(Deliverance, The Emerald Forest),* who also wrote and produced the autobiographical film, has said he was determined to strip away the mythologizing that surrounds the memory of the war and describe it the way he experienced it: as a time of almost ecstatic anarchy. The result is a film that's full of humor, affection, and incongruities. Bill Rohan, played by seven-year-old Sebastian Rice-Edwards, learns about sex, death, love, hypocrisy, and the foibles of adults as he prowls the ruins of bombed houses on Rosehill Avenue. His childlike father (David Hayman) is off chasing patriotic dreams of glory from behind a military clerk's typewriter; his teenage sister (Sammi Davis) runs wild; his mother (Sarah Miles) can't cope; and everything in the end turns out all right. A *comedy*—albeit bittersweet—about the Blitz? As difficult as that may be to imagine, Boorman makes it real, with the help of fine performances by all. *(Elizabeth Brevitz)*

PASSION (Jean-Luc Godard; 1984). *Not available on video*

SHOOT THE MOON (1982). In this story about the emotional loose ends that remain when a modern marriage disintegrates, Diane Keaton plays Faith Dunlap, wife of fifteen years to Albert Finney's George Dunlap and mother of their four daughters. They live in messy, rambling splendor in the suburbs north of San Francisco, where the urban tangle of freeways and development gives way to a breathtakingly beautiful rustic landscape. Nevertheless, the Dunlaps' is *not* a happy home. Finney moves out and takes a lover (Karen Allen); the children stubbornly try to bring their parents back together; and Faith slowly adjusts to her new, independent existence. Nothing can prepare them or you for the emotional rampages that follow. Directed by Alan Parker from an original screenplay by Bo Goldman, *Shoot the Moon* features memorable star turns from Keaton and Finney and top-notch support from Peter Weller, as Keaton's love interest, and Dana Hill, as the angry oldest daughter.   *(Kitty Bowe Hearty)*

SID & NANCY (1986). The antic director Alex Cox—Britain's answer to Oliver Stone—presents the life, times, and premature death of the undertalented Sex Pistol Sid Vicious. Sid obviously never saw Nicholas Ray's *Knock on Any Door,* in which John Derek's credo was "Live fast, die young, and leave a good-looking corpse." The movie doesn't show his death (it's satisfied with the appalling end of his companion, the eponymous Nancy, inadvertently stabbed to death by the terminally stoned Sid), but he never cared much for appearances, if this account is to be believed. Cox takes us on a lurid, sometimes funny, and ultimately affecting tour of the punk underworld of the '70s (London on a nickel bag a day). Brilliant performances by Gary Oldman as Sid and Chloe Webb as Nancy.
(Peter Biskind)

SOPHIE'S CHOICE (1982). Alan J. Pakula's maddeningly faithful screen adaptation of William Styron's novel is slow, depressing, and boring for most of its greath length, but it is also a movie of shattering power shot through with moments of singular beauty, and it possesses one overriding virtue: a magnificent performance by Meryl Streep in the title role of the Holocaust-haunted Polish Catholic heroine. When she cries, as she does often in this movie, her skin goes waxy, her eyes turn pink like a hamster, her nose gets as red as Rudolph's. She plays so many variations on the theme of pain, she's a one-woman symphony of suffering. Her Polish accent is impeccable, and we understand at once why the two male leads are mad for her. Kevin Kline plays one, a demented Brooklyn Jew, and Peter MacNicol the other, a young, Waspy aspiring writer. This mid-'80's ethnic allegory, a prequel or twin to *Enemies, A Love Story,* has a strange moral: Old World Jews and guilt-ridden Catholics are locked in a mutually self-destructive embrace incomprehensible to New World Wasps, who stand by helplessly and watch or, if they're lucky, transform the experience into art. *(Peter Biskind)*

TESS (1980). Perhaps Nastassja Kinski is a bit too beautiful to play a lowly English farm laborer. Mistreated milkmaid, maybe. But here's Kinski (and her pout) as Thomas Hardy's oxymoronic noble peasant heroine, doomed by fate and society's inherent unfairness. Once the innocent maiden loses her innocent maidenhood to the cruel hands (and whatever) of an aristocratic "cousin," she suffers through one betrayal after another, wearing the weighty burdens of her pride, her loyalty, and her sins like a hangman's noose. A girl can take only so much, however, and in despair, Tess sells out —but not without a fight. The blood dripping down through the ceiling at the climax of this Roman Polanski movie doesn't quite match the epic sweep of Hardy's *Tess of the d'Urbervilles,* but on most other counts, the Oscar-winning production (Best Cinematography, Costume Design, and Art Direction) scores high marks. If anything, it equals, if not surpasses, the arresting beauty of its young star.

(*Jodie Burke*)

VERONIKA VOSS (Rainer Werner Fassbinder; 1982). *Not available on video*

ZELIG (1983). Although Woody Allen's more conventional films, such as *Hannah and Her Sisters,* which he can do with his eyes closed, have gotten the lion's share of the critical credit, it is actually his offbeat, unpredictable movies, such as *Zelig* and *The Purple Rose of Cairo,* that are the most extraordinary. These are the films in which Allen plays with the conventions of movies and emerges as the most singular, most original mind working in Hollywood. Unlike dreary avant-garde films that share the same ambitions, Allen knows how to have fun and thus fashions an entertainment along the way. Of these films, *Zelig* is the most spectacular—breathtakingly experimental and hugely funny at the same time. A combination of *The Elephant Man* and *Dead Men Don't Wear Plaid, Zelig* is the story of an insecure, chameleon-like shlepper who takes on the protective coloration of his environment. He's the man who would be everyone, and Allen flawlessly integrates him into newsreels from the '20s and '30s so that he can rub shoulders with the likes of Babe Ruth, Eugene O'Neill, and Adolf Hitler. Throughout, Allen rings changes on his favorite themes—therapy, Jewish-

ness, masculinity, love—and, while he's at it, metaphorically answers the critics who savaged him for *Stardust Memories, Interiors,* and the like.

(*Peter Biskind*)

23.

6 POINTS

A NOS AMOURS (1984). The French have a peculiar knack for churning out dramas about the sexual escapades of nubile fifteen-year-old girls; what distinguishes this one is the skillful direction of Maurice Pialat and a remarkable debut performance by the youthful Sandrine Bonnaire. Bonnaire plays Suzanne, a restless nymphette whose string of empty physical encounters does little to satisfy her obvious need for more meaningful attachments. And her loveless family is no help, either. When Suzanne comes home after curfew, her neurotic mother launches into maniacal tantrums, and her father (played marvelously by Pialat himself) cannot intervene because he has flown the coop to live with his mistress. At times Pialat's direction errs on the side of melodrama, particularly during a few unintentionally comical quarrel scenes in which family members vigorously spit at one another (typically French!). But elsewhere Pialat is a master of the subtle touch, the understated revelation. And Bonnaire has a natural talent for expressing her character's inherent ambiguities—she's charming, smug, vulnerable, childish, and wise. She's also sexually charged, even when she's talking quietly with her father or sharing a cigarette with a female schoolmate.

(*Christopher Bagley*)

THE '80S (1983). Chantal Akerman's all-dancing, all-singing jigsaw puzzle is a musical in the way that *Stranger Than Paradise* is a road film—it's an ironic, playful reworking (or disassembling) of a popular genre. Dense and fragmentary, the first hour of this film/video, fiction/documentary hybrid is culled from hours of rehearsal tapes. Roles are auditioned, routines blocked out, songs recorded. There's a cubist logic to Akerman's raw, sensuous montage (a kind of valentine to performers) which gloriously climaxes à la Busby Berkeley with a half-hour series of lavish production numbers. Lines, scenes, dances, and miscellaneous bits of business fall into place as the members of the cast sing and cavort their way through the Toison d'or (Golden Fleece) shopping mall, absurdly extolling the transcendent power of love. Akerman tackles one of the oldest clichés of movie musical comedies—namely that of putting on a show—turns it inside out, and gives it a new lease on life.

(J. Hoberman)

LAW OF DESIRE (1987). Graphic sex, outrageous plot contrivances, romantic violence—everything is just a throwaway in the movies of Spanish virtuoso Pedro Almodóvar. His *Law of Desire* is an irresistible mishmash of the above ingredients and much more. Eusebio Poncela plays a celebrated, jet-set gay film director trying to get over a failed relationship with a bisexual youth. Poncela's sister is a transsexual actress (played by Almodóvar's once-favored heroine. Carmen Maura) who lives with her preteen daughter. (Maura is technically the girl's father; the mother, a lesbian, is played in the movie by a transsexual actress—get it?) Enter Antonio Banderas, a naïve young man obsessed with Poncela and his films. Banderas, embracing fate, manages to meet and seduce the director, and

then, employing the same persistent macho sweetness with which he courts Victoria Abril in Almodóvar's *Tie Me Up! Tie Me Down!*, he insinuates himself into every corner of Poncela's world. Although the result —murder and suicide—is tragic, the ironies abound. Almodóvar flirts so often with absurdity that what happens in *Law of Desire* often feels tabloid-silly, almost numbing, a perception that the self-important bohemians of Poncela's entourage would find more humiliating than failure.

(Howard Karren)

MATEWAN (1987). It's not hard to spot the bad guys in *Matewan*. They're the ones who hold a boy at gunpoint during dinner, laugh in church, and act so incredibly slimy, it's hard to understand why anyone would come within ten feet of them. (They wear black hats, too.) The movie is writer-director John Sayles's version of the labor war fought between striking miners and their coal company in the tiny town of Matewan, West Virginia, in 1920. *Matewan* is a somber tale, sealed with tragedy, but the context is personal, not political. What's remarkable about the movie is the way Sayles tempers the cut-and-dry polarization of characters. As he sees it, the history of the union is, above all, the story of individuals: the solidly antiunion preacher, played by Sayles himself; the Communist labor agitator, played by birdlike Chris Cooper ("There ain't but two sides to this world—them that work and them that don't. You work; they don't"); and Few Clothes, the leader of the black miners, played by James Earl Jones. One short scene exemplifies Sayles's approach: An Italian miner plays his mandolin by the fire one night. In the shadows behind him, two locals pluck and strum at their guitar and violin; the Italian beckons them to join him. After a bit, a black miner chimes in on the harmonica. The music strengthens as they play. And then the shooting begins.

(Elise Mac Adam)

MISSISSIPPI BURNING (1988). It's a fact that in 1964, three young civil-rights activists, two white, one black, were murdered by the KKK-infil-trated police of Neshoba County, Mississippi. Yet in this fictionalized account of the aftermath, blacks are relegated to the background—for some viewers, an irredeemable flaw. For others, the story that director Alan Parker *does* tell is a searing tour de force. He focuses on two mis-matched white heroes, FBI men Gene Hackman and Willem Dafoe, as they overcome philosophical differences about investigating a crime in the bigoted South. Parker translates this simple Hollywood story line into vi-suals seething with such emotion that even the familiar Klan icon of the burning cross recovers some of its original shock value and dread. *Missis-sippi Burning* woos its audience in much the same way that Hackman teases information from a deputy's wife: Despite a tacit understanding of its aims, you never doubt the sincerity of the seduction.   (Caroline Kirk)

PARTING GLANCES (1986). This startlingly accomplished low-budget film, produced by and for the gay community (writer-director Bill Sher-wood died of AIDS in 1990), has, in fact, more to say to heterosexual au-diences about love among adults than most of the Hollywood fare aspiring to do just that. *Parting Glances* is the first fictional film to convey with three-dimensional candor how the heirs of gay liberation live; Sherwood has the visual flair and dramatic re-straint of a veteran talent. Michael (Richard Ganoung), a book editor who lives on New York City's Upper West Side with his Ken-doll lover, Robert (John Bolger), has reached a turning point in his life. Robert has accepted a long-term job in Africa, and both men are uncertain their rela-tionship will withstand the separation. Michael also has an ex, Nick (Steve Buscemi, in a beautifully modulated performance), the boyish hipster whom Michael, in his heart, has never given up. And Nick has AIDS, a fact he accepts glumly, without fanfare. Though poor Michael loves both Robert and Nick, in mutually exclu-sive yet equally important ways, he must confront the imminent depar-ture of both men from his life. And confront it he does—wistfully, thor-oughly, honestly.   (Howard Karren)

A ROOM WITH A VIEW (1986). The exceptionally talented trio of director James Ivory, producer Ismail Mer-chant, and screenwriter Ruth Prawer Jhabvala bring to the screen E. M. Forster's 1908 novel of a young En-glishwoman's awakening to passion. Lucy Honeychurch (Helena Bonham Carter) visits Florence properly chap-eroned by her prudish cousin Char-lotte Bartlett (Maggie Smith), who keeps one strict Victorian eye peeled on Lucy's every movement. At their pension, Lucy and Charlotte encoun-ter Mr. Emerson (Denholm Elliott) and his son, George (Julian Sands)—an eccentric duo who enjoy decorat-ing old ladies with cornflowers and are not the slightest bit appalled by the uninhibited habits of the native Italians. Complications arise during a picnic, when Charlotte witnesses George stealing a kiss from Lucy. Of course, the two ladies take the first train out the next morning. Back in England, Lucy settles into her homey but dull suburban-gentry lifestyle and agrees to marry a scholarly snob named Cecil Vyse (perfectly priggish Daniel Day-Lewis). That is, until George arrives and tries to kiss her some more. Before long, George, the Reverend Beebe (Simon Callow), and Lucy's restless brother, Freddy (Rupert Graves), have thrown off all their clothes to romp and splash in a pond. Shocking! *(Jodie Burke)*

STAND BY ME (1986). Four twelve-year-old boys (Wil Wheaton, River Phoenix, Corey Feldman, and Jerry O'Connell) set out on a journey into the woods to find the body of a dead boy, and along the way, they test and confirm their manhood, bravery, and friendship. With so many weighty coming-of-age themes woven into the script (based on a short story by Stephen King), *Stand By Me* teeters on the brink of becoming awfully serious at times, but director Rob Reiner skillfully guides the viewer through all the soul searches with a light and funny touch. Well, sort of light—some may object to the boys' frequently foul language. Watch for the swamp scene—you'll never dream what the leeches latch on to. The four leads are outstanding; also on hand are Kiefer Sutherland as a mean teenager, lovable John Cusack as an older brother, and Richard Dreyfuss as the narrator—Wheaton grown up—who tells the story as an extended flashback. *(Jodie Burke)*

THE THIN BLUE LINE (1988). Not since *Blood Simple* has the creepy, sinister side of Texas been captured as nakedly as it is in Errol Morris's breakthrough documentary, *The Thin Blue Line*. In 1976, a Dallas policeman was murdered, and even though a small-town hood named David Harris said that he's duh one who popped duh trigger, a jury chose to believe his *second* version of what happened—that it was Randall Adams, a hitchhiker Harris had picked up, who had the cold blood, not he. In good-ol'-boy twang (as chilling as death when heard with the ominous Philip Glass score), smiling Texas law keepers claim that Harris, with an extensive criminal history, is an innocent youth and Adams, with no previous record, is a killer who "creeps at night." And even though in the final interview Harris as much as says—again—that he is the killer, the Big D po-lice (whose reputation is at stake) think filmmaker Morris is just a'meddlin'. "Sometimes I think it's the ultimate episode of *The Twilight Zone*," Morris has said of *The Thin Blue Line*. Certainly the prosecution's bizarre (and hardly believable) surprise witnesses—and Morris's startling restagings of the murder—are worthy of Rod Serling's wild imagination. Adams, however, didn't imagine his life sentence; as a result of this movie's release, his case was reopened and he was eventually set free. *(Bruce Bibby)*

THE THREE CROWNS OF THE SAILOR (Raúl Ruiz; 1984). *Not available on video*

24.

5 POINTS

DINER (1982). Barry Levinson's *Diner* achieves a heroic feat: It makes something compelling and non–white bread out of ordinary middle-class life, circa the late 1950s. There are no Spielbergian gremlins or extraterrestrials or (this being John Waters's territory, Baltimore) three-hundred-pound drag queens to give the story an artificial boost, just a group of confused and scared young men who convene at a local diner to play the same roles they've played for years—only now they're outgrowing them. Kevin Bacon, Daniel Stern, Timothy Daly, the surprisingly passable Steve Guttenberg, and the terminally nonchalant Mickey Rourke impersonate guys who don't know what they're going to do with their lives and don't know a thing about women. Ellen Barkin is smashing as one such creature, who drives husband Stern insane by misfiling his rock 'n' roll and R&B records. You'll seldom see a more affectionate or more accurate depiction of much-maligned but—given what a cold, cruel world this is—completely necessary male bonding.   *(John Clark)*

DREAMCHILD (1985). Who else but Dennis Potter, the author of the emotionally twisted television masterpieces *Pennies From Heaven* and *The Singing Detective,* would think of writing a screenplay about the child lust of *Alice in Wonderland*'s Lewis Carroll (the pseudonym for the Reverend Charles Dodgson, played by Ian Holm) from the point of view of the real-life Alice as an old woman (Coral Browne)? Alice, who has come to Columbia University in the 1930s to honor the centenary of Carroll's birth, hates vulgar America and is haunted by the memories of her Victorian childhood. Haunted, that is, until she comes to terms with Dodgson's gift of love. Gavin Millar directed; the inventively fleshed-out Carroll creatures are by Jim Henson.   *(Howard Karren)*

FROM THE POLE TO THE EQUATOR (Yervant Gianikian and Angela Ricci Lucchi; 1988). *Not available on video*

LILI MARLEEN (Rainer Werner Fassbinder; 1981). *Not available on video*

LITTLE DORRIT (1988). If you find yourself trapped in a bleak house with nothing but time (how about six hours?) on your hands, settle in with a spot of tea and Christine Edzard's astonishing adaptation of Charles Dickens's *Little Dorrit.* An immense film shot in a small studio on London's docks, it pairs Derek Jacobi (as Arthur Clennam) with Alec Guinness (William Dorrit) and introduces young Sarah Pickering in the title role. On top of this inspired casting (which also includes Joan Greenwood, in her final film appearance, as Clennam's puritanical mother, and Roshan Seth as the ratlike rent collector Pancks, who *squeezes* the tenants of Bleeding Heart Yard), the score of Verdi music will carry you to Victorian London's greedy heights, then plunge you to its depths, where the Dorrits reign as the royal family of the debtors' prison. Most interesting of all is the film's unfolding in two parts. Part I, *Nobody's Fault,* is the riches-to-rags and rags-to-riches story of nice-guy Arthur Clennam and Little Dorrit, seen through his eyes. Part II, *Little Dorrit's Story,* is the same tale, only it's told through *her* eyes.

(Jodie Burke)

MEPHISTO (1981). You may think you've seen all the movies about Nazi Germany that you care to, but this Hungarian Oscar winner, directed by István Szabó, is truly different, offering an unusual milieu (the German theater), insinuatingly casual pacing, and a brilliant performance by Klaus Maria Brandauer. Brandauer has plenty of territory to conquer as Hendrik, a provincial-repertory actor with ambitions to match Hitler's and a personal code that bends to admit any behavior, any political position, any tie that will further his career. Opening just before the triumph of the National Socialist party, *Mephisto* is shot in shades of gray and brown that become bloodied by the scarlet of Nazi banners. Hendrik, a member of a leftist theater group, throws off "cultural Bolshevism" when he sees the opportunity to become the biggest star of the new regime. According to Nazi artistic thinking, Shakespeare may still be performed, being "classic, like the Greeks," but Hamlet, that most Aryan of heroes, must be expunged of all weakness, doubt, and hesitation—a challenge that Hendrik embraces. German art must be rid of the "mendacious, degenerate taste of the loud-mouthed culture," he parrots, never pausing to consider what he is sanctioning. In the end, though, Hendrik is trapped in his signature role of Mephistopheles, that tool of the Devil, pleading, "What do they want of me? I'm only an actor."

(Elizabeth Brevitz)

OUT OF AFRICA (1985). Meryl Streep, flawlessly accented once again, is Danish author Isak Dinesen—the pen name for Karen Blixen—who as a young woman marries her titled cousin (Klaus Maria Brandauer) and abandons a comfortable but stifling life in Denmark to accompany him to Kenya. The two get along but are not very much in love; what turns this masterful Sydney Pollack movie (with Oscars for Best Picture, Direction, Adapted Screenplay, Cinematography, Original Score, and Sound) into a grand romance is the entrance of handsome Robert Redford as a terminally independent adventurer. True to its source—Dinesen's memoirs—the movie shows some early feminist consciousness. With virtually no help, Blixen sets up a coffee plantation and a school for native children and establishes humane relationships with local Africans. Snubbed by her male compatriots, she is later toasted by them at the local men's club. But the key to the movie's spectacle is David Watkins's gifted cinematography, which starkly contrasts the beauty of Africa to the repressive imperialism of European society. (Jodie Burke)

PIXOTE (1981). Pixote is pronounced pee-shote, at least by the delinquents, cops, drug dealers, and prostitutes who inhabit the reformatory, slums, and brothels where the title character whiles away his childhood. This film is a Third World (Brazilian) version of Truffaut's bleak, autobiographical The 400 Blows, which means it's about fresh-faced kids being stomped on by adults, starting with their parents. "Since you won't get me the stuff [marijuana], how's about getting my mother," says ten-year-old Pixote to his grandfather, who is visiting him in reform school. "If you find her before I do," the old man replies, "let me know." When Pixote escapes from the school, where rape, glue-sniffing, and beatings are the norm, he has no choice but to return to the streets, where, as a minor, he steals, deals, pimps, and eventually murders with impunity. Needless to say, this is not for the fainthearted, but director Hector Babenco somehow keeps events at a distance, and sometimes they are so outrageous and horrifying that Pixote becomes a black comedy. In the best neorealist fashion, Babenco cast an authentic street urchin, Fernando Ramos da Silva, as the "hero." Da Silva, unlike Truffaut, did not survive his youth—he was killed by the Brazilian police in 1987.

(John Clark)

RAIDERS OF THE LOST ARK (1981). It used to bring on the heebie-jeebies when a deadly tarantula planted itself on an unsuspecting movie hero. Then Raiders came along. It used to be goose-bump city when a character intimately interfaced with a coil of deadly snake flesh . . . before *Raiders*. And once upon a time, a singular skeleton dropping in on a heroine sparked adequate trauma. No more. *Raiders of the Lost Ark* came along and set new standards for cliff-hangers and the willies. Here, we get a torso *covered* with tarantulas, a room *slithering* with snakes, a cavern *teeming* with dropping skeletons—not to mention a cave that spits lethal darts and spikes, a stampeding native tribe, a crew of evil Nazis, and the mysterious forces inside an ark that holds the tablets of the Ten Commandments. George Lucas and director Steven Spielberg broke new ground here by taking an old-fashioned adventure—a professor-archeologist fights off Nazis as he searches for the lost ark—telling it in an old-fashioned way, and then adding every new cinematic trick and firework in the book. It's a moving comic book with an ideal hero in Indiana Jones (Harrison Ford)—the personification of higher education as well as pure machismo. That is, when he's not asking the terrifying question "Snakes. . . . Why did it have to be snakes?" *(Rob Medich)*

THÉRÈSE (1986). Only a few filmmakers have done it convincingly—Robert Bresson *(Diary of a Country Priest)* and Carl Theodor Dreyer *(The Passion of Joan of Arc)* come to mind—but Alain Cavalier manages in *Thérèse* to dramatize the life of a saint, a full-blooded person with uncompromising religious faith. The screenplay is based on the diaries of Thérèse Martin, a young French girl who died of tuberculosis in a Carmelite convent in 1897 and was canonized twenty-eight years later. Like all Carmelite nuns, Thérèse (Cathérine Mouchet) devotes her life to Jesus Christ. But she is only fifteen, and her devotion is characterized by all the giggles and obsessions of a schoolgirl crush. Her desire to be one of His holy brides (she even wears a wedding dress when joining the convent) is unshakable; even as her body deteriorates from disease, her intense physical suffering is transformed into sacrificial joy. Just as Dreyer did with Joan of Arc, Cavalier shoots Thérèse's story against featureless backdrops, accentuating the serenity and simplicity of her calling. No attempt is made to hide the sexual repression and neurosis of convent life, but there's no need to—Thérèse's martyrdom is perfectly realized in Mouchet's face, so thoroughly human yet transparent with happiness and love. *(Caroline Kirk)*

TOUTE UNE NUIT (1982). Set in blandest Brussels one steamy summer night, Chantal Akerman's austere, sweetly nutty urban nocturne is fashioned from the shards of two dozen pulverized melodramas. There could be eight million stories in this naked city. (It's the Belgian director's fragmented version of *La Ronde* or maybe a structuralist-materialist update of *A Midsummer Night's Dream*.) With camera and characters moving in and out of traffic, *Toute une nuit* jumps from narrative situation to narrative situation. Men leave women, women leave men, insomniacs stare at the ceiling. The artful posing and zap-TV format suggest the collaboration of Gertrude Stein and Cindy Sherman. The deadpan tone is at once poetic and jokey. Just before dawn a thunderstorm passes through. And just after daybreak, one woman comes home and pops into bed beside her sleeping husband—just in time for the alarm to go off. *(J. Hoberman)*

HARDWARE

BUYING A VCR

If It Were Easy, They Wouldn't Call It Hardware

———•———

BY BOB BREWIN

Trying to figure out which VCR to buy as home video enters its second full decade consists of a brain-numbing trip through enough acronyms to delight a Pentagon bureaucrat. (And let's hope perestroika never develops to the state where the Russians start exporting VCRs here, since Cyrillic has more letters than English.)

Back in the good old late '70s —an era of innocence in which hardly anyone would ever think of linking the words "junk" and "bond" together—VCR selection consisted of two choices, VHS or Betamax. Deciding which format to choose was relatively simple. Beta offered (according to the techies) better quality, while the VHS format delivered longer recording time: six hours maximum for VHS versus four hours for Beta.

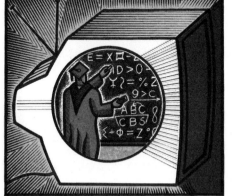

TOM GRAJEK

America, naturally, chose quantity over quality, propelling VHS to such a position of market dominance that more and more prerecorded video suppliers don't even bother to offer product in the Beta format. Even Sony, developer of Beta, now markets VHS VCRs, while still producing enough high-end Beta machines to satisfy the dwindling but loyal Betaphile market. (Betaphiles are the kind of people who, I'm sure, order vegetables at a restaurant and expect to receive five artfully arranged miniature carrots.)

Installing a VCR of either format back in the early days of home video was still relatively simple (but slightly more difficult than changing the blades on a Cuisinart): Plug the TV antenna (or cable wire) into the VCR; plug the *one* thick black wire that came with the VCR into the TV antenna terminal; plug in the power; set the TV on channel three or four; and sit down to watch *Attack of the Killer Tomatoes* without commercial interruption.

Those early VCRs didn't have many of the features now available. Sound was mono—*bad* mono, as a matter of fact—and picture resolution was so murky it was hard to figure out exactly which people really were doing what to each other, especially in the early "adult" tapes that dominated the prerecorded video market during its infancy.

Now, even mid-range VCRs boast stereo sound, while high-end machines promise to deliver far better picture quality than broadcast television. Prices in home video's second decade—for the astute shopper—remain low. (Anyone who pays the full suggested retail price for a VCR in the 1990s either is a fool or shops on Rodeo Drive.)

But while VCR quality has improved and prices have dropped (in constant dollars) since the late '70s, buying and installing one has become both confusing and confounding. You'd think the predominance of the VHS format would have simplified the selection process. Well, it hasn't. You can blame the proliferation of subformats and add-ons, each with its own forest of acronyms and initials.

Walk into a video hardware store and you're faced with a choice of VHS, Super VHS, VHS-C, Beta, ED Beta, 8mm, and Hi8. Add to this an alphabetical thicket of options, including Hi-Fi, Dolby Surround, VHS HQ, PIP, MTS, and SAP, then set it all to music and you have a high-tech version of supercalifragilisticexpialidocious.

Once you haul one of these super-califragilistic VCRs home, get ready for a trip to Radio Shack for wire—*lots* of wire. Hi-Fi VCRs need a connection to a stereo amplifier in order to utilize the special Hi-Fi soundtrack. This requires a minimum of thirteen wires to make the amplifier and TV connections. Add another Hi-Fi VCR (for making copies) and soon the spaghetti mass of wires needed to hook all this stuff up becomes what one of my former wives referred to as the Thing That Lives Behind the Television Set (TTLBTTS).

Hooking up two Hi-Fi VCRs and a TV creates a TTLBTTS with twenty-one wires. Add in power cords and the wires leading from the stereo amplifier to a CD player and a turntable, and the TTLBTTS consists of thirty-six wires. Throw in a Dolby Surround system, and it's back to Radio Shack for two more speaker wires and a couple more amplifier wires—you'll end up with some forty wires writhing behind the TV.

Since wire neophytes often buy the wrong wire, sooner or later you'll end up, like me, with a Wire Bag—a high-tech version of an old-fashioned ball of string. I throw odd, mismatched bits of wire into the Wire Bag in hopes that as I upgrade or add items to the TTLBTTS I'll get lucky and find a piece of wire I need in the bag, rather than having to fork over more money to Radio Shack. At this stage, it also might be a good idea to buy stock in the Tandy Corporation, owner of Radio Shack.

But wait. Don't let visions of a wildly contorted and out of control TTLBTTS scare you away from participating fully in home video's second full decade. The process can be demystified and the tools made accessible.

First know your terms and acronyms.

BETA AND VHS. The original tape formats. You need to know that the prime difference between the two is the VHS cassette is larger than Beta's. This allows manufacturers to cram more tape into the VHS shell than into Beta's, which gives VHS more playing time. If you're stuck for dinner conversation, you might want to observe that the Beta "U" wrap is gentler on tape handling than the VHS "M" wrap. (The Beta tape travels in a U-shaped path around the video heads, while the VHS tape travels in what techies refer to as a more tortuous, M-shaped path around the heads.)

HEADS. Brass cylinders inside the VCR which read the information on the tape. The more heads a VCR has, the better it can hold a still picture or go in slow-motion or fast-forward while the image is on-screen. Top-of-the-line VCRs sport four heads.

ED BETA AND S-VHS. These stand for Extended Definition Beta and Super VHS. Ordinary Beta and VHS machines deliver about 240 lines of horizontal resolution to the 525-line television screen. S-VHS can deliver 400-plus lines of resolution while ED-Beta machines deliver 500-plus lines. The more lines, the better the picture. Unfortunately, few prerecorded video distributors have released tapes in either of these formats, so you're paying a premium to record off-the-air pictures with greater clarity. Both ED Beta and S-VHS achieve higher resolution by boosting the signal carrier frequency and splitting the brightness and color signals, feeding each from separate outputs on the VCR to separate inputs on the TV.

HQ. This is a technology designed to increase the resolution of standard VHS VCRs. To work best, VCRs should be equipped with all three HQ circuits. There are more people in the world who truly comprehend Einstein's theory of relativity than there are video salesmen who can tell you how many HQ circuits a particular VCR contains.

8MM AND HI8. Yet another tape format, this too backed by Sony. At about two-thirds the size of the ½-inch tape packed into both Beta and VHS tape shells, 8mm first found a niche in the camcorder market, where the small size of its cassettes meant smaller and lighter cameras. Look for Sony, which recently spent $3.4 billion to acquire Columbia Pictures, to release a lot of prerecorded tapes in the 8mm format.

Hi8 is the high-resolution version of 8mm (about 400 lines). Both 8mm and Hi8 can handle a digital stereo soundtrack, though the dynamic range is smaller than that of a CD.

VHS-C. The VHS camp's answer to 8mm. This downsized version of the VHS cassette shell can be used in smaller, lighter camcorders, but it requires an adapter for playback in a standard VHS deck.

MTS. Multichannel Television Sound, or a very long way to say "stereo TV." This Federal Communications Commission—backed standard allows television stations to broadcast programs in stereo while mono sets remain unaffected. One of the MTS channels is called SAP, for Separate Audio Program. Most SAP programming to date has been rather sappy (ahem), and many stations have yet to exploit it. New Jersey Public Television uses it to broadcast audio programming for the blind, while

WNET in New York has developed more ambitious plans for the SAP channel, including foreign-language simulcasts and broadcasts of the BBC World Service. A VCR with MTS capability makes it easy to record stereo broadcasts on the Hi-Fi track of VHS and Beta machines equipped with such a feature.

Hi-Fi. Not necessarily stereo. Sometimes not very Hi *or* Fi, either. When first introduced, both VHS and Beta VCRs recorded the soundtrack on a narrow, linear band at the bottom of the videotape. Sony and then JVC developed a method of interweaving a high-fidelity audio signal with the video signal across the entire tape width. This Hi-Fi signal can deliver a superior stereo sound—that is, *if* the source material was recorded in stereo. (Don't expect to magically hear *Casablanca* in true stereo sound.) Old movie soundtracks do, however, have less tape hiss when recorded in Hi-Fi. To get the maximum amount of enjoyment out of a truly stereo Hi-Fi tape, you really have to hook up your Hi-Fi VCR to a stereo amplifier. (Or play it through a stereo TV which has a built-in audio amplifier and quality speakers.)

Dolby Surround. Want to hear the Batmobile carom off all four walls of the home entertainment room? You'll need a Dolby Surround decoder to extract the rear-channel information, as well as an extra stereo amplifier (usually included), two more speakers, and a mess of wire. Beware of "surround" decoders which don't bear the Dolby trademark—plain vanilla surround doesn't do the job as well.

Dolby noise reduction. If you buy a VCR sporting this feature, I'd like to introduce you to a guy with a deal on a bridge. Dolby stereo–equipped VCRs usually sport a much lower price than Hi-Fi VCRs—and for good reason. Before Sony developed the Hi-Fi recording method, some VHS manufacturers decided to offer stereo capability by splitting the already thin linear track in half and then combating the tape hiss by adding Dolby noise reduction circuits. No hi and no fi in these beasts. Don't buy one. If you do, the kids will be as humiliated as if you dropped them off at the private school in a Toyota.

Digital. By the end of the '90s, people will be the only stuff left on the planet that are still analog, but until then, when you buy a VCR with the word "digital" plastered all over it, keep in mind that what you're buying is digital effects, not true digital recording. To make VCRs truly digital you need to have truly digital TV screens, which will only require the scrapping of the entire U.S. television broadcast system. (Then again, laserdiscs are digitally *recorded,* and JVC offers a truly digital *sound* system for its Super VHS VCRs.)

Until then, what digital VCRs *can* perform is some interesting tricks, using computer circuits to allow the viewer to store, manipulate, or enhance standard analog pictures. A common digital function is picture-in-picture (PIP), which allows you to watch a main program with another channel inset into a corner. Some VCRs come equipped with PIP functions that allow display of nine pictures at one time—getting an extra seven eyes is the viewer's problem.

Now that you're acronym qualified (AQ), you're almost ready to deal intelligently with a video store salesman. But before you decide what kind of VCR you want to buy, you should figure out what kind of machine best suits your needs. *That* will be determined by factors that at first don't seem to have anything to do with the VCR.

TYPE OF TV. Do you have a TV already equipped with MTS stereo, a state-of-the-art remote control, and 155-channel tuner? If so, you might get by with a VCR minus the bells and whistles you've already paid to put on your TV. Does the TV already sport a nine-picture PIP function? If so, you don't need the same function on the VCR—unless you absolutely love the novelty value of having nine extra tiny PIP-within-PIP pictures decorating your TV screen.

If you own an older TV set that does not have all the latest features, then make the plunge for the higher-end VCR with the idea that you'll probably use it as the main control center for your system. For example, if the old TV does not have MTS capability and you plan to buy a VCR, a few more dollars will give you MTS capability for both recording and viewing—instead of tuning in with the TV, you'll tune in with the stereo-equipped VCR.

Does your TV have direct "video in" and "video out" plugs? If not, accept the fact that you'll be sacrificing resolution by using the RF (radio frequency) cables to send signals from the VCR to the TV. (When using the RF cables, the VCR acts as a mini-transmitter, passing along the signal from a port on the VCR to the antenna plug or terminal on the TV.)

Unless your TV has special S-VHS plugs, don't even bother thinking about an S-VHS, ED-Beta, or Hi8 VCR. Without those plugs, you'll lose some of the clarity achieved by the VCRs' separation of color and brightness signals.

THE CABLE TV PROBLEM. If you have cable TV, you already *know* you have a problem. Wait until you add a VCR to the mix.

The cable industry, for the most part, seems unaware of the invention of the VCR or conveniently chooses to ignore a potentially rival medium. VCR manufacturers have tried to accommodate the cable industry by developing "cable ready" machines, whose 155-channel tuners are designed to pick up "normal" cable industry channeling schemes.

These machines are "ready" in about the same way that sixteen-year-old boys are ready: For either to work, they have to find someone or something that's accommodating. Call your cable company to determine what kind of channelization it uses. Even if the cable company's scheme will accommodate the ready VCR, you'll need to look for one that has a "loop through" circuit, which feeds the scrambled channels back to the cable box for decoding.

If your cable company's channels do not correspond to the channels on cable-ready VCRs, the cable-ready feature is worthless. You'll end up using the company's cable converter as a tuner.

Want to record MTS stereo programs off the air? Find out if your cable company "passes" along the MTS signals. (A few years back, the National Cable TV Association estimated it would take billions of dollars —more than enough to buy each cable company its own Stealth bomber—to reconfigure the nation's existing cable systems to carry MTS signals.) Some cable companies put stereo TV signals on the FM radio band. This means you're going to have to locate the FM tuner and the VCR together and engage in a Rube Goldbergian wiring exercise to make it all work.

YOUR AUDIO NEEDS. If you plan to purchase a low-end, mono-only VCR, skip this section. However, if you want to tap into all that both MTS and Hi-Fi sound offer, you need to think audio even though your intention was just to go video. Assess your stereo system. Since VCR "audio out" and "audio in" ports plug into the tape recorder ports of a stereo amplifier, you need to find out if you have any spare tape-jack plugs.

If you already own a cassette tape deck, it's likely that your stereo amp does not have any jacks to spare. This means buying a new stereo amp/tuner. I recommend "audio/video" tuners and amplifiers, which have plugs, ports, and jacks galore, including plugs for both VCR audio and video, allowing easy dubbing from one machine to another.

Many of these machines also feature FM/TV presets which allow automatic tuning of a cable channel and its companion FM audio soundtrack. Many of these high-end amplifiers also include Dolby Surround circuitry and a built-in rear-channel amplifier. While such gear is expensive, it is a neat, packaged solution to hooking all that audio and video gear together.

Some final thoughts gained from experience.

Buy a machine with on-screen programming. This feature allows you to set all the functions of your VCR—especially all the programs you want the VCR to record daily over the three months you plan to be in India visiting your spiritual master—with the remote control. If you don't buy a machine with such a feature, you'll spend many an intolerable hour scrunched on your knees trying to manipulate Lilliputian-sized buttons with Brobdingnagian fingers while going blind trying to focus on a liquid crystal display capable of being read only by eagle-eyed Marine snipers.

Don't expect a video salesman to know *anything*. He's there to move iron, not to inform—let alone satisfy —the customer. This is a transaction where the buyer must first be aware, then *beware*. Shop for prices. VCRs—especially mid-range machines—have more or less become commodity items. Shop around for the best price for the machine that best fits your needs. Then buy.

Oh yeah—and find an empty bag to be your Wire Bag. You'll be surprised how fast it fills up.

Index of Mail-Order Video Distributors

Compiled by
Judy Alk Karren

•

GENERAL

CABIN FEVER ENTERTAINMENT
100 West Putnam Avenue
Greenwich, CT 06830
1-800-55-FEVER

CAPTAIN BIJOU
P.O. Box 87
Toney, AL 35773
205-852-0198

CBS VIDEO CLUB
P.O. Box 1112
Dept. GH6
Terre Haute, IN 47811-1112
1-800-CBS-4804

CONGRESS VIDEO
1776 Broadway
Suite 1010
New York, NY 10019
1-800-VHS-TAPE

CRITIC'S CHOICE VIDEO
P.O. Box 549
Department KAP
Elk Grove Village, IL 60009
1-800-367-7765

MARKETING INTERNATIONAL
833 Summer Street
Stamford, CT 06905
1-800-624-6233

MGM/UA DIRECT
P.O. Box 5686
Denver, Colorado 80217
1-800-443-5500

MODERN TALKING PICTURE SERVICE
500 Park Street North
St. Petersburg, FL 33709
1-800-237-4599

MOVIES UNLIMITED
6736 Castor Avenue
Philadelphia, PA 19149
1-800-523-0823

Pacific Arts Video
50 North La Cienega Boulevard
Suite 210
Beverly Hills, CA 90211
1-800-538-5856
213-657-2233

Random House Home Video
400 Hahn Road
Westminster, MD 21157
1-800-733-3000

Special Interest Video
475 Oberlin Avenue South
CN 2112
Lakewood, NJ 08701-1062
1-800-522-0502

Time-Life Home Video
P.O. Box 8520
Harrisburg, PA 17105
1-800-255-8433

21st Genesis
15820 Arminta Street
Van Nuys, CA 91406
1-800-344-1060
810-787-0660

ART

Art/NY
138 Prince Street
New York, NY 10012
212-966-7446

Art on Video
12 Havermeyer Place
Greenwich, CT 06830
1-800-533-5278
Beta

Evergreen Video Society
213 West 35th Street
New York, NY 10001
1-800-225-7783

Facets Video
1517 West Fullerton Avenue
Chicago, IL 60614
1-800-331-6197
312-281-9075

Home Vision/Public Media Video
P.O. Box 800
Concord, MA 01742
1-800-262-8600
Beta

Kultur
121 Highway 36
West Long Branch, NJ 07764
1-800-4-KULTUR
201-229-2343
Beta

Lagoon Video
P.O. Box 5730
Santa Monica, CA 90405
213-823-4024

V.I.E.W. Video
34 East 23rd Street
New York, NY 10010
1-800-843-9843
212-674-5550
Beta, 8mm, laserdisc

AVANT-GARDE

Evergreen Video Society
213 West 35th Street
New York, NY 10001
1-800-225-7783

Lagoon Video
P.O. Box 5730
Santa Monica, CA 90405
213-823-4024

Mystic Fire Video
P.O. Box 1202
Montauk, NY 11954
1-800-727-8433

BLACK

Ms Print Plus
199-19 Linden Boulevard
St. Albans, NY 11412
718-527-2417

CHILDREN'S FILMS

CHILDREN'S CIRCLE
Newton Turnpike
Weston, CT 06883
1-800-KIDS-VID
203-222-0002

CINEMA PRODUCTS VIDEO
7410 Santa Monica Boulevard
West Hollywood, CA 90046
1-800-VID-TAPE
213-850-6500

FAMILY HOME ENTERTAINMENT
15400 Sherman Way
P.O. Box 10124
Van Nuys, CA 91410-0124
1-800-PLAY-FHE

FRIES HOME VIDEO
6922 Hollywood Boulevard
Los Angeles, CA 90028
1-800-248-1113 (info only)
213-201-8800
213-466-2266
Beta

FRONT-ROW VIDEO
P.O. Box 5032
Edison, NJ 08837
1-800-666-2800
201-225-8896

JUST FOR KIDS
6320 Canoga Avenue
17th floor
penthouse suite
Woodland Hills, CA 91365
818-715-1980
Beta

TWIN TOWER ENTERPRISES
18720 Oxnard Street
Suite 101
Tarzana, CA 91356
1-800-553-4321

V.I.E.W. VIDEO
34 East 23rd Street
New York, NY 10010

1-800-843-9843
212-674-5550
vhs, beta, 8mm laserdisc

CLASSICS

BLACKHAWK FILMS
12636 Beatrice Street
Los Angeles, CA 90066
1-800-826-2295

CAPTAIN BIJOU
P.O. Box 87
Toney, AL 35773
205-852-0198

EVERGREEN VIDEO SOCIETY
213 West 35th Street
New York, NY 10001
1-800-225-7783

KINO ON VIDEO
333 West 39th Street
New York, NY 10018
212-629-6880

RHINO VIDEO
2225 Colorado Avenue
Santa Monica, CA 90404
1-800-432-0020

21ST GENESIS
15820 Arminta Street
Van Nuys, CA 91406
1-800-344-1060
818-787-0660

VIDEO DIMENSIONS
530 West 23rd Street
New York, NY 10011
212-929-6135

VIDEO YESTERYEAR
Box C
Sandy Hook, CT 06482
1-800-243-0987

VIDEOTAKES
187 Parker Avenue
P.O. Box 648
Manasquan, NJ 08736
1-800-526-7002
201-528-5000

COOKING

VIDEOCRAFT CLASSICS
P.O. Box 8529
FDR Station
New York, NY 10150
212-246-9849

CULT

MPI HOME VIDEO
15825 Rob Roy Drive
Oak Forest, IL 60452
1-800-323-0442
312-687-7881

MYSTIC FIRE VIDEO
P.O. Box 1202
Montauk, NY 11954
1-800-727-8433
Beta

RHINO VIDEO
2225 Colorado Avenue
Santa Monica, CA 90404
1-800-432-0020

21ST GENESIS
15820 Arminta Street
Van Nuys, CA 91406
1-800-344-1060
818-787-0660

**TAMARELLE'S INTERNATIONAL
FILMS**
P.O. Box 1249
Chico, CA 95927
1-800-356-3577
916-895-3429

DOCUMENTARY

BRIGHTON VIDEO
250 West Fifth Street
Suite 2421
New York, NY 10019
1-800-542-5554
212-315-2502

EVERGREEN VIDEO SOCIETY
213 West 35th Street
New York, NY 10001
1-800-225-7783

KINO ON VIDEO
333 West 39th Street
New York, NY 10018
212-629-6880

LAGOON VIDEO
P.O. Box 5730
Santa Monica, CA 90405
213-823-4024

MPI HOME VIDEO
15825 Rob Roy Drive
Oak Forest, IL 60452
1-800-323-0442
312-687-7881

MYSTIC FIRE VIDEO
P.O. Box 1202
Montauk, NY 11954
1-800-727-8433
vhs, beta

PUBLIC MEDIA VIDEO
P.O. Box 800
Concord, MA 01742
1-800-262-8600
Beta

SIGNALS (PBS)
274 Fillmore Avenue East
St. Paul, MN 55107
1-800-669-9696

TIME-LIFE BOOKS AND MUSIC
1450 East Parham Road
Richmond, VA 23280
1-800-621-7026

V.I.E.W. VIDEO
34 East 23rd Street
New York, NY 10010
1-800-843-9843
212-674-5550
Beta, 8mm, laserdisc

WILLOW MIXED MEDIA
P.O. Box 194
Glenford, NY 12433
914-657-2914

FOREIGN FILMS

CINEVISTA
353 West 39th Street
Suite 404
New York, NY 10018
1-800-447-0196
212-947-4373

CONNOISSEUR VIDEO COLLECTION
8436 West Third Street
Suite 600
Los Angeles, CA 90048
213-653-8873

CORINTH
34 Gansevoort Street
New York, NY 10014
1-800-221-4720
212-463-0305
Beta

FACETS VIDEO
1517 West Fullerton Avenue
Chicago, IL 60614
1-800-331-6197
312-281-9075

HOME FILM FESTIVAL
P.O. Box 2032
Scranton, PA 18501
1-800-258-3456
1-800-633-3456 (in PA)

INTERAMA VIDEO CLASSICS
301 West 53rd Street
Suite 19E
New York, NY 10019
212-977-4830
Beta

KINO ON VIDEO
333 West 39th Street
New York, NY 10018
212-629-6880

NEW YORKER VIDEO
16 West 61st Street
11th Floor
New York, NY 10023
212-247-6110

TAMARELLE'S INTERNATIONAL FILMS
P.O. Box 1249
Chico, CA 95927
1-800-356-3577
916-895-3429

U. S. GOVERNMENT FILMS

NATIONAL AUDIOVISUAL CENTER
8700 Edgeworth Drive
Capitol Heights, MD 20743-3701
1-800-638-1300
301-763-1896

MODERN TALKING PICTURE SERVICE
5000 Park Street North
St. Petersburg, FL 33709
1-800-237-4599

HEALTH/ FITNESS

CINERGY ENTERTAINMENT
858 12th Street
Suite 8
Santa Monica, CA 90403
1-800-237-9661 (outside CA)
213-451-2513

HEALING ARTS HOME VIDEO
1223 Third Street
Suite C
Santa Monica, CA 90401
1-800-722-7347
213-458-9797
Beta

V.I.E.W. VIDEO
34 East 23rd Street
New York, NY 10010
1-800-843-9843
212-674-5550
Beta

HISTORY

INTERNATIONAL HISTORIC FILMS
Box 29035
Chicago, IL 60629
312-927-2900
Beta

READER'S DIGEST
Pleasantville, NY 10570
1-800-431-1246

INSTRUCTIONAL

DIY VIDEO CORPORATION
P.O. Box 36565
Charlotte, NC 28236
704-342-9608

PREMIERE HOME VIDEO
6824 Melrose Avenue
Los Angeles, CA 90038
1-800-525-4313
213-934-8903

TAMARELLE'S INTERNATIONAL FILMS
P.O. Box 1249
Chico, CA 95927
1-800-356-3577
916-895-3429

VIDEO LEARNING LIBRARY
7201 Haven Avenue
Suite E
Alta Loma, CA 91701
1-800-383-8811

VIDEOTAKES
187 Parker Avenue
P.O. Box 648
Manasquan, NJ 08736
1-800-526-7002

JUDAICA

ALDEN FILMS
P.O. Box 449
Clarksburg, NJ 08510
201-462-3522
vhs, beta

ERGO MEDIA
P.O. Box 2037
Teaneck, NY 07666
201-692-0404
Beta

NATIONAL CENTER FOR JEWISH FILM
Brandeis University
Lown Building, Room 102
Waltham, MA 02254
617-899-7044

MUSIC

CABIN FEVER ENTERTAINMENT
100 West Putnam Avenue
Greenwich, CT 06830
1-800-55-FEVER

DCI MUSIC VIDEO
541 Avenue of the Americas
New York, NY 10011
1-800-342-4500
212-924-6624

FRIES HOME ENTERTAINMENT
6922 Hollywood Boulevard
Los Angeles, CA 90028
1-800-248-1113
213-201-6800
213-466-2266

MPI HOME VIDEO
15825 Rob Roy Drive
Oak Forest, IL 60452
1-800-323-0442
312-687-7881

RHAPSODY FILMS
P.O. Box 179
30 Charlton Street
New York, NY 10014
212-243-0152

RHINO VIDEO
2225 Colorado Avenue
Santa Monica, CA 90404
213-828-1980

URBAN VIDEO NETWORK (JAZZ)
P.O. Box 5207
East Orange, NJ 07017
201-675-7281

VIDEO ARTISTS INTERNATIONAL
2112 Broadway
Suite 415
New York, NY 10023
1-800-338-2566

V.I.E.W. VIDEO
34 East 23rd Street
New York, NY 10010
1-800-843-9843
212-674-5550

NATURE

BULLFROG FILMS
Oley, PA 19547
1-800-543-FROG
vhs, beta

ENVIRONMENTAL VIDEO
P.O. Box 577
Manhattan Beach, CA 90266
1-800-332-1140
213-515-3302

NATIONAL AUDUBON SOCIETY
950 Third Avenue
New York, NY 10022
212-832-3200

NATIONAL GEOGRAPHIC SOCIETY
Education Service
Washington, DC 20036
1-800-368-2728

PUBLIC MEDIA VIDEO
P.O. Box 800
Concord, MA 01742
1-800-262-8600
Beta

TIME-LIFE BOOKS AND MUSIC
1450 East Parham Road
Richmond, VA 23280
1-800-621-7026

NEW AGE

MYSTIC FIRE VIDEO
P.O. Box 1202
Montauk, NY 11954

1-800-727-8433
Beta

PERFORMING ARTS

CORINTH
34 Gansevoort Street
New York, NY 10014
1-800-221-4720
212-463-0305
Beta

FACETS VIDEO
1517 West Fullerton Avenue
Chicago, IL 60614
1-800-331-6197
312-281-9075

HOME VISION/PUBLIC MEDIA VIDEO
P.O. Box 800
Concord, MA 01742
1-800-262-8600
Beta

KULTUR
121 Highway 36
West Long Branch, NJ 07764
1-800-4-KULTUR
201-229-2343
Beta

MYSTIC FIRE VIDEO
P.O. Box 1202
Montauk, NY 11954
1-800-727-8433
Beta

VIDEO ARTISTS INTERNATIONAL
2112 Broadway
Suite 415
New York, NY 10023
1-800-338-2566

RELIGIOUS

FOCUS ON THE FAMILY
Pomona, CA 91799
1-800-A-FAMILY
714-620-8500

VANGUARD VIDEO
6535 East Skelly Drive
Tulsa, OK 74145
1-800-331-4077

VISION VIDEO
2030 Wentz Church Road
Box 540
Worcester, PA 19490
1-800-523-0226

SPANISH LANGUAGE

CLUB-VID (VID DIMENSION)
424 South C Street
Madera, CA 93638
1-800-233-0089

DATEL
12901 Coral Tree Place
Los Angeles, CA 90066
1-800-666-5088

MILLION DOLLAR VIDEO
5900 Wilshire Boulevard
Suite 500
Los Angeles, CA 90036
1-800-888-9940
213-933-1616

SPORTS

BABE WINKELMAN PRODUCTIONS
P.O. Box 407
Brainerd, MN 56401
218-963-4424

BENNETT MARINE VIDEO
730 Washington Street
Marina del Rey, CA 90292
1-800-262-8862
213-821-3329

BEST FILM AND VIDEO
98 Cutter Mill Road
Great Neck, NY 11021
1-800-527-2189
516-487-4515

CABIN FEVER ENTERTAINMENT
100 West Putnam Avenue

Greenwich, CT 06830
1-800-55-FEVER

COLISEUM VIDEO
430 West 54th Street
New York, NY 10019
1-800-288-8130
212-489-8130

DIAMOND ENTERTAINMENT
833 Summer Street
Stamford, CT 06905
1-800-624-6233

J2 COMMUNICATIONS
10850 Wilshire Boulevard
Suite 1000
Los Angeles, CA 90024
1-800-521-7797
213-474-J2J2

MAJOR LEAGUE BASEBALL PRODUCTIONS
1212 Avenue of the Americas
New York, NY 10036
212-921-8100

NFL FILMS VIDEO
330 Fellowship Road
Mt. Laurel, NJ 08054
1-800-NFL-TAPE
609-778-1600

TROPHY VIDEO
2814 Hickory Street
Yorktown Heights, NY 10598
1-800-992-3362
914-245-1728

TELEVISION SHOWS

CORINTH
34 Gansevoort Street
New York, NY 10014
1-800-221-4720
Beta

MPI HOME VIDEO
15825 Rob Roy Drive
Oak Forest, IL 60452
1-800-323-0442
312-687-7881

MYSTIC FIRE VIDEO
P.O. Box 1202
Montauk, NY 11954
1-800-727-8433
Beta

RHINO VIDEO
2225 Colorado Avenue
Santa Monica, CA 90404
213-828-1980

VIDEO DIMENSIONS
530 West 23rd Street
New York, NY 10011
212-929-6135

TRAVEL

BEST FILM AND VIDEO
98 Cutter Mill Road
Great Neck, NY 11021
1-800-527-2189
516-487-4515

HOUSE OF TYROL
P.O. Box 909
Alpenland Center
Helen Highway

75 North
Cleveland, GA 30528
1-800-241-5404 (orders only)
404-865-5115

INTERNATIONAL VIDEO NETWORK
2242 Comino Ramon
San Ramon, CA 94583
415-866-1121

READER'S DIGEST
Pleasantville, NY 10570
1-800-431-1246

TAMARELLE'S INTERNATIONAL FILMS
P.O. Box 1249
Chico, CA 95927
1-800-356-3577
916-895-3429

WESTERNS

HOLLYWOOD'S ATTIC
138 Fifth Avenue
Pelham, NY 10803
1-800-3-OLDIES

INDEX OF
MOVIE
TITLES

———●———

Other credits: Screenplay by John Piel-meyer, based on his play; cinematography by Sven Nykvist
VHS availability: GoodTimes Home Video
Religion in Extremis, p. 195

THE AGONY AND THE ECSTASY
(1965)
140 min.; Color
Director: Carol Reed
Cast: Charlton Heston, Rex Harrison
Other credits: Screenplay by Philip Dunne, based on the novel by Irving Stone; music by Alex North
VHS availability: CBS/Fox Video
Artists, p. 94

ALICE IN THE CITIES
(1974)
110 min.; BW
In German; English subtitles
Director: Wim Wenders
Cast: Rüdiger Vogler, Yella Rottländer
Other credits: Screenplay by Wenders and Veith der Furstenberg; cinematography by Robby Müller
VHS availability: Pacific Arts Video
Tales of Three Cities, p. 37

ALIEN
(1979)
117 min.; Color
Director: Ridley Scott
Cast: Sigourney Weaver, John Hurt, Harry Dean Stanton
Academy Awards: Best Visual Effects
Other credits: Screenplay by Dan O'Ban-non; story by O'Bannon and Ronald Shusett; music by Jerry Goldsmith
VHS availability: CBS/Fox Video
Sci-Fi, p. 109

ALIENS
(1986)
136 min.; Color
Director: James Cameron
Cast: Sigourney Weaver, Carrie Henn, Michael Biehn
Academy Awards: Best Visual Effects, Best Sound Effects Editing
Other credits: Screenplay by Cameron; story by Cameron, David Giler, and

Walter Hill, based on characters created by Dan O'Bannon and Ronald Shusett
VHS availability: CBS/Fox Video
Sci-Fi, p. 109

ALL ABOUT EVE
(1950)
138 min.; BW
Director: Joseph L. Mankiewicz
Cast: Bette Davis, George Sanders, Anne Baxter
Academy Awards: Best Picture, Best Di-rection (Mankiewicz), Best Screenplay (Mankiewicz), Best Supporting Actor (Sanders), Best Sound Recording
VHS availability: Key Video
Directors' Choice I, p. 18
Journalists, p. 169

ALL OF ME
(1984)
93 min.; Color
Director: Carl Reiner
Cast: Steve Martin, Lily Tomlin
Other credits: Screenplay by Phil Alden Robinson and Henry Olek, based on the novel *Me Too* by Ed Davis
VHS availability: HBO Video
Directors' Choice I, p. 15

ALL THE KING'S MEN
(1949)
109 min.; BW
Director: Robert Rossen
Cast: Broderick Crawford, Mercedes McCambridge, John Ireland
Academy Awards: Best Picture, Best Actor (Crawford), Best Supporting Ac-tress (McCambridge)
Other credits: Screenplay by Rossen, based on the novel by Robert Penn Warren
FYI: McCambridge's movie debut
VHS availability: RCA/Columbia Pic-tures Home Video
Politics, p. 89

ALL THE PRESIDENT'S MEN
(1976)
138 min.; Color
Director: Alan J. Pakula
Cast: Robert Redford, Dustin Hoffman, Jason Robards

Academy Awards: Best Adapted Screenplay (William Goldman), Best Supporting Actor (Robards)
Other credits: Based on the book by Carl Bernstein and Bob Woodward; cinematography by Gordon Willis
VHS availability: Warner Home Video
Journalists, p. 167

ALPHAVILLE
(1965)
98 min.; BW
In French; English subtitles
Director: Jean-Luc Godard
Cast: Eddie Constantine, Anna Karina
Other credits: Screenplay by Godard; cinematography by Raoul Coutard
VHS availability: Connoisseur Video Collection
Tales of Three Cities, p. 38

ALTERED STATES
(1980)
102 min.; Color
Director: Ken Russell
Cast: William Hurt, Blair Brown
FYI: "Sidney Aaron" credited as screenwriter after Paddy Chayefsky had his name removed
VHS availability: Warner Home Video
TV Actors in the Movies, p. 64

AMADEUS
(1984)
158 min.; Color
Director: Miloš Forman
Cast: F. Murray Abraham, Tom Hulce, Elizabeth Berridge
Academy Awards: Best Picture, Best Actor (Abraham), Best Direction (Forman), Best Adapted Screenplay (Peter Shaffer), Best Art Direction, Best Costume Design, Best Makeup.
Other credits: Based on Shaffer's play
VHS availability: HBO Video
The Greatest Movies of the '80s,
p. 224

AN AMERICAN IN PARIS
(1951)
131 min.; Color
Director: Vincente Minnelli

Cast: Gene Kelly, Oscar Levant, Leslie Caron
Academy Awards: Best Picture, Best Story and Screenplay (Alan Jay Lerner), Best Cinematography (Alfred Gilks), Best Scoring of a Musical
VHS availability: MGM/UA Home Video
Tales of Three Cities, p. 38
Artists, p. 98

ANDY WARHOL'S DRACULA
(1974)
93 min.; Color
Director: Paul Morrissey
Cast: Udo Kier, Joe Dallesandro
FYI: Originally shot in 3-D
VHS availability: Rental only
Virgins, p. 121

A NOS AMOURS
(1984)
102 min.; Color
In French; English subtitles
Director: Maurice Pialat
Cast: Sandrine Bonnaire, Dominique Besnehard, Pialat
Other credits: Screenplay by Pialat and Arlette Langmann
VHS availability: Facets Video
The Greatest Movies of the '80s,
p. 233

ASHES AND DIAMONDS
(1958)
105 min.; BW
In Polish; English subtitles
Director: Andrzej Wajda
Cast: Zbigniew Cybulski, Ewa Krzyzanowska, Adam Pawlikowski
Other credits: Screenplay by Wajda and Jerzy Andrzejewski, based on Andrzejewski's novel
VHS availability: Nelson Entertainment
Critics' Choice, p. 26

ATLANTIC CITY
(1981)
87 min.; Color
Director: Louis Malle
Cast: Burt Lancaster, Susan Sarandon, Kate Reid, Robert Joy

Other credits: Screenplay by John Guare
FYI: Shot in Atlantic City as the first casinos were being constructed
VHS availability: Paramount Home Video
The Greatest Movies of the '80s, p. 226

THE ATOMIC CAFE
(1982)
88 min.; Color
Documentary
Directors: Kevin Rafferty, Jayne Loader, Pierce Rafferty
VHS availability: Rental only
Critics' Choice, p. 26

AU REVOIR LES ENFANTS
(1987)
103 min.; Color
In French; English subtitles
Director: Louis Malle
Cast: Gaspard Manesse, Raphael Fejto
Other credits: Screenplay by Malle
VHS availability: Orion Home Video
The Greatest Movies of the '80s, p. 230

AUTUMN LEAVES
(1956)
108 min.; BW
Director: Robert Aldrich
Cast: Joan Crawford, Cliff Robertson, Vera Miles
VHS availability: RCA/Columbia Pictures Home Video
Enhancing Your Bad Moods, p. 29

L'AVVENTURA
(1960)
145 min.; BW
In Italian; English subtitles
Director: Michelangelo Antonioni
Cast: Gabriele Ferzetti, Monica Vitti, Lea Massari
Other credits: Screenplay by Elio Bartolini, Tonino Guerra, and Antonioni
VHS availability: Connoisseur Video Collection
Slow Movies/Fast Films, p. 150

THE AWFUL TRUTH
(1937)
92 min.; BW
Director: Leo McCarey
Cast: Cary Grant, Irene Dunne, Ralph Bellamy
Academy Awards: Best Direction (McCarey)
Other credits: Based on the play by Arthur Richman
VHS availability: RCA/Columbia Pictures Home Video
Love and Marriage, p. 58
Screwball Comedies, p. 186

B

BABETTE'S FEAST
(1987)
102 min.; Color
In Danish; English subtitles
Director: Gabriel Axel
Cast: Stéphane Audran, Jean-Philippe Lafont
Academy Awards: Best Foreign Language Film
Other credits: Screenplay by Axel, based on a story by Isak Dinesen
FYI: The first Danish film to win Best Foreign Language Film
VHS availability: Orion Home Video
The Greatest Movies of the '80s, p. 231

BACK STREET
(1961)
107 min.; Color
Director: David Miller
Cast: Susan Hayward, John Gavin, Vera Miles
Other credits: Based on the novel by Fannie Hurst
FYI: Back Street was filmed twice before: in 1932, with Irene Dunne and John Boles; and in 1941, with Margaret Sullavan and Charles Boyer
VHS availability: MCA/Universal Home Video
Triangles, p. 157

THE BIRDS
(1963)
120 min.; Color
Director: Alfred Hitchcock
Cast: Tippi Hedren, Rod Taylor, Jessica Tandy
Other credits: Screenplay by Evan Hunter, based on the story by Daphne du Maurier; music by Bernard Herrmann
FYI: Hitchcock appears in the beginning, in front of a San Francisco pet store
VHS availability: MCA/Universal Home Video

BLACK NARCISSUS
(1947)
99 min.; Color
Directors: Michael Powell, Emeric Pressburger
Cast: Deborah Kerr, David Farrar, Sabu, Jean Simmons
Academy Awards: Best Color Cinematography, Best Color Art Direction
Other credits: Screenplay by Powell and Pressburger, based on the novel by Rumer Godden
VHS availability: Rental only

BLADE RUNNER
(1982)
118 min.; Color
Director: Ridley Scott
Cast: Harrison Ford, Sean Young, Rutger Hauer
Other credits: Based on the novel *Do Androids Dream of Electric Sheep?* by Philip K. Dick; music by Vangelis
VHS availability: Nelson Entertainment

BLOODY MAMA
(1970)
90 min.; Color
Director: Roger Corman
Cast: Shelley Winters, Robert De Niro, Bruce Dern
VHS availability: Vestron Video

BLOW OUT
(1981)
107 min.; Color
Director: Brian De Palma
Cast: John Travolta, Nancy Allen
Other credits: Screenplay by De Palma; cinematography by Vilmos Zsigmond
VHS availability: Rental only

BLUE HAWAII
(1961)
101 min.; Color
Director: Norman Taurog
Cast: Elvis Presley, Joan Blackman, Angela Lansbury
VHS availability: CBS/Fox Video

BLUE VELVET
(1986)
120 min.; Color
Director: David Lynch
Cast: Kyle MacLachlan, Dennis Hopper, Isabella Rossellini
Other credits: Screenplay by Lynch; cinematography by Fred Elmes, music by Angelo Badalamenti
VHS availability: Warner Home Video

BOB LE FLAMBEUR
(1955)
102 min.; BW
In French; English subtitles
Director: Jean-Pierre Melville
Cast: Roger Duchesne, Isabelle Corey, Daniel Cauchy
VHS availability: RCA/Columbia Pictures Home Video

BODY HEAT
(1981)
113 min.; Color
Director: Lawrence Kasdan
Cast: William Hurt, Kathleen Turner, Ted Danson

Other credits: Screenplay by Kasdan
VHS availability: Warner Home Video
Winter Antidotes, p. 79

BONNIE AND CLYDE
(1967)
111 min.; Color
Director: Arthur Penn
Cast: Faye Dunaway, Warren Beatty, Gene Hackman, Estelle Parsons
Academy Awards: Best Supporting Actress (Parsons), Best Cinematography (Burnett Guffey)
Other credits: Screenplay by Robert Benton and Robert Newman
VHS availability: Warner Home Video
Trompe l'Oeil, p. 47

DAS BOOT
(1982)
145 min.; Color
In German; English subtitles; dubbed version *(The Boat)*
Director: Wolfgang Petersen
Cast: Jürgen Prochnow, Herbert Gronemeyer, Klaus Wennemann
Other credits: Screenplay by Petersen, based on the novel by Lothar-Günther Buchheim
VHS availability: RCA/Columbia Pictures Home Video
The Greatest Movies of the '80s, p. 229

BOUDU SAVED FROM DROWNING
(1932)
87 min.; BW
In French; English subtitles
Director: Jean Renoir
Cast: Michel Simon, Charles Grandval, Marcelle Hainia
Other credits: Screenplay by Renoir, based on a play by René Fauchois
FYI: Remade as *Down and Out in Beverly Hills* in 1986
VHS availability: Facets Video
Tales of Three Cities, p. 38

THE BOUNTY
(1984)
130 min.; Color
Director: Roger Donaldson

Cast: Anthony Hopkins, Mel Gibson, Laurence Olivier, Daniel Day-Lewis
Other credits: Screenplay by Robert Bolt; music by Vangelis
VHS availability: Vestron Video
Critics' Choice, p. 20

BOYFRIENDS AND GIRLFRIENDS
(1988)
102 min.; Color
In French; English subtitles
Director: Eric Rohmer
Cast: Emmanuelle Chaulet, Sophie Renoir, Eric Viellard, François-Eric Gendron, Anne-Laure Meury
Other credits: Screenplay by Rohmer
FYI: The sixth and final installment of Rohmer's "Comedies and Proverbs" series
VHS availability: Orion Home Video
The Greatest Movies of the '80s, p. 226

BREAKER MORANT
(1980)
107 min.; Color
Director: Bruce Beresford
Cast: Edward Woodward, Jack Thompson, Bryan Brown
VHS availability: LIVE Home Video
TV Actors in the Movies, p. 64

BREAKFAST AT TIFFANY'S
(1961)
115 min.; Color
Director: Blake Edwards
Cast: Audrey Hepburn, George Peppard, Patricia Neal, Mickey Rooney
Academy Awards: Best Song ("Moon River")
Other credits: Screenplay by George Axelrod, based on the novel by Truman Capote
VHS availability: Paramount Home Video
Food, p. 48
Censorship, p. 177

THE BREAKFAST CLUB
(1985)
97 min.; Color
Director: John Hughes
Cast: Molly Ringwald, Anthony Mi-

chael Hall, Emilio Estevez, Judd Nelson, Ally Sheedy
Other credits: Screenplay by Hughes
FYI: Cameos by Anthony Michael Hall's mother and sister
VHS availability: MCA/Universal Home Video
School Days, p. 68

BREAKING AWAY
(1979)
100 min.; Color
Director: Peter Yates
Cast: Dennis Christopher, Dennis Quaid, Daniel Stern, Jackie Earle Haley
Academy Awards: Best Screenplay (Steve Tesich)
VHS availability: CBS/Fox Video
School Days, p. 68
Underdogs, p. 162

THE BRIDE OF FRANKENSTEIN
(1935)
75 min.; BW
Director: James Whale
Cast: Boris Karloff, Elsa Lanchester, Colin Clive, Valerie Hobson
VHS availability: MCA/Universal Home Video
Directors' Choice I, p. 14

BRINGING UP BABY
(1938)
102 min.; BW
Director: Howard Hawks
Cast: Cary Grant, Katharine Hepburn
Other credits: Screenplay by Dudley Nichols and Hagar Wilde, story by Wilde
FYI: Hepburn's dog, George, is played by Asta of *Thin Man* fame
VHS availability: Turner Home Entertainment
Screwball Comedies, p. 186

BROADCAST NEWS
(1987)
131 min.; Color
Director: James L. Brooks
Cast: Holly Hunter, Albert Brooks, William Hurt
FYI: Jack Nicholson makes a brief, un-

credited appearance as a network anchor
VHS availability: CBS/Fox Video
Journalists, p. 169

BROADWAY DANNY ROSE
(1984)
86 min.; BW
Director: Woody Allen
Cast: Allen, Mia Farrow, Nick Apollo Forte
Other credits: Screenplay by Allen; cinematography by Gordon Willis
VHS availability: Vestron Video
Tales of Three Cities, p. 37

THE BROOD
(1979)
90 min.; Color
Director: David Cronenberg
Cast: Samantha Eggar, Oliver Reed
Other credits: Screenplay by Cronenberg
VHS availability: Nelson Entertainment
Family Troubles, p. 122

BUDDY, BUDDY
(1981)
96 min.; Color
Director: Billy Wilder
Cast: Jack Lemmon, Walter Matthau
Other credits: Screenplay by Wilder, adapted from the 1974 French-Italian movie, *A Pain in the A—,* starring Lino Ventura and Jacques Brel
VHS availability: Rental only
Enhancing Your Bad Moods, p. 33

THE BUGS BUNNY/ROAD RUNNER MOVIE
(1979)
92 min.; Color
Compilation of animated shorts
Directors: Chuck Jones, Phil Monroe
VHS availability: Rental only
Directors' Choice I, p. 14

C

CABARET
(1972)
128 min.; Color
Director: Bob Fosse

Cast: Liza Minnelli, Joel Grey, Michael York
Academy Awards: Best Actress (Minnelli), Best Supporting Actor (Grey), Best Direction (Fosse), Best Cinematography (Geoffrey Unsworth), Best Art Direction, Best Sound, Best Film Editing, Best Score (Ralph Burns)
Other credits: Based on the Broadway musical by John Kander and Fred Ebb
VHS availability: CBS/Fox Video
Directors' Choice I, p. 15
Musicals, p. 103

CALAMITY JANE
(1953)
101 min.; Color
Director: David Butler
Cast: Doris Day, Howard Keel, Allyn McLerie
Academy Awards: Best Song ("Secret Love")
VHS availability: Warner Home Video
Good and Evil, p. 85

THE CANDIDATE
(1972)
109 min.; Color
Director: Michael Ritchie
Cast: Robert Redford, Melvyn Douglas, Peter Boyle
Other credits: Screenplay by Jeremy Larner
VHS availability: Warner Home Video
Directors' Choice I, p. 18
Politics, p. 91

CAN'T STOP THE MUSIC
(1980)
118 min.; Color
Director: Nancy Walker
Cast: Steve Guttenberg, Valerie Perrine, Bruce Jenner
FYI: Featuring the Top 40 hits of the disco group the Village People
VHS availability: HBO Video
The '70s, p. 130

CAN YOU HEAR THE LAUGHTER?
(1979)
100 min.; Color
TV movie; sometimes subtitled *The Story of Freddie Prinze*

Director: Burt Brinckerhoff
Cast: Ira Angustain, Kevin Hooks, Randee Heller
VHS availability: Rental only
The '70s, p. 129

CARAVAGGIO
(1986)
93 min.; Color
Director: Derek Jarman
Cast: Nigel Terry, Sean Bean
Other credits: Screenplay by Jarman
VHS availability: Facets Video
Artists, p. 96

CARNAL KNOWLEDGE
(1971)
96 min.; Color
Director: Mike Nichols
Cast: Jack Nicholson, Art Garfunkel, Candice Bergen, Ann-Margret
Other credits: Screenplay by Jules Feiffer; cinematography by Giuseppe Rotunno
VHS availability: Nelson Entertainment
School Days, p. 68

CARRIE
(1976)
97 min.; Color
Director: Brian De Palma
Cast: Sissy Spacek, Piper Laurie, John Travolta, Amy Irving, Nancy Allen
Other credits: Screenplay by Lawrence D. Cohen, based on the novel by Stephen King
VHS availability: MGM/UA Home Video
Enhancing Your Bad Moods, p. 34
School Days, p. 71
Religion in Extremis, p. 198

CAT ON A HOT TIN ROOF
(1958)
108 min.; Color
Director: Richard Brooks
Cast: Elizabeth Taylor, Paul Newman, Burl Ives
Other credits: Screenplay by Brooks and James Poe, based on the play by Tennessee Williams

VHS availability: MGM/UA Home Video

Censorship, p. 177

CAUGHT
(1949)
88 min.; BW
Director: Max Ophuls
Cast: James Mason, Barbara Bel Geddes, Robert Ryan
Other credits: Screenplay by Arthur Laurents, based on the novel *Wild Calendar* by Libbie Block; cinematography by Lee Garmes
VHS availability: Republic Pictures Home Video

Triangles, p. 157

THE CHASE
(1966)
135 min.; Color
Director: Arthur Penn
Cast: Robert Redford, Jane Fonda, E. G. Marshall, Marlon Brando
Other credits: Screenplay by Lillian Hellman, based on the novel and play by Horton Foote
VHS availability: GoodTimes Home Video

Small Towns, p. 136

CHERRY, HARRY, AND RAQUEL
(1969)
71 min.; Color
Director: Russ Meyer
Cast: Charles Napier, Uschi Digard
VHS availability: RM Films International

Winter Antidotes, p. 79

CHINATOWN
(1974)
131 min.; Color
Director: Roman Polanski
Cast: Jack Nicholson, Faye Dunaway, John Huston
Academy Awards: Best Screenplay (Robert Towne)
Other credits: Music by Jerry Goldsmith
VHS availability: Paramount Home Video

Tales of Three Cities, p. 40

CHOOSE ME
(1984)
106 min.; Color
Director: Alan Rudolph
Cast: Keith Carradine, Lesley Ann Warren, Geneviève Bujold
Other credits: Screenplay by Rudolph
VHS availability: Media Home Entertainment

Critics' Choice, p. 23

CIAO! MANHATTAN
(1973)
90 min.; BW
Director: John Palmer
Cast: David Weisman, Edie Sedgwick
VHS availability: Pacific Arts Video

Fame, p. 112

CITIZEN KANE
(1941)
119 min.; BW
Director: Orson Welles
Cast: Orson Welles, Joseph Cotten, Dorothy Comingore
Academy Awards: Best Screenplay (Welles and Herman J. Mankiewicz)
Other credits: Cinematography by Gregg Toland
FYI: Welles's directorial and cinematic debut
VHS availability: Turner Home Entertainment

Directors' Choice I, p. 12

CITIZENS BAND
(1977)
98 min.; Color
Director: Jonathan Demme
Cast: Paul Le Mat, Ann Wedgeworth, Candy Clark
Other credits: Screenplay by Paul Brickman
FYI: Rereleased as *Handle With Care*
VHS availability: Rental only

Critics' Choice, p. 21

THE COLOR PURPLE
(1985)
152 min.; Color
Director: Steven Spielberg
Cast: Whoopi Goldberg, Oprah Winfrey, Danny Glover, Margaret Avery

Other credits: Screenplay by Menno Meyjes, based on the novel by Alice Walker; music by Quincy Jones
VHS availability: Warner Home Video
Underdogs, p. 164

CONVOY
(1978)
110 min.; Color
Director: Sam Peckinpah
Cast: Kris Kristofferson, Ali MacGraw, Ernest Borgnine
VHS availability: Rental only
The '70s, p. 131

THE COTTON CLUB
(1984)
127 min.; Color
Director: Francis Ford Coppola
Cast: Richard Gere, Diane Lane, Gregory Hines
Other credits: Screenplay by Coppola and William Kennedy
FYI: Richard Gere plays his own cornet solos
VHS availability: Nelson Entertainment
Slow Movies/Fast Films, p. 153

COUP DE TORCHON
(1981)
128 min.; Color
In French; English subtitles
Director: Bertrand Tavernier
Cast: Philippe Noiret, Isabelle Huppert, Stéphane Audran
Other credits: Screenplay by Tavernier and Jean Aurenche, based on the novel *Pop. 1280* by Jim Thompson; music by Philippe Sarde
VHS availability: Facets Video
Critics' Choice, p. 24

CRIMES OF PASSION
(1984)
101 min.; Color
Director: Ken Russell
Cast: Kathleen Turner, Anthony Perkins, John Laughlin
Other credits: Screenplay by Barry Sandler
VHS availability: New World Video
Censorship, p. 174

CUTTER'S WAY
(1981)
105 min.; Color
Director: Ivan Passer
Cast: Jeff Bridges, John Heard, Lisa Eichhorn
Other credits: Music by Jack Nitzsche
FYI: Originally released as *Cutter and Bone*
VHS availability: MGM/UA Home Videos
Critics' Choice, p. 21

D

DAMES
(1934)
90 min.; BW
Director: Ray Enright
Cast: Joan Blondell, Dick Powell, Ruby Keeler, Zasu Pitts
Other credits: Choreography by Busby Berkeley
VHS availability: Key Video
Musicals, p. 101

DANGEROUS LIAISONS
(1988)
120 min.; Color
Director: Stephen Frears
Cast: Glenn Close, John Malkovich, Michelle Pfeiffer
Academy Awards: Best Adapted Screenplay (Christopher Hampton), Best Costume Design
Other credits: Based on Hampton's play *Les Liaisons Dangereuses,* adapted from the Choderlos de Laclos novel
VHS availability: Warner Home Video; letterboxed
The Greatest Movies of the '80s, p. 220

DANTON
(1983)
136 min.; Color
In French; English subtitles
Director: Andrzej Wajda

Cast: Gérard Depardieu, Wojciech Pszoniak
FYI: Wajda's first film made outside Poland
VHS availability: RCA/Columbia Pictures Home Video
The Greatest Movies of the '80s,
p. 223

DAVID COPPERFIELD
(1955)
130 min.; BW
Director: George Cukor
Cast: Freddie Bartholomew, W. C. Fields, Lionel Barrymore
Other credits: Based on the Dickens novel
FYI: Before Fields was hired, Charles Laughton was initially contracted to play Micawber
VHS availability: MGM/UA Home Video
An Elegant Hollywood Threesome,
p. 140

DAWN OF THE DEAD
(1979)
126 min.; Color
Director: George A. Romero
Cast: David Emge, Ken Foree
Other credits: Screenplay by Romero
FYI: The second installment of Romero's "Dead" trilogy; the entire movie was shot after hours in a Pennsylvania shopping mall.
VHS availability: HBO Video
Enhancing Your Bad Moods,
p. 34

DAYS OF WINE AND ROSES
(1962)
117 min.; BW
Director: Blake Edwards
Cast: Jack Lemmon, Lee Remick
Academy Awards: Best Song ("Days of Wine and Roses")
Other credits: Screenplay by J. P. Miller, based on his teleplay; music by Henry Mancini
VHS availability: Warner Home Video
Enhancing Your Bad Moods,
p. 28

THE DAY THE EARTH STOOD STILL
(1951)
92 min.; BW
Director: Robert Wise
Cast: Patricia Neal, Michael Rennie
Other credits: Music by Bernard Herrmann
VHS availability: CBS/Fox Video
Sci-Fi, p. 107

DEAD OF WINTER
(1987)
100 min.; Color
Director: Arthur Penn
Cast: Mary Steenburgen, Roddy McDowell
VHS availability: Rental only
Trompe l'Oeil, p. 43

DEAD RINGERS
(1988)
115 min.; Color
Director: David Cronenberg
Cast: Jeremy Irons, Geneviève Bujold
Other credits: Screenplay by Cronenberg and Norman Snider, based on the book *Twins* by Bari Wood and Jack Geasland
VHS availability: Media Home Entertainment
The Greatest Movies of the '80s,
p. 220

THE DECLINE OF THE AMERICAN EMPIRE
(1986)
101 min.; Color
In French; English subtitles
Director: Denys Arcand
Cast: Pierre Curzi, Remy Girard, Yves Jacques, Daniel Brière, Dominique Michel, Louise Portal, Dorothée Berryman, Geneviève Rioux, Gabriel Arcand
Other credits: Screenplay by Arcand
VHS availability: MCA/Universal Home Video
Food, p. 51

THE DEER HUNTER
(1978)
183 min.; Color
Director: Michael Cimino
Cast: Robert De Niro, Christopher

Walken, John Savage, Meryl Streep, John Cazale
Academy Awards: Best Picture, Best Supporting Actor (Walken), Best Direction (Cimino), Best Sound, Best Film Editing
Other credits: Cinematography by Vilmos Zsigmond; music by John Williams
VHS availability: MCA/Universal Home Video

Small Towns, p. 136

DETOUR
(1945)
69 min.; BW
Director: Edgar G. Ulmer
Cast: Tom Neal, Ann Savage
VHS availability: Video Yesteryear

Critics' Choice, p. 25

DINER
(1982)
110 min.; Color
Director: Barry Levinson
Cast: Steve Guttenberg, Kevin Bacon, Mickey Rourke, Ellen Barkin, Timothy Daly, Daniel Stern
Other credits: Screenplay by Levinson
FYI: Levinson's directorial debut
VHS availability: MGM/UA Home Video

Food, p. 49
The Greatest Movies of the '80s, p. 236

DINNER AT EIGHT
(1933)
113 min.; BW
Director: George Cukor
Cast: Jean Harlow, Marie Dressler, Billie Burke, John Barrymore, Lionel Barrymore, Wallace Beery
Other credits: Based on the Broadway play by Edna Ferber and George S. Kaufman
VHS availability: MGM/UA Home Video

Trompe l'Oeil, p. 45

THE DIRTY DOZEN
(1962)
150 min.; Color
Director: Robert Aldrich

Cast: Lee Marvin, Ernest Borgnine, Charles Bronson, John Cassavetes, Telly Savalas
Academy Awards: Best Sound Effects
VHS availability: MGM/UA Home Video

The Twelve Days of Christmas, p. 183

THE DISCREET CHARM OF THE BOURGEOISIE
(1972)
100 min.; Color
In French; English subtitles
Director: Luis Buñuel
Cast: Fernando Rey, Delphine Seyrig, Stéphane Audran, Bulle Ogier
Academy Awards: Best Foreign Language Film
Other credits: Screenplay by Buñuel and Jean-Claude Carrière
VHS availability: Media Home Entertainment

Food, p. 49

D.O.A.
(1949)
83 min.; BW
Director: Rudolph Maté
Cast: Edmond O'Brien, Pamela Britton, Luther Adler
Other credits: Music by Dmitri Tiomkin
FYI: Remade in 1988 with Dennis Quaid and Meg Ryan
VHS availability: Video Yesteryear

Tales of Three Cities, p. 39

DR. STRANGELOVE, OR HOW I LEARNED TO STOP WORRYING AND LOVE THE BOMB
(1964)
93 min.; BW
Director: Stanley Kubrick
Cast: Peter Sellers, George C. Scott, Sterling Hayden
Other credits: Screenplay by Kubrick, Terry Southern, and Peter George, loosely based on George's novel *Red Alert*
VHS availability: RCA/Columbia Pictures Home Video

Directors' Choice I, p. 16

E

Cast: Judy Garland, Fred Astaire, Peter Lawford, Ann Miller
Academy Awards: Best Score (Musical)
FYI: A two-and-a-half-year-old Liza Minnelli appears in the final scene
VHS availability: MGM/UA Home Video
An Elegant Hollywood Threesome,
p. 146

EATING RAOUL
(1982)
83 min.; Color
Director: Paul Bartel
Cast: Bartel, Mary Woronov, Robert Beltran
Other credits: Screenplay by Bartel and Richard Blackburn
VHS availability: CBS/Fox Video
Food, p. 52

ECHO PARK
(1986)
93 min.; Color
Director: Robert Dornhelm
Cast: Susan Dey, Tom Hulce, Michael Bowen
VHS availability: Paramount Home Video
TV Actors in the Movies, p. 63

8½
(1963)
135 min.; BW
In Italian; English subtitles
Director: Federico Fellini
Cast: Marcello Mastroianni, Claudia Cardinale, Anouk Aimée
FYI: Fellini's eighth-and-a-half film, counting co-directing credits as halves
VHS availability: MPI Home Video
Directors' Choice I, p. 12
The Twelve Days of Christmas,
p. 183

THE '80S
(1983)
82 min.; Color
In French; English subtitles
Director: Chantal Akerman
Cast: Aischa Bentebouche, Francesca Best, Warre Borgmans

Other credits: Screenplay by Akerman and Jean Gruault
VHS availability: Facets Video
The Greatest Movies of the '80s,
p. 233

EIGHT MEN OUT
(1988)
119 min.; Color
Director: John Sayles
Cast: John Cusack, David Strathairn, John Mahoney, D. B. Sweeney, Sayles
Other credits: Screenplay by Sayles, based on the book by Eliot Asinof
VHS availability: Orion Home Video
The Twelve Days of Christmas,
p. 182

8 MILLION WAYS TO DIE
(1986)
115 min.; Color
Director: Hal Ashby
Cast: Jeff Bridges, Rosanna Arquette, Andy Garcia
Other credits: Screenplay by Oliver Stone and David Lee Honey
VHS availability: CBS/Fox Video
Critics' Choice, p. 21

11 HARROWHOUSE
(1974)
98 min.; Color
Director: Aram Avakian
Cast: Charles Grodin, Candice Bergen, James Mason
VHS availability: Playhouse Video
The Twelve Days of Christmas,
p. 183

ELMER GANTRY
(1960)
145 min.; Color
Director: Richard Brooks
Cast: Burt Lancaster, Jean Simmons, Arthur Kennedy, Shirley Jones
Academy Awards: Best Actor (Lancaster), Best Supporting Actress (Jones), Best Adapted Screenplay (Brooks)
Other credits: Based on the novel by Sinclair Lewis
VHS availability: MGM/UA Home Video
Religion in Extremis, p. 196

THE EMERALD FOREST
(1985)
113 min.; Color
Director: John Boorman
Cast: Powers Boothe, Meg Foster, Charley Boorman
Other credits: Cinematography by Philippe Rousselot
FYI: Charley Boorman is John Boorman's son
VHS availability: Nelson Entertainment
Winter Antidotes, p. 76

ENTER THE DRAGON
(1973)
97 min.; Color
Director: Robert Clouse
Cast: Bruce Lee, John Saxon, Jim Kelly
VHS availability: Warner Home Video
Directors' Choice II, p. 203

ERASERHEAD
(1978)
90 min.; BW
Director: David Lynch
Cast: Jack Nance, Charlotte Stewart, Allen Joseph, Jeanne Bates
Other credits: Screenplay by Lynch; cinematography by Fred Elmes
FYI: Lynch's first feature
VHS availability: Rental only
Slow Movies/Fast Films, p. 149

E.T. THE EXTRA-TERRESTRIAL
(1982)
115 min.; Color
Director: Steven Spielberg
Cast: Dee Wallace, Henry Thomas, Drew Barrymore
Other credits: Screenplay by Melissa Mathison; score by John Williams
FYI: Largest-grossing movie ever
VHS availability: MCA/Universal Home Video
The Greatest Movies of the '80s, p. 214

THE EXORCIST
(1973)
121 min.; Color
Director: William Friedkin
Cast: Ellen Burstyn, Max von Sydow, Jason Miller, Linda Blair
Academy Awards: Best Adapted Screenplay (William Peter Blatty), Best Sound
Other credits: Based on Blatty's novel
VHS availability: Warner Home Video
Religion in Extremis, p. 198

EYE OF THE NEEDLE
(1981)
112 min.; Color
Director: Richard Marquand
Cast: Donald Sutherland, Kate Nelligan
Other credits: Screenplay by Stanley Mann, based on the novel by Ken Follett; music by Miklos Rozsa
VHS availability: MGM/UA Home Video
The Ten Most Underrated Movies of the '80s, p. 104

F

A FACE IN THE CROWD
(1957)
125 min.; BW
Director: Elia Kazan
Cast: Andy Griffith, Patricia Neal, Walter Matthau, Anthony Franciosa, Lee Remick
Other credits: Screenplay by Budd Schulberg, based on his short story "The Arkansas Traveler"
VHS availability: Warner Home Video
Politics, p. 89
Fame, p. 111

FAHRENHEIT 451
(1967)
111 min.; Color
Director: François Truffaut
Cast: Julie Christie, Oskar Werner
Other credits: Based on the novel by Ray Bradbury
FYI: Truffaut's only film in English
VHS availability: MCA/Universal Home Video
Trompe l'Oeil, p. 42

FANNY AND ALEXANDER
(1983)
197 min.; Color

In Swedish, English subtitles; dubbed version
Director: Ingmar Bergman
Cast: Gunn Wallgren, Pernilla Allwin, Bertil Guve
Academy Awards: Best Art Direction, Best Costume Design, Best Foreign Language Film
Other credits: Cinematography by Sven Nykvist
FYI: Bergman's last film made for theatrical release
VHS availability: Nelson Entertainment
The Greatest Movies of the '80s, p. 216

FASTER, PUSSYCAT! KILL! KILL!
(1965)
84 min.; BW
Director: Russ Meyer
Cast: Tura Satana, Lori Williams, Haji
VHS availability: RM Films International
Critics' Choice, p. 26

FAST TIMES AT RIDGEMONT HIGH
(1982)
92 min.; Color
Director: Amy Heckerling
Cast: Sean Penn, Jennifer Jason Leigh, Judge Reinhold, Phoebe Cates
Other credits: Screenplay by Cameron Crowe, based on his novel
FYI: Eric Stoltz and Anthony Edwards make their film debuts
VHS availability: MCA/Universal Home Video
School Days, p. 70

FEMALE TROUBLE
(1974)
95 min.; Color
Director: John Waters
Cast: Divine, Mink Stole, Edith Massey
Other credits: Screenplay by Waters
VHS availability: Rental only
Trompe l'Oeil, p. 45
Family Troubles, p. 126

FINAL CHAPTER—WALKING TALL
(1977)
112 min.; Color
Director: Jack Starrett

Cast: Bo Svenson, Margaret Blye, Forrest Tucker
VHS availability: Vestron Video
The '70s, p. 131

THE FISH THAT SAVED PITTSBURGH
(1979)
102 min.; Color
Director: Gilbert Moses
Cast: Julius Erving, Jonathan Winters, Stockard Channing
VHS availability: Warner Home Video
The '70s, p. 130

FIVE CORNERS
(1988)
92 min.; Color
Director: Tony Bill
Cast: Jodie Foster, Tim Robbins, John Turturro
Other credits: Screenplay by John Patrick Shanley
VHS availability: Cannon Video
The Twelve Days of Christmas, p. 181

THE FLY
(1958)
94 min.; Color
Director: Kurt Neumann
Cast: Al (David) Hedison, Patricia Owens, Vincent Price
VHS availability: Turner Home Entertainment
Sci-Fi, p. 109

THE FLY
(1987)
100 min.; Color
Director: David Cronenberg
Cast: Jeff Goldblum, Geena Davis, John Getz
Other credits: Screenplay by Charles Edward Pogue and Cronenberg
FYI: Cronenberg makes a cameo appearance as a gynecologist
VHS availability: CBS/Fox Video
Sci-Fi, p. 109
Journalists, p. 171

FORBIDDEN PLANET
(1956)
98 min.; Color

Director: Fred McLeod Wilcox
Cast: Walter Pidgeon, Anne Francis, Leslie Nielsen
VHS availability: MGM/UA Home Video

Sci-Fi, p. 108

FOREIGN CORRESPONDENT
(1940)
119 min.; BW
Director: Alfred Hitchcock
Cast: Joel McCrea, Laraine Day, Herbert Marshall, George Sanders
VHS availability: Warner Home Video

Journalists, p. 167

THE 400 BLOWS
(1959)
99 min.; BW
In French; English subtitles
Director: François Truffaut
Cast: Jean-Pierre Léaud, Claire Maurier, Albert Rémy
Other credits: Screenplay by Truffaut and Marcel Moussy; story by Truffaut
FYI: Léaud's character, Antoine Doinel, was featured in four more Truffaut comedies—*Love at Twenty* ("Antoine and Colette" episode), *Stolen Kisses, Bed and Board,* and *Love on the Run*
VHS availability: Key Video

Tales of Three Cities, p. 39

THE 4TH MAN
(1979)
104 min.; Color
In Dutch; English subtitles
Director: Paul Verhoeven
Cast: Jeroen Krabbé, Renée Soutendijk, Thom Hoffman
VHS availability: Media Home Entertainment

The Twelve Days of Christmas,
p. 181

FRENCH POSTCARDS
(1979)
92 min.; Color
Director: Willard Huyck
Cast: Miles Chapin, Blanche Baker, David Marshall Grant, Debra Winger
Other credits: Screenplay by Huyck and Gloria Katz

VHS availability: Paramount Home Video

School Days, p. 70

FRENZY
(1972)
116 min.; Color
Director: Alfred Hitchcock
Cast: Jon Finch, Barry Foster, Barbara Leigh-Hunt, Alec McCowen
Other credits: Screenplay by Anthony Shaffer, based on the novel *Goodbye Piccadilly, Farewell Leicester Square* by Arthur Le Bern
VHS availability: MCA/Universal Home Video

Food, p. 50

FRITZ THE CAT
(1972)
78 min.; Color
X-rated animated feature based on the cartoon characters of R. Crumb
Director: Ralph Bakshi
VHS availability: Rental only

The '70s, p. 129

FUNNY FACE
(1957)
103 min.; Color
Director: Stanley Donen
Cast: Audrey Hepburn, Fred Astaire, Kay Thompson
FYI: Astaire's character is based on photographer Richard Avedon, who was the movie's visual consultant
VHS availability: Paramount Home Video
An Elegant Hollywood Threesome,
p. 147

FUNNY GIRL
(1968)
155 min.; Color
Director: William Wyler
Cast: Barbra Streisand, Omar Sharif, Kay Medford
Academy Awards: Best Actress (Streisand)
Other credits: Based on the Broadway musical biography of Fanny Brice

FYI: Streisand created role on stage
VHS availability: RCA/Columbia Pictures Home Video

Fame, p. 113

F/X
(1986)
106 min.; Color
Director: Robert Mandel
Cast: Bryan Brown, Brian Dennehy, Diane Venora
VHS availability: HBO Video

Critics' Choice, p. 24

G

GASLIGHT
(1944)
84 min.; BW
Director: George Cukor
Cast: Ingrid Bergman, Charles Boyer, Joseph Cotten, Angela Lansbury
Academy Awards: Best Actress (Bergman), Best Art Direction
VHS availability: MGM/UA Home Video

Love and Marriage, p. 56

GENTLEMEN PREFER BLONDES
(1953)
91 min.; Color
Director: Howard Hawks
Cast: Marilyn Monroe, Jane Russell, Charles Coburn
Other credits: Screenplay by Charles Lederer, based on the stage musical by Anita Loos and Joseph Fields, adapted from Loos's book
VHS availability: CBS/Fox Video

Trompe l'Oeil, p. 46

GEORGE STEVENS: A FILMMAKER'S JOURNEY
(1984)
110 min.; Color
Documentary
Director: George Stevens, Jr.
VHS availability: Rental only

Critics' Choice, p. 24

GEORGY GIRL
(1966)
100 min.; BW
Director: Silvio Narizzano
Cast: James Mason, Alan Bates, Lynn Redgrave, Charlotte Rampling
Other credits: Screenplay by Margaret Forster and Peter Nichols, based on Forster's novel; costumes by Mary Quant; lyrics to the song "Georgy Girl" by actor Jim Dale
VHS availability: RCA/Columbia Pictures Home Video

Virgins, p. 119

GIANT
(1956)
201 min.; Color
Director: George Stevens
Cast: Elizabeth Taylor, Rock Hudson, James Dean
Academy Awards: Best Direction (Stevens)
Other credits: Based on the novel by Edna Ferber
FYI: Dean's last film
VHS availability: Warner Home Video

Winter Antidotes, p. 75

GILDA
(1946)
110 min.; BW
Director: Charles Vidor
Cast: Rita Hayworth, Glenn Ford, George Macready
VHS availability: Rental only

Triangles, p. 159

THE GODFATHER, 1902–1954: THE COMPLETE EPIC
(1981)
450 min.; Color
This combined version of *The Godfather* and *The Godfather, Part II* was created for television
Director: Francis Ford Coppola
Cast: Marlon Brando, Al Pacino, Robert De Niro, Robert Duvall, James Caan, Diane Keaton
VHS availability: Paramount Home Video

Winter Antidotes, p. 74

GONE WITH THE WIND
(1939)
222 min.; Color
Director: Victor Fleming
Cast: Vivien Leigh, Clark Gable, Olivia de Havilland, Leslie Howard, Hattie McDaniel, Butterfly McQueen
Academy Awards: Best Picture, Best Actress (Leigh), Best Supporting Actress (McDaniel), Best Direction (Fleming), Best Screenplay (Sidney Howard), Best Film Editing, Best Art Direction, Best Color Cinematography (Ernest Haller and Ray Rennehan)
Other credits: Based on the novel by Margaret Mitchell; produced by David O. Selznick
FYI: The most successful Hollywood picture until the 1970s
VHS availability: MGM/UA Home Video
An Elegant Hollywood Threesome, p. 141

THE GOOD, THE BAD, AND THE UGLY
(1967)
161 min.; Color
Director: Sergio Leone
Cast: Clint Eastwood, Eli Wallach, Lee Van Cleef
Other credits: Music by Ennio Morricone
VHS availability: CBS/Fox Video
Slow Movies/Fast Films, p. 151

THE GRADUATE
(1967)
105 min.; Color
Director: Mike Nichols
Cast: Anne Bancroft, Dustin Hoffman, Katharine Ross
Academy Awards: Best Direction (Nichols)
Other credits: Songs by Simon and Garfunkel; screenplay by Buck Henry and Calder Willingham, based on the novel by Charles Webb
VHS availability: Nelson Entertainment
Love and Marriage, p. 54
Virgins, p. 117

GRAND ILLUSION
(1937)
111 min.; BW
In French; English subtitles
Director: Jean Renoir
Cast: Jean Gabin, Pierre Fresnay, Erich von Stroheim
Other credits: Screenplay by Renoir and Charles Spaak
VHS availability: Connoisseur Video Collection
Directors' Choice II, p. 201

THE GRAPES OF WRATH
(1940)
120 min.; BW
Director: John Ford
Cast: Henry Fonda, Jane Darwell, John Carradine
Academy Awards: Best Supporting Actress (Darwell), Best Direction (Ford)
Other credits: Screenplay by Nunnally Johnson, based on the novel by John Steinbeck; cinematography by Gregg Toland
VHS availability: CBS/Fox Video
Directors' Choice II, p. 202

THE GROUP
(1966)
150 min.; Color
Director: Sidney Lumet
Cast: Candice Bergen, Joan Hackett, Elizabeth Hartman, Joanna Pettet, Kathleen Widdoes, Jessica Walter
Other credits: Screenplay by Sidney Buchman, based on the novel by Mary McCarthy
FYI: Lumet's father, Barach, plays Mr. Schneider
VHS availability: Rental only
School Days, p. 66

H

HAIL MARY
(1985)
107 min.; Color
In French; English subtitles

Director: Jean-Luc Godard
Cast: Myriem Roussel, Thierry Rode, Juliette Binoche
Other credits: Screenplay by Godard
VHS availability: Vestron Video

Virgins, p. 121

HAIR
(1979)
121 min.; Color
Director: Miloš Forman
Cast: John Savage, Treat Williams, Beverly D'Angelo
Other credits: Screenplay by Michael Weller, based on the Broadway musical by Gerome Ragni, James Rado, and Galt MacDermot
VHS availability: MGM/UA Home Video

Musicals, p. 103

HAMLET
(1948)
153 min.; BW
Director: Laurence Olivier
Cast: Olivier, Jean Simmons, Eileen Herlie
Academy Awards: Best Picture, Best Actor (Olivier), Best Art Direction, Best Costume Design
Other credits: Screenplay by Alan Dent, based on the Shakespeare play
VHS availability: Paramount Home Video

Trompe l'Oeil, p. 46

HAMMETT
(1982)
97 min.; Color
Director: Wim Wenders
Cast: Frederic Forrest, Peter Boyle, Marilu Henner
FYI: Wenders's *The State of Things* (1982) is a fictional account of the troubles he had shooting *Hammett* for executive producer Francis Coppola
VHS availability: Warner Home Video

Critics' Choice, p. 27

HANNAH AND HER SISTERS
(1986)
106 min.; Color
Director: Woody Allen

Cast: Allen, Michael Caine, Mia Farrow, Dianne Wiest
Academy Awards: Best Supporting Actor (Caine), Best Supporting Actress (Wiest), Best Screenplay (Allen)
Other credits: Cinematography by Carlo di Palina
FYI: The film uses Farrow's Central Park West apartment as a location and seven of her children as actors
VHS availability: HBO Video

The Greatest Movies of the '80s, p. 215

THE HAPPY HOOKER
(1975)
96 min.; Color
Director: Nicholas Sgarro
Cast: Lynn Redgrave, Jean-Pierre Aumont, Lovelady Powell, Nicholas Pryor
Other credits: Based on the autobiographical book by Xaviera Hollander
VHS availability: Rental only

The '70s, p. 129

A HARD DAY'S NIGHT
(1964)
85 min.; BW
Director: Richard Lester
Cast: John Lennon, Paul McCartney, George Harrison, Ringo Starr
FYI: The Beatles' movie debut
VHS availability: Rental only

Fame, p. 113

THE HARDER THEY COME
(1973)
98 min.; Color
In Jamaican argot; English subtitles
Director: Perry Henzell
Cast: Jimmy Cliff, Carl Bradshaw, Janet Bartley
Other credits: Screenplay by Henzell and Trevor D. Rhone
FYI: Cliff sings several original songs
VHS availability: HBO Video

Fame, p. 110

HARPER VALLEY P.T.A.
(1978)
102 min.; Color
Director: Richard Bennett

Cast: Barbara Eden, Ronny Cox, Nanette Fabray
VHS availability: Vestron Video
The '70s, p. 132

THE HARRAD EXPERIMENT
(1973)
88 min.; Color
Director: Ted Post
Cast: James Whitmore, Tippi Hedren, Don Johnson
Other credits: Based on the novel by Robert H. Rimmer
VHS availability: Rental only
TV Actors in the Movies, p. 64

THE HEARTBREAK KID
(1972)
104 min.; Color
Director: Elaine May
Cast: Charles Grodin, Jeannie Berlin, Cybill Shepherd
Other credits: Screenplay by Neil Simon, based on a story by Bruce Jay Friedman
FYI: Berlin is May's daughter
VHS availability: Media Home Entertainment
Love and Marriage, p. 54

HEAVEN HELP US
(1985)
104 min.; Color
Director: Michael Dinner
Cast: Andrew McCarthy, Mary Stuart Masterson, Donald Sutherland
VHS availability: HBO Video
School Days, p. 69

HERE COMES MR. JORDAN
(1941)
93 min.; BW
Director: Alexander Hall
Cast: Robert Montgomery, Evelyn Keyes, Claude Rains
FYI: Remade as *Heaven Can Wait* (1978)
VHS availability: Rental only
Directors' Choice I, p. 17

THE HIDDEN
(1987)
96 min.; Color
Director: Jack Sholder

Cast: Michael Nouri, Kyle MacLachlan, Ed O'Ross
VHS availability: Media Home Entertainment
The Ten Most Underrated Movies of the '80s, p. 104

HIGH PLAINS DRIFTER
(1975)
105 min.; Color
Director: Clint Eastwood
Cast: Eastwood, Verna Bloom, Marianna Hill
VHS availability: MCA/Universal Home Video
Small Towns, p. 137

HIGH SIERRA
(1941)
100 min.; BW
Director: Raoul Walsh
Cast: Humphrey Bogart, Ida Lupino, Alan Curtis, Arthur Kennedy
Other credits: Screenplay by John Huston and W. R. Burnett, based on Burnett's novel
FYI: Remade as *Colorado Territory* (1949) and *I Died a Thousand Times* (1955)
VHS availability: Rental only
Crime, p. 190

THE HILLS HAVE EYES
(1978)
87 min.; Color
Director: Wes Craven
Cast: Sue Lanier, Robert Houston, Virginia Vincent
VHS availability: Rental only
Family Troubles, p. 126

THE HILLS HAVE EYES II
(1985)
88 min.; Color
Director: Wes Craven
Cast: Michael Berryman, John Laughlin, Tamara Stafford
VHS availability: HBO Video
Family Troubles, p. 126

HIS GIRL FRIDAY
(1940)
92 min.; BW

Director: Howard Hawks
Cast: Cary Grant, Rosalind Russell, Ralph Bellamy
Other credits: Screenplay by Charles Lederer, based on the play *The Front Page* by Ben Hecht and Charles MacArthur
VHS availability: Video Yesteryear
Slow Movies/Fast Films, p. 152

HOLIDAY
(1938)
93 min.; BW
Director: George Cukor
Cast: Cary Grant, Katharine Hepburn, Doris Nolan, Lew Ayres
FYI: Remake of a 1930 film, based on the play by Philip Barry, with Ann Harding, Robert Ames, and Mary Astor
VHS availability: RCA/Columbia Pictures Home Video
An Elegant Hollywood Threesome, p. 141

HOMETOWN U.S.A.
(1979)
93 min.; Color
Director: Max Baer
Cast: Gary Springer, David Wilson, Brian Kerwin
VHS availability: Vestron Video
The '70s, p. 132

THE HONEYMOON KILLERS
(1970)
108 min.; BW
Director: Leonard Kastle
Cast: Shirley Stoler, Tony LoBianco, Mary Jane Higby, Doris Roberts
VHS availability: Vestron Video
Crime, p. 190

HOPE AND GLORY
(1987)
113 min.; Color
Director: John Boorman
Cast: Sebastian Rice-Edwards, Geraldine Muir, Sarah Miles, David Hayman, Sammi Davis
Other credits: Screenplay by Boorman; cinematography by Philippe Rousselot
VHS availability: Nelson Entertainment
The Greatest Movies of the '80s, p. 231

THE HORSE'S MOUTH
(1958)
93 min.; BW
Director: Ronald Neame
Cast: Alec Guinness, Kay Walsh
Other credits: Screenplay by Guinness, based on the novel by Joyce Cary
VHS availability: Nelson Entertainment
Artists, p. 99

THE HURRICANE
(1937)
102 min.; BW
Director: John Ford
Cast: Jon Hall, Raymond Massey, Dorothy Lamour, Mary Astor
VHS availability: Nelson Entertainment
An Elegant Hollywood Threesome, p. 144

HURRICANE
(1979)
119 min.; Color
Director: Jan Troell
Cast: Jason Robards, Jr., Mia Farrow, Max von Sydow, Dayton Ka'ne
Other credits: Cinematography by Sven Nykvist; music by Nino Rota
VHS availability: Paramount Home Video
An Elegant Hollywood Threesome, p. 144

HUSH . . . HUSH, SWEET CHARLOTTE
(1964)
133 min.; BW
Director: Robert Aldrich
Cast: Bette Davis, Olivia de Havilland, Joseph Cotten, Mary Astor
VHS availability: Key Video
An Elegant Hollywood Threesome, p. 145

I

THE IDOLMAKER
(1980)
119 min.; Color
Director: Taylor Hackford

Cast: Ray Sharkey, Tovah Feldshuh, Peter Gallagher
VHS availability: MGM/UA Home Video
Fame, p. 113

I MARRIED A WITCH
(1942)
76 min.; BW
Director: René Clair
Cast: Veronica Lake, Fredric March, Susan Hayward
VHS availability: Warner Home Video
Good and Evil, p. 80

IMITATION OF LIFE
(1959)
124 min.; Color
Director: Douglas Sirk
Cast: Lana Turner, John Gavin, Sandra Dee, Susan Kohner, Juanita Moore
Other credits: Based on the novel by Fannie Hurst
FYI: Remake of the 1934 movie starring Claudette Colbert; Sirk's last film
VHS availability: MCA/Universal Home Video
Family Troubles, p. 124

IN COLD BLOOD
(1967)
134 min.; BW
Director: Richard Brooks
Cast: Robert Blake, Scott Wilson, John Forsythe
Other credits: Screenplay by Brooks, based on the true-life novel by Truman Capote
VHS availability: RCA/Columbia Pictures Home Video
Crime, p. 190

THE INCREDIBLE SHRINKING MAN
(1952)
81 min.; BW
Director: Jack Arnold
Cast: Grant Williams, Randy Stuart, April Kent
VHS availability: MCA/Universal Home Video
Sci-Fi, p. 109

INDIANA JONES AND THE TEMPLE OF DOOM
(1984)
118 min.; Color
Director: Steven Spielberg
Cast: Harrison Ford, Kate Capshaw
Academy Awards: Best Visual Effects
Other credits: Screenplay by Willard Huyck and Gloria Katz; music by John Williams
VHS availability: Paramount Home Video
Slow Movies/Fast Films, p. 153

IN THE HEAT OF THE NIGHT
(1967)
109 min.; Color
Director: Norman Jewison
Cast: Sidney Poitier, Rod Steiger, Warren Oates
Academy Awards: Best Picture, Best Actor (Steiger), Best Adapted Screenplay (Stirling Silliphant), Best Film Editing (Hal Ashby), Best Sound
Other credits: Based on the novel by John Ball; cinematography by Haskell Wexler; music by Quincy Jones
VHS availability: MGM/UA Home Video
Small Towns, p. 139

INVASION OF THE BODY SNATCHERS
(1956)
80 min.; BW
Director: Don Siegel
Cast: Kevin McCarthy, Dana Wynter, Larry Gates
Other credits: Based on the novel *The Body Snatchers* by Jack Finney
VHS availability: Republic Pictures Home Video
Enhancing Your Bad Moods, p. 30
Sci-Fi, p. 109

INVASION OF THE BODY SNATCHERS
(1978)
115 min.; Color
Director: Philip Kaufman
Cast: Donald Sutherland, Brooke Adams, Leonard Nimoy, Jeff Goldblum
Other credits: Screenplay by W. D.

Richter; cinematography by Michael Chapman
FYI: Kevin McCarthy, star of the 1956 original, makes a cameo appearance
VHS availability: MGM/UA Home Video

Sci-Fi, p. 109

IT LIVES AGAIN
(1978)
91 min.; Color
Director: Larry Cohen
Cast: Frederic Forrest, Kathleen Lloyd
Other credits: Screenplay by Cohen
VHS availability: Warner Home Video

Enhancing Your Bad Moods,
p. 35

IT'S ALIVE!
(1974)
91 min.; Color
Director: Larry Cohen
Cast: John Ryan, Sharon Farrell, Andrew Duggan
Other credits: Screenplay by Cohen
VHS availability: Warner Home Video

Enhancing Your Bad Moods,
p. 35

IT'S A WONDERFUL LIFE
(1946)
129 min.; BW
Director: Frank Capra
Cast: James Stewart, Donna Reed, Lionel Barrymore, Gloria Grahame
Other credits: Music by Dmitri Tiomkin
VHS availability: Republic Pictures Home Video

Director's Choice II, p. 202

IT SHOULD HAPPEN TO YOU
(1954)
81 min.; BW
Director: George Cukor
Cast: Judy Holliday, Peter Lawford, Jack Lemmon
Other credits: Screenplay by Garson Kanin
VHS availability: RCA/Columbia Pictures Home Video

Tales of Three Cities, p. 36

IVAN THE TERRIBLE, PART I
(1943)
96 min.; BW
In Russian; English subtitles
Director: Sergei Eisenstein
Cast: Nikolai Cherkasov
Other credits: Screenplay by Eisenstein; music by Sergei Prokofiev
VHS availability: Facets Video

Slow Movies/Fast Films, p. 151

I WALKED WITH A ZOMBIE
(1943)
69 min.; BW
Director: Jacques Tourneur
Cast: James Ellison, Francis Dee, Tom Conway
VHS availability: Media Home Entertainment

Winter Antidotes, p. 76

I WANT TO LIVE!
(1958)
120 min.; BW
Director: Robert Wise
Cast: Susan Hayward, Simon Oakland, Virginia Vincent, Theodore Bikel
Academy Awards: Best Actress (Hayward)
VHS availability: MGM/UA Home Video

Enhancing Your Bad Moods,
p. 30

J

JASON AND THE ARGONAUTS
(1963)
104 min.; Color
Director: Don Chaffey
Cast: Todd Armstrong, Honor Blackman, Nancy Kovack, Gary Raymond
Other credits: Music by Bernard Herrmann; special effects by Ray Harryhausen
VHS availability: RCA/Columbia Pictures Home Video

Winter Antidotes, p. 78

JEAN DE FLORETTE
(1986)
122 min.; Color

In French; English subtitles
Director: Claude Berri
Cast: Yves Montand, Gérard Depardieu, Daniel Auteuil
Other credits: Screenplay by Berri and Gérard Brach, based on the novel by Marcel Pagnol
FYI: Manon of the Spring, the second half of this two-part film, was released separately in the United States
VHS availability: Orion Home Video
Small Towns, p. 138

JOHNNY GUITAR
(1954)
110 min.; Color
Director: Nicholas Ray
Cast: Joan Crawford, Sterling Hayden, Mercedes McCambridge
Other credits: Screenplay by Philip Yordan, based on the novel by Roy Chanslor
VHS availability: Republic Pictures Home Video
Critics' Choice, p. 25

JULES AND JIM
(1962)
104 min.; BW
In French; English subtitles
Director: François Truffaut
Cast: Jeanne Moreau, Oskar Werner, Henri Serre
Other credits: Screenplay by Truffaut and Jean Gruault, based on the novel by Henri-Pierre Roche; cinematography by Raoul Coutard; music by Georges Delerue
VHS availability: Key Video
Triangles, p. 155

JUST BETWEEN FRIENDS
(1986)
110 min.; Color
Director: Allan Burns
Cast: Mary Tyler Moore, Ten Danson, Christine Lahti
Other credits: Screenplay by Burns
VHS availability: HBO Video
TV Actors in the Movies, p. 60

JUST TELL ME WHAT YOU WANT
(1985)
112 min.; Color
Director: Sidney Lumet
Cast: Ali MacGraw, Alan King, Myrna Loy
Other credits: Screenplay by Jay Presson Allen, based on her novel
VHS availability: Warner Home Video
The Ten Most Underrated Movies of the '80s, p. 105

K

KAGEMUSHA
(1980)
159 min.; Color
In Japanese; English subtitles
Director: Akira Kurosawa
Cast: Tatsuya Nakadai
Other credits: Screenplay by Kurosawa and Masato Ide
VHS availability: CBS/Fox Video
The Greatest Movies of the '80s, p. 225

THE KILLING FIELDS
(1984)
141 min.; Color
Director: Roland Joffé
Cast: Sam Waterston, Haing S. Ngor, John Malkovich
Academy Awards: Best Supporting Actor (Ngor), Best Cinematography (Chris Menges), Best Film Editing
Other credits: Screenplay by Bruce Robinson, based on *The New York Times Magazine* article "The Death and Life of Dith Pran" by Sydney Schanberg
VHS availability: Warner Home Video
Journalists, p. 169
The Greatest Movies of the '80s, p. 225

THE KILLING OF SISTER GEORGE
(1968)
138 min.; Color
Director: Robert Aldrich
Cast: Susannah York, Beryl Reid, Coral Browne

Other credits: Based on the play by Frank Marcus
VHS availability: Rental only
Triangles, p. 159

KIND HEARTS AND CORONETS
(1949)
104 min.; BW
Director: Robert Hamer
Cast: Alec Guinness, Dennis Price, Joan Greenwood, Valerie Hobson
Other credits: Screenplay by Hamer and John Dighton, based on the novel *Noblesse Oblige* by Roy Horniman
VHS availability: HBO Video
Trompe l'Oeil, p. 41

KING KONG
(1933)
100 min. (103 min. uncut); BW
Directors: Merian C. Cooper, Ernest B. Schoedsack
Cast: Fay Wray, Robert Armstrong, Bruce Cabot
FYI: Cooper and Schoedsack make a cameo appearance as pilots of the plane that downs Kong
VHS availability: Turner Home Entertainment
Tales of Three Cities, p. 37
Censorship, p. 173

KING LEAR
(1971)
137 min.; BW
Director: Peter Brook
Cast: Paul Scofield, Irene Worth, Jack MacGowran
Other credits: Screenplay by Brook, based on the Shakespeare play
VHS availability: Rental only
Family Troubles, p. 125

THE KING OF COMEDY
(1983)
109 min.; Color
Director: Martin Scorsese
Cast: Robert De Niro, Jerry Lewis, Sandra Bernhard
Other credits: Screenplay by Paul D. Zimmerman; music by Robbie Robertson

VHS availability: RCA/Columbia Pictures Home Video
Enhancing Your Bad Moods,
p. 34
Fame, p. 113
The Greatest Movies of the '80s,
p. 224

L

THE LADY EVE
(1941)
94 min.; BW
Director: Preston Sturges
Cast: Barbara Stanwyck, Henry Fonda, Charles Coburn
Other credits: Screenplay by Sturges, based on the play *The Faithful Heart* by Monckton Hoffe
FYI: Remade in 1956 as *The Birds and the Bees*
VHS availability: MCA/Universal Home Video
Critics' Choice, p. 25
Screwball Comedies, p. 187

THE LAST HURRAH
(1958)
110 min.; BW
Director: John Ford
Cast: Spencer Tracy, Jeffrey Hunter, Basil Rathbone, Pat O'Brien
Other credits: Screenplay by Frank S. Nugent, based on the novel by Edwin O'Connor
VHS availability: RCA/Columbia Pictures Home Video
Politics, p. 90

LAST SUMMER
(1969)
97 min.; Color
Director: Frank Perry
Cast: Barbara Hershey, Richard Thomas, Bruce Davison, Cathy Burns
Other credits: Screenplay by Eleanor Perry, based on the novel by Evan Hunter
VHS availability: Key Video
Triangles, p. 156

THE LOST WEEKEND
(1945)
101 min.; BW
Director: Billy Wilder
Cast: Ray Milland, Jane Wyman, Philip Terry
Academy Awards: Best Picture, Best Actor (Milland), Best Direction (Wilder), Best Screenplay (Wilder and Charles Brackett)
Other credits: Based on the novel by Charles R. Jackson; music by Miklos Rozsa
VHS availability: MCA/Universal Home Video
Underdogs, p. 165

LOVE STREAMS
(1984)
141 min.; Color
Director: John Cassavetes
Cast: Gena Rowlands, Cassavetes, Diahnne Abbott
Other credits: Screenplay by Ted Allan and Cassavetes, based on Allan's play
VHS availability: MGM/UA Home Video
The Greatest Movies of the '80s, p. 226

M

MACAO
(1952)
80 min.; BW
Director: Josef von Sternberg
Cast: Robert Mitchum, Jane Russell, William Bendix, Gloria Grahame
FYI: Nicholas Ray directed some of the final scenes.
VHS availability: Rental only
Winter Antidotes, p. 78

MACBETH
(1971)
140 min.; Color
Director: Roman Polanski
Cast: Jon Finch, Francesca Annis, Martin Shaw
Other credits: Screenplay by Polanski and Kenneth Tynan, based on the Shakespeare play
FYI: Polanski's first movie after his wife, Sharon Tate, was murdered
VHS availability: RCA/Columbia Pictures Home Video
Good and Evil, p. 81

THE MACK
(1973)
110 min.; Color
Director: Michael Campus
Cast: Max Julian, Don Gordon, Richard Pryor
VHS availability: Nelson Entertainment
Directors' Choice I, p. 17

MACON COUNTY LINE
(1974)
89 min.; Color
Director: Richard Compton
Cast: Alan Vint, Cheryl Waters, Max Baer, Jr., Joan Blackman
VHS availability: Nelson Entertainment
The '70s, p. 133

MAD MAX
(1979)
93 min.; Color
Dubbed in American English
Director: George Miller
Cast: Mel Gibson, Joanne Samuel, Hugh Keays-Byrne
Other credits: Screenplay by Miller and James McCausland; story by Miller and Byron Kennedy
VHS availability: Video Treasures
Slow Movies/Fast Films, p. 152

MALCOLM
(1986)
86 min.; Color
Director: Nadia Tass
Cast: Colin Friels, John Hargreaves, Lindy Davies
VHS availability: Vestron Video
Critics' Choice, p. 23

THE MALTESE FALCON
(1941)
100 min.; BW
Director: John Huston
Cast: Humphrey Bogart, Mary Astor,

Peter Lorre, Sydney Greenstreet, Elisha Cook, Jr.
Other credits: Screenplay by Huston, based on the novel by Dashiell Hammett
FYI: Huston's directorial debut; Greenstreet's first talkie
VHS availability: CBS/Fox Video

Directors' Choice I, p. 18
An Elegant Hollywood Threesome, p. 145

THE MANCHURIAN CANDIDATE
(1962)
126 min.; BW
Director: John Frankenheimer
Cast: Frank Sinatra, Laurence Harvey, Angela Lansbury
Other credits: Screenplay by George Axelrod and Frankenheimer, based on the novel by Richard Condon
VHS availability: MGM/UA Home Video

Politics, p. 91

MANHATTAN
(1979)
96 min.; BW
Director: Woody Allen
Cast: Allen, Diane Keaton, Michael Murphy, Mariel Hemingway
Other credits: Screenplay by Allen and Marshall Brickman; cinematography by Gordon Willis; music by George Gershwin
VHS availability: MGM/UA Home Video; letterboxed

Directors' Choice I, p. 18

THE MAN WHO KNEW TOO MUCH
(1956)
120 min.; Color
Director: Alfred Hitchcock
Cast: James Stewart, Doris Day
Academy Awards: Best Song ("Que Sera, Sera")
Other credits: Music by Bernard Herrmann
FYI: A remake of Hitchcock's own 1938 British movie of the same title, starring Leslie Banks, Edna Best, and Peter Lorre

VHS availability: MCA/Universal Home Video

Good and Evil, p. 85

THE MAN WHO SHOT LIBERTY VALANCE
(1962)
119 min.; BW
Director: John Ford
Cast: James Stewart, John Wayne, Vera Miles, Lee Marvin
VHS availability: Paramount Home Video

Directors' Choice I, p. 14

THE MAN WITH TWO BRAINS
(1983)
93 min.; Color
Director: Carl Reiner
Cast: Steve Martin, Kathleen Turner, David Warner
Other credits: Screenplay by Reiner, Martin, and George Gipe; cinematography by Michael Chapman
FYI: Sissy Spacek provided the voice for the brain
VHS availability: Warner Home Video
The Ten Most Underrated Movies of the '80s, p. 105

MARJOE
(1972)
88 min.; Color
Documentary
Directors: Howard Smith and Sarah Kernochan
VHS availability: RCA/Columbia Pictures Home Video

Religion in Extremis, p. 197

MARTIN
(1979)
95 min.; Color
Director: George A. Romero
Cast: John Amplas, Lincoln Maazel, Christine Forrest
Other credits: Screenplay by Romero
VHS availability: HBO Video

Family Troubles, p. 127

MARTY
(1955)
91 min.; BW

Director: Delbert Mann
Cast: Ernest Borgnine, Betsy Blair, Esther Minciotti
Academy Awards: Best Picture, Best Actor (Borgnine), Best Direction (Mann), Best Screenplay (Paddy Chayefsky)
VHS availability: MGM/UA Home Video
Love and Marriage, p. 54

THE MASQUE OF THE RED DEATH
(1964)
86 min.; Color
Director: Roger Corman
Cast: Vincent Price, Hazel Court, Jane Asher
Other credits: Based on the Edgar Allan Poe story; cinematography by Nicolas Roeg
VHS availability: Rental only
Good and Evil, p. 83

MASS APPEAL
(1984)
100 min.; Color
Director: Glenn Jordan
Cast: Jack Lemmon, Zeljko Ivanek, Charles Durning
Other credits: Screenplay by Bill C. Davis, based on his play
VHS availability: MCA/Universal Home Video
The Ten Most Underrated Movies of the '80s, p. 105

MATEWAN
(1987)
130 min.; Color
Director: John Sayles
Cast: Chris Cooper, Will Oldham, James Earl Jones, David Strathairn
Other credits: Screenplay by Sayles; cinematography by Haskell Wexler
VHS availability: Warner Home Video
The Greatest Movies of the '80s, p. 234

MEET ME IN ST. LOUIS
(1944)
113 min.; Color
Director: Vincente Minnelli

Cast: Judy Garland, Margaret O'Brien, Mary Astor
Academy Awards: Special award to O'Brien as outstanding child actress
VHS availability: MGM/UA Home Video
Musicals, p. 102
Family Troubles, p. 125

MELVIN AND HOWARD
(1980)
95 min.; Color
Director: Jonathan Demme
Cast: Paul Le Mat, Jason Robards, Mary Steenburgen
Academy Awards: Best Supporting Actress (Steenburgen), Best Screenplay (Bo Goldman)
VHS availability: MCA/Universal Home Video
Critics' Choice, p. 22

MEPHISTO
(1981)
135 min.; Color
In German; English subtitles
Director: István Szabó
Cast: Klaus Maria Brandauer, Krystyna Janda
Academy Awards: Best Foreign Language Film
Other credits: Screenplay by Szabó and Peter Dobal, based on the novel by Klaus Mann
VHS availability: HBO Video
The Greatest Movies of the '80s, p. 237

MILLHOUSE: A WHITE COMEDY
(1971)
90 min.; BW
Documentary
Director: Emile de Antonio
VHS availability: MPI Home Video
Politics, p. 92

THE MIRACLE OF MORGAN'S CREEK
(1944)
99 min.; BW
Director: Preston Sturges
Cast: Eddie Bracken, Betty Hutton, William Demarest
Other credits: Screenplay by Sturges

FYI: Remade in 1958 as *Rock-a-Bye Baby,* directed by Frank Tashlin and starring Jerry Lewis, Marilyn Maxwell, and Connie Stevens
VHS availability: Paramount Home Video

Virgins, p. 119

THE MIRACLE OF THE BELLS
(1948)
120 min.; BW
Director: Irving Pichel
Cast: Fred MacMurray, Valli, Frank Sinatra, Lee J. Cobb
Other credits: Screenplay by Ben Hecht, Quentin Reynolds, and Dewitt Bodeen, based on the novel by Russell Janney
VHS availability: Republic Pictures Home Video

Religion in Extremis, p. 197

THE MIRROR CRACK'D
(1980)
105 min.; Color
Director: Guy Hamilton
Cast: Angela Lansbury, Elizabeth Taylor, Kim Novak, Tony Curtis, Rock Hudson
Other credits: Screenplay by Jonathan Hales and Barry Sandler, based on the novel *The Mirror Crack'd From Side to Side* by Agatha Christie
VHS availability: HBO Video

The Ten Most Underrated Movies of the '80s, p. 105

MRS. SOFFEL
(1984)
110 min.; Color
Director: Gillian Armstrong
Cast: Diane Keaton, Mel Gibson, Matthew Modine
Other credits: Screenplay by Ron Nyswaner; cinematography by Russell Boyd
FYI: Australian Armstrong's first American movie
VHS availability: MGM/UA Home Video

Enhancing Your Bad Moods, p. 29

MISSISSIPPI BURNING
(1988)
125 min.; Color
Director: Alan Parker
Cast: Gene Hackman, Willem Dafoe, Frances McDormand
Academy Awards: Best Cinematography (Peter Biziou)
Other credits: Screenplay by Chris Gerolmo
VHS availability: Orion Home Video

The Greatest Movies of the '80s, p. 235

MR. AND MRS. SMITH
(1941)
95 min.; BW
Director: Alfred Hitchcock
Cast: Carole Lombard, Robert Montgomery, Gene Raymond
VHS availability: Turner Home Entertainment

Screwball Comedies, p. 187

MR. SMITH GOES TO WASHINGTON
(1939)
129 min.; BW
Director: Frank Capra
Cast: James Stewart, Jean Arthur, Claude Rains
Academy Awards: Best Original Story (Lewis Foster)
FYI: Condemned by the U.S. Senate; U.S. Ambassador to Britain Joseph P. Kennedy tried to prevent its release in Europe.
VHS availability: Rental only

Politics, p. 87
Underdogs, p. 164

THE MODERNS
(1988)
128 min.; Color
Director: Alan Rudolph
Cast: Keith Carradine, Geneviève Bujold, John Lone
Other credits: Screenplay by Rudolph and Jon Bradshaw
VHS availability: Nelson Entertainment

Artists, p. 100

MOGAMBO
(1953)
115 min.; Color
Director: John Ford
Cast: Clark Gable, Ava Gardner, Grace Kelly
FYI: Remake of Victor Fleming's 1932 *Red Dust* (see), starring Gable (in the same role), Jean Harlow and Mary Astor
VHS availability: MGM/UA Home Video
Triangles, p. 157

MONTY PYTHON'S LIFE OF BRIAN
(1979)
93 min.; Color
Director: Terry Jones
Cast: Graham Chapman, John Cleese, Terry Gilliam, Eric Idle, Jones, Michael Palin
Other credits: Screenplay by Chapman, Cleese, Gilliam, Idle, Jones, and Palin
VHS availability: Rental only
Religion in Extremis, p. 196

MONTY PYTHON'S THE MEANING OF LIFE
(1983)
107 min.; Color
Director: Terry Jones
Cast: Graham Chapman, John Cleese, Terry Gilliam, Eric Idle, Jones, Michael Palin
Other credits: Screenplay by Chapman, Cleese, Gilliam, Idle, Jones, and Palin
VHS availability: MCA/Universal Home Video
Food, p. 50

THE MOON'S OUR HOME
(1936)
76 min.; BW
Director: William A. Seiter
Cast: Margaret Sullavan, Henry Fonda, Beulah Bondi
VHS availability: KVC Entertainment
Screwball Comedies, p. 186

THE MORNING AFTER
(1986)
103 min.; Color
Director: Sidney Lumet
Cast: Jane Fonda, Jeff Bridges, Raul Julia
Other credits: Cinematography by Andrzej Bartkowiak
VHS availability: Warner Home Video
Critics' Choice, p. 23

MOVIE MOVIE
(1978)
107 min.; Color and BW
Director: Stanley Donen
Cast: George C. Scott, Red Buttons, Ann Reinking, Harry Hamlin
Other credits: Screenplay by Larry Gelbart and Sheldon Keller
VHS availability: Rental only
TV Actors in the Movies, p. 62

THE MUSIC MAN
(1962)
151 min.; Color
Director: Morton Da Costa
Cast: Robert Preston, Shirley Jones, Buddy Hackett, Hermione Gingold, Ronny Howard
Academy Awards: Best Adapted Score (Ray Heindorf)
Other credits: Screenplay by Marion Hargrove, based on the stage musical by Meredith Willson and Franklin Lacey
VHS availability: Warner Home Video
Small Towns, p. 137

MY BEAUTIFUL LAUNDRETTE
(1986)
94 min.; Color
Director: Stephen Frears
Cast: Daniel Day-Lewis, Saeed Jaffrey, Roshan Seth, Gordon Warnecker
Other credits: Screenplay by Hanif Kureishi
VHS availability: Warner Home Video
Critics' Choice, p. 23

MY BODYGUARD
(1980)
96 min.; Color
Director: Tony Bill
Cast: Chris Makepeace, Adam Baldwin, Matt Dillon

FYI: Bill's directorial debut
VHS availability: CBS/Fox Video
School Days, p. 69

MY DINNER WITH ANDRE
(1981)
110 min.; Color
Director: Louis Malle
Cast: Wallace Shawn, Andre Gregory
Other credits: Screenplay by Shawn and Gregory
VHS availability: Pacific Arts Video
Food, p. 49
The Greatest Movies of the '80s,
p. 221

MY FAVORITE WIFE
(1940)
88 min.; BW
Director: Garson Kanin
Cast: Cary Grant, Irene Dunne, Randolph Scott, Gail Patrick
FYI: Remade in 1963 as *Move Over Darling,* starring Doris Day and James Garner
VHS availability: Republic Pictures Home Video
Screwball Comedies, p. 187

MY FAVORITE YEAR
(1982)
92 min.; Color
Director: Richard Benjamin
Cast: Peter O'Toole, Mark Linn-Baker, Jessica Harper, Joseph Bologna
Other credits: Screenplay by Norman Steinberg and Dennis Palumbo; story by Palumbo
VHS availability: MGM/UA Home Video
The Ten Most Underrated Movies of the '80s, p. 105

MY LIFE AS A DOG
(1987)
101 min.; Color
In Swedish; English subtitles
Director: Lasse Hallström
Cast: Anton Glanzelius, Anki Lidem, Melinda Kinnaman

VHS availability: Paramount Home Video
The Greatest Movies of the '80s,
p. 229

THE MYSTERY OF PICASSO
(1955)
85 min.; Color
In French; English subtitles
Documentary
Director: Henri-Georges Clouzot
VHS availability: Vestron Video
Artists, p. 97

N

NASHVILLE
(1975)
139 min.; Color
Director: Robert Altman
Cast: Keith Carradine, Ronee Blakley, Keenan Wynn, Lily Tomlin, Ned Beatty, Geraldine Chaplin, Karen Black, Shelley Duvall, Henry Gibson, Barbara Harris
Academy Awards: Best Song ("I'm Easy")
Other credits: Screenplay by Joan Tewkesbury; music by Richard Baskin
VHS availability: Paramount Home Video
Fame, p. 114

THE NATURAL
(1984)
134 min.; Color
Director: Barry Levinson
Cast: Robert Redford, Glenn Close, Barbara Hershey
Other credits: Screenplay by Roger Towne and Phil Dusenberry, based on the novel by Bernard Malamud; cinematography by Caleb Deschanel; music by Randy Newman
VHS availability: RCA/Columbia Pictures Home Video
Slow Movies/Fast Films, p. 150

O

ODE TO BILLY JOE
(1976)
108 min.; Color
Director: Max Baer
Cast: Robby Benson, Glynnis O'Connor, Joan Hotchkis
Other credits: Based on Bobbie Gentry's 1967 hit song
VHS availability: Warner Home Video
The '70s, p. 133

OKLAHOMA!
(1955)
143 min.; Color
Director: Fred Zinnemann
Cast: Gordon MacRae, Shirley Jones, Gloria Grahame
Other credits: Based on the Broadway musical by Richard Rodgers and Oscar Hammerstein II, with choreography by Agnes de Mille
VHS availability: CBS/Fox Video
Musicals, p. 103

LOS OLVIDADOS
(1950)
88 min.; BW
In Spanish; English subtitles
Director: Luis Buñuel
Cast: Estela Inda, Roberto Cobo
Other credits: Made in Mexico
VHS availability: Connoisseur Video Collection
Critics' Choice, p. 25

ONCE UPON A TIME IN AMERICA
(1984)
227 min.; Color
Director: Sergio Leone
Cast: Robert De Niro, James Woods, Elizabeth McGovern
Other credits: Music by Ennio Morricone
VHS availability: Warner Home Video
Directors' Choice I, p. 17
The Greatest Movies of the '80s,
p. 222

ONCE UPON UPON A TIME IN THE WEST
(1969)
165 min.; Color
Director: Sergio Leone
Cast: Henry Fonda, Claudia Cardinale, Jason Robards, Charles Bronson
Other credits: Screenplay by Leone and Sergio Donati; story by Dario Argento, Bernardo Bertolucci, and Leone; music by Ennio Morricone
VHS availability: Paramount Home Video
Winter Antidotes, p. 76

ONE CRAZY SUMMER
(1986)
93 min.; Color
Director: Savage Steve Holland
Cast: John Cusack, Linda Warren, Demi Moore
Other credits: Screenplay by Holland; animation by Bill Kupp
VHS availability: Warner Home Video
Winter Antidotes, p. 79

ONE FLEW OVER THE CUCKOO'S NEST
(1975)
133 min.; Color
Director: Miloš Forman
Cast: Jack Nicholson, Louise Fletcher, Brad Dourif
Academy Awards: Best Picture, Best Actor (Nicholson), Best Actress (Fletcher), Best Direction (Forman), Best Adapted Screenplay (Lawrence Hauben and Bo Goldman)
Other credits: Based on the novel by Ken Kesey; music by Jack Nitzsche
VHS availability: HBO Video
The Twelve Days of Christmas,
p. 180

ORDINARY PEOPLE
(1980)
123 min.; Color
Director: Robert Redford
Cast: Donald Sutherland, Mary Tyler Moore, Timothy Hutton, Judd Hirsch
Academy Awards: Best Supporting Actor (Hutton), Best Direction (Redford), Best Adapted Screenplay (Alvin Sargent)

Other credits: Based on the novel by Judith Guest
VHS availability: Paramount Home Video
Family Troubles, p. 123

OUT OF AFRICA
(1985)
161 min.; Color
Director: Sydney Pollack
Cast: Meryl Streep, Robert Redford, Klaus Maria Brandauer
Academy Awards: Best Picture, Best Direction (Pollack), Best Adapted Screenplay (Kurt Luedtke), Best Cinematography (David Watkin), Best Art Direction, Best Original Score (John Barry), Best Sound
Other credits: Based on the writings of Isak Dinesen
VHS availability: MCA/Universal Home Video
The Greatest Movies of the '80s, p. 238

THE OUT-OF-TOWNERS
(1970)
97 min.; Color
Director: Arthur Hiller
Cast: Jack Lemmon, Sandy Dennis, Anne Meara
Other credits: Screenplay by Neil Simon; music by Quincy Jones
VHS availability: Paramount Home Video
Underdogs, p. 163

OUTRAGEOUS!
(1977)
100 min.; Color
Director: Richard Benner
Cast: Craig Russell, Hollis McLaren
Other credits: Screenplay by Benner, based on the story "Making It" by Margaret Gibson
VHS availability: RCA/Columbia Pictures Home Video
Trompe l'Oeil, p. 43
Fame, p. 114

P

PAINTERS PAINTING
(1972)
116 min.; BW and Color
Documentary about the New York art scene, 1940–70
Director: Emile de Antonio
VHS availability: Mystic Fire Video
Artists, p. 97

THE PALM BEACH STORY
(1942)
90 min.; BW
Director: Preston Sturges
Cast: Claudette Colbert, Joel McCrea, Mary Astor, Rudy Vallee
Other credits: Screenplay by Sturges
VHS availability: MCA/Universal Home Video
Screwball Comedies, p. 188

THE PARALLAX VIEW
(1974)
102 min.; Color
Director: Alan J. Pakula
Cast: Warren Beatty, Hume Cronyn, William Daniels, Paula Prentiss
Other credits: Screenplay by David Giler and Lorenzo Semple, Jr., based on the novel by Loren Singer; cinematography by Gordon Willis
VHS availability: Paramount Home Video
Politics, p. 91
Journalists, p. 167

THE PARENT TRAP
(1961)
124 min.; Color
Director: David Swift
Cast: Hayley Mills, Maureen O'Hara, Brian Keith
Other credits: Screenplay by Swift, based on the novel *Das doppelte Lottchen* by Erich Kastner; cinematography by Lucien Ballard
VHS availability: Rental only
Trompe l'Oeil, p. 41
Family Troubles, p. 124

PARTING GLANCES
(1986)
90 min.; Color
Director: Bill Sherwood
Cast: Richard Ganoung, John Bolger, Steve Buscemi
Other credits: Screenplay by Sherwood
VHS availability: Key Video

PATHS OF GLORY
(1957)
86 min.; BW
Director: Stanley Kubrick
Cast: Kirk Douglas, Ralph Meeker, Adolphe Menjou
Other credits: Screenplay by Kubrick, Calder Willingham, and Jim Thompson, based on the novel by Humphrey Cobb
VHS availability: Rental only

PENNIES FROM HEAVEN
(1981)
107 min.; Color
Director: Herbert Ross
Cast: Steve Martin, Bernadette Peters, Christopher Walken, Vernel Bagneris
Other credits: Screenplay by Dennis Potter, based on his British TV series, which starred Bob Hoskins; cinematography by Gordon Willis
VHS availability: MGM/UA Home Video

PERSONA
(1966)
81 min.; BW
In Swedish; English subtitles
Director: Ingmar Bergman
Cast: Liv Ullmann, Bibi Andersson
Other credits: Screenplay by Bergman; cinematography by Sven Nykvist
VHS availability: Facets Video

THE PHILADELPHIA STORY
(1940)
112 min.; BW
Director: George Cukor
Cast: Katharine Hepburn, James Stewart, Cary Grant
Academy Awards: Best Actor (Stewart), Best Screenplay (Donald Ogden Stewart)
Other credits: Based on the Broadway play by Philip Barry, in which Hepburn created her role
FYI: Grant donated his salary to the British War Relief Fund; remade as the 1956 musical *High Society,* starring Grace Kelly, Frank Sinatra, and Bing Crosby
VHS availability: MGM/UA Home Video

THE PICTURE OF DORIAN GRAY
(1945)
110 min.; BW and Color
Director: Albert Lewin
Cast: George Sanders, Hurd Hatfield, Donna Reed
Academy Awards: Best Cinematography (Harry Stradling)
Other credits: Screenplay by Lewin, based on the novel by Oscar Wilde
VHS availability: MGM/UA Home Video

PILLOW TALK
(1959)
105 min.; Color
Director: Michael Gordon
Cast: Rock Hudson, Doris Day, Tony Randall, Thelma Ritter
Academy Awards: Best Story and Screenplay (Russell Rouse, Clarence Greene, Stanley Shapiro, and Maurice Richlan)
VHS availability: MCA/Universal Home Video

PIXOTE
(1981)
127 min.; Color

In Portuguese; English subtitles
Director: Hector Babenco
Cast: Fernando Ramos da Silva; Marília Pera
Other credits: Screenplay by Babenco and Jorge Duran, based on the novel *Infância dos Mortos* by Jose Louzeiro
VHS availability: Rental only
Directors' Choice II, p. 201
The Greatest Movies of the '80s, p. 238

A PLACE IN THE SUN
(1951)
122 min.; BW
Director: George Stevens
Cast: Montgomery Clift, Elizabeth Taylor, Shelley Winters, Raymond Burr
Academy Awards: Best Direction (Stevens), Best Screenplay (Michael Wilson and Harry Brown), Best Cinematography (William C. Mellor), Best Score (Franz Waxman)
Other credits: Based on the novel *An American Tragedy* by Theodore Dreiser
VHS availability: Paramount Home Video
Enhancing Your Bad Moods, p. 30

PLAN 9 FROM OUTER SPACE
(1959)
79 min.; BW
Director: Edward D. Wood, Jr.
Cast: Bela Lugosi, Gregory Walcott, Tom Keene
VHS availability: Media Home Entertainment
Directors' Choice I, p. 15

PLATOON
(1986)
120 min.; Color
Director: Oliver Stone
Cast: Tom Berenger, Willem Dafoe, Charlie Sheen
Academy Awards: Best Picture, Best Direction (Stone), Best Film Editing, Best Sound

Other credits: Cinematography by Ralph Richardson
VHS availability: Vestron Video
The Greatest Movies of the '80s, p. 215

PLAYERS
(1979)
120 min.; Color
Director: Anthony Harvey
Cast: Ali MacGraw, Dean-Paul Martin, Maximilian Schell
Other credits: Costumes by Calvin Klein and Richard Bruno
VHS availability: Paramount Home Video
The '70s, p. 130

PLAY IT AGAIN, SAM
(1972)
87 min.; Color
Director: Herbert Ross
Cast: Woody Allen, Diane Keaton, Tony Roberts
Other credits: Screenplay by Allen, based on his play
VHS availability: Paramount Home Video
Fame, p. 114

PLAY MISTY FOR ME
(1971)
102 min.; Color
Director: Clint Eastwood
Cast: Eastwood, Jessica Walter, Donna Mills, John Larch
VHS availability: MCA/Universal Home Video
Enhancing Your Bad Moods, p. 31

PLAYTIME
(1967)
108 min.; Color
Director: Jacques Tati
Cast: Tati, Barbara Dennek, Jacqueline Lecomte
Other credits: English dialogue by Art Buchwald
VHS availability: Nelson Entertainment
Tales of Three Cities, p. 38

PLENTY
(1985)
124 min.; Color
Director: Fred Schepisi
Cast: Meryl Streep, Sting, Charles Dance, Tracey Ullman
Other credits: Screenplay by David Hare, based on his play
VHS availability: HBO Video
TV Actors in the Movies, p. 61

THE PLOUGHMAN'S LUNCH
(1983)
100 min.; Color
Director: Richard Eyre
Cast: Jonathan Pryce, Tim Curry, Rosemary Harris
VHS availability: Nelson Entertainment
Food, p. 48

PRETTY BABY
(1978)
109 min.; Color
Director: Louis Malle
Cast: Brooke Shields, Keith Carradine, Susan Sarandon
Other credits: Screenplay by Polly Platt; story by Platt and Malle; based on the memoirs of photographer E. J. Bellocq; cinematography by Sven Nykvist
VHS availability: Paramount Home Video
Virgins, p. 117

PRIZZI'S HONOR
(1985)
129 min.; Color
Director: John Huston
Cast: Jack Nicholson, Kathleen Turner, Anjelica Huston, William Hickey
Academy Awards: Best Supporting Actress (Huston)
Other credits: Screenplay by Richard Condon and Janet Roach, based on the novel by Condon; music by Alex North
VHS availability: Vestron Video
The Greatest Movies of the '80s, p. 223

THE PRODUCERS
(1968)
88 min.; Color
Director: Mel Brooks
Cast: Zero Mostel, Gene Wilder, Dick Shawn, Kenneth Mars
Academy Awards: Best story and screenplay (Brooks)
FYI: Brooks's directorial debut
VHS availability: Nelson Entertainment
Directors' Choice I, p. 16
Directors' Choice II, p. 204

PSYCHO
(1960)
109 min.; BW
Director: Alfred Hitchcock
Cast: Anthony Perkins, Janet Leigh, John Gavin
Other credits: Screenplay by Joseph Stefano, based on the novel by Robert Bloch; music by Bernard Herrmann (using only string instruments)
VHS availability: MCA/Universal Home Video
Directors' Choice I, p. 16

THE PURPLE ROSE OF CAIRO
(1985)
82 min.; Color
Director: Woody Allen
Cast: Mia Farrow, Jeff Daniels, Danny Aiello
Other credits: Screenplay by Allen; cinematography by Gordon Willis
FYI: Michael Keaton was originally cast in the Daniels role
VHS availability: Vestron Video
Trompe l'Oeil, p. 42

Q

THE QUIET MAN
(1952)
129 min.; Color
Director: John Ford
Cast: John Wayne, Maureen O'Hara, Barry Fitzgerald, Victor McLaglen
Academy Awards: Best Direction (Ford), Best Cinematography (Winton C. Hoch and Archie Stout)
VHS availability: Republic Pictures Home Video
Directors' Choice II, p. 200

R

RADIO DAYS
(1987)
85 min.; Color
Director: Woody Allen
Cast: Dianne Wiest, Josh Mostel, Julie Kavner, Mia Farrow
Other credits: Screenplay by Allen; cinematography by Carlo di Palma; production designed by Santo Loquasto
VHS availability: HBO Video
The Ten Most Underrated Movies of the '80s, p. 106

RAGING BULL
(1980)
128 min.; BW and Color
Director: Martin Scorsese
Cast: Robert De Niro, Cathy Moriarty, Joe Pesci
Academy Awards: Best Actor (De Niro); Best Film Editing
Other credits: Screenplay by Paul Schrader and Mardik Martin, based on the Jake LaMotta autobiography; cinematography by Michael Chapman
FYI: De Niro gained fifty pounds to play LaMotta in middle age.
VHS availability: HBO Video
Underdogs, p. 165
Director's Choice II, p. 201
The Greatest Movies of the '80s, p. 213

RAIDERS OF THE LOST ARK
(1981)
115 min.; Color
Director: Steven Spielberg
Cast: Harrison Ford, Karen Allen, Denholm Elliott
Academy Awards: Best Art Direction; Best Sound; Best Film Editing; Best Visual Effects
Other credits: Screenplay by Lawrence Kasdan; story idea by George Lucas and Philip Kaufman
VHS availability: Paramount Home Video
The Greatest Movies of the '80s, p. 238

RAIN MAN
(1988)
140 min.; Color
Director: Barry Levinson
Cast: Dustin Hoffman, Tom Cruise, Valeria Golino
Academy Awards: Best Picture, Best Actor (Hoffman), Best Direction (Levinson), Best Original Screenplay (Ronald Bass and Barry Morrow)
VHS availability: MGM/UA Home Video
The Greatest Movies of the '80s, p. 227

RAISING ARIZONA
(1987)
92 min.; Color
Director: Joel Coen
Cast: Nicholas Cage, Holly Hunter, Trey Wilson, John Goodman, Randall "Tex" Cobb
Other credits: Screenplay by Joel and Ethan Coen; cinematography by Barry Sonnenfeld
VHS availability: CBS/Fox Video
Directors' Choice II, p. 204
The Greatest Movies of the '80s, p. 225

RAN
(1985)
161 min.; Color
In Japanese; English subtitles
Director: Akira Kurosawa
Cast: Tatsuya Nakadai, Mieko Harada
Academy Awards: Best Costume Design
Other credits: Screenplay by Kurosawa, Hideo Ogani, and Masato Ide, based on Shakespeare's play *King Lear*
VHS availability: CBS/Fox Video
The Greatest Movies of the '80s, p. 219

REBEL WITHOUT A CAUSE
(1955)
111 min.; Color
Director: Nicholas Ray
Cast: James Dean, Sal Mineo, Natalie Wood, Jim Backus

FYI: Dean died shortly before the movie was released
VHS availability: Warner Home Video
Family Troubles, p. 127

RED BEARD
(1965)
185 min.; BW
In Japanese; English subtitles
Director: Akira Kurosawa
Cast: Toshiro Mifune, Yuzo Kayama
VHS availability: Facets Video
Directors' Choice II, p. 203

RED DUST
(1932)
83 min.; BW
Director: Victor Fleming
Cast: Clark Gable, Jean Harlow, Mary Astor
FYI: Remade by John Ford in 1953 as *Mogambo* (see), starring Gable (in the same role), Ava Gardner, and Grace Kelly
VHS availability: MGM/UA Home Video
An Elegant Hollywood Threesome, p. 143

THE RED SHOES
(1948)
133 min.; Color
Director: Michael Powell and Emeric Pressburger
Cast: Moira Shearer, Anton Walbrook, Marius Goring
Academy Awards: Best Score (Brian Easdale), Best Art Direction
Other credits: Screenplay by Powell, Pressburger, and Keith Winter
VHS availability: Paramount Home Video
Directors' Choice I, p. 13

REMBRANDT
(1936)
84 min.; BW
Director: Alexander Korda
Cast: Charles Laughton, Gertrude Lawrence, Elsa Lanchester
VHS availability: Nelson Entertainment
Artists, p. 94

REPO MAN
(1984)
92 min.; Color
Director: Alex Cox
Cast: Emilio Estevez, Harry Dean Stanton, Vonetta McGee
Other credits: Screenplay by Cox
VHS availability: MCA/Universal Home Video
Tales of Three Cities, p. 40

THE RETURN OF MARTIN GUERRE
(1982)
111 min.; Color
In French; English subtitles
Director: Daniel Vigne
Cast: Gérard Depardieu, Nathalie Baye, Roger Planchon
Other credits: Screenplay by Vigne and Jean-Claude Carrière
VHS availability: Nelson Entertainment
Small Towns, p. 136

RETURN OF THE JEDI
(1983)
133 min.; Color
Director: Richard Marquand
Cast: Mark Hamill, Harrison Ford, Carrie Fisher, Billy Dee Williams
Academy Awards: Best Visual Effects
Other credits: Screenplay by Lawrence Kasdan and George Lucas; story by Lucas
VHS availability: CBS/Fox Video
Underdogs, p. 162

RICH AND FAMOUS
(1981)
117 min.; Color
Director: George Cukor
Cast: Jacqueline Bisset, Candice Bergen, Hart Bochner
Other credits: Screenplay by Gerald Ayres
FYI: Cukor's last film; a remake of *Old Acquaintance* (1943), starring Bette Davis and Miriam Hopkins
VHS availability: MGM/UA Home Video
An Elegant Hollywood Threesome, p. 143

THE RIGHT STUFF
(1983)
193 min.; Color
Director: Philip Kaufman
Cast: Sam Shepard, Scott Glenn, Ed Harris, Dennis Quaid, Fred Ward
Academy Awards: Best Sound, Best Film Editing, Best Sound Effects Editing
Other credits: Screenplay by Kaufman, based on Tom Wolfe's book; cinematography by Caleb Deschanel
FYI: Chuck Yeager makes a cameo appearance
VHS availability: Warner Home Video
The Greatest Movies of the '80s, p. 220

RIO BRAVO
(1959)
141 min.; Color
Director: Howard Hawks
Cast: John Wayne, Dean Martin, Ricky Nelson, Angie Dickinson
VHS availability: Warner Home Video
Directors' Choice II, p. 200

THE ROAD WARRIOR
(1981)
94 min.; Color
Director: George Miller
Cast: Mel Gibson, Bruce Spence, Vernon Wells
FYI: Released outside the United States as *Mad Max 2*
VHS availability: Warner Home Video
The Greatest Movies of the '80s, p. 217

ROBOCOP
(1987)
103 min.; Color
Director: Paul Verhoeven
Cast: Peter Weller, Nancy Allen, Ronny Cox
VHS availability: Orion Home Video
Slow Movies/Fast Films, p. 154
The Greatest Movies of the '80s, p. 227

ROCK 'N' ROLL HIGH SCHOOL
(1979)
93 min.; Color
Director: Allan Arkush

Cast: P. J. Soles, Vincent Van Patten, Mary Woronov, the Ramones
Other credits: Music by the Ramones
VHS availability: Rental only
School Days, p. 70

ROCKY
(1976)
119 min.; Color
Director: John G. Avildsen
Cast: Sylvester Stallone, Talia Shire, Burgess Meredith, Carl Weathers
Academy Awards: Best Picture, Best Direction (Avildsen), Best Film Editing
Other credits: Screenplay by Stallone
VHS availability: MGM/UA Home Video
Underdogs, p. 161

A ROOM WITH A VIEW
(1986)
115 min.; Color
Director: James Ivory
Cast: Maggie Smith, Helena Bonham Carter, Denholm Elliott, Julian Sands, Daniel Day-Lewis
Academy Awards: Best Adapted Screenplay (Ruth Prawer Jhabvala), Best Art Direction, Best Costume Design
Other credits: Based on the novel by E. M. Forster
VHS availability: CBS/Fox Video
The Greatest Movies of the '80s, p. 235

THE ROSE
(1979)
134 min.; Color
Director: Mark Rydell
Cast: Bette Midler, Alan Bates, Frederic Forrest
Other credits: Screenplay by Bo Goldman, William Kerby, and Michael Cimino; story by Kerby; cinematography by Vilmos Zsigmond
VHS availability: CBS/Fox Video
Fame, p. 112

ROSEMARY'S BABY
(1968)
136 min.; Color
Director: Roman Polanski

Cast: Mia Farrow, John Cassavetes, Ruth Gordon
Academy Awards: Best Supporting Actress (Gordon)
Other credits: Screenplay by Polanski, based on the novel by Ira Levin
VHS availability: Paramount Home Video
Directors' Choice I, p. 16
Good and Evil, p. 80

ROXANNE
(1987)
107 min.; Color
Director: Fred Schepisi
Cast: Steve Martin, Daryl Hannah, Rick Rossovich
Other credits: Screenplay by Martin, based on the play *Cyrano de Bergerac* by Edmond Rostand
VHS availability: RCA/Columbia Pictures Home Video
Triangles, p. 156

ROYAL WEDDING
(1951)
93 min.; Color
Director: Stanley Donen
Cast: Fred Astaire, Jane Powell, Peter Lawford, Sarah Churchill
Other credits: Screenplay by Alan Jay Lerner
FYI: Donen's first solo directing credit
VHS availability: MGM/UA Home Video
An Elegant Hollywood Threesome, p. 146

THE RULING CLASS
(1972)
154 min.; Color
Director: Peter Medak
Cast: Peter O'Toole, Alistair Sim, Arthur Lowe, Coral Browne
Other credits: Screenplay by Peter Barnes, based on his play
VHS availability: Nelson Entertainment
Religion in Extremis, p. 197

RUTHLESS PEOPLE
(1986)
93 min.; Color
Director: Jim Abrahams

Cast: Bette Midler, Danny DeVito, Helen Slater, Judge Reinhold
Other credits: Screenplay by Dale Launer
VHS availability: Rental only
Underdogs, p. 165

S

SABOTEUR
(1942)
108 min.; BW
Director: Alfred Hitchcock
Cast: Priscilla Lane, Robert Cummings, Norman Lloyd
VHS availability: MCA/Universal Home Video
TV Actors in the Movies, p. 63

SABRINA
(1954)
113 min.; BW
Director: Billy Wilder
Cast: Humphrey Bogart, Audrey Hepburn, William Holden
Academy Awards: Best Costume Design
Other credits: Screenplay by Wilder, Samuel Taylor, and Ernest Lehman, based on the play *Sabrina Fair* by Taylor
VHS availability: Paramount Home Video
Triangles, p. 155

SALVADOR
(1986)
123 min.; Color
Director: Oliver Stone
Cast: James Woods, Jim Belushi, John Savage, Michael Murphy
Other credits: Screenplay by Stone and Richard Boyle; cinematography by Robert Richardson
VHS availability: Vestron Video
Critics' Choice, p. 20
Journalists, p. 170
The Greatest Movies of the '80s, p. 222

SAMSON AND DELILAH
(1949)
128 min.; Color
Director: Cecil B. De Mille

Cast: Hedy Lamarr, Victor Mature, George Sanders, Angela Lansbury
Academy Awards: Best Art Direction, Best Costume Design
VHS availability: Paramount Home Video

THE SANDPIPER
(1965)
116 min.; Color
Director: Vincente Minnelli
Cast: Elizabeth Taylor, Richard Burton, Eva Marie Saint, Charles Bronson
Academy Awards: Best Song ("The Shadow of Your Smile")
VHS availability: MGM/UA Home Video

SCARFACE
(1932)
90 min.; BW
Director: Howard Hawks
Cast: Paul Muni, Ann Dvorak, George Raft, Boris Karloff
Other credits: Screenplay by Ben Hecht, Seton I. Miller, John Lee Mahin, W. R. Burnett, and Fred Palsey, based on the novel by Armitage Trail
FYI: Remade in 1983 by Brian De Palma, starring Al Pacino
VHS availability: MCA/Universal Home Video

SCENES FROM A MARRIAGE
(1974)
168 min.; Color
In Swedish; English subtitles; dubbed version
Director: Ingmar Bergman
Cast: Liv Ullmann, Erland Josephson, Bibi Andersson
Other credits: Screenplay by Bergman; cinematography by Sven Nykvist
FYI: Originally produced as a six-episode, 300-minute TV series for Swedish television.
VHS availability: RCA/Columbia Pictures Home Video

THE SEARCHERS
(1956)
119 min.; Color
Director: John Ford
Cast: John Wayne, Jeffrey Hunter, Vera Miles, Ward Bond, Natalie Wood
Other credits: Screenplay by Frank S. Nugent, based on the novel by Alan LeMay
VHS availability: Warner Home Video

SECRET HONOR
(1984)
80 min.; Color
Director: Robert Altman
Cast: Philip Baker Hall
Other credits: Based on the play by Donald Freed and Arnold M. Stone
VHS availability: Vestron Video

THE SEDUCTION OF JOE TYNAN
(1979)
107 min.; Color
Director: Jerry Schatzberg
Cast: Alan Alda, Barbara Harris, Meryl Streep
Other credits: Screenplay by Alda
VHS availability: MCA/Universal Home Video

THE SERVANT
(1964)
115 min.; BW
Director: Joseph Losey
Cast: Dirk Bogarde, James Fox, Sarah Miles, Wendy Craig
Other credits: Screenplay by Harold Pinter, based on a novel by Robin Maugham
VHS availability: HBO Video

SEVEN DAYS IN MAY
(1964)
118 min.; BW
Director: John Frankenheimer
Cast: Burt Lancaster, Kirk Douglas, Fredric March, Ava Gardner
Other credits: Screenplay by Rod Serling,

based on the novel by Fletcher Knebel and Charles Waldo Bailey II
VHS availability: Rental only
Politics, p. 91

THE SEVEN SAMURAI
(1954)
141 min. (208 min. uncut); BW
In Japanese; English subtitles
Director: Akira Kurosawa
Cast: Toshiro Mifune, Takashi Shimura, Yoshio Inaba
FYI: Remade in 1960 as *The Magnificent Seven*
VHS availability: Nelson Entertainment
The Twelve Days of Christmas,
p. 182

THE SEVENTH SEAL
(1956)
96 min.; BW
In Swedish; English subtitles
Director: Ingmar Bergman
Cast: Max von Sydow, Gunnar Björnstrand, Bibi Andersson
Other credits: Screenplay by Bergman, based on his play *Tramalning*
VHS availability: Nelson Entertainment
Religion in Extremis, p. 194

SEXTETTE
(1978)
91 min.; Color
Director: Ken Hughes
Cast: Mae West, Timothy Dalton, Dom DeLuise, Tony Curtis, Ringo Starr
Other credits: Screenplay by Herbert Baker, based on the play by West
VHS availability: Media Home Entertainment
The Twelve Days of Christmas,
p. 182

SHAFT
(1971)
100 min.; Color
Director: Gordon Parks
Cast: Richard Roundtree, Moses Gunn, Charles Cioffi
Academy Awards: Best Song ("Theme from *Shaft*")
Other credits: Music by Isaac Hayes

VHS availability: MGM/UA Home Video
Tales of Three Cities, p. 36

SHAMPOO
(1975)
109 min.; Color
Director: Hal Ashby
Cast: Warren Beatty, Julie Christie, Goldie Hawn, Jack Warden, Lee Grant, Carrie Fisher
Academy Awards: Best Supporting Actress (Grant)
Other credits: Screenplay by Beatty and Robert Towne; cinematography by Laszlo Kovacs
FYI: Fisher's film debut
VHS availability: GoodTimes Home Video
Underdogs, p. 165

THE SHINING
(1980)
142 min.; Color
Director: Stanley Kubrick
Cast: Jack Nicholson, Shelley Duvall, Danny Lloyd, Scatman Crothers
Other credits: Screenplay by Kubrick and Diane Johnson, based on the novel by Stephen King
VHS availability: Warner Home Video
The Greatest Movies of the '80s,
p. 229

SHOAH
(1985)
503 min.; Color
In various languages; English subtitles
Documentary
Director: Claude Lanzmann
VHS availability: Paramount Home Video
Winter Antidotes, p. 75
The Greatest Movies of the '80s,
p. 216

SHOOT THE MOON
(1982)
123 min.; Color
Director: Alan Parker
Cast: Albert Finney, Diane Keaton, Karen Allen, Peter Weller, Dana Hill

Other credits: Screenplay by Bo Goldman
VHS availability: MGM/UA Home Video

THE SHOP ON MAIN STREET
(1965)
128 min.; BW
In Czech; English subtitles
Directors: Jan Kadar, Elmar Klos
Cast: Josef Kroner, Ida Kaminska, Han Slivkova
Academy Awards: Best Foreign Language Film
VHS availability: RCA/Columbia Pictures Home Video

SID & NANCY
(1986)
111 min.; Color
Director: Alex Cox
Cast: Gary Oldman, Chloe Webb, Drew Schofield
Other credits: Screenplay by Cox and Abbe Wool
FYI: The opening scenes were shot in the Chelsea Hotel room where Sid Vicious stayed
VHS availability: Nelson Entertainment

SILK STOCKINGS
(1957)
117 min.; Color
Director: Rouben Mamoulian
Cast: Fred Astaire, Cyd Charisse, Janis Paige, Peter Lorre
Other credits: Musical score by Cole Porter; based on the Broadway musical, an adaptation of the 1939 film *Ninotchka*
FYI: Mamoulian's last completed film
VHS availability: MGM/UA Home Video

SINGIN' IN THE RAIN
(1952)
102 min.; Color
Directors: Stanley Donen and Gene Kelly
Cast: Kelly, Donald O'Connor, Debbie Reynolds, Jean Hagen
Other credits: Screenplay by Adolph Green and Betty Comden
FYI: The set for Kelly's mansion is decorated with remnants from the production of *Flesh and the Devil* (1927), starring John Gilbert and Greta Garbo
VHS availability: MGM/UA Home Video

SISTERS
(1973)
93 min.; Color
Director: Brian De Palma
Cast: Margot Kidder, Jennifer Salt, Charles Durning
Other credits: Screenplay by De Palma and Louisa Rose; story by De Palma; music by Bernard Herrmann
VHS availability: Rental only

SIXTEEN CANDLES
(1984)
93 min.; Color
Director: John Hughes
Cast: Molly Ringwald, Anthony Michael Hall, Michael Schoeffling, Paul Dooley
Other credits: Screenplay by Hughes
FYI: Hughes's directorial debut
VHS availability: MCA/Universal Home Video

SLEEPER
(1973)
88 min.; Color
Director: Woody Allen
Cast: Allen, Diane Keaton
Other credits: Screenplay by Allen and Marshall Brickman
VHS availability: MGM/UA Home Video

A STREETCAR NAMED DESIRE
(1951)
122 min.; BW
Director: Elia Kazan
Cast: Vivien Leigh, Marlon Brando, Kim Hunter, Karl Malden
Academy Awards: Best Actress (Leigh), Best Supporting Actor (Malden), Best Supporting Actress (Hunter), Best Art Direction
Other credits: Screenplay by Tennessee Williams, adapted by Oscar Saul, based on Williams's play
VHS availability: Warner Home Video
Censorship, p. 175

STREET SMART
(1987)
97 min.; Color
Director: Jerry Schatzberg
Cast: Christopher Reeve, Morgan Freeman, Kathy Baker, Mimi Rogers
Other credits: Screenplay by David Freeman
VHS availability: Media Home Entertainment
Journalists, p. 171

THE STUFF
(1985)
93 min.; Color
Director: Larry Cohen
Cast: Michael Moriarty, Andrea Marcovicci, Garrett Morris
Other credits: Screenplay by Cohen
VHS availability: R & G Video
Food, p. 52

SUBURBIA
(1984)
96 min.; Color
Director: Penelope Spheeris
Cast: Timothy Eric O'Brien, Grant Miner, Michael Bayer
VHS availability: Vestron Video
Tales of Three Cities, p. 40

SUMMER OF '42
(1971)
102 min.; Color
Director: Robert Mulligan
Cast: Jennifer O'Neill, Gary Grimes, Jerry Houser

Academy Awards: Best Original Score (Michel Legrand)
VHS availability: Warner Home Video
Virgins, p. 119

SUMMER STOCK
(1950)
109 min.; Color
Director: Charles Walters
Cast: Judy Garland, Gene Kelly, Eddie Bracken, Gloria De Haven, Phil Silvers
VHS availability: MGM/UA Home Video
Musicals, p. 102

SUNDAY BLOODY SUNDAY
(1971)
110 min.; Color
Director: John Schlesinger
Cast: Glenda Jackson, Peter Finch, Murray Head, Peggy Ashcroft
Other credits: Screenplay by Penelope Gilliatt
VHS availability: Rental only
Triangles, p. 159

A SUNDAY IN THE COUNTRY
(1984)
94 min.; Color
In French; English subtitles
Director: Bertrand Tavernier
Cast: Louis Ducreux, Sabine Azéma, Michael Aumont
Other credits: Screenplay by Bertrand and Colo Tavernier
VHS availability: MGM/UA Home Video
Artists, p. 99

SUNSET BOULEVARD
(1950)
110 min.; BW
Director: Billy Wilder
Cast: William Holden, Gloria Swanson, Erich von Stroheim
Academy Awards: Best Story and Screenplay (Charles Brackett, Billy Wilder, and D. M. Marshman, Jr.), Best Score (Franz Waxman), Best Art Direction
FYI: Buster Keaton makes a cameo appearance as an aging silent star; the film clip screened within the movie is from *Queen Kelly,* a 1928 silent movie di-

rected by Stroheim and starring Swanson
VHS availability: Paramount Home Video

SWEET DREAMS
(1985)
115 min.; Color
Director: Karel Reisz
Cast: Jessica Lange, Ed Harris, Ann Wedgeworth
VHS availability: HBO Video

SWEET SMELL OF SUCCESS
(1957)
96 min.; BW
Director: Alexander Mackendrick
Cast: Burt Lancaster, Tony Curtis, Susan Harrison
Other credits: Screenplay by Clifford Odets and Ernest Lehman, based on a short story by Lehman; cinematography by James Wong Howe; music by Elmer Bernstein
VHS availability: MGM/UA Home Video

SWING TIME
(1936)
103 min.; BW
Director: George Stevens
Cast: Fred Astaire, Ginger Rogers, Victor Moore, Eric Blore
Academy Awards: Best Song ("The Way You Look Tonight")
Other credits: Music by Jerome Kern; choreography by Hermes Pan
VHS availability: Turner Home Entertainment

T

TARZAN, THE APE MAN
(1932)
99 min.; BW
Director: W. S. Van Dyke
Cast: Johnny Weissmuller, Maureen O'Sullivan
Other credits: Screenplay by Cyril Hume and Ivor Novello, based on the characters created by Edgar Rice Burroughs
VHS availability: MGM/UA Home Video

TAXI DRIVER
(1976)
113 min.; Color
Director: Martin Scorsese
Cast: Robert De Niro, Cybill Shepherd, Jodie Foster
Other credits: Screenplay by Paul Schrader; cinematography by Michael Chapman; music by Bernard Herrmann
VHS availability: GoodTimes Home Video

TEACHER'S PET
(1958)
120 min.; BW
Director: George Seaton
Cast: Clark Gable, Doris Day, Gig Young
VHS availability: Rental only

10
(1979)
122 min.; Color
Director: Blake Edwards
Cast: Dudley Moore, Julie Andrews, Bo Derek, Brian Dennehy
Other credits: Screenplay by Edwards; music by Henry Mancini
VHS availability: Warner Home Video

THE TEN COMMANDMENTS
(1956)
220 min.; Color
Director: Cecil B. De Mille
Cast: Charlton Heston, Yul Brynner, Anne Baxter, Edward G. Robinson, Yvonne de Carlo
Academy Awards: Best Special Effects

Other credits: Music by Elmer Bernstein
FYI: De Mille's last movie
VHS availability: Paramount Home Video

TEN FROM YOUR SHOW OF SHOWS
(1973)
92 min.; BW
Compilation of material from the TV series *Your Show of Shows*
Director: Max Liebman
VHS availability: Media Home Entertainment

TERMS OF ENDEARMENT
(1983)
132 min.; Color
Director: James L. Brooks
Cast: Debra Winger, Shirley MacLaine, Jack Nicholson, Jeff Daniels
Academy Awards: Best Picture, Best Actress (MacLaine), Best Supporting Actor (Nicholson), Best Direction (Brooks), Best Adapted Screenplay (Brooks)
Other credits: Based on the novel by Larry McMurtry; cinematography by Andrzej Bartkowiak
VHS availability: Paramount Home Video

TESS
(1980)
170 min.; Color
Director: Roman Polanski
Cast: Nastassja Kinski, Leigh Lawson, Peter Firth
Academy Awards: Best Cinematography (Geoffrey Unsworth and Ghislain Cloquet), Best Art Direction, Best Costume Design
Other credits: Screenplay by Polanski, Gérard Brach, and John Brownjohn, based on the novel *Tess of the d'Urbervilles,* by Thomas Hardy; music by Philippe Sarde

FYI: Cinematographer Unsworth died during the filming; Cloquet took over
VHS availability: RCA/Columbia Pictures Home Video

THÉRÈSE
(1986)
91 min.; Color
In French; English subtitles
Director: Alain Cavalier
Cast: Cathérine Mouchet, Sylvie Habault, Aurore Prito
Other credits: Screenplay by Cavalier and Camille de Casabianca; cinematography by Philippe Rousselot
VHS availability: Facets Video

THESE THREE
(1936)
93 min.; BW
Director: William Wyler
Cast: Miriam Hopkins, Merle Oberon, Joel McCrea, Bonita Granville
Other credits: Screenplay by Lillian Hellman, based on her play *The Children's Hour;* cinematography by Gregg Toland
FYI: Remade by Wyler in 1962 as *The Children's Hour,* starring Audrey Hepburn and Shirley MacLaine
VHS availability: Nelson Entertainment

THE THIN BLUE LINE
(1988)
96 min.; Color
Documentary
Director: Errol Morris
Other credits: Music by Philip Glass
VHS availability: HBO Video

THE THIN MAN
(1934)
93 min.; BW
Director: W. S. Van Dyke

Cast: William Powell, Myrna Loy, Maureen O'Sullivan
Other credits: Screenplay by Albert Hackett and Frances Goodrich, based on the novel by Dashiell Hammett; cinematography by James Wong Howe
VHS availability: MGM/UA Home Video
Screwball Comedies, p. 185

THE THING
(1951)
87 min.; BW
Director: Christian Nyby and (uncredited) Howard Hawks
Cast: Kenneth Tobey, James Arness, Margaret Sheridan
Other credits: Screenplay by Charles Lederer, based on the story "Who Goes There," by John Wood Campbell, Jr.; music by Dmitri Tiomkin
FYI: Remade in 1982 by John Carpenter
VHS availability: Turner Home Entertainment
Sci-Fi, p. 107

THE THIRD MAN
(1950)
104 min.; BW
Director: Carol Reed
Cast: Joseph Cotten, Orson Welles, Alida Valli, Trevor Howard
Academy Awards: Best Cinematography (Robert Krasker)
Other credits: Screenplay by Graham Greene; music by Anton Karas
VHS availability: Media Home Entertainment
Directors' Choice I, p. 13

THIS ISLAND EARTH
(1955)
86 min.; Color
Director: Joseph Newman
Cast: Jeff Morrow, Faith Domergue, Rex Reason
VHS availability: MCA/Universal Home Video
Sci-Fi, p. 108

THIS IS SPINAL TAP
(1984)
82 min.; Color
Director: Rob Reiner
Cast: Christopher Guest, Michael McKean, Harry Shearer, Reiner
Other credits: Screenplay and music by Guest, McKean, Shearer, and Reiner
VHS availability: Nelson Entertainment
The Greatest Movies of the '80s, p. 227

THREE BROTHERS
(1982)
113 min.; Color
In Italian; English subtitles
Director: Francesco Rosi
Cast: Philippe Noiret, Charles Vanel, Michele Placido, Vittorio Mezzogiorno
Other credits: Screenplay by Rosi and Tonino Guerra, based on the story "The Third Son" by A. Platonov; cinematography by Pasqualino De Santis
VHS availability: Nelson Entertainment
The Greatest Movies of the '80s, p. 228

THREE DAYS OF THE CONDOR
(1975)
117 min.; Color
Director: Sydney Pollack
Cast: Robert Redford, Faye Dunaway, Cliff Robertson, Max von Sydow
Other credits: Screenplay by Lorenzo Semple, Jr., and David Rayfiel, based on the novel *Six Days of the Condor* by James Grady
VHS availability: Paramount Home Video
The Twelve Days of Christmas, p. 180

THE TIN DRUM
(1979)
142 min.; Color
In German; English subtitles
Director: Volker Schlöndorff
Cast: David Bennent, Mario Adorf, Angela Winkler
Academy Awards: Best Foreign Language Film
Other credits: Screenplay by Franz Seitz, Schlöndorff, Jean-Claude Carrière, and Günter Grass, based on Grass's novel
VHS availability: Warner Home Video
Food, p. 49

Academy Awards: Best Original Song Score (Henry Mancini and Leslie Bricusse)
Other credits: Screenplay by Edwards, based on the 1933 German film *Viktor und Viktoria*
VHS availability: MGM/UA Home Video

Trompe l'Oeil, p. 44

VIDEODROME
(1983)
90 min.; Color
Director: David Cronenberg
Cast: James Woods, Sonja Smits, Deborah Harry
Other credits: Screenplay by Cronenberg
VHS availability: MCA/Universal Home Video

Enhancing Your Bad Moods, p. 33

VIVA KNIEVEL!
(1977)
106 min.; Color
Director: Gordon Douglas
Cast: Evel Knievel, Gene Kelly, Lauren Hutton
VHS availability: Warner Home Video

The '70s, p. 128

W

WAIT UNTIL DARK
(1967)
108 min.; Color
Director: Terence Young
Cast: Audrey Hepburn, Alan Arkin, Richard Crenna, Efrem Zimbalist, Jr.
Other credits: Screenplay by Robert Carrington and Jane Howard Carrington, based on the play by Frederick Knott; music by Henry Mancini
VHS availability: Warner Home Video

Underdogs, p. 161

WAR OF THE WORLDS
(1953)
85 min.; Color
Director: Byron Haskin

Cast: Gene Barry, Ann Robinson, Les Tremayne
Academy Awards: Best Special Effects
Other credits: Screenplay by Barre Lyndon, based on the novel by H. G. Wells; produced by George Pal
VHS availability: Paramount Home Video

Sci-Fi, p. 108

THE WAY WE WERE
(1973)
118 min.; Color
Director: Sydney Pollack
Cast: Barbra Streisand, Robert Redford, Bradford Dillman
Academy Awards: Best Song ("The Way We Were"), Best Original Score (Marvin Hamlisch)
Other credits: Screenplay by Arthur Laurents, based on his novel
VHS availability: RCA/Columbia Pictures Home Video

Love and Marriage, p. 59

A WEDDING
(1978)
125 min.; Color
Director: Robert Altman
Cast: Lillian Gish, Desi Arnaz, Jr., Vittorio Gassman
VHS availability: Key Video

Love and Marriage, p. 55

WEST SIDE STORY
(1961)
151 min.; Color
Directors: Robert Wise and Jerome Robbins
Cast: Natalie Wood, Richard Beymer, Russ Tamblyn, Rita Moreno, George Chakiris
Academy Awards: Best Picture, Best Supporting Actor (Chakiris), Best Supporting Actress (Moreno), Best Direction (Wise and Robbins), Best Cinematography (Daniel L. Fapp), Best Art Direction, Best Costume Design, Best Film Editing, Best Sound, Best Scoring of a Musical
Other credits: Based on the Broadway

musical (book by Arthur Laurents, music by Leonard Bernstein, lyrics by Stephen Sondheim, choreography by Robbins)
FYI: Wood's singing voice is dubbed by Marni Nixon
VHS availability: MGM/UA Home Video
Directors' Choice II, p. 202

WHAT EVER HAPPENED TO BABY JANE?
(1962)
132 min.; BW
Director: Robert Aldrich
Cast: Bette Davis, Joan Crawford
Academy Awards: Best Costume Design
Other credits: Screenplay by Lukas Heller, based on the novel by Henry Farrell
VHS availability: Warner Home Video
Enhancing Your Bad Moods, p. 32

WHITE HEAT
(1949)
114 min.; BW
Director: Raoul Walsh
Cast: James Cagney, Virginia Mayo, Edmond O'Brien, Margaret Wycherly
Other credits: Music by Max Steiner
VHS availability: MGM/UA Home Video
Crime, p. 191

WHO FRAMED ROGER RABBIT
(1988)
103 min.; Color
Director: Robert Zemeckis
Cast: Bob Hoskins, Christopher Lloyd, Joanna Cassidy
Other credits: Screenplay by Jeffrey Price and Peter S. Seaman, based on the novel *Who Censored Roger Rabbit?* by Gary K. Wolf; animation directed by Richard Williams
Academy Awards: Special award to Williams
VHS availability: Touchstone Home Video
The Greatest Movies of the '80s, p. 217

THE WILD BUNCH
(1969)
134 min. (uncut 143 min.); Color
Director: Sam Peckinpah
Cast: William Holden, Ernest Borgnine, Robert Ryan, Warren Oates
Other credits: Screenplay by Walon Green and Peckinpah; story by Green and Roy N. Sickner; cinematography by Lucien Ballard; music by Jerry Fielding
VHS availability: Warner Home Video
Censorship, p. 174

WILD IN THE STREETS
(1968)
97 min.; Color
Director: Barry Shear
Cast: Shelley Winters, Christopher Jones, Hal Holbrook, Richard Pryor
VHS availability: HBO Video
Politics, p. 90

WINGS OF DESIRE
(1988)
130 min.; BW and Color
In German; English subtitles
Director: Wim Wenders
Cast: Bruno Ganz, Peter Falk, Solveig Dommartin, Otto Sander
Other credits: Screenplay by Wenders and Peter Handke; cinematography by Henri Alékan
VHS availability: Orion Home Video
The Greatest Movies of the '80s, p. 214

WINTER KILLS
(1979)
97 min.; Color
Director: William Richert
Cast: Jeff Bridges, John Huston, Anthony Perkins, Sterling Hayden, Eli Wallach
Other credits: Screenplay by Richert, based on the novel by Richard Condon; cinematography by Vilmos Zsigmond; music by Maurice Jarre
VHS availability: Nelson Entertainment
Politics, p. 92

WISE BLOOD
(1979)
108 min.; Color
Director: John Huston
Cast: Brad Dourif, Harry Dean Stanton, Daniel Shor
Other credits: Screenplay by Benedict Fitzgerald, based on the novel by Flannery O'Connor; music by Alex North
VHS availability: MCA/Universal Home Video
Religion in Extremis, p. 195

THE WITCHES OF EASTWICK
(1987)
118 min.; Color
Director: George Miller
Cast: Jack Nicholson, Cher, Susan Sarandon, Michelle Pfeiffer, Veronica Cartwright
Other credits: Screenplay by Michael Cristofer, based on the novel by John Updike; cinematography by Vilmos Zsigmond; score by John Williams
VHS availability: Warner Home Video
Good and Evil, p. 81

WITNESS
(1985)
112 min.; Color
Director: Peter Weir
Cast: Harrison Ford, Kelly McGillis, Lukas Haas
Academy Awards: Best Original Screenplay (William Kelley, Pamela Wallace, and Earl W. Wallace), Best Film Editing
Other credits: Music by Maurice Jarre
VHS availability: Paramount Home Video
The Greatest Movies of the '80s, p. 221

THE WIZARD OF OZ
(1939)
101 min.; Color and BW
Director: Victor Fleming
Cast: Judy Garland, Ray Bolger, Bert Lahr, Jack Haley, Margaret Hamilton
Academy Awards: Best Song ("Over the Rainbow"), Best Original Score (Herbert Stothart)

VHS availability: MGM/UA Home Video
Directors' Choice I, p. 17

WOLF AT THE DOOR
(1987)
90 min.; Color
Director: Henning Carlsen
Cast: Donald Sutherland, Max von Sydow, Valerie Morea
Other credits: Screenplay by Christopher Hampton; story by Carlsen and Jean-Claude Carrière
VHS availability: Key Video
Artists, p. 95

WOMAN OF THE YEAR
(1942)
112 min.; BW
Director: George Stevens
Cast: Spencer Tracy, Katharine Hepburn, William Bendix, Fay Bainter
Academy Awards: Best Original Screenplay (Michael Kanin and Ring Lardner, Jr.)
VHS availability: MGM/UA Home Video
Journalists, p. 168

THE WOMEN
(1939)
132 min.; BW and Color
Director: George Cukor
Cast: Norma Shearer, Joan Crawford, Rosalind Russell, Paulette Goddard, Joan Fontaine
Other credits: Screenplay by Anita Loos and Jane Murfin, based on the play by Clare Boothe
VHS availability: MGM/UA Home Video
Love and Marriage, p. 58

WOODSTOCK
(1970)
184 min.; Color
Documentary
Director: Michael Wadleigh
Academy Awards: Best Documentary
VHS availability: Warner Home Video
Fame, p. 114

WORKING GIRL
(1988)
113 min.; Color
Director: Mike Nichols
Cast: Harrison Ford, Melanie Griffith, Sigourney Weaver, Joan Cusack, Alec Baldwin
Academy Awards: Best Song ("Let the River Run")
Other credits: Screenplay by Kevin Wade; cinematography by Michael Ballhaus; music by Carly Simon
VHS availability: CBS/Fox Video
Underdogs, p. 163

THE WRONG MAN
(1956)
105 min.; BW
Director: Alfred Hitchcock
Cast: Henry Fonda, Vera Miles, Anthony Quayle
Other credits: Screenplay by Maxwell Anderson and Angus MacPhail, based on "The True Story of Christopher Emmanuel Balestrero" by Anderson; music by Bernard Herrmann
VHS availability: Warner Home Video
Enhancing Your Bad Moods, p. 30

X

X, Y AND ZEE
(1972)
110 min.; Color
Director: Brian G. Hutton
Cast: Elizabeth Taylor, Michael Caine, Susannah York, Margaret Leighton
Other credits: Screenplay by Edna O'Brien
VHS availability: RCA/Columbia Pictures Home Video
Triangles, p. 158

Y

THE YEAR OF LIVING DANGEROUSLY
(1982)
115 min.; Color

Director: Peter Weir
Cast: Mel Gibson, Sigourney Weaver, Linda Hunt
Academy Awards: Best Supporting Actress (Hunt)
Other credits: Screenplay by David Williamson, Weir, and C. J. Koch, based on Koch's novel; music by Maurice Jarre; cinematography by Russell Boyd
VHS availability: MGM/UA Home Video
Winter Antidotes, p. 78
Journalists, p. 169

YENTL
(1983)
134 min.; Color
Director: Barbra Streisand
Cast: Streisand, Mandy Patinkin, Amy Irving
Academy Awards: Best Song Score (Michel Legrand, Alan and Marilyn Bergman)
Other credits: Screenplay by Streisand and Jack Rosenthal, based on the short story "Yentl, the Yeshiva Boy" by Isaac Bashevis Singer
VHS availability: CBS/Fox Video
Trompe l'Oeil, p. 44

YOJIMBO
(1961)
110 min.; BW
In Japanese; English subtitles
Director: Akira Kurosawa
Cast: Toshiro Mifune, Eijiro Tono, Seizaburo Kawazu
VHS availability: Nelson Entertainment
Directors' Choice I, p. 13
Directors' Choice II, p. 203

YOU'RE A BIG BOY NOW
(1966)
96 min.; Color
Director: Francis Ford Coppola
Cast: Peter Kastner, Elizabeth Hartman, Geraldine Page, Julie Harris
Other credits: Screenplay by Coppola, based on the novel by David Benedictus
VHS availability: Warner Home Video
Virgins, p. 116

Z